Richard Kagan, PhD

Rebuilding Attachments with Traumatized Children
Healing from Losses, Violence, Abuse, and Neglect

Pre-publication REVIEWS, COMMENTARIES, EVALUATIONS . . .

"Perhaps no other author communicates better than Dr. Kagan the conviction that severely abused and neglected children can be helped to overcome the impact of earlier trauma. In *Rebuilding Attachments with Traumatized Children* he writes clearly and compellingly about successful therapy with severely traumatized children, and also shares a detailed supplemental resource for helping these children, *Real Life Heroes: A Life Storybook for Children*. This workbook illustrates Dr. Kagan's creative therapeutic skills and provides a tool for other therapists who work with abused, neglected, and abandoned children, and with the adults who now provide them a safe environment. Central to Kagan's approach is his belief that 'trauma therapy is not focused on a child exposing painful feelings, but rather a means to help him or her learn how to tell the story of what happened *without* reliving, day after day, the traumas of the past.' This book offers a sound working model of how to help children 'reclaim their past and rewrite their future.' All who work with abused and neglected children should be grateful to Dr. Kagan for sharing his creative melding of relevant knowledge and creative technique, and, of course, for reaffirming our hope that even the most severely traumatized children can be helped."

Kenneth W. Watson, MSW
Retired social worker;
trainer, consultant, and writer

More pre-publication
REVIEWS, COMMENTARIES, EVALUATIONS . . .

"Dr. Kagan provides a much-needed compilation of the most current theory and practice related to understanding and working with traumatized children and the families raising them. He does this with both passion and compassion within a practice framework aimed at strengthening healthy child development and family relations with children who have experienced a history of instability and uneven developmental stimulation as well as multiple moves and unexplained relationship disruptions.

Dr. Kagan details how the earliest neglectful experiences may interfere with the brain's ability to develop sequentially and to function optimally. He also explains how children with early deprivation and instability can respond to relearning experiences later in life to help them build resiliency, form secure attachments, learn to self-satisfy, and function more effectively and consistently in a family setting.

The author addresses the current challenges of permanency planning within a context of shorter legal timeframes for planning and decision-making about where children will grow up. Although he makes a compelling case that children do not have the time to wait for the parenting they need, he does not rush to discount the potential for change, rebuilding attachments, and healing within birth families. Yet, when children must move on, he proposes a solid clinical framework for helping them form new relationships with nurturing adults—adults with whom they can learn to trust, safely tell their stories, and move forward with the developmental business of childhood. Dr. Kagan provides insightful examples of how parents (birth, foster, and adoptive) can help children become their own heroes by providing a safe space to tell their stories and make the burden of past trauma more bearable.

This book provides hope where there too often is none—enlightening parents, social workers, and therapists alike to increase the odds of favorable developmental outcomes for children through safe, planned, collaborative interventions."

Sarah B. Greenblatt, MSEd, MS, ACSW
Director, The Casey Center for Effective Child Welfare Practice,
Casey Family Services,
New Haven, Connecticut

"Dr. Richard Kagan, a recognized expert in working with traumatized children, has written a truly impressive book. Not only does the book contain a wealth of information for understanding the complex issues faced by traumatized youngsters, but it also offers specific interventions that can be used to help these children and their caregivers become more hopeful and resilient. Dr. Kagan's compassion and empathy for traumatized children are apparent throughout the book and it is little wonder that he is so skilled in connecting with them. In addition, the workbook *Real Life Heroes* provides an excellent therapeutic resource. I am certain that this book will be read and reread by professionals engaged in improving the lives of at-risk youth."

Robert Brooks, PhD
Faculty, Harvard Medical School;
Co-author of *Raising Resilient Children, Nurturing Resilience in Our Children,* and *The Power of Resilience*

NOTES FOR PROFESSIONAL LIBRARIANS AND LIBRARY USERS

This is an original book title published by The Haworth Maltreatment and Trauma Press, an imprint of The Haworth Press, Inc. Unless otherwise noted in specific chapters with attribution, materials in this book have not been previously published elsewhere in any format or language.

CONSERVATION AND PRESERVATION NOTES

All books published by The Haworth Press, Inc. and its imprints are printed on certified pH neutral, acid free book grade paper. This paper meets the minimum requirements of American National Standard for Information Sciences-Permanence of Paper for Printed Material, ANSI Z39.48-1984.

Rebuilding Attachments with Traumatized Children

Healing from Losses, Violence, Abuse, and Neglect

Rebuilding Attachments with Traumatized Children
Healing from Losses, Violence, Abuse, and Neglect

Richard Kagan, PhD

HMTP

The Haworth Maltreatment and Trauma Press®
An Imprint of The Haworth Press, Inc.
New York • London • Oxford

Published by

The Haworth Maltreatment and Trauma Press, an imprint of The Haworth Press, Inc., 10 Alice Street, Binghamton, NY 13904-1580.

PUBLISHER'S NOTE
Identities and circumstances of individuals discussed in this book have been changed to protect confidentiality.

Cover design by Marylouise Doyle.

Library of Congress Cataloging-in-Publication Data

Kagan, Richard.
Rebuilding attachments with traumatized children : healing from losses, violence, abuse, and neglect / Richard Kagan.
p. cm.
Includes bibliographical references and index.
ISBN 0-7890-1543-9 (alk. paper)—ISBN 0-7890-1544-7 (pbk. : alk. paper)
1. Attachment disorder in children—Treatment. 2. Child abuse—Treatment. 3. Abused children—Rehabilitation. I. Title.

RJ507.A77K34 2004
618.92'891—dc21

2003005268

For Michelle, Josh, Michael, and Cindy
and
all those with the courage to reach out to troubled children
with caring, commitment, and homes "ever after"

ABOUT THE AUTHOR

Richard Kagan, PhD, has twenty-seven years of post-doctoral experience in child and family, mental health, and substance abuse services as a therapist, consultant, trainer, researcher, and director of psychological services, research, and professional development programs. He is Director of Psychological Services for Parsons Child and Family Center in Albany, New York, and Clinical Director/Principal Investigator for Parsons Child Trauma Study Center, a community services site for the National Child Traumatic Stress Network. He has also served as a consulting psychologist for county departments of social services, and several child and family service agencies.

Dr. Kagan is the author or co-author of *Families in Perpetual Crisis; Turmoil to Turning Points: Building Hope for Children in Crisis Placements;* and *Wounded Angels: Lessons from Children in Crisis.* He has published more than twenty articles, chapters, and papers on practice and research issues in family systems work, child welfare, adoption, professional development, program evaluation, and quality improvement in family service agencies.

CONTENTS

Preface

For the past twenty-seven years, I have worked with children in crisis: boys found hanging by their fingers from second-story windows, their legs swaying over the concrete below and girls who kicked, hit, and bit. Many of these children frightened teachers, physicians, social workers, and their parents with dangerous behaviors. The children I met were placed into emergency foster families after a school nurse discovered severe welts or a neighbor reported that the children next door had gone for days without a parent at home, begging or stealing the food they needed. Others were placed into psychiatric hospitals or residential treatment programs after threatening their parents with butcher knives or lighting fires that destroyed their homes or entire buildings.

Children were referred to my agency because they had been severely neglected, physically or sexually abused, or were at high risk of severely hurting themselves or others. Often, their stealing, hitting, running away, defiance, and rages created crises in their schools, neighborhoods, and communities, crises that matched the turmoil in their homes.

My colleagues and I were contracted to help these children and their families rebuild their lives, to strengthen caring, nurturing, and guidance, to stop the violence, and to protect communities. We worked to keep children in their families whenever possible, to reunite families of children who had left their homes, and to find new families for children who could not return to their parents.

High risk was the criteria for funding. Referrals were limited to children on the brink of harm to themselves or others. I met their parents, their grandparents, their aunts, and their uncles. I listened to their screams, felt their despair, and experienced their rages in their homes, classrooms, and my office. I listened to the pitch and tone of each child's voice, watched for patterns and rhythms in behavior, and tried to understand the message in each child's story. I watched as they drew pictures of hearts and hands reaching out to a drug-addicted parent or ran to hug a grandparent, and I listened as they begged to see a sibling. I learned how the crises enveloping these children covered a drive for a caring and nurturing family.

Children who have experienced repeated traumas often show little trust in themselves or anyone else. Their lives may appear to revolve in serial crises that progressively destroy even a sense of hope. Yet, these children also teach us important lessons about making the most of our lives. Many of them have learned at a tender age about love and loss, commitment and abandonment, safety and violence, loyalty and betrayal, and what is necessary in life at any age. They carry lessons that can help us all.

Without interventions from caring adults, the sweetness, caring, and beauty in these children often remains buried under the storms of their families' struggles. When these struggles cannot be contained in their homes, their crises spill out into their schools, neighborhoods, and communities.

I have learned from children in crisis how each of us needs to feel valued and to have someone we can trust enough to allow us to share our deepest feelings and beliefs. They showed me the yearning for attachments to overcome the traumas in their families, even while they demonstrated how they could not trust. Children showed me that they needed more than nice clothes, the latest toys, and a roof over their head. Week after week, these children searched for adults who cared enough to teach them how to succeed at school, on the playground, in the streets, and in future jobs; to celebrate their triumphs; to pull them up off the ground when they failed; and to be there day after day.

The greatest challenge I experienced with children in crisis was the task of rebuilding enduring attachments to adults who could provide these children with the caring, nurturing, and guidance they so desperately needed to believe in, for the present and into the future. I learned that many children, very naturally, were afraid to face what they saw as monsters from their past or present. I could not simply ask a child or a parent to tell his or her life story. For a frightened child, this was perceived as being asked to do something both impossible and terrifying, such as forging a raging river. For such children, and often their parents as well, safety had been an illusion, adults could not be trusted, and survival meant having to make it on your own.

I grew up with a sense of heroes, men and women[1] who dared to risk themselves in order to protect and care for others. I grew up with stories of John F. Kennedy as a war hero, Superman on TV, and James Bond in the movies. We were taught in school that teachers, clergy, and police officers would help you when you were in trouble. More important, I grew up with family members who were heroes in real life. My grandparents escaped the persecution of Jews in Russia. My birth father died after service in World War II, part of the generation including my adoptive father and uncle who defeated fascism. I learned from my Jewish heritage that each of us has the responsibility to make the world a little better. My mom was waiting at home for my siblings and me after school because she believed that nothing was more important than raising children. My adoptive father taught me about the excitement of discovering antibiotics that saved people's lives. I grew up believing that we could push the limits of our understanding, and with perseverance and struggle, we could build a better world.

The children I met in my work had often lost any sense of heroes in their world. Some witnessed their parents pursue drugs and the sudden or steady erosion of the stability that had held their families together. Breakfasts, dinners, and bedtime stories were lost, often followed by abuse and degradation. Homelessness meant moving over and over, transferring from school to school, and learning that nothing would last. Other children learned that parents or other caregivers could explode any moment, run away, or sink into a stupor from which they could not be awoken. These children often lost their parents, grandparents, aunts, uncles, and cousins, as well as their family's heritage. But most never gave up a wish to be loved and treated as someone special. My colleagues and I were able to see these same children blossom again when they finally formed a new bond with someone they could trust.

I developed the *Real Life Heroes* storybook and this book to help troubled children step back from what often feels like the raging rivers of their lives and to work with a psychotherapist to build a sense of support from significant people in their past, the present, and for the future. Guided by committed, caring adults, children can find a place along each river where the water is still, shallow, and able to be crossed. Each story of support for children, and each example of how children helped others, forms a steppingstone for crossing even a river. Together, these stories help children shape beliefs in themselves as heroes in their own lives. With caring and committed adults, children can rekindle their hopes and learn to succeed.

This book includes a therapeutic framework based on attachment and trauma research, assessment tools, and a workbook that can help children develop self-esteem and overcome difficult experiences in their lives. The focus of both the text and the workbook is on overcoming the impact of traumas and utilizing life-story work to understand the perspectives of children in distress, to discover strengths in their families, and to rebuild connections and hope. The permanency interventions and creative arts approach engages children (ages six to twelve) to create their own autobiographies with a wide range of activities including drawings, photographs, music, dance, videotape, posters, crafts, game cards, and narrative. School counselors and psychotherapists can use these assessment and therapeutic resources to help a child replace a self-image of weakness or victimization with feelings of validation and competence.

Drawings, storytelling, music, and other creative arts provide wonderful ways to help children foster a sense of mastery, positive values, and a sense of pride. By working together to share life experiences, caring adults can help a child develop the courage and understanding that he or she needs to move beyond worries or fears from the past. The life-story workbook provides a framework for adults to show that they care enough about a child to face difficult times and keep on going.

This book highlights and preserves moments in which important people in a child's family and community showed they cared, moments in a child's life that signify how he or she was valued. The workbook and storytelling approach provides a resource practitioners in schools, mental health programs, and child and family service agencies can use to engage caring adults to work together with a child who has experienced traumas or neglect. Practitioners, parents, grandparents, foster parents, adoptive parents, and mentors can use this book to show children that they can learn from the past, resolve problems in the present, and build a better future.

This is a book about summoning the courage and commitment children need to surmount losses, separations, violence, and neglect. The intent is not to simply tell a child's life story, but rather, to rebuild a story of people who care for a child based on strength, courage, and belonging. The heroes (male and female) in this book are real people who define what it means for a child to have a family, to overcome hardships, and to live within a community.

Acknowledgments

I could never have written this book without the help of my family, friends, and colleagues. I especially want to thank my wife Laura Kagan, and daughter, Michelle, for putting up with my obsession with this book. My wife's practical wisdom as a parent and forensic psychologist permeates this book. Michelle edited references, appendixes, and the workbook. My son Joshua helped edit initial drafts. My son Michael and my brother, Glenn, helped edit the workbook.

Rebuilding Attachments with Traumatized Children builds on the premises of the permanency-based model of family therapy developed with Shirley Schlosberg, my co-author for *Families in Perpetual Crisis* (1989) and former director of Parsons Prevention Program. Emphasis on life-story work was inspired by use of life stories in older-child adoption by Claudia Jewett (1978), by storytelling therapies including Gardner (1975), by trauma therapists including Figley (1989) and van der Kolk, McFarlane, and Weisaeth (1996), and by narrative family therapies developed by White and Epston (1990) and Freedman and Combs (1996). This book was shaped by Robert Geffner who encouraged me to develop a book on research and practice to guide practitioners in life-story work and use of the *Real Life Heroes* workbook, building on current research on the impact of trauma. His guidance, support, and criticism were essential in keeping this book on target. My production editors at The Haworth Press, Peg Marr, Dawn Krisko, and Catherine Kempf, fine-tuned the manuscript and kept this work on schedule.

Staff and supervisors at Parsons Child and Family Center tested use of the workbook with children as part of therapy sessions and provided critical feedback that led to the final product. Judy Riopelle printed, bound, and circulated copies of the workbook, an immense task that was essential for testing and revisions. I am indebted to Sudha Hunziker and Ron Gerhard for help in refining early drafts of the workbook and text. I will always be grateful to Sudha for her understanding of the difficulty of writing this book, for her expertise from years of work in foster family care, and for prodding me to finish the manuscript. Mary McHugh connected me with the writing of Joseph Campbell and provided me with outlines of storytelling approaches to therapy. Joe Benamati helped me with outlines of Figley's trauma therapy and updated references on trauma and trauma therapy including practical applications in residential treatment. Diane Rosenbaum-Weisz and John O'Grady helped with suggestions on enlarging the family roots worksheet. Kathy Tambasco provided invaluable help with computer applications and graphics. Dennis Chapko rescued the accompanying life storybook from technical problems. Stephen Lawton helped me with the hero concept and workbook. Sylvia Dettmer helped me focus on the practical side of life in foster families. Robin Sorriento kept me real and focused, when I became overwhelmed with my day-to-day work and the difficulties of our work with families in crisis.

Suzanne d'Aversa, Mary Purdy, Carrie Blanchard, Erin Christopher-Sisk, Amy Anneling, and Denise Minnear helped edit later versions of this book, providing valuable critiques and additions from their experience as practitioners in foster family care, adoption, and prevention of placement programs. Suzanne d'Aversa inspired me with her practical wisdom from a quarter century of work with families who have adopted children and helped me refine sections on attachment therapy for children as part of our work together on creating a post-adoption training seminar for practitioners. Suzanne was also responsible for my inclusion of a chapter in the workbook tracing moves in a child's life. Mary and Carrie inspired me with their courage in working with distressed and sometimes threatening families. Denise contributed pearls of practical wisdom from her experience as both a foster care social worker and an adoptive parent. Amber Douglas, Mary Purdy, Norm Sweet, Robin Sorriento, and Anita Taboh helped me edit the curriculum outline and make final revisions for the *Real Life Heroes* storybook.

This book was truly based on all that I have learned in twenty-seven years of work with families, foster parents, and colleagues. I thank them all for the courage they have shared to overcome adversity.

The author wishes to thank the National Child Traumatic Stress Network and the Center for Mental Health Services, Substance Abuse and Mental Health Services Administration, U.S. Deparatment of Health and Human Services for funding research on the effectiveness of the *Real Life Heroes* workbook and curriculum with traumatized children. The author is grateful to Joe Benamati, Amber Douglas, and John Hornik, for their help in developing a pilot research study to research the effectiveness of this model as part of the Parsons Child Trauma Study Center. The author is especially grateful to Amy Scheele for helping to research references and prepare materials for this project.

PART I: LIFELINES

Chapter 1

Attachment

There is no such thing as a baby; there is a baby and someone.

D. W. Winnicott

TRAUMA DAMAGE TO NEURODEVELOPMENT

Life and Death: An Example

Tracy's eyes sparkled and locked onto my own from the moment I met her. I was struck by her chunky cheeks, carefully braided hair, and cute button nose. Tracy smiled up at me as though she had known me for forever.

"This is Tracy," her county social worker announced. Four-and-a-half-year-old Tracy reached out her hand and gently placed it into mine. Then, without a look behind at her social worker, Tracy began walking with me past doors, up stairs, through halls to my office, her steps confident and secure, her chin tilted upward, and her golden brown eyes gazing upward at me. I thought of Little Orphan Annie.

Tracy lived with her mother for her first eighteen months and then lived for two years with a friend of her mother's who brought her to child protective services, saying she could no longer care for her. Tracy was placed with a foster family where she had been living for almost a year. I asked Tracy to draw pictures of her foster mother, her biological mother, and her mother's friend. She smiled up at me and began to draw primitive sketches, even for her age, huge heads for each figure taking up half a page each, an imaginary line separating each of her mothers.

Each figure had immense, bulging oval eyes. On the picture of her mother, Tracy sketched a jagged slash through her mother's eye, her memory. (I later learned that Tracy's mother had cut her in the face with a knife.) Her mother's friend was drawn with similar jagged scars on the sides of her face.

After sketching her three mothers, I asked Tracy to include herself. She drew a smaller oval head than she had drawn for her mothers, but she included the same bulging eyes. Tracy added two short lines for legs, just as she had in the other pictures. Then, Tracy's face tensed and she pursed her lips. She bore down on her black marker and began scribbling from left to right, zigzag slashes, repeated over and over until she had totally obliterated her drawing.

"Me." Tracy said simply. She smiled, gazing up again into my eyes.

Tracy was going to be evicted from her foster family. Her foster mother was a manager with a demanding schedule and had bravely offered to care for school-age children who could not live in their own families. The county case worker had begged her to take Tracy on a temporary, emergency basis. Weeks stretched into months, and Tracy was no closer to having a secure or lasting home. A year went by. Tracy's foster mother said she could not keep Tracy any longer. She had worked out a way to provide day care but she could no longer manage what caring for Tracy had done to her own life. Tracy screamed every night, a piercing howl that fractured her foster mother's sleep. She was exhausted.

Tracy showed me how the loss of a parent is similar to the obliteration of a child's identity and his or her very being. Despite losing three mothers, Tracy had not given up. She held my hand and gazed at me with an appealing smile. She was still looking for someone to love her.

I have seen hundreds of girls and boys such as Tracy–infants, toddlers, young children, adolescents, and young adults who continue to search. Although they have learned that they cannot trust, deep down they keep wishing for someone to love them.

ATTACHMENT THEORY AND RESEARCH

Shaping a Life

Dependence on an parent is a fact of life for all children, and in fact, all primates. Humans, by nature, have the longest period of dependence of any animal and simply do not survive without the twenty-four-hour-a-day care and support of their parents. Attachment to a caring parent means survival. Abandonment to a young child means death.

Bonding begins before conception. The security of a child's future life begins with the resources a mother and father bring with them. The parents' relationships, wealth, heritage, and community can support or constrain their union and their ability to support their child. Was this conception sanctioned or unsanctioned? Will the newborn be accepted and cared for, neglected, or rejected by parents, grandparents, extended family, neighbors, educators, and community leaders? What does the fetus represent, not only to the mother and father, but to the extended families now united through the growing embryo who forms the future of both families? Are the parents living in a neighborhood with playgrounds, enriched schools, and after-school activities or an impoverished battleground dominated by rival gangs and drug dealers. The answers form the emotional and social cradle that nourishes or impedes an infant's growth.

The brain has developed, according to neurological researchers (Schore, 1994, 2003a; Siegel, 1999, 2003), in sequence from more primitive functions such as the brain stem, which manages basic autonomic functions, to the limbic system, with the hippocampus mediating memory and learning, the amygdala processing emotional memories, and the anterior cingulate working rather like a coordinator of bodily responses to higher-level thinking. The prefrontal cortex provides verbal (left hemisphere) and visual, tonal, and emotional reasoning (right hemisphere), and the cortex serves many distinct functions necessary for visual, auditory, and affective processing. Some connections in the brain are classified as life critical and develop with little adaptation in order to manage basic life functioning such as the infant's heart rate and breathing. Higher-level connections have been found to be shaped by experiences (Siegel, 1999; Schore, 1994; Perry, 2001). Brain growth builds from conception with each stage of growth forming the foundation for higher levels of functioning.

Neurobiologists have discovered how the infant's brain is altered by chemicals experienced in utero. Prenatally stressed infants may have difficult temperaments resulting from environmental stress, poor nutrition, and toxic chemicals on their developing nervous systems. A pregnant woman stressed from traumas produces increased hormones, such as cortisol. These hormones strengthen her body in the short term but increase the likelihood of blocking development of connections in the fetus's developing brain or decreasing the number of brain cells. Parts of the brain needed for memory and learning (e.g., the hippocampus) may be impaired. Studies have shown how cortisol decreases memory ability and the ability to sustain attention.

Similarly, norepinephrine, a critical hormone for self-protection, can have an adverse effect on infants and fetuses. Norepinephrine brings a human to the "fight-or-flight" level needed for survival. Too much, however, can lead to panic. If the infant is exposed to high levels of norepinephrine, the level of agitation can become a persistent state in which he or she is always on guard looking for threats and expecting harm. High levels of norepinephrine increase excitable neurons. The infant's system essentially becomes sensitized and even normal stressors can ignite the preprogrammed stress response generated by the development in utero or early infancy with too much norepinephrine. This has been called *kindling,* a level of neuronal excitability caused by repeated stress.

After birth, brain development continues to be shaped by environmental factors that stimulate the organization of neural interconnections (Kotulak, 1996; Shore, 1997; Siegel, 1999). Researchers have classified some neural connections as experience-expectant and thus greatly impacted by culture, heritage, nurture, and the experiences of a child. Experiences of the fetus and young child have a major impact on the cultivation and pruning of neural synapses, and key experiences have been found to be necessary within extended time periods, sometimes called *windows of opportunity,* for optimal development of different brain centers.

Stress on a parent and child accordingly impacts the infant's developing brain in different ways at different stages of development. The absence of stimulation through profound neglect, such as a baby being left in its crib, or over stimulation from trauma (e.g., abuse or violence) can result in the failure of the infant to complete certain tasks and distort development of neuronal functions. This is one of the reasons why siblings who experience violence, sickness, or loss at different ages respond to the same trauma in different ways. Parents may misunderstand how one child, who was one year old at the time of violence in the family, became hyperactive and was later expelled from kindergarten for aggressive behavior, while an older child, who was eight years old at the time of the violence, was able to continue to succeed at school, even though the child became preoccupied with the care and protection of a parent at home.

Overemphasis on the impact of damage during prenatal experiences can also lead policymakers and funding bodies to give up on children seen as irreparably damaged in utero. In the late 1980s, it was feared that babies born to crack-addicted mothers would be maimed for life. Instead, it has been learned that the family's environment *after birth* may have a stronger effect on a child's temperament than the experience of cocaine in utero. Schore (2001) found that as many synapses develop in the nine months after birth as in the nine months in utero. Accordingly, the level of stress experienced growing up with a mother who was or had been crack-addicted, may have a stronger impact on a child's brain than the infant's experience of cocaine in utero. Well after an infant's diagnosis as having fetal cocaine or fetal alcohol effects, parenting, educational, and therapeutic interventions make a tremendous difference in his or her life.

A child's early years have now been well publicized as critical. The public, however, has been less informed about how a child's environment continues to shape brain development well through adolescence (Thompson and Nelson, 2001) and into young adulthood. Brain centers most relevant for cognition and higher-order thinking operations such as problem solving, reasoning, self-regulation, and strategic thinking develop well into adolescence. Moreover, the adult brain also has been found to *re*organize based on life experiences (Greenough and Black, 1992; Elbert et al., 1995; Ramachandran, 1995) with growth of new neurons occurring through-out the life span (Eriksson et al., 1998; Gould, 1999). Although brain growth is especially vulnerable during the prenatal period and a child's early years, the lifelong process of brain development presents opportunities for remediation.

Windows for Growth

Watching a new parent cradle an infant is a beautiful sight. The infant signals its needs through a whimper or cry. The parent responds with a smile, a caress, a nipple, or a bottle, removing pain and satisfying the needs of the infant. Eye to eye, coo matching coo, the infant feels united with a parent, building a linkage over time and the foundation for trust (Erikson, 1986). Attachment is an interactive process (Schore, 2003a; Siegel, 2003), brain to brain, limbic system to limbic system, a synchronicity of parent and child. Attachment in the child's first three years centers on communication between the right brains of both parent and child, especially visual, face-to-face images of one another, touch, and tone of voice. These experiences form indelible memories in a child's limbic system, long before a child develops the capacity to utilize language, including expectations of whether parents will respond to distress, whether the child will be soothed, and whether parents can modulate their own emotions at times of stress.

In the first stages of development, the infant's needs must come first, but the infant-parent dyad is controlled by the nurturing parent, typically the mother. This is the stage of development where the brain stem and thalamus are being shaped. The infant absorbs the care from the parent and essentially absorbs the self-regulatory system of the parent. When the infant is cared for fully, the infant grows up feeling wanted. When the infant experiences a lack of response, his or her regulatory system fails and the infant may die.

Infants learn whether they can trust that their needs will be met. They are shaped by the sensitivity and responsiveness of their parents. Those who experience a high level of stress at this point of development will often develop a state of hyperarousal. Infants who experience intermittent care learn that the world is unpredictable and become unpredictable in their own lives. Those who experience angry parents become frightened and easily triggered to rage. Infants who experience parents who are depressed and nonresponsive often tend to withdraw, and show a decrease in positive emotions.

From four to six months, the cerebellum and thalamus develop at a high rate. At this point, the infant needs to send clear signals to affect the necessary relationship with the parent. He or she mirrors the gaze and interactions of the parent, and the parent mimics and mirrors the child. Ideally, the infant experiences an attunement between the parent and his or her own behavior.

This is a wonderful stage in which the infant begins to show delight and positive excitement. On the other hand, the infant who has not received the care and stimulation needed will begin to avoid contact with his or her parent and show subdued or inhibited behavior. The infant who experiences inconsistent care will often act chaotic in his or her own behaviors. The infant who experiences a parent who periodically becomes abusive will often avert his or her gaze from the parent and demonstrate the fear learned from his or her parent's rages.

From six to twelve months, the prefrontal cortex develops at a rapid pace. This is the bridge between the survival functions of the limbic system and the higher-level cognitive functioning of the cortex. The development of regulatory functions is shaped by a child's experiences during these critical months. The process of attachment between infant and parent is especially critical from eight to eighteen months. The child learns whether the parent can be relied upon.

The child learns from the parent how to manage problems and stressors. With each month of development, the child increasingly takes a stronger role in signaling what he or she needs. The parent's response to these signals demonstrates whether the child can count on the world around him or her or must try to take control on his or her own of a world that seems out of control. In reality, no parent provides perfect attunement to a child, just as no parent or child lives in a stress-free world. The infant who experiences a sensitive, predictable, and reliable parent learns that his or her parent will regulate intense emotions.

Social and Emotional Development

Mahler, Pine, and Bergman (1975) and Greenspan and Lieberman (1988) described the developmental process of attachment and its impact on a child's cognitive, social, and emotional development. Schore (1994) denoted the critical impact of a mother and child's relationship on the physical development of the brain building the child's framework for future inter- and intrapersonal development. Schore stressed how attunement between a parent and child facilitated growth of the limbic system during the first year. Caregivers provide experiences that regulate hormones in the child and in turn shape gene transcription (Schore, 1997). Interactional experiences modulate genetic development and shape brain circuitry.

From twelve to twenty-four months, the child exercises a great deal of independent action. The parent's attunement provides the foundations for discipline, social skills, and the development of self-control. Researchers have also described the role of separation and shame in shaping a child's ability to integrate a sense of self that incorporates both good and bad behavior. When a child experiences a parent breaking attunement after misbehavior, he or she becomes anxious. Reprimands and withdrawal of attention induce discomfort in the child, that, in turn, shapes his or her behavior. This is critical in terms of developing inhibitory circuits.

Discipline within a caring, nurturing relationship helps the infant learn self-regulation and self-control. The parent scolds or withdraws affection, *and* then *re*attunes. *Re*attunement affirms the child's security with his or her parent. The child calms and over time learns how to regulate his or her own responses in order to keep the parent's attunement. The parent's *re*attunement helps a child develop a sense of autonomy within the security of a continuing bond. The child learns right from wrong and how to succeed. As the child develops, this learning progresses into verbal communication and use of words to understand and regulate his or her own behavior. Without *re*attunement, the child learns to live in an unstable, insecure, and often dangerous world in which his or her relationship to the parent is always at risk.

Contrary to popular assumptions, babies who are picked up often when they are young actually cry less when they are older. Moreover, the widespread assumption in many Western cultures that young children must separate from their parents in order to become independent may in fact impair the development of security, competency, and ability for relationships for both girls (Surrey, 1991) and boys (Silverstein and Rashbaum, 1994; Garbarino, 1999; Gurian, 1997).

Attachment forms the foundations for a child's future relationships, learning, and expectations. The strength of a child's attachment shapes his or her emotional regulatory system and fosters exploration and mastery, feelings of self-confidence, empathy, language development, reasoning processes, and the ability to manage and resolve conflicts. The consistency of care, empathy, and commitment of a parent allows the child to progress steadily through developmental stages, steadily building vital skills of self-regulation, understanding, and competence.

Jerome Kagan (1998) described development as being similar to the growth of a tree. Step by step, stage by stage, the child builds upon what came before. From a family and community perspective, the roots of the tree can be dense, thick, and supportive, or weak, fragmented, and fragile. The strength of a child's roots and stem symbolize the attachment the child experienced in his or her early years. A strong, fixed stem and widespread, deep roots can withstand heavy winds and temporary droughts. The roots and the stem form the basis for the branching and foliage, thick or thin. The foliage, in turn, provides the nutrients to rebuild and maintain the tree.

Optimal growth and development of a child requires protection, nurture, and guidance provided with the security of a lifetime commitment from caring adults in the child's family and community. The parents' presence and encouragement support the child to go forth, to learn, to explore, and to develop skills (Ramey and Ramey, 1998). The child who is insecure will cling or shy away. Parents and caretakers nurture the child's basic cognitive development, helping him or her develop skills through practice and rehearsal, promote flexible problem solving, protect the child from overwhelming, stimulate language and verbal capacities, and reinforce the child's development.

In reality, of course, parents are often not in tune with their children's feelings and needs. What is important is how parents and children *repair* the relationship after missteps in the dance of their relationship (Easterbrooks, 1998). Children learn to say they are "sorry" from parents who are strong enough to recognize when they make mistakes and apologize. Children need to learn that their relationships will be reaffirmed no matter what happens. This is why bedtime rituals, the gentle snuggle and story time or the good-night hug and kiss, are so important. In contrast, shaming and humiliation lead children to distrust themselves and the adults who try to care for them.

In "still-face" experiments (cited by Easterbrooks, 1998), researchers videotaped babies interacting with their parents who, at a certain point, were instructed to become still-faced and show no response to their babies. The babies protested and, if they still did not get a response, they withdrew or tried to provoke a response again. When the parents began to act again in a normal manner, babies typically protested to their parents. In this way, the babies clearly signaled that what the parents had been doing, acting still-faced in the experiment, was inappropriate and frightening.

The "still-face" experiments were meant to mimic how a child experiences a depressed parent. If the parent continued to act in a depressed manner, experiments found that the baby continued to withdraw and essentially acted depressed. Babies who had experienced inconsistent relationships tended to give up easier. After a time of experiencing still-faced parents, infants showed signs of being unable to regulate their environment, a breakdown in their ability to manage. Babies cried or became unable to perform tasks that they earlier could accomplish, such as stacking a block. Babies in these experiments regressed in their use of language often within in minutes.

Babies show us what they need. Parents act as the base from which infants or young children explore the world. Children who are held can quickly stop crying and recover. Toddlers with strong attachments will follow their parents' suggestions. Toddlers also show they have a strong attachment by the affection they show their parents. Attached children utilize their parents' faces as a signal for information and look to their parents quickly in any case of anxiety, such as the introduction of a stranger into their environment. In contrast, insecure children often appear to stay where they are and cry when upset, to show anger at the parent, or to rarely ask for help. Children with insecure attachments may cry to get their parents' attention or to cling in a manner showing they must be the center of their parents' attention in order to be safe. Other children with insecure attachments may wander off.

A child's behavior signals what kind of attachment he or she has experienced. The child who appears inhibited and focuses his or her attention almost exclusively on the gestures and verbalizations of the adult has often learned to anticipate adult responses with the hope of getting what he or she needs from an inconsistent adult, perhaps a parent consumed by his or her own problems. A child who acts wild or in a destructive manner may have learned that this is what he or she needs to do in order to get attention or anything at all. Preschool children who seek attention and affection from strangers often have not had a secure relationship and have learned that they must rely on whatever attention they can get from the adults in their environment.

Care and Nurture

The attachment process is repeated through the child's life, hour by hour, day by day, in progressively more complex sequences that continue into adulthood and then form the basis for how the next generation is raised. Cicchetti (1989) surmised that dysfunctional attachments may be a significant factor in the continuation of maltreatment from generation to generation.

Care and nurture build trust (Bowlby, 1988; Erikson, 1986; Ainsworth et al., 1978; Fraiberg, 1980). Lack of care and nurture generate helplessness, hopelessness, and anger. The greater the trust created, the greater the ability of the child to handle feelings of need and his or her overall feelings of security. Conversely, the lower the trust developed, the greater the child's ever-present sense of unfulfilled need, anxiety, and agitation.

Bonding to the parent before and after birth forms the blueprint for all future relationships. The child who grows up fearful of whether or how a parent will respond tends to inhibit expression of feelings and thoughts. These children watch carefully for clues to see when it is safe to speak up and ask for help. The child who gets very little tends to give up, to shut down, and may die as in the failure to thrive syndrome. The child who experiences unpredictability and periodic rageful responses by his or her parents will tend to become self-focused, aggressive, uncaring about others, and will learn to do whatever is necessary to get what is desired. Such a child learns to survive in a hostile world where caring and nurture mean stealing, manipulation, and deceit as a way of life.

Healthy attachments (Pastzor, Leighton, and Blome, 1993) have been associated with development of a conscience, impulse control, self-esteem, getting along with others, self-awareness, thinking skills, and age-appropriate developmental abilities. Children with strong attachments show us that they feel guilt, shame, or anxiety after doing something hurtful to others and that they can accept responsibility for what they do wrong, set limits on their own behaviors, plan ahead, understand consequences, and work to achieve their goals. Attached children typically show pride in their accomplishments and can accept praise and have fun without going wild or getting into trouble. They can give and receive affection and do not have to be in control of all situations.

Parents need to demonstrate skills and knowledge including an understanding of a child's needs, empathy for the child, child-management skills, and advocacy skills. All of this, however, will not be enough if a parent cannot exercise self-control. The parent must demonstrate the ability to regulate his or her own feelings and then pass this on to the child. Management of frustration, patience, self-seeking, and a sense of humor make parenting possible. Children need parents to provide consistency with flexibility to stand up for them and protect them in all areas of their lives. The child learns from a parent to deal with dimensions of time including past, present, and future. Children need parents who can tolerate them asserting themselves and model effective problem-solving skills. Most of all, the child needs a caring adult who shows day after day that he or she is valued. This commitment anchors children to their families and communities and forms the foundation for empathy.

Parents and caretakers promote the basic cognitive development for children, reinforce development of skills, help them develop skills through practice and promotion of new options, protect them from painful events such as inordinate punishment or harm from others, and stimulate language and verbal capacities. All of this impacts the neurobiology of children at critical stages of development (Schore, 1994, 2001, 2003a,b; Siegel, 1999, 2003). The neurobiology, in turn, impacts what children are capable of doing, how they respond to their environments, and the responses they engender from peers and adults. In summary, the parent-child attachment shapes a child's neurobiology, which, in turn, impacts the child's relationships in an ongoing cycle throughout his or her life.

ATTACHMENT AND BEHAVIOR PATTERNS

Lack of a strong attachment between a child and a parent has been correlated with failure to thrive, conduct disorder, anxiety and depression, poor social skills, borderline personality disorder, affect regulation and self-control problems, low frustration tolerance, short attention span, poor concentration and problem-solving skills, poor peer relations, limited ability to adapt to adversity, social aggression, and disruptive behavior disorders.

The "Strange Situation" Test

Patterns of attachment have been classified by an infant's response to the "strange situation," a test of his or her responses to reunion with a parent after two brief separations (Ainsworth et al., 1978). These patterns reflect the quality of a mother-child attachment during the first year (Ainsworth et al., 1978; Isabella and Belsky, 1991).

Secure infants actively look for contact with caregivers, are calmed by their mothers, and are then able to explore their surroundings. Secure children demonstrate pleasure when they see their mothers and relax in their presence. Parents provide a secure base for children to explore and learn. In contrast, *insecure-avoidant* infants will avoid their mothers when mothers re-enter the room. Instead, these children focus on objects and their play. Their behavior shows a distance or detachment from their mothers and this pattern of attachment has been linked to babies who have experienced their mothers rebuffing their babies' calls for contact or comforting. Infants who have experienced inconsistent parenting tend to respond to the "strange situation" by seeking contact with their mothers, and at the same time angrily resisting them. These babies, described as *insecure-ambivalent,* may demonstrate angry, avoidant, or highly immature and dependent behaviors during their reunions with mothers. They may have difficulty exploring and instead become extremely passive.

Secure, insecure-avoidant, and insecure-ambivalent infants demonstrate an organized strategy for coping with the stress of their mothers leaving the room and working toward the goal of regaining proximity with their mothers (Main and Solomon, 1990; Solomon and George, 1996). Secure children directly approach their mothers when stressed. Insecure-avoidant and insecure-ambivalent children may pull away or use angry resistant behavior to reengage parents. These responses appear constricted but function in an organized manner to reduce their stress.

Main and Solomon (1986) found that children who had been traumatized by age one, often show contradictory behaviors (e.g., backing toward the parent instead of moving directly toward the parent, face forward).

> One infant hunched her upper body and shoulders at hearing her mother's call, then broke into extravagant laugh-like screeches with an excited forward movement. Her braying laughter became a cry and distress-face without a new intake of breath as the infant hunched forward. Then suddenly, she became silent, blank, and dazed. (p. 119)

These children often demonstrate contradictory behaviors. They may start to approach their parents, then appear disoriented and abruptly turn away. They do not have an organized strategy for regaining proximity and care from their parents in times of stress and have been described as having *disorganized attachments* (Main and Solomon, 1990). Some toddlers act in highly controlling manners, in ways that appear punitive to parents, or as if, these children have learned that they must assume the parenting role. Other children may show compulsively compliant behaviors with almost no visible sense of autonomy, or apprehension, confusion, and no expectation of cause and consequence in their lives.

Children with chaotic, disorganized attachments seem unable to integrate experiences of conflict in their primary relationships (Solomon and George, 1999). Their behavior tends to oscillate and reflects their experiences that primary responses do not work to ease their distress. These infants and toddlers show confusion and apprehension in common situations where other children with secure attachments have learned to expect comfort and soothing. Instead of calming, children with chaotic disorganized attachments may become more distressed with proximity to caretakers.

Schore (2001) reviewed research that demonstrates how disorganized attachments lead to severe orbitalfrontal pruning and the lack of critical neural connections necessary for learning how to cope and manage stress. Excessive parcellation and death of neural cells leads to a lack of ability to regulate hormone production by the hypothalamus and impedes affective regulation. Stress hormones released in the midst of traumas activate fast, "low road" amygdala connections that provide very little information, provoke immediate survival responses, and over time become the child's primary pattern of responding, weakening "high road," neural connections involving the child's prefrontal cortex and hippocampus that would provide the child with more sensory information and more effective coping responses (LeDoux, 2002). Schore maintained that parent-child relationship trauma blocks both the dendritic growth and astrocyte proliferation. Neurological studies have found that the astrocytic processes around the synapses are directly impacted by the young child's social environment (Jones and Greenough, 1996).

Schore (1996, 1997, 2001) argued that excessive pruning of limbic circuits results in inefficient regulation of subcortical systems. Excessive parcellation would reduce the child's ability to experience positive feelings and lead to vulnerability to hypoarousal (e.g., depression). In addition, Schore described how severe parcellation of the medial orbitofrontal areas and the inhibitory medial tegmental forebrain-midbrain circuit would impede a child's ability to contain hyperarousal, to calm, and to avoid uncontrolled terror and rage. Impairment of the orbitalfrontal lobes is especially critical (Schore, 1994, 2003a) for self-regulation, including affect modulation, since this is the only area of the brain that is linked to the limbic system, the cortex, and the autonomic nervous system by one neuron. The right orbitofrontal region operates as a regulatory endpoint for both branches of the autonomic nervous system (ANS). The sympathetic branch of the ANS serves as an "accelerator," while the parasympathetic branch works as a "brake."

Traumatized children display deficits in social and emotional information processing and may overreact or freeze when faced with stress. Faces in particular may trigger chaotic behavior in infants who have experienced abuse or neglect. Images of angry faces are believed to be stored in the right amygdala and the sounds of angry voices in the left (Schore, 2001). Schore (2003a) hypothesized that children who experience rejection in parent-child relationships often demonstrate underarousal of their autonomic nervous system and that this could predispose a child to developing an antisocial personality. Children who grow up with an abusive parent demonstrate excessive arousal and develop a predisposition for disorganization and symptoms of borderline personality disorder. An infant growing up with a disorganized, chaotic attachment may respond to the sight of a parent returning with trance-like behavior (e.g., freezing for twenty seconds or oscillating between approaching and moving away from a parent) (Schore, 2001).

Affect regulation by the right orbitalfrontal brain is largely formed by age two. The traumatic impact of living with inconsistent and often neglectful or abusive parenting directly impairs the child's developing nervous system. Children growing up without a secure and organized attachment show signs from infancy of emotional dysregulation and reliance on primitive modes of autoregulation (e.g., denial, dissociation, and avoidance). The excessive pruning also impairs connections between the right and left prefrontal cortex inhibiting a child's ability to understand and develop cognitive and language-based solutions to problems. Over time, disorganized attachments lead to symptoms of post-traumatic stress disorder and borderline and antisocial personality disorders (Schore, 2001; Main, 1996).

Disorganized behavior patterns have been associated with frightening or frightened parenting behaviors (Main and Hess, 1990) as well as to interactions with hostile and intrusive mothers (Lyons-Ruth et al., 1991). Young children who begin showing a disorganized and controlling pattern of behavior have frequently experienced maltreatment (Carlson et al., 1989). Parents of children with these behaviors have been described as often failing to protect their children and often feeling helpless in their roles as parents (Solomon and George, 1996).

Parents who have lost attachment figures in their own lives are especially vulnerable to problems in raising their children. Their children's attachment-seeking behavior may trigger painful memories of their parents that have not been resolved. They may become disoriented and unable to care for or comfort their children. Parents may also respond in a frightening or frightened manner toward their children (Main, 1991; Main and Hesse, 1990, 1992; Main and Solomon, 1990). Similarly, parents who remain traumatized from violence perpetuated by siblings or a child's other parent may react with detachment, rage, or ambivalence when triggered by the developing images, gestures, tone of voice, or other nonverbal behaviors of their child.

Finally, the strange situation may elicit a pattern of behaviors that reflect a *tenuous or nonattachment*. These children show almost no searching behavior for their missing parents, show no protest at separation, and when reunited with their parents, may wander around the room appearing oblivious to their parents' actions. Such children may whimper, but do not look to their parents for assistance or comfort. For these children, parents appear as impersonal objects with little significance for their lives.

Research with the strange situation paradigm found that children who lived with abuse or neglect showed ambivalent, avoidant, or disorganized attachments with their primary parents (Cicchetti, 1989). Disorganized attachments appear linked with both disturbed caregiving and their experiences with multiple unfamiliar placements (Jacobsen and Miller, 1999). This has created a dilemma for authorities seeking to maintain bonds between children and mothers diagnosed with mental illnesses and at the same time to protect these children from maltreatment. Research on children of mentally ill mothers has found that these children appear at high risk both when they remain with their mothers and also when they are separated from them (Silverman, 1989). The physical location (or placement) of a child does not, by itself, address the child's need for a healthy attachment.

In a study of children of mothers diagnosed with mental illnesses, Jacobsen and Miller (1999) found that 35 percent of the children showed disorganized controlling behaviors and 35 percent showed tenuous or no attachments. Mothers of *tenuous/nonattached* children did not seem able to recognize their children as individuals. These mothers had significantly smaller support networks than parents of the *disorganized/controlling* children, typically just one person who could help them with parenting. Loss of that one person put the mothers at high risk of isolation and loneliness. Mothers of children in the *disorganized attachment* group glorified descriptions of their children and their relationships with them, and their children tended to speak idealistically about their mothers.

Frequent changes in caregivers and persistent neglect from primary caregivers has been linked to the development of disorganized or disorganized/controlling attachments or children with tenuous or no attachments.

Crittenden and Ainsworth (1989) described how withholding close bodily contact accounted for anxious and avoidant attachment patterns.

ATTACHMENT AND BEHAVIOR PROBLEMS

Lack of attachment has been correlated with failure to thrive, conduct disorder, anxiety and depression, borderline personality disorder, social aggression, disruptive behavior disorder, and deficits in social skills, affect regulation, self-control, frustration tolerance, attention span, concentration, problem solving, and adaptations to adversity. A child's attachment pattern becomes associated with behaviors that lead to further problems with parents and other caregivers. The young child may elicit harsh discipline by caregivers and punishments that, in turn, lead to further behavior problems and additional rejection and abuse. The damage to a child mounts as he or she becomes mired in cycles of loneliness and punishment. Often, the child's contribution to behavior problems increases over time as he or she experiences rejection and violence (Steinhauer, 1974). Placement away from home can confirm a child's sense of being worthless or abandoned, leading to increased rejection and increased behavioral problems. These, in turn, may lead to additional separations, *re*placements, and further difficulties in interactions with adults and caretakers.

Unresolved separations and the cumulative experience of rejection contribute to a child's increasing behavior problems. Toddlers who experience inconsistency or even abuse, develop the kinds of behaviors often seen in children labeled as oppositional defiant disorder and later in adults classified as borderline or antisocial personality disorders (Peterson, 1994). In research studies, the lack of security in preschool boys was found to be the best predictor of oppositional defiant disorder (Speltz et al., 1995), and insecure attachments may play a primary role in the formation of conduct disorders (Greenberg, Speltz, and DeLyen, 1993).

Attachment problems can continue into adulthood and affect an individual's relationships. For instance, Scott and Cordova (2002) found that adults who grew up with more secure attachments tended to have better adjustments in their marriages and fewer indicators of depression. Marital partners with an avoidant attachment style tended to have more dysfunctional marriages and more depressive symptoms.

Hughes (1997) compiled a list of behavioral symptoms of children with significant attachment difficulties based on research and clinical experience. These symptoms include:

- a compulsive need to control others, including caregivers, teachers, and other children;
- intense lying, even when "caught in the act";
- poor response to discipline: aggressive or oppositional-defiant;
- lack of comfort with eye contact (except when lying);
- physical contact (wanting too much or too little);
- interactions lack mutual enjoyment and spontaneity;
- body functioning disturbances (eating, sleeping, urinating, defecating);
- increased attachment produces discomfort and resistance;
- indiscriminately friendly and charming; easily replaced relationships;
- poor communication: many nonsense questions and chatter;
- difficulty learning cause/effect, poor planning and/or problem solving;
- lack of empathy, little evidence of guilt and remorse for others;
- ability to see only the extremes (all good or all bad);
- habitual dissociation or hypervigilence; and
- pervasive shame, with extreme difficulty reestablishing a bond following conflict (pp. 30-31).

Reactive Attachment Disorders

The DSM-IV (APA, 1994) delineates criteria for diagnosing reactive attachment disorders when a child demonstrates severely impaired and inappropriate interpersonal relations starting before the age of five. Children may present as constricted by consistently failing to seek or respond to relationships, or as, the opposite, when children demonstrate indiscriminate relationships with others and multiple superficial attachments. The diagnosis of reactive attachment disorder is also based on children's experiences of neglect in the care provided to meet their basic needs, as well as multiple changes in caregivers that block development of secure attachments. Not surprisingly, children with attachment disorders tend to see adults who try to exercise authority (Peterson, 1994) as untrustworthy, dishonest, self-centered, rejecting, inconsistent, stupid, and not really caring. These children have learned to expect parents, foster parents, relatives, teachers, and other authorities to become rejecting or abusive.

Attachment problems vary in severity depending on a child's experiences and age. Young children who have experienced repeated rejections, abandonment, abuse, and neglect typically show the worst effects. The younger the child is when attachment breaks down, the more disturbed the child may be. Similarly, the more frequently a child experiences the breakdown or failure of attachments, the greater the symptoms of attachment disorder.

FACILITATING ATTACHMENT

Wisdom Through the Ages

All cultures have developed ways to promote care for the young. A Navaho adage admonishes, "He who acts wild, careless, is like a man without relatives." An African adage (Rattrey, 1956) warns, "When a chicken separates itself from the rest, a hawk will get it."

From a biological perspective, all babies begin life with two parents as well as extended family with aunts, uncles, and grandparents to provide care. This allows for backups in case something happens with one of the primary adult caregivers for a child. Fathers, often neglected in discussions of education and social services, are critical and correlated in study after study with positive growth and development including academic achievement of children. Grandparents, aunts, uncles, older siblings, and cousins can play a major role in enhancing a child's resilience and success. Government and businesses can support or undermine the parenting, education, and guidance of children. Policies, regulations, and financial structures impact the daily life of parents and children.

A Lifetime Commitment

We can see the attachment process unfold when a loving parent cares for an infant. As the infant looks into the parent's eyes, the child sees that he or she is recognized. The child coos, sighs, or cries and the parent responds with a caress, a smile, or mimics the infant's sound or gesture. With each response, the infant feels validated and real. The parent and child often breathe in unison. The skin of the mother of a newborn changes temperature (cited by Hughes, 1998b) to cool or warm a naked baby place skin to skin. The child literally sees a reflection of himself or herself in the parent's face, eye to eye, skin to skin. The infant begins life as part of a relationship that will shape every aspect of his or her being.

Attunement is associated with the prefrontal limbal cortex (Schore, 1994). This is also the area of the brain shut down the most during stress and trauma. Parents teach the child how to self-soothe in times of stress. Children who learn that they will be cared for learn to care about others. Children who do not experience this recognition and validation learn to see themselves as a dark hole, without value, or simply bad. Children become overwhelmed with grief. If they do not receive help, they may never be able to surmount the pain of their losses. They grow physically, but close to the surface, the pain lingers, similar to an unhealed wound. We see it in toddlers, six year olds, adolescents, and adults. The need for attachment continues throughout our lives.

Poised and assertive, eighteen-year-old Rebecca stated her intent to get her GED (general equivalency diploma), begin a job, save some money, and consider college for the next fall. Rebecca had impressed my colleagues with her confidence, the self-care evident in her clothing, and her ability to look adults directly in the eye. She elucidated to me her achievements to date and her pride in earning the highest privileges allowed in her group care facility.

I gently asked about family members she wanted to see and any family members who had supported her. Rebecca looked down and away. She described trying to reunite with her mother after several years in placement. I asked what happened. Tears formed in her eyes. Rebecca lifted her head but couldn't stop herself. She began to sob.

Rebecca's mother left her when Rebecca was three years old. Rebecca never understood what happened. The next years of her life were marred by sex abuse and violence, but Rebecca had endured and held on to her wish to live once again with her mother. When Rebecca heard that her mother had returned, she felt hope once again and moved back with her. They lived together for several months before her mother cast her out, calling her "worthless" and "no good."

Rebecca, with tears in her eyes, described how her mother, once again, did not call, write, or even send a card at her last birthday. In fact, her mother had never recognized any birthdays that Rebecca could remember.

Infants and children demonstrate how they need adults who will raise them to maturity and remain committed to their well-being. Parents are not interchangeable. Children removed from their *psychological* parents experience insecurity and are often hampered in their social, emotional, and cognitive development. This is critical when considering custody cases or parental plans to have someone else such as a grandparent raise the child for the first few years, followed by removal from that substitute parent, and return to the biological parent. For a child, "return" of custody to birth parents may represent transfer to a stranger and the shock of disorientation.

Reuniting may be desirable for a parent who returns with a wish to regain his or her child, but what may seem good for a parent, may entail massive losses for a child. He or she may lose primary ties to psychological parents often coupled with lost friendships and ties to schools, neighbors, and religious institutions. The child's foundation of trust can be shattered. A biological parent's legal rights may not be healthy or in the best interest of the child (Goldstein, Freud, and Solnit, 1973). A parent's verbalized wishes to resume parenting after several years of absence or neglect, may reflect the parent's needs or, in some cases, the parent's response to pressure from family members or the community. The child's need for an enduring attachment over time is all too often not addressed in court proceedings that emphasize genetic over psychological parenting.

Attunement with a child requires a commitment to care over time. Parenting is not a verbalized promise; it is something parents do, day in and day out, 24/7, with love, validation, and work, through the good times and the bad. Children learn whether they can trust their parents to be there in the future. This forms their expectations of permanency.

In reality, no relationship lasts forever. Death, disease, wars, and natural disasters take their toll. Children can grow and thrive with the expectation of a bonded relationship lasting into the future. They learn to get past losses with the help of supportive relationships and the opportunities to rebuild attachments.

Permanency is an expectation built on trust and commitment, tested in adversity. False promises and unreal bonds do not work, even if they are written on a legal document or codified on a case record. Children are naturally loyal to their parents and may cling to fantasies or wishes for reunion. But, in the hard times, children learn the difference between their wishes/fantasies of idealized parents and the reality of who they can count on for help. Children find out who can be trusted in the middle of a dark lonely night when they are lying sick in bed and week after week when they struggle to learn at school and when their parents have to struggle with bills, cars breaking down, and paying the rent.

Indicators of Attachment

In checking for attachment, we look for signs at all ages about whether a child can be soothed by a parent and the child's reaction to the absence of a parent. An eighteen-month-old with healthy attachment will typically turn his or her head and look back if a parent leaves the room. An eighteen-month-old with little attachment may not seem to care or may simply climb into any adult's lap, indiscriminately moving from stranger to stranger. We can observe attachment and skill development with eighteen-month-old toddlers by demonstrating how to stack two blocks and then asking the child to do the same (Brazelton, 1974). Some toddlers will stack the blocks and then look up at the adult, as if to say, "How great I am." Other toddlers will appear cognitively unable to process information and unable to learn. Toddlers with attachment problems may demonstrate that they know what the adult is asking by beginning to stack the blocks but then slide the blocks by each other and look up, as if to say, "See, I'm no good. Reject me . . ."

Other signs of attachment (Carson and Goodfield, 1988) include whether a child spontaneously looks for a hug or affection from a parent or significant adult. Does the child show age-appropriate space, not always clingy, and not always attached? Does the child learn to explore and show curiosity? Does the child show empathy or sensitivity to others? Can the child have fun without ending up upset or aggressive? Does the child model after peers to get adult reinforcement?

Attachment can also be observed by how a child can utilize a parent as a base for security (Waters and Deane, 1985). Attached children will recover quickly from minor hurts and insults when held by their parents. They will look to their parents if they are unsure and use clues from their faces to help master a task. Attached children will spontaneously hug or put their arms around a parent.

Attached children demonstrate confidence. We see this in how they approach a task or challenge, from a toddler stacking blocks to an adolescent tackling a chemistry exam. Attached children have a positive view of their potential in the world. They are involved in fewer conflicts and show an ability to resolve them and solve problems.

Learning the Truths of Life

Infants, toddlers, and young children learn the truths of their lives—who they can trust, who really cares, and who just pretends. Bonding is tested in times of pain and risk. When a child feels discomfort, he or she calls for help. The infant can do little more than cry. The older child may call for help, curse, or slam a door. If the parent recognizes the child's call for help and comforts the child, he or she learns safety, to trust others, to belong, and to care about others. Secure attachments (Siegel, 2003) are based on contingent communication, including sharing of emotions, reflections by adults using words to describe experiences, repairing disruptions between parent and child, and helping children develop coherent life stories. A parent needs to perceive their child's signals calling for attention or help, understand the child's experiences, and respond in an effective and timely manner. A young child bases his or her security on the ability of primary adults to keep themselves both available and emotionally regulated. Children watch their parents carefully. Most communication is right brain to right brain: eye contact, facial appearance, posture, gestures, tone of voice, and touch. Adults help children learn to develop their own capacity to perceive the world and experience a broad range of emotions by sharing and increasing positive experiences, and, similarly, sharing and reducing negative experiences and difficult feelings, e.g., loss, anger, regret, fear. By adding words to experiences, adults teach children to develop their own left-brain capacity for language-based reasoning, to question, understand, cope, and self-regulate. Over time, parents can help children develop the capacity to conceive their own life in an organized and comprehensive manner, which gives a child a sense of identity and competence.

Healthy attachments (Pastzor, Leighton, and Blome, 1993) have been associated with development of a conscience, impulse control, self-esteem, getting along with others, self-awareness, thinking skills, and age-appropriate developmental abilities. Children with a strong attachment show feelings of guilt, shame, or anxiety after doing something hurtful to others. They accept responsibility for what they do wrong; can set limits on their own behaviors; can think or plan ahead; and can think and understand consequences. Such children also show pride in their accomplishments and can accept praise and have fun without going wild or getting into trouble. Attached children can give and receive affection and do not have to be in control of all situations.

Children also learn the truths of life from their parents' reactions to adversity. When children see parents become distressed in the course of their daily lives, children signal their own distress. Children watch their parents carefully to learn whether parents can manage their own stress and continue to soothe their children. When parents do not respond to children's cries, or reject their children, children learn to expect discomfort in life. Such children learn to see themselves as powerless and worthless. They learn to look at adults and caregivers as hurtful, uncaring, or not to be trusted.

Insecurely attached children learn that they must be in control or they will die. This belief guides their behaviors in ways that may not be understood by other adults. These children may withdraw or act enraged. They may lie, steal, and even deny what they have done when they are caught in the act. They have learned that real feelings must be hidden, both to protect themselves and because they are too difficult to experience.

Children who have experienced insecure attachments often act in ways that make no sense to other people. Their behavior is similar to the stripes on a zebra. In a zoo, a lone zebra's stripes seem illogical and crazy. On the plains of Africa, the same zebra's stripes flow in a distorting image to protect the zebra in a herd running from predators.

Children in crisis often cannot tell us what has happened. They may even lie to protect parents or siblings and their wish to reunite. But, children's behavior almost always will show us what we need to know about the reality of their attachments and safety within their home and community. Their behaviors can be used as clues to both underlying problems and solutions (Kagan, 2003).

PROMOTING RESILIENCE

Resilience is not a static attribute but rather functions as a multidetermined and ever-changing product of interacting forces within an individual's family, social groups, community, society, and world (Waller, 2001). Competence and resilience have been linked with individual, family, and extrafamilial supports (Masten and Coatsworth, 1998). Individual factors associated with resilience include: good intellectual functioning, special talents, an easygoing disposition, an appealing sociable demeanor, faith, and a person's belief in self-efficacy and feelings of self-confidence and self-esteem. These individual characteristics have also been associated with relationship factors and environmental supports that foster resilience (Masten and Coatsworth, 1998) including: a close relationship to a caring parent figure; parenting with warmth, structure, and high expectations of the child; socioeconomic resources; caring adults who provide consistent parenting that is warm and structured with high expectations; ties to extended family members; connections to adults outside the family; involvement with prosocial organizations; and effective schools. Factors linked to resilience appear tied together in a growth-enhancing cycle benefiting the child fortunate enough to be raised with a strong family and community network providing support, safety, nurture, and stimulation.

Masten (2001) found that contrary to popular belief, resilience develops from very ordinary adaptational processes and is not limited to remarkable individuals. Current reviews of research on resilience (Masten, 2001; Luthar, Cicchetti, and Becker, 2000; Wyman et al., 2000) identified a small number of factors that were found to be the most critical for promoting resilience, including

- positive connections to caring and competent adults within a youth's family or community;
- development of cognitive and self-regulation abilities;
- positive beliefs about oneself;
- motivation to act effectively in one's environment.

Supportive connections help buffer an individual against the worst effects of trauma (Herman, 1992) and serve as "inoculations against adversity" (Schimmer, Personal Communication, 1999). The greatest threats to resilience (Masten, 2001) appear to follow the breakdown of protective systems: damage to brain development and cognitive skills, parent/caregiver and child relationships, cognitive abilities to regulate emotions and behaviors, and motivation to interact with one's environment and to learn and develop new skills. In situations of severe adversity, poor parenting and poor cognitive skills increase the risk of antisocial behavior, and normative intellectual skills and parenting seem to protect the child and foster growth of competence even in conditions of adversity. Studies of resilience have found that maladaptive behavioral patterns develop when adversity is severe and the child lacks protective resources such as good parenting, socioeconomic resources, and intellectual abilities (Masten, 2001).

Efforts to build or rebuild attachments are most successful with younger children and with children who still dare to demonstrate a desire for attachments and can reciprocate affection and caring. Adolescents very naturally seek greater autonomy and may resist efforts to create bonded relationships. Still, many adolescents long for attachments and can be engaged in work to rebuild trust.

The approach outlined in this book is especially designed for children with a wide range of attachment problems. The *Real Life Heroes* workbook can be modified to help both young children and adolescents. The focus of this approach centers on building, or rebuilding, a child's attachments as primary interventions to prevent and overcome secondary behavioral problems.

Celebrations

The other day, I went to a bar mitzvah (the Jewish ritual to celebrate the transition of a thirteen-year-old into the responsibilities of adulthood). In Jewish life this means leading the Sabbath service and taking on responsibilities, mitzvat, which stress helping others. For families, of course, the event marks the change from the baby-faced child to the adolescent. Whiskers replace chunky cheeks. A driver's license is often only three years away. Children grow at an alarming rate and demand more privileges. For parents, the transition is both wonderful and at the same times marks a loss. They watch their children change before their eyes and know that the days of caring for and guiding the young child have come to an end.

I watched as the son of friends honored aunts and uncles, grandparents, cousins, and his forty closest friends followed by a slide show accompanied by music showing his life from birth to age thirteen. I was struck by all the photographs of this boy with different family and extended-family members. Photograph after photograph documented people who cared about this boy. Each photograph showed someone with a smile leaning forward, their arm around the youth, and a look on their face that told everyone watching that they saw this youth as special. So special, indeed, that his parents had lit up his name in lights and 150 people had gathered to celebrate his transition into young adulthood.

A week later, I was sitting in the offices of Child Protective Services and introduced myself to a fifty-five-year-old grandmother. "I'm exhausted," she responded in a soft, hoarse voice. She had been given custody of her grandson, Anthony, five months before. Anthony's mother died of AIDS, and they had been estranged from his grandmother for many years. Anthony had never known his father or any relatives on his father's side of his family. With the death of his mother, Anthony had been moved 500 miles north to live with the only known relative. His grandmother told me she was planning to retire. "I am alone and I'm too old for this." In a fit of anger, she had struck her grandson across the face, leaving a bruise.

Two boys: one with so many resources in his life, the other on the brink of homelessness. Anthony's bruise formed a visible mark of his family's trauma. Anthony had lost critical family members even before he was born, and now his last family tie was breaking.

CONCLUSION

The link between parent and child forms a lifeline that protects a child from harm and fosters growth and development. Strong attachments to caring parents lead to successful children. Each attachment adds to a child's strength and resilience. The stronger the child's relationships, the more likely he or she is to overcome adversity in life and to become productive as an adult, contributing, in turn, to the welfare of the community.

Rebuilding broken lifelines means listening to children and learning how to respond to their needs for nurture, consistency, predictability, safety, and discipline within an enduring and bonded relationship to primary parents. Efforts by an adult to control a child's behaviors are typically only successful for limited periods of time, usually when the adult in charge is watching and able to overpower the child. Attachment-related behavior problems require attachment-centered interventions.

In the following chapters, I describe the experience of attachment and neglect from a child's perspective, the impact of trauma on neurological functioning, factors leading to neglect, obstacles that hinder care for children at risk, and how we can utilize the lessons children teach us to rebuild lifelines for children in crisis.

Chapter 2

Angel or Demon?

It is better to see oneself as a sinner in a world ruled by the good Lord, than as a saint in a world ruled by the Devil.

W. R. D. Fairbairn

TWO BOYS

Billy's Story

Billy[1] liked to ride down his driveway on his tricycle, pumping his little legs as fast as he could. He was a three-and-a-half-years-old, a cute little guy with a bright smile, sparkling eyes, and chunky little cheeks. Billy was all motion, fearless on his little tricycle. Speed meant fun. Billy pretended he was a knight with the power of the wind brushing against his cheeks. He was the master of the most powerful vehicle in the universe and faster than any boy had ever dared to go.

Billy zoomed past the tree at the end of the driveway, past the marker where Mom and Dad told him to always stop. As Billy headed for the corner, he pedaled faster and faster, a little too fast. He raced on, started his turn, planning to skid expertly in a tight circle, just as he had seen racers make turns on a televised off-road competition.

Suddenly, Billy lost his balance. He flipped to the left and lost his grip on the handlebars. Billy slammed into the cement and skidded to a halt in the dirt and gravel. Billy looked down at his arms and legs. Blood oozed out from under the dirt. His knee stung with pain He felt his chin ache and his shoulder throb. Billy hurt all over, but the worst part was the burning pain in his knee.

Looking down, Billy saw red drops, his blood. He was sure his insides were coming out. Billy stared at his wounded knee and for a moment, his whole body stiffened. A panicky scream grew from his stomach upward into his lungs. For Billy, the bright red blood represented his life force draining away.

Billy pulled himself up and headed for his front door, forcing his legs to move through the pain, one foot in front of the other, jerky steps with stiff legs. With every step, bursts of fire surged upward from his knee. Billy almost stopped but something propelled him faster and faster. His eyes locked on to the doorknob. Tears streamed down his cheeks and mixed with drops of blood on his chin.

Billy reached the front door and cried out with every ounce of breath in his lungs. His eyes swept left and right searching for Mom, Dad, Grandpa, somebody. Where were they?

Billy heard footsteps. His head and his eyes went down, pointing toward his bloody knee. His mouth tightened into his deepest frown. Billy's whole body shuddered with each breath. He was the embodiment of pain, a wounded soul searching for salvation.

Billy saw his mom's legs and feet running toward him. In a flash, she opened the door, reached out, and enveloped him. She lifted him up and pulled him tightly against her chest, holding his cheek next to hers. Billy's tears streamed onto his mother's face. He felt her gentle kiss on his forehead.

Billy ached all over. With each sob, he checked to make sure his mom knew how much he hurt. Cindy, Billy's mom, carried him to the sink, gently washed his cuts, and covered them with a soothing ointment. She stroked his back, hugged him lightly, and put a bandage on his knee, not just an ordinary bandage, but a magic bandage with pictures of Billy's favorite hero. Billy felt his mom's touch, steady and warm. He knew that he was not alone.

"I'll just stay close to Mom," he thought to himself. He was feeling safe again with his mother's hugs, the soothing ointment, and just being close to her. It was better that way. He would promise Mom and Dad to stay close forever. Never leave their sight. Billy's mind drifted off. He could be a little baby again, even give up racing his bike. He would just stay next to his Mom and Dad. That way he could be safe from the pain of cuts and crashing tricycles. No more blood, ever.

Billy let out a sigh and his whole body shuddered. He never, ever wanted to hurt so bad again.

Cindy gave him another hug. He felt the pain in his knee start to go down. The hugs were like magic. For a second, he'd feel okay. But then, he felt the sting again. Not so bad now, but still there. Billy saw the bright bandage covering his wound. There was no more blood leaking out. His knee was safe.

Billy looked up at his mom. He could see a teardrop in the corner of his Mom's eyes. "I should have been watching you," Cindy continued. "I went to get the phone. Next time, I'll keep it with me while I watch you ride your bike." Billy saw her face change from the creased wrinkles that showed her worried side to the firmer lines that meant he'd better listen. Billy shuddered again and looked down, putting on his hurt look.

"Look at me," Cindy said. She looked him in the eyes.

"Don't go past the end of the driveway! Go slow when you turn." Her voice was stern. It was a lesson on how to be safe.

Billy watched TV for the next hour. He heard his mother making dinner in the kitchen. Carefully picking up his hurt knee, Billy trudged slowly to the doorway. Then he stopped, gazing at his mother and the kitchen, as though he was seeing her for the first time. His eyes were down, just a bit, his mouth shaped into a moping look.

"You can go out," Cindy said, but Billy just stood there. "Go back out. Remember the rules I told you. I'll be watching." Billy walked slowly to the door, looking back over his shoulder to see if his mom was really there. "Go ahead." She smiled.

Billy's knee hurt when he started to ride again. But, riding his tricycle felt good. Billy kept looking up to the front door. And, a few minutes later, he saw his mom's face. Not the worried look. Not an angry look. Just plain old mom.

Billy felt okay inside. He had learned that he should ride on, be a boy again, and that Mom and Dad cared enough to make sure he followed the rules and stayed safe. Billy learned that we make mistakes, we can get hurt, and we can cry. But, we pick ourselves up, help each other, and we go on.

Billy learned from every spill, every accident, every adventure. Some lessons stuck in his mind more than others. Together they formed lessons about managing pain, about who you can trust, and how to deal with pain.

As with Billy, we too have learned the most important lessons in pain. We learned to feel, to recover, to carry on. We learned whether or not we could trust the most important people in our lives. Through accidents and illnesses, life's serial assaults, we learned crucial lessons. And, as siblings, parents, aunts, uncles, grandparents, teachers, and neighbors, we have taught these lessons to those around us.

Tommy's Story

Four-year-old Tommy sometimes played with Billy in their preschool program. Tommy had a cute upturned little nose and sparkling blue eyes. His blond hair, ready grin, and smudgy face led family friends to call him "a real boy." Tommy liked hearing that. It made him feel strong.

Tommy's dad had always told him, "Be a man." Tommy was good with his hands, just like his dad. He liked to draw, paint, and build things out of blocks and clay. He prided himself on climbing higher than any of the other boys on the school's jungle gym. He was the bravest of the boys.

One day, Tommy, as with his friend Billy, rode his bike a little too fast, crashed, and skinned his knee. Running to the front door, tears in his eyes, blood on his knee, Tommy saw his mother in the living room, bent over his new baby brother. Tommy yanked open the door, slamming it against the wall as he ran into the room. He had learned long ago there was no use waiting around for his mom or dad to answer his cries. Dad was never around anymore, and for the past year, Mom had brought in a new boyfriend, his baby brother's father, someone else who stole his mom's time.

Tommy lurched toward his mother, his whole body throbbing with pain. He couldn't wait. Tommy charged into his mother from behind.

Marie, Tommy's mom, felt the blow to her bad leg, the one she had injured last year when her boyfriend smashed their car. She fell forward, hitting her hip on the wooden frame of the couch, barely catching herself before she crushed her new baby. The baby screamed.

Marie felt a stabbing pain in her hip, and was reminded of the months of pain from the car accident. She whirled around, her mouth curled in fury.

"Stop it! You almost *killed* your brother! Don't you *look* before you do anything? How *stupid* can you be?" Without looking at Tommy, she turned back to the baby, carefully picking him up. She needed to settle him down if she was going to get her work done.

"There, there. Don't you mind that nasty old brother of yours. I know you'll be much more considerate when *you* grow up."

Tommy's heart sank into his stomach. His whole body felt heavy, old. He shuddered. Tears formed in his eyes. Tommy quickly turned away. He would not let her see him cry.

"No use anyway. She doesn't care!" he thought to himself. Tommy trudged silently toward the door, head down, tears streaming down his face.

Lessons

Tommy, too, had learned a lesson. For many children, crying over a scraped knee means getting a whack with a hand, belt, or board, and hearing Mom, Dad, or a grandparent scream at you, "Don't be a sissy!" "Don't bother me right now!" "Can't you see I'm busy with your brother?" "You kids are driving me nuts." "One more problem and I'm out of here." "Now get back outside and play. . . . If I don't get some peace, I'm putting you all in a home."

Tommy stumbled back out the door. He was numb, in a daze. He heard the door slam shut behind him. Suddenly, all the pain in his knee came back with a burning pulse. It wouldn't go away. Tommy's nerves lit up. His knee was on fire.

Tommy's head went down, his eyes narrowed, and the tears stopped. He had learned a vital lesson for survival in his family: "Don't upset Mom or Dad at all costs." Tommy learned to ignore the pain in his leg. He kept his mouth shut. Tommy learned to carry on, pretending nothing happened.

"Don't even think about it!" Tommy ordered himself. "Don't look at the blood! Nothing stops me!" he repeated to himself. "Nothing. Nothing!"

Tommy shut down his pain and narrowed his mind. He got back on his tricycle and climbed back up to the top of the driveway. He was a man of action. This time when he roared down the driveway he was not trying to be a great race car driver. He was a WWF (World Wrestling Federation) wrestler. The biggest and the strongest. Afraid of nothing! Tougher than blood. "I am *the* man! Nobody gets in *my* way!" he said to himself, remembering a line his mother's last boyfriend liked to say. Tommy was making his getaway. He would zoom away from Mom, his baby brother, everything!

Tommy still felt the burning cut on his knee. But, the faster he went, the less he thought about the pain. The wind felt great. He was master once again, searching for even more power. He was going faster than any four year old ever dared. Tommy rounded the corner and headed out into the street. The world was his domain.

A car turned onto the street as Tommy zoomed out. The driver was Billy's mother, her mind preoccupied with the hundred and one things she had to do before dinner, problems at work, worries about the kids, planning for the weekend. Suddenly, she saw a shadow low on the ground, a moving object. Instinctively, she slammed on the brakes. The brakes squealed and the car jerked to a stop, throwing her head backward. She looked ahead and watched the shadow become a little boy darting across the road. A few more feet and she would have hit him. Cindy winced and quickly looked over her shoulder to check on Billy sitting in his car seat in the backseat. Cindy sighed and turned back to the road ahead.

Tommy didn't see the car and didn't even sense how he could have been hit. He was just going faster, heading off alone into the setting sun.

Good Son/Bad Son

Later in the day, or later in the week, Tommy heard a very different message from Marie. "Come here baby," cooed the same parent who had shunned him hours before. "Rub Mommy's back . . . You're my sweetie . . . You're Mama's special one . . . None of the others are worth a damn . . . I could never make it without you." Tommy was drawn into his special role, a companion who watched over and cared for his mom. He became his mother's guard.

"I'm her back," he told himself. Tommy felt warm again inside. The memories of the scraped knee and her rejection were blocked.

"I love my mommy!" he'd tell anyone who asked about his mother. "It's the two of us. Mom and me against everybody."

Tommy grew up with two conflicting but powerful messages from Marie: "I love you; you're a part of me" and "Get out! I hate you." Tommy lived with both messages and split his own identity into two parts.[2] Tommy, the "good" son, was always there for his mom, ready night and day to hold, serve, and care for her. The "bad" son acted out the fear and rage he saw in his mother's glare and heard in the harshness of her voice as she scolded him, often repeating his mom's angry side and the voices of the men in his life, especially Clyde, his mom's latest boyfriend, the one who hit his mom.

Tommy called his teacher a "fucking bitch," using the words Clyde used with just the same loud, angry voice. He smacked the girl in front of him in the lunch line as hard as he could. When no one was looking, he took some money and cookies from another child's cubby. "Why not?" he said to himself. His baby brother grabbed his stuff and no one stopped him. His mom's boyfriend had broken his toy car. He told his mom. No one did anything.

THE IMPACT OF NEGLECT AND VIOLENCE

Trust

I have met many boys and girls similar to Tommy, children who have learned to "shut down" their feelings and to ignore pain. They have learned to not trust adults and fend for themselves. In the worst cases, this lesson was learned in utero, with fathers who shoved a pregnant girlfriend into walls or down stairs, with mothers who cursed the growing child in their bodies and tried to remove the baby with alcohol, drugs, or even hitting their bellies. In other families, such as Tommy's, the rejection came later.

Nothing is more important than having people who care enough about a child to commit themselves to providing time and effort and simply being available when he or she needs comfort and guidance. Every child needs someone who is crazy about him or her (Bronfenbrenner, 1979).

Growing up unwanted and often alone, children learn that caring for others is a luxury. They learn to "do what they need to do" in order to get by, often just as their parents do.

Children raised by abusive and neglectful parents grow up in an agitated state of alarm and a "biological paradox" (Hesse et al., 2003) between a child's inherent drive to seek nurture and affinity with the same person who creates feelings of terror. Such children are typically unable to regulate the conflicting drives to simultaneously approach and avoid their parent. Clinically, these children present as alternating between charming, loving, sweet, and quick changes to anger, withdrawal, and avoidance. This split reflects the child's unresolved need to both attach and defend (Kagan, 1996). Over time, this split leads to a pattern in which the child and his or her family appear to be moving in and out of crises, with children, siblings, and parents alternating between intimacy and avoidance, often with increasing danger that brings in outside authorities. Families may appear from the outside to be spinning in crises and about to disrupt, yet crises function at the same time to help children and their parents avoid dealing with unbearable fears of abandonment or death.

Children such as Tommy were fortunate to have felt loved in their first two years, before they started moving around so much and getting into so much trouble. Tommy learned that caring was for babies. Sometimes their moms or dads gave them warm hugs and presents, and sometimes they forgot dinner or birthdays. It all depended on what was going on in *their* lives. The children just couldn't count on them. They had to listen and obey. These children learned to take care of themselves and depend on no one.

Festering Wounds

Tommy was able to brush himself off and get back on to his bike. His cuts and bruises were nothing compared to his memories of Mom and Clyde's fights, and nothing at all, compared to the scars of children growing up with guns, knives, and threats of killing.

Unresolved violence festers in a family similar to an open wound. Without the care and protection of caring adults, the wound is open to infection. Children who grow up in such homes feel helpless to make things better. Without parents who are able and caring enough to protect them, children may seek out relationships with peers, older youths, and adults who offer them attention, listen to their complaints, and demonstrate at least some concern and nurture. Such children can be easily seduced into acting like their new friends. Drugs, sex, harassment of other people, or stealing may seem a small price for inclusion into a group with new friendships and a sense, finally, of identity with people who want you.

Easy access to unregistered guns and ammunition fosters rapid escalations of violence. The fist fights and occasional stabbings of previous years have given way to deadlier battles spawned by the availability of handguns and assault weapons and the lack of consistent prosecution of adults, including parents and relatives, who allow or children access to guns.

Children such as Tommy are often drawn to others who have also learned that "no one cares." Excitement and danger replace the love and caring they cannot find in their families. Violence from movies, video games, and the neighborhood seeps in, filling the void left by missing adults in their lives and teaching children to be tough, to strike out first, and that the winner will be the one who cares the least about anyone. Neglect at home leaves a child open to whatever he or she finds on the street. Anything becomes better than nothing. The excitement of the street makes a youth feel alive and temporarily relieves the emptiness inside.

With every act of defiance at school, Tommy draws reprimands, criticism, shame, and rejections. Step by step he becomes the bad boy in his preschool, a problem child in first grade, a serious behavior problem by third grade, a troublemaker by fifth grade, defiant and out of control in middle school, and part of a "wannabe" gang and a drop-out by age sixteen. Diagnostic labels change from adjustment disorder to oppositional defiant disorder to antisocial personality disorder, as Tommy grows older and his aggression becomes more threatening to adults. When a teacher's reprimands no longer work, Tommy is sent out the door, to the principal's office, and later as he gets older, to the detention center, to residential treatment, or to the criminal justice system.

Shattered Hearts and Minds

All too often, children such as Tommy also experience physical abuse in their homes or communities. Beatings and sexual abuse scar children for life. But, even worse, they often have no one to turn to, no one to help them heal. They learn that violations of their bodies are part of life.

Attachments can be broken down when children experience multiple and repeated disruptions in caregiving that may result from a range of problems including parental illness, postpartum depression, abuse and neglect, developmental disorders, overwhelmed parents whose own basic needs are not met, or parents who lack awareness or sensitivity to their child's needs (Becker-Weidman, 2001).

Abuse by peers and adults in the community can destroy any remaining trust in the goodness and belief in morality and decency in the world. Their very spirit becomes shattered and split. If no one helps them escape pain and violence, they feel betrayed, not just by their families, but by everyone.

Survival necessitates a hard shell and a tough attitude to manage the betrayals and unpredictable violence. "You can't hurt me." "I don't feel anything" become their mantras. Otherwise, these children would become lost in their helplessness, pain, or, even worse, their shame for what has happened, especially the memories of sex or violence that they dare not tell anyone.

Trauma shatters a child's perceptions of the world, similar to a rock breaking the windows in their bedrooms. The shattered glass represents the pieces of a child's experience. One piece may represent the images of Mom and Dad fighting. A second holds the sweet pungent smell of marijuana. A third piece represents the pressure in the child's chest as his or her heart beats fiercely, faster and faster, until the child feels as though he or she will explode from within. A fourth holds shrill voices of anger. And, a fifth, the words of rage, the curses and obscenities hurled outward like lances as his or her parents struggled. Altogether, the trauma is unbearable. To survive, the child must break it apart into pieces, pieces that can never be allowed to reconnect. In this way trauma works like a shattered mirror (Gil, 1991, 1996) reflecting the child's broken life and shattered identity.

Normal physiological responses to trauma (Lerner and Shelton, 2001b) include increased blood pressure, faster heart beat, trouble breathing, chest pains, fatigue, fainting, shock symptoms, and cardiac palpitations. Emotional responses (Lerner and Shelton, 2001b) include severe anxiety, or a stunned numbing, denial or shock, dissociation, a dazed look, emptiness, irritability, depression, grief, terror, or feeling alone. Cognitive responses include impaired concentration, short attention span, forgetfulness, and confusion. Traumatized individuals may *re*play the experience of trauma in their minds and appear disoriented to what is going on around them. Behavioral responses include impulsivity, inability to sit still, accentuated startle responses, spacing out, withdrawal, or noncommunication.

In the days following an acute loss, numbing is typically followed by "yearning and searching" (Lerner and Shelton, 2001a). The individual may be preoccupied with loss and show signs of anxiety, insomnia, and a poor appetite. Images or sounds may be interpreted as signs of the lost person's presence. In the weeks and months following a loss or trauma, an individual may appear disorganized and show anger and depression. In normal grief processes, these stages will lead eventually to reorganization and reattachment. However, without the security of attachment, the grief process is blocked and the individual may cycle in and out of crises (Kagan and Schlosberg, 1989). Crises may become a way of life as the individual remains locked in stages of denial and rage.

TRAUMA AND NEUROLOGICAL FUNCTIONING: THEORY AND RESEARCH

Trauma and the Brain

MRI (magnetic resonance imaging) studies of adults with post-traumatic stress disorder (PTSD) have discovered how areas of the brain associated with smell, touch, visual images, and other sensations are lit up as the frontal lobes representing verbal reasoning remain depressed (Van der kolk, McFarlane, and Weisaeth, 1996). Traumatic experiences in early childhood have been found to lead to ongoing hypersensitivity in regions of the brain containing corticotropin releasing factor (CRF) (Heit, Graham, and Nemeroff, 1999). Children who experience abuse and neglect are prone to acute stress responses that are not controlled by normal regulatory systems. Normally, the hypothalamus releases CRF in stressful situations. CRF stimulates production in the adrenal glands of adrenocorticotropic hormone (ACTH). ACTH, in turn, stimulates increased concentration in the blood of glucocorticoids that signals the hypothalamus to stop releasing CRF. When this feedback loop is blocked, children and adults appear to function with a persistent acute stress response. Children who have experienced early childhood traumas are often easily triggered by stressors in life and plunge back into states of acute chronic stress. This hypersensitivity to stressors makes them especially vulnerable to PTSD and depression (Heit, Graham, and Nemeroff, 1999).

Porges (1996) described three levels of neurological responses when an individual is threatened with danger. Each level functions to promote safety and survival. Optimally, children utilize the highest and most effective level, the social nervous system which relies on the ventral vagal system. Development of social skills and success in engaging social support work together to promote safety and security. Children have a natural drive to engage adults; however, developing the social nervous system requires nonverbal communication with a trusted caregiver, involving voice, eyes, and facial expressions.

When dangers in a child's life cannot be managed by social interactions, he or she is unable to develop a secure attachment. The child learns to rely on the next, more primitive, level of neurological responsiveness to danger. This middle level in Porges theory, the sympathetic-adrenal system, creates the "fight-of-flight" responses to danger characterized by increased breathing, heart rate, readiness to act, and decreased digestion. When the child remains unsafe with this level of responses, he or she will resort to the most basic level, the dorsal vagal system. A child who is not able to find safety through social interactions or fight-or-flight responses will resort to shutting down and immobilization. In animals, this basic level functions to immobilize the individual and essentially to fake death.

Abuse and neglect in childhood leads to excessive stress hormone secretion, which in turn can impair development of mental abilities. Excessive cortisol secretion on a sustained basis can result in the death of neuronal cells (Siegel, 2003). Recent studies show that prolonged exposures to threat lead to electrophysiological abnormalities (Teicher et al., 1997) and smaller intracranial and cerebral volumes, i.e., a reduction in overall brain size (DeBellis, Baum, et al., 1999; DeBellis, Keshavavan, et al., 1999). In addition, early childhood abuse has been shown to lead to impaired growth of the corpus callosum, the connective tissue between the right and left prefrontal lobes (De Bellis, Baum, et al., 1999; DeBellis, Keshavavan, et al., 1999). Teicher (2002) found that the cerebellar vermis may be impaired, reducing its ability to soothe limbic centers in the brain. Moreover, the hippocampus may be reduced in size, which would reduce the child's ability to encode stimuli into explicit memory and also reduce the child's ability to develop a sense of identity (Siegel, 2003). Abnormalities are accentuated when traumatic exposures occur early in life, are severe, and persist (Perry, 2001). Perry (2001) described how the brain changes in a "use-dependent" manner and stores and retrieves information from experience in a "state-dependent" manner. A child growing up in a persisting state of arousal cannot sit and learn in a classroom.

Traumatized children are often labeled as learning disabled and appear to function with more primitive cognitive reasoning and problem-solving abilities, including reliance on aggression as a means of coping. Reading nonverbal signals is often accentuated and can become a relative strength, although traumatized children often misinterpret nonverbal cues. Direct eye contact may be perceived as aggression, a friendly touch on the shoulder may signal the beginning of sex abuse. Children living with ongoing fear have a different orientation to time. The child's sense of future is reduced. Such children have little capacity to think of future consequences or rewards because of the imperative of maintaining a high state of arousal as a matter of survival. Thinking about behaviors is also very difficult or even impossible as the child remains in a state of alarm. The cerebral cortex is cut off from regulating the brain and the brain stem reacts impulsively, reflexively, and often aggressively to perceived threats. Traumatized children react to signals that have little impact on others (e.g., eye contact for more than a second, a hand raised toward the child, a curt command from a teacher). Other children remain calm, but traumatized children move into "kill or be killed" responses (Perry, 2001).

Protection of children and child-rearing practices shape every society. When children are neglected, poorly educated, and exposed to violence they grow into adults who develop or perpetuate a reactive, restrictive, and violent society. Children who grow up unprotected from terror and violence are stunted in creativity and abstract abilities (Perry, 2001).

A review of empirical studies (Buka et al., 2001) found that males, ethnic minorities, and children growing up in cities were at increased risk of experiencing violence in their families or communities. Higher incidence of depression, PTSD, aggression, and acting-out behavioral problems was found among children and adolescents who witnessed violence. The impact of experiencing violence was modified by family support, domestic violence, and family conflict. Other studies found that the less the availability of parents, the greater likelihood of behavioral problems when children experience trauma (Burton et al., 1994). The greater availability of families and the greater the communication, the better children were able to recover from trauma (Green et al., 1991). The capacity to perceive a better future, hope that life will improve, and strongly held spiritual beliefs were also associated with better outcomes after exposure to traumatic crises (Overcash et al., 1966; Calhoun et al., 2000).

Life or Death

With severe, life-threatening trauma, words, thoughts, and feelings cannot be brought together. It is as if the helplessness of the moment necessitates cutting off verbal reasoning. The horror of the battle, a rape, or parents fighting becomes too much to bear. Witnessing the beatings of siblings or a parent shatters any sense of security. Children draw pictures of their homes with jagged and piercing glass in broken windows, knife-shaped objects, and large sharply pointed fingers on parents' hands.

Abused children are threatened with isolation or harm to family members or themselves if they disclose. When sexual abuse has occurred, factors found to delay disclosure may include: the severity of traumatization, belief in obedience to adults, mistrust of people, fear of social rejection, and fear of social systems (e.g., the police criminal justice system). Factors that promoted disclosure include media attention to childhood sexual abuse and personal achievements (Somer and Szwarcberg, 2001).

Violence is especially devastating when preschool children experience a physical penetration or violation of their bodies, and the sight of blood on themselves or someone they love. Many tough-looking youths, described as aggressive by their teachers or guardians, have become teary-eyed recalling memories from when they were three to five years old and watched or heard their parents, or often, a mother and a boyfriend, fight. Some remembered trying to pull their father off their mother and being shoved aside, knocked into a wall, where they remained frozen in fear. These "tough" youths remembered crying as they watched their father and mother hit each other, feeling helpless to do anything. Helplessness, in their minds, became a pervasive belief in their own worthlessness. They could not stop the fighting. They could not protect the parents or siblings they loved. The worst part, often, was when they saw the blood emerging from the bruises on their mother's face, or their father's cut and bleeding hand as he ran from the house after being stabbed by their mother.

Young children see blood as the life force draining from the body of the person they love. They are shocked at the vulnerability of the big, powerful parent who they count on for everything they need. Young children have no understanding of how a body can heal. Their belief in magic cannot overcome the screams and suffering of a parent or sibling in agony.

Blood represents death or at least the threat of death. This belief is accentuated in action video games where blood comes out of figures to represent that they have been killed. When children who play such video games or who watch violent movies see blood come out of a family member, they naturally believe that the mother, father, or brother they love is about to die. Moreover, violent games and movies perpetuate a belief that the world is full of inescapable violence.

A child's development requires a core sense of safety and the consistency of a nurturing, predictable home. All of this is shattered with the sight of blood or the sounds of an adult or older sibling threatening to kill someone, especially a sibling or parent the child loves. Without resolution and renewal of safety, the child's social and emotional development is blocked. The child continues to rely upon more primitive responses to perceptions of risk, rather than developing neural connections that foster greater perception of what is happening and consequently greater possibilities and flexibility for coping. Trauma impairs encoding and integration of sensory, emotional, and perceptual experiences into verbal memory and conceptualization of the child's identity (Siegel, 2003). He or she keeps growing physically, but inside, the clock remains fixed on the time when the child's core sense of nurture ended.

Children are very adaptive. They will mold their identity and very being to survive in a desolate world. Beliefs about safety, what they can do, how the world works, and what the future holds in store will be transformed by trauma. Life-threatening violence often leads to flashbacks, nightmares, and anxiety shown by their high level of arousal, hypervigilence, and agitation. Violence leads to other physiological changes shown by their excitability, distractibility, impulsiveness, and attention-deficit problems. Researchers have also found a link between dissociation and depersonalization in delinquent youths with a history of neglect and abuse (Carrion and

Steiner, 2000). These are the symptoms of PTSD in children, a pattern of behaviors learned to cope with unresolved danger.

By definition (American Psychiatric Association, 1994), children with PTSD have experienced events outside the realm of normal human experience that are often perceived by children as life threatening. These traumatic events include family violence and multiple out-of-home placements. Children can develop PTSD as victims, witnesses, perpetrators, or a combination of experiences. Typically, children with PTSD avoid reminders of traumas by impulsive responses to perceived threats. They show physiological reactivity such as headaches or stomachaches when faced with reminders of traumatic experiences. They experience intrusive thoughts or memories, and they may shut down their feelings and present with constricted or blunted affect. Traumatized children often show perceptual distortions and expressive language problems (Terr, 1983, 1990) that, in turn, impede their ability and success at school and in developing social relationships.

Traumatized children often act as sentries watching for the slightest sound or tightening lips on an adult that signaled in the past that another cycle of violence was about to begin. Survival for these children means reacting quickly to any gesture or tone of voice that may mean danger. This helps them feel some sense of control at home and their hypervigilence is often reinforced when they are the first to warn a parent, rush siblings to a bedroom, or call 911. The children, in effect, become for a moment, the family's heroes, until someone gets hurt and helplessness sets in again. Even after placement into another home, traumatized children will often reenact the worst episodes, or wake up in the night screaming for help, convinced in a dream state that the violence is happening again and again.

Trauma-induced physiological changes are most damaging from conception and during the child's first years. The signs and symptoms of disorganized attachment and trauma become a way of life. And, each recurrence of violence and loss confirms for the child that his or her world is chaotic and dangerous.

When their primary caregivers have been violent, children will often emotionally numb themselves and avoid thinking about or forget the worst incidents. Their interests become diminished. Time comes to mean only the present. The past is too painful to think about and the future is impossible to imagine as more than just the same chaos and violence. Hope fades away. Children shut down.

Yet, they have a tremendous capacity to survive and heal. The horror can be overcome. Children keep signaling for help for a long time. Those who received some love in their first years can often survive even repeated traumas and keep on struggling for several years before giving up. A little love can go a long way.

Our challenge is to make it safe enough to put the pieces of the puzzle back together. This means helping adults in the child's life to become strong enough to help a child, and usually the child's siblings, to face the pain of the past and recover the promise of a future. Therapy means facing, mastering, and changing the story of their lives.

CONCLUSION

Children such as Tommy learn to be both angels and demons. They learn to take their message to school, to the street, to neighbors, to each of us.

When he zoomed into the street, Tommy was already at age four showing his neighborhood that he was alone and acting in dangerous ways. He neglected his own safety just as he experienced his mother ignoring his call for help and sending him out of their home without appropriate rules and supervision to keep him safe. Tommy was thrust into a crisis. He didn't cause the problems in his family, but he learned to contribute to them, both as a good, loving son *and* as a child in trouble.

If we look at Tommy as a demon, we have already lost the battle. If we look at him as sending us a message, we have a chance to help him and his family change their story.

Chapter 3

The Curse of Neglect

Our children are being raised by appliances.

Bill Moyers

INTRODUCTION

May 6, 1999

I spent the morning conducting a court-ordered assessment with Greg, a twelve-year-old boy. Just a few days earlier, Greg had allegedly lit a fire under his bed, destroying his family's apartment and causing extensive damage to most of the building. Twenty people were now homeless.

"Didn't my mother tell you? I shut down!" Greg demanded as he strutted into the office. He talked about "Dad 1" and "Dad 2." Characters in his stories sounded like crime statistics: "Male, teenage. Female, adult." Greg stressed his high tolerance for pain but could not sit still for more than a few minutes. He became agitated at the mention of family members. Liz, his mother, smiled and described her ordeal of securing new housing after the fire. She blamed Greg's friend for the fire, even though the police were convinced her son had started the blaze. Greg had been setting fires since he was four years old.

Later, when I saw Greg alone, I invited him to act out a little story with small family dolls including a father, a mother, and a four-year-old boy. Greg dropped his stone-faced scowl and grabbed the figures. He stripped the figures of their clothes and within a few minutes was dramatizing a story of beatings and sex, a whirlwind of violence and rage enacted in detail around the entire room. In the end, two boys joined together to beat the dad and throw away the mom.

Liz denied that anything had happened to Greg when he was little. She never worried about leaving him with his father, "Dad 1," even though she had known he often used drugs. Except, she recalled, for the time Greg's father beat her older daughter into a bloody pulp. When Greg saw his sister bloodied, he was nearly four years old. Liz had to save her daughter's life. She kicked Greg's father out of the house, but soon afterward allowed him to come back. He stayed until he began seeing another woman. For Liz, the apartment fire was just another hassle in her life, another in a long series of crises that began from her earliest days and extended through three marriages and the burden of raising Greg and his two sisters with no help from their fathers. She was nonchalant about the damage, just glad to find a new apartment. Neither Greg nor his mother showed any concern for their homeless neighbors.

"I'm not worried about Greg," Liz said. "He puts out the fires he starts."

However, the police were more than worried. And so was I. Greg had been overheard telling another boy he wanted to burn the building down. The police were convinced Greg was the only one who could have set the fire. I was convinced Greg had experienced enough sex and violence by age four to fill him with a simmering rage and need for power. Shut down was Greg's way of holding back all the pain and anger. By age twelve, he had become a master at it. I met with Greg's mother and tried to explain my concern. Reluctantly, she agreed and said she was willing to place Greg in a residential treatment program and work in counseling to help Greg get over whatever caused him to start setting fires. I left the session pleased with her shift to cooperation. However, Greg was still a time bomb and his mother had never stuck with any counseling program to help her children. I shuddered slightly when I thought of their new neighbors. I knew I wouldn't want to live next to Greg.

Research on Violent Youth

Research on violent youths has consistently found significant correlations with children's experiences of abuse and neglect, particularly experiences of chronic abuse from a very young age (Ewing 2001; Karr-Morse and Wiley, 1997). Brazelton (1997, p. xiii) described how "experiences in infancy which result in the child's inability to regulate strong emotions are too often the overlooked source of violence in children and adolescents." Children who experience repeated rejections in early childhood may develop a tendency for underarousal of their autonomic nervous systems and a predisposition to antisocial behaviors (Schore, 2003a). On the other hand, children who are physically abused may develop tendencies for excessive arousal of their autonomic nervous systems and a predisposition to show symptoms of disorganized behavior often described as borderline personality disorder (Schore, 2003a).

Reduced empathy has also been found to be correlated with experiences of different types of maltreatment (Cicchetti and Toth, 1995; Feshbach, 1989; Kolko, 1992), and with delinquent behavior by adolescents (Eckenrode, Powers, and Garbarino, 1997). Childhood abuse or neglect was found to increase the likelihood of arrest as a juvenile by 53 percent, as an adult by 38 percent, and for a violent crime by 38 percent (Widom, 1992).

In my office that afternoon after seeing Greg, I received an e-mail alert. The city's chief of police warned that a gang had been threatening to carry out random acts of violence in one section of the city over the next five days. The agency directors canceled all home visits and meetings in the area.

Later that afternoon, I saw a seventeen-year-old girl with a beautiful smile and bright eyes. Maureen had stopped running away and smoking marijuana. She had been doing well for the past six months in a group care program with caring youth counselors around her twenty-four hours a day, special tutoring, and two psychotropic medications to quell her agitation, worries, intrusive memories, and inability to sleep. Maureen was highly verbal, bright, and a strong advocate for herself. In the course of our session, I showed her a picture of a frightened girl and asked her to make up a brief story. Within seconds, Maureen began to shake as if she was vibrating in her chair, both arms crossed over and clutching her stomach as she nervously rocked back and forth. Maureen looked down, then to the side of the room, away from the picture.

"I don't know." Maureen's voice quivered and paused.

"She's scared." Another long pause, Maureen seemed shivered up and down her body. Her voice dropped to a quavering whisper. "I don't know."

Maureen looked at the floor. "I've got to get to work by 3:00," she said, changing the subject, but she kept shaking.

I headed home thinking of how many hurt children I saw every week.

"We had a bomb threat at school today," my own seventeen-year-old child announced at dinner. "I left class to go to the bathroom, came back, and the door was locked. I had to knock on the door. My teacher peeked through the window. She called out through door, 'Who's there?' Her voice was shaking. She was *really* scared."

A rumor was spreading around school that a boy was telling people he was going to blow up the junior prom that Saturday.

"Teachers have been locking the doors."

"Isn't that the boy from your second grade soccer team?" I asked. I had been an assistant coach and remembered the name. "Wasn't he the one I had to stop from running around and hitting the other kids with his plastic shin guard?"

Our high school was just one of countless schools checking out bomb threats in the days and weeks following murders of students at Columbine High School by two of their classmates. A police officer had already been stationed in the school for the past two years because of concerns over student violence. The rumor in our high school turned out to be untrue. However, the fear was real. Inner-city schools had already become accustomed to periodic bursts of violence. Now, the image of safety in suburban schools was shattered.

Violence and intimidation spread when the root causes are shrouded in silence. Most youth violence has been found to be related to repeated experiences of violence in the home, abuse, neglect, and domestic violence. Maltreatment of children affects us all when it is allowed to fester unchecked or is shrouded in silence. This is the curse of neglect. It spreads. It hits home. It degrades every neighborhood and every life.

A Dog in Disgrace

The curse of neglect penetrates with a subtle but devastating force. Charles Dickens (1987) captured its power in *Great Expectations,* when a young boy, Pip, feels the sting of his caretaker's scorn.

> She came back with some bread and meat and a little mug of beer. She put the mug down on the stones of the yard, and gave me the bread and meat *without looking at me,* as insolently as if I were a dog in disgrace.

> I was so humiliated, hurt, spurned, offended, angry, sorry—I cannot hit upon the right name for the smart—God knows what its name was—that tears started in my eyes. The moment they sprang there, the girl looked at me with a quick delight in having been the cause of them.
>
> But when she was gone, I looked about for a place to hide my face in. . . . As I cried, I kicked the wall, and took a hard twist of my hair; so bitter were my feelings, and so sharp was the smart without a name, that needed counteraction. (p. 57)

Dickens understood the vulnerability we all feel and the shame that drives children (or adults) to run and hide themselves in a corner, under a bed, somewhere where no one will see the ugliness. Over time, omissions and lack of recognition make children feel they are worthless. Neglect teaches children that they are not worthy of being cared for, that they deserve whatever traumas happen to them. Later, children learn to cover their shame with a mask. The rage simmers and burns within them until hope is gone. Then, it is too late for the simple embrace that could have kept a child's love alive.

HOW NEGLECT DISRUPTS ATTACHMENT

Dangerous Words

Calling children derogatory names may be more damaging than physical abuse. Words penetrate their sense of being and shape their perceptions of who they are, who cares about them, and what they can be. Calling children names such as "slut, bitch, fucker, or asshole" abuses their core sense of self and leaves children feeling cursed by the people they need the most. When a four-year-old boy was removed by Child Protective Services (CPS) for repeated sex abuse and neglect, his mother told him, "I'm not worried. I'll just make another baby." This boy learned that parents and children were interchangeable and every parent was likely to abandon him sooner or later.

Too often, the price of admission to correctional facilities and mental health programs is to ignore the neglect that led to behavior problems. Labels of psychopathology and delinquency often hide the wounds of neglect. He's a juvenile delinquent. She's bipolar. If we stick to the jargon, we miss the reality underneath. We can try to rehabilitate the offender or treat the disorder. But, these labels can feed the curse of neglect. Children become identified as problems, rather than persons.

Similarly, state-mandated goals of "return home" or "independent living" may make sense for funding agencies, but for the child who continues to fear Dad's beatings or who feels totally unwanted and worthless, these words represent a message of doom. An eight-year-old boy placed in a crisis residence was overheard begging his father, "I want to go home. Just stop the sex." Children may long to go home and be loved, but also need to hear that their fears are recognized.

Too often, children end up feeling cursed once again by the adult world.

Rebecca tried to get help at age three and age five by telling teachers she had been touched on her private parts. Nothing was done. For a year, her older sister was placed in a residential treatment center for behavior problems and returned home. Nothing changed. At age twelve, Rebecca told a teacher that the devil was chasing her in her bedroom every night. Within a week, she was placed in a private psychiatric hospital. Two weeks later, she was transferred to a state psychiatric hospital because her father lacked insurance and then after two months, she was moved to a crisis residence. When I saw Rebecca, she wrote to me about how her father and her father's friend would come into her bedroom and have sexual relations with her.

Later, after listening to our concerns, the CPS worker finally said to Rebecca, "I'm not sure what was going on. I want you to stay here (in our crisis residence) and then we'll find another program where you can stay for now."

"But do I have to go home?" Rebecca begged, tears forming in her eyes.

"Not for now," her CPS worker replied as she got up to leave. "That's all I can say."

Rebecca's parents had refused all services. But, the CPS worker would not believe Rebecca. She had been labeled schizophrenic. She still woke up screaming every night, sometimes unable to differentiate her nighttime dreams from reality. But Rebecca could tell us now that it was really her father. However, Rebecca's CPS worker did not think she could win a case in court. Rebecca was not a good witness and the presiding judge had a long-established record of doubting children's accounts of sex abuse.

Words such as "for now" perpetuate impermanence and neglect. Rebecca was only twelve and well behind her grade level in understanding and reasoning ability. But Rebecca understood what "for now" meant. She could go into a group care facility "for now" and then be returned to her father, just like her sister. Nowhere was safe. Rebecca's nightmare was very real. In a world where CPS made decisions based on winning in court, the most severely damaged children typically were the worst witnesses and thus the least likely to be protected.

Nobody's Child

"Nobody cares." I've heard these words from so many children, adolescents, and young adults that I worry about becoming callused myself. So much pain, and seemingly, so few who care.

Rejection is the greatest curse. Repeated rejection means death to an infant. For the toddler and young child, rejection builds a core of rage stored deep inside that shapes his or her understanding of the world. The child grows physically into a young adult, but it's only a thin veneer covering the emptiness inside. The feeling of being unwanted eats away at his or her inner being. When a child's core trust in his or her parents is broken, the child feels ripped into parts. One side of the child still longs to love Mom and Dad. The other side rages at what the parents did. Every interaction with peers and adults becomes a test of whether or not someone is "for me or against me." And, every response becomes a life or death question, a matter of urgency. "Be for me, and I will love and adore you. Oppose me and you will spike a rage that no one can endure."

We have a window of opportunity marked by a child's kindness and caring. We can reach out to a child, or let the child go. Dickens captured this challenge in *A Christmas Carol* (Dickens, 1980). Scrooge was confronted with the images of a boy and a girl.

> Yellow, meager, ragged, scowling, wolfish; but prostrate, too, in their humility. Where graceful youth should have filled their features out, and touched them with its freshest tints, a stale and shriveled hand, like that of age, had pinched and twisted them and pulled them into shreds. Where angels might have sat enthroned, devils lurked, and glared out menacing. . . .
>
> "This boy is Ignorance. This girl is Want. Beware of them both, and all of their degree, but most all beware this boy, for on his brow I see that written which is Doom, unless the writing be erased. . . ." cried the spirit to Scrooge.
>
> "Have they no refuge or resource?" cried Scrooge.
>
> "Are there no prisons?" said the Spirit, turning on him for the last time with his own words. "Are there no workhouses?" (pp. 90-91)

Nobody's child becomes everybody's nightmare.

NEGLECT AND THE SOCIAL SERVICE SYSTEM

Answering the Call

Neglect builds on secrecy and isolation reinforced by fear. Tommy in Chapter 2 learned to not talk about what was going on in his home. That would be an act of disloyalty (Boszormenyi-Nagy and Spark, 1984) and a violation of his wish for the love he wanted from his parents. If no adults are brave enough to look at what has happened and to help a child voice the truth, the child will act it out, some how, some way. This is the child's call for help. The call may be strong at first, then die down to a whimper, a rare moment of honesty, or periodically emerge with an explosion.

> Daisy, a fifteen-year-old girl surrendered by her mother and living in her fourth foster family, shared with me how her "attitude" would get her into screaming battles with her foster mother. They would argue and battle until her foster mother would send Daisy to her room.
>
> Daisy had grown up needing to be tough in order to survive the drinking, drugs, beatings by her father, and sexual molestation by her mother. It was a tough shell. But Daisy whispered to me that, when she is sitting in her room at night, "I feel like crying." Daisy kept her tears, her soft side, hidden. She wished her foster mother could see how bad she felt for causing so much trouble, but Daisy was afraid. Mothers in her life cursed her, threatened suicide, or ran away.

Daisy was reaching out. She kept trying, guided by the understanding and strength of her foster mother, social workers, and staff who didn't give up.

Hurt children don't just magically change their behaviors. First, they have to show us the worst parts of their lives to see if we, the adults, can really handle the pain, fear, and shame they carry inside. It is a test of our commitment, a test of whether attachment is possible.

Children give us many chances to pass the test. But over time the honest moments and the openness to building or rebuilding a relationship fade away. Detachment, anger, and lack of caring settle in. The lack of caring marks a youth who has learned to live without hope, to truly believe in his or her guts that he or she is alone and always will be. Neglect over time reflects the impoverishment of the child's world. Policies, beliefs, and administrative procedures in mental health, social services, and juvenile justice systems can inadvertently reinforce a child's isolation and seemingly confirm his or her beliefs that the homes, schools, and communities are unjust, unfair, and undeserving of an honest response.

If we miss a child's message and see only problem behaviors, we will fail the test. Worse, we can easily be drawn in as parents, professionals, or authorities to foster further neglect, channeled to work in restricted paths and procedures. The power of a child's extended family, ethnic group, religious affiliations, and community organizations is often ignored. Instead, family members, practitioners, and organizations may be brought in to help in splintered, uncoordinated efforts.

Parents may demand placement and behavioral or medical treatment of a child who is seen as threatening a family's stability. Child care workers often feel pressured to be police officers of sorts. Nurses may be brought in to administer PRN ("as needed") medications to calm and restrain children in crises. Teachers find themselves suspending and expelling students. Foster parents call their agencies in the middle of the night to get a child out of their homes. Probation and criminal justice counselors are asked to teach youths new skills and send them back to the same environment that spawned their offenses. Family-preservation workers may be asked to help a family indicated for neglect but without the support of overburdened CPS workers who close "the case," or the funding to provide concrete support or specific therapeutic interventions. Parent advocate programs may provide concrete supportive services to overwhelmed parents after children have been diagnosed with mental illnesses but often without provision of intensive family therapy or work on parent-child relationships contributing to children's behaviors. Domestic violence and anger-management counselors often work to help one spouse, or the parents together, without involvement of children in the development of safety plans. Shelters protect battered spouses and focus blame on the more aggressive partner, but may overlook the neglect, or abuse of children inflicted by a battered spouse. Mental health professionals are often limited to truncated assessments of children or parents and crisis management. Alcohol and drug treatment programs typically separate parents from children, leaving children to "wait and see" if their parents relapse or maintain sobriety.

All of these services have merit and can be partially effective. However, splintered services often end up leaving children and parents further apart and the breakdown of a parent-child-family bond is often left untouched.

Betrayal

Neglect is not simple. It is rarely a matter of cold indifference by cruel people. Parents almost always have a desire to help their children and especially to give their children more than they received as children. Authorities work hard to protect children and enforce the laws. Unfortunately, children can easily get lost in day-to-day struggles and shortages of time and services.

Drugs and alcohol are particularly devastating in their power to overwhelm parents' natural drive to care for their children. Prejudice and racism wound children and constrict their vision of what is possible for children similar to themselves. Economic policies foster financial and psychological impoverishment by implementing regulations and tax laws that favor the wealthy and take away services needed by those trying to break out of poverty.

Service providers struggle to engage hurt and angry children, parents, and families. All too often, though, effective interventions are thwarted or undermined by policies and regulations focused on cutting costs in the short run and addressing the politics of the moment, rather than the needs of children. Programs may be evaluated and funded based on narrow and limited outcomes, with practitioners limited to one particular form of intervention. For instance, some family-preservation programs were limited to short-term home-based interventions with contracts contingent on success in keeping children in biological families, rather than focusing on the best interests of children and parents for safe, nurturing homes. Family preservation or reunification is usually the best outcome, but may not be in the best interests of many children, parents, or communities.

Service providers can also become caught up in demands from government agencies to prioritize monitoring, documentation, and reporting of parent violations and take on the responsibility for CPS, rather than working with both parents' strengths *and* problems. With CPS units chronically underfunded and frequently lacking capacity for careful evaluations and monitoring, practitioners at child and family agencies are often expected to fill the void. Parents may seek help and instead experience scrutiny with little support available for helping them manage very real stresses, or validation of their desire to rebuild their families. Parents may pull away, seek out advocates for themselves, and focus their energy on fighting authorities.

Adversarial battles among parents, agencies, and service providers can sap services that could have gone into helping parents *and* children. Children can often end up left on their own, waiting months and years for their parents and guardians to settle battles in courts overwhelmed with cases waiting for adjudication.

When authorities appear to allow, to close their eyes, or even to support neglect or abuse, children are very likely to give up hope for someone to protect them, to help their families, and to validate the good parts they carry inside. Omissions hurt just as much as the hitting and the threats. Lack of help can cement a child's understanding that secrets must be kept and no one can be trusted.

Eight-year-old Max tripped a boy in his class. "It was an accident," he claimed. Max was sent once again to the principal's office. Max's mother, Tanya, was called and arrived an hour later.

Tanya complained about being called so many times at work. She could lose her job. She turned and cursed at her son.

"Look at me when I speak!" she demanded.

Max snickered under his breath and looked down.

Tanya's hand went back. She pulled out a small stick and struck him hard on his back. Max could feel the stick dig into his skin through his shirt. His eyes smarted. His back stung. Tears formed on his face. Max saw the principal and a teacher watching the beating. His whole head began to burn.

"What did the principal do?" I asked Max.

"Nothing. She just watched," Max replied, a cold look in his eyes.

Max had learned an important lesson. He was on his own. Even the principal, the supreme power of the school, didn't seem to care and appeared to do nothing to prevent or stop the beating. If Tanya had struck the principal, assault charges would have been filed. CPS was involved with the family, but Tanya left no marks on Max and thus the incident did not qualify as abuse. Max experienced how children are often treated as second-class citizens and left unprotected.

In Max's eyes, the principal had endorsed his mother's whippings. After that, Max changed. Talking out of turn, teasing, and poking other children became knocking over desks, throwing rocks at girls, and spitting at his teacher.

Max was suspended. His mother asked the judge to place him in a treatment center as a PINS (person in need of supervision). By definition, such a statement would appear to represent Tanya's admission that she could not provide the supervision and care Max needed. However, in court, it was Max who was held solely responsible for his actions. To Max, the whole world did not care, so neither did he.

Children feel betrayed when parents and other adults in their lives watch but do nothing. How can a child feel safe when the adults allow the neglect to go on? Neighbors and communities condone neglect when they turn their heads and pretend they do not see the impoverishment of children's lives or the violence that destroys families. Neglect becomes a nightmare with no end. Children living in this nightmare feel cursed by the world around them. Betrayal and neglect break a child's spirit, the natural instincts to seek nurture from adults and to care for others. In its place, the child searches for power. Neglected children learn to manipulate, to charm, to lie, and if necessary, to steal or to attack, whatever it takes to feel in control.

Children may still succeed if their talents and skills are recognized and fostered by caring teachers, coaches, relatives, or community leaders. But, children who experience failure in their schools and communities, as well as their homes, may tap into a power that children raised with neglect know all too well. This is the force of threats and violence. Children who grow up with no prospect of succeeding in the approved world can still gain power by becoming masters of everything their neighbors fear.

STATISTICS AND RESEARCH ON ABUSE AND NEGLECT

Facts and Figures (United States)

- Approximately 20 percent of all children lived in poverty in 1997 and 2.7 million children were living in extreme poverty (Freedman, 1999).
- The U.S. Department of Health and Human Services (2001) reported that 826,000 children were found after investigations to have been victims of child abuse or neglect in 1999. The highest victimization

rates were reported for children in the birth to age three group (13.9 per 1,000 children). The average time from the start of a CPS investigation to provision of service was 47.4 days.

- In 1999, 220,000 children were placed into foster care after CPS investigations, 78 percent after substantiated reports of abuse or neglect requiring removal from their homes (U.S. Department of Health and Human Services, 2001).
- In 1999, an estimated 1,100 children died from abuse or neglect, approximately 1.62 deaths per 100,000 children (U.S. Department of Health and Human Services, 2001). Gelles (1997) found that half of the children killed by parents or caretakers were killed after the child became known to CPS.
- Over 3.3 million children lived in homes in which domestic violence occurred in 1997 (Kaufman, 1999).
- By age eighteen, the average American youth has seen over 50,000 murders or attempted murders on TV (Landau, 1990).
- Studies found that up to 90 percent of individuals with serious problems such as alcohol or drug abuse, criminal or gang involvement, emotional disorders, mental illness, prostitution, teenage pregnancy, sexual offenses, suicide, alcohol and drug abuse, school failures, sexual dysfunction, school dropouts, violent crime, and "run away" behavior were victims of child abuse (Phillips, 1998).

Research on Abuse and Neglect

An increasing volume of research has found damaging effects of violence on children, leading to multiple problems including PTSD, anxiety disorders, substance abuse, depression, and delinquency (Boney-McCoy and Finkelhor, 1995, 1996; Widom and Morris, 1997; Widom and Shepard, 1996). The impact of repeated violations of a child's body has been found to be especially damaging. Saunders et al. (1992) found nearly 50 percent of child rape victims in their study met the criteria for major depressive episode as adults. Hanson et al. (2001) found that women who reported both physical injury and life threats had higher rates of lifetime and current PTSD and lifetime major depressive episode than did those reporting only life threat or neither life threat nor injury. In their study, experiences of aggravated assault defined as the victim's perception that the perpetrator intended death or serious injury and actual physical injury were the factors most predictive of PTSD, even after controlling for rape.

Physically abused children showed significantly higher levels of depressive symptoms and suicidality than children who were neither neglected nor abused, or children who were neglected but not abused (Finzi et al., 2001). In this study, physically abused children were found to have more behavioral problems, were at higher risk of self-injury, saw themselves as bad, felt guilty, were more isolated, believed they had no friends, and often appeared to be restless, undisciplined, embroiled in conflicts, and were unable to handle loneliness. In contrast, neglected children without evidence of physical abuse were found (Finzi et al., 2001) to show greater signs of insomnia, loss of appetite, and more pain but lower risk taking and a reluctance to risk bodily harm to self.

Studies have also found that children exposed to violence have decreased IQs, increased school problems, increased learning disabilities, and an increased likelihood of using drugs to manage their feelings (Putnam, 2003). The annual direct and indirect costs of children's abuse has been estimated between $60 and 100 billion (Putnam, 2003). Many abused children manage to function in school, but they also demonstrate an inner emptiness and a fear of falling apart and succumbing to the terror they hold inside. Abused children may hurt themselves as means of self-stimulation or to reenact the painful experience (Rosen, 1991; van der Kolk, Perry, and Herman, 1991). In a study of adolescents, physical abuse was correlated with high levels of suicidality (Bensley et al., 1999). Physically abused adolescents experience a world marked by violence and helplessness (Kaplan et al., 1999). They may internalize their parents' aggression, identifying with the perpetrator of violence and victimizing others, or take on the role of victims themselves, shown by suicidal behavior.

Experiences of unpredictable aversive stimulation, such as physical or sexual assault, without the opportunity to escape lead to a learned sense of helplessness and depressive symptoms (Gold, 1986; Seligman, Maier, and Solomon, 1971; Seligman, 1973). Sexual abuse by an adult leaves a child with strong feelings of helplessness and a decrease in his or her self-efficacy and ability to cope (Finkelhor and Browne,1985; Finkelhor, 1988; McCann and Pearlman, 1990). Abused children often develop feelings that they are different or bad. Perpetrators have been found to reinforce this belief and further reduce self-esteem and increase depression in children (Briere and Runtz, 1988). Feelings of worthlessness and shame, in turn, contribute to depression (Beck, 1976). Moreover, the experience of assault as a child has been found to increase the risk of *re*victimization and increased PTSD and depression in women (Messman and Long, 1996).

Depression in children is often demonstrated primarily by aggression, rage, and anxiety (Cytryn and McKnew, 1974; Kazdin, 1990). Physical abuse has also been found to be associated with heightened levels of depression in adolescents (Lewinsohn et al., 1994), in psychiatrically hospitalized children (Cohen, Spirito, et al., 1966), and correlated with major depression disorder in adulthood (Bifulco, Brown, and Harris, 1994).

Depressive symptoms and conduct disorders of physically abused adolescents have been described (Pelcovitz et al., 1994) as PTSD symptoms resulting from repetitive exposure to trauma. A damaged self-image, suicidal potential, and sense of guilt have been found as long-term impairments of abused children that often persist throughout their development (Kaplan et al., 1999). Moreover, acute symptoms of depression, suicidality, and aggression have been found to reflect ongoing trauma and threats of violence (Finzi et al., 2001).

CONCLUSION

Neglect robs children of the nurture and respect they need to feel valued and able to succeed within the rules of our society. Children will struggle for months and years to reclaim love and nurture. With too much neglect, the love fades and rage seeps into its place.

Lack of attachment can lead to the deaths of infants. Severely neglected babies close down, stop eating, and gradually wither away. These are the "failure to thrive" babies who have learned that they cannot regulate their lives in a world that is too inconsistent and harsh for survival.

Attachment is not only a life-or-death question for infants and toddlers. Children with weak, insecure, or chaotic attachments grow up angry, with little empathy for others. They act like starving individuals, desperate and impulsive with no room from their perspective to care about the needs of others.

Invalidation and violence distort each stage of a child's development. Insecure bonding and violence form a breeding ground for misbehavior, defiance, and antisocial acts. The child learns that closeness means risk, that touch means violation of one's body, that feelings mean unbearable pain. Children who grow up without attachment become a risk for themselves and for everyone in their families, their jobs, and anyone passing through their neighborhoods.

By replacing neglect with commitment and care, parents, practitioners, and caring adults can rebuild the security our families and communities need in order to thrive. However, before we can transform neglect into nurture, we need to overcome the obstacles that have blocked these children and their parents, relatives, and neighbors who have wanted to help.

PART II: REBUILDING ATTACHMENTS

Chapter 4

Breaking the Curse

> The task of listening to every voice is not for saints alone; it is not too hard for ordinary people, in ordinary times.
>
> Vivian Paley

INTRODUCTION

Neglect marks the breakdown of attachment. A gap grows between parent and child, and if not checked, the gap can grow into a gulf between the child and siblings, relatives, peers, and adults in the community. Neglect robs our children of their dreams, hides our angels, and leaves our neighborhoods impoverished.

A hurt child almost always means that a parent, grandparent, or other caring relative is also hurting and just as stuck in a life of crises. To help a child who has had an insecure attachment, we need to *re*pair the attachment, and *re*establish that critical pairing of child to parent. If a child cannot be reunited with a biological parent or relative, we need to find a substitute parent willing and able to help a child bridge the gap between trust and distrust, renewed hope and despair.

Fighting neglect takes courage and commitment. When children have experienced threats and pain, it is almost a given that they will need to test adults in their lives to see if they can face the life they knew. When children have been traumatized in their early years, bedtimes and nights may be the most critical times to *re*establish trust and help children get past the very real nightmares of their past. Parents and substitute parents provide the critical twenty-four-hour-a-day care that defines whether a child's life of neglect, loss, or trauma has really ended. They are on the front line bearing the heaviest load in this fight.

Parents and substitute parents need support from relatives and their communities. The pain of attachment crises is usually too difficult for a parent or parent substitute to face alone. Children who have experienced attachment disruptions have learned that adults fail. A caring adult working alone is no-ble but vulnerable. Children and parents (or substitute parents) succeed when they have the backing and support to overcome the gaps in a child's life. Family preservation, bonding, postadoptive services, and family-centered agencies can pull together family members, caring adults in the community, and professionals (child protective workers, psychologists, social workers, family support workers, child care workers, physicians, nurses, teachers, mentors, CASA [Court Appointed Special Advocates] volunteers, law guardians, and judges) to overcome the forces of neglect.

Rebuilding attachments means mobilizing family members and caring adults to meet the needs of children at risk, but we must first overcome the myths that often disrupt adults from answering a child's call for help and *re*-pairing family ties. Otherwise, caring adults often find themselves working alone with the pain of multigenerational traumas and feeling oppressed by family members, agencies, and community leaders who should be supporting them.

Prickers and Vines

When Tommy in Chapter 2 felt the sting of his mother's anger, he burst out of their home. He pumped the pedals of his bike faster and faster, literally driving the pain of his bleeding knee away with each thrust of his legs.

Tommy may as well have been in a trance. And, just as in a fairy tale, a wall was growing up around him, a tall hedge of prickly vines that kept everyone away. Each thorn and tangled vine grew from beliefs pervading Tommy's family *and* their community. "Mind your own business." "Don't ask. Don't tell." "It's none of our business." "Bad seed." "Nothing helps!"

We must overcome our own constricted vision and the dogmas we carry inside our heads, the words, phrases, and beliefs that stop us from doing what otherwise would be very natural, to help a child and to help a neighbor in distress. The child in trouble is often caught, like an entranced princess behind a seemingly impenetrable barrier. The child seems cursed, even doomed. And, just as in a fairy tale, the challenge of healing Tommy meant finding a hero or heroine to break through the thorns and fight off the forces that had imprisoned hope.

Heroes and heroines break down walls of despair. The magic of kisses and hugs could wake the gentle boy sleeping inside Tommy. But that would mean overcoming the prickers and vines that keep parents, relatives, and neighbors away. The prickers and vines are part of the curse that leads children such as Tommy into the streets.

To find the hurt child inside, we have to break through the myths of our times. We have to be stronger *and* help family members become stronger than the "prickers and vines" that envelop lost children.

MYTHS THAT PERPETUATE ABUSE AND NEGLECT

"Nothing Helps"

Probably the most devastating myths of our times are that nothing can be done to prevent neglect, or that children who were victimized by abuse will grow up to be abusers. If nothing works, then it does not pay for legislators or taxpayers to invest in services or programs for neglected children.

Studies[1] have demonstrated how parent-infant therapy, home visiting, parent-child bonding programs, trauma therapies, early childhood education programs, mentoring, and multifaceted family and community interventions have helped parents and children overcome neglect and traumas,[2] change destructive behaviors, and prevent future neglect and abuse. Simple, one-shot actions are not enough, and too often, truncated services are studied with disappointing results. The most successful programs combine family-based interventions designed to rebuild trust with parents (or, if necessary, substitute parents), social skills training, education programs geared to enhance each child's abilities, and community activities with one-to-one links for youths and parents.

"Wait and See"

It is very tempting to give a young mother and father a lot of time to figure out how to care for their children. All too often in families with chronic violence and neglect, the babies are the last to be placed into substitute homes with relatives or foster families. Children under three are not able to call for help or tell adults what is happening in their homes.

Caring practitioners often want to give parents additional time to work things out and are able to engage parents to begin working on change. In a home with domestic violence, a husband and wife may work to stop the fighting over the course of several years. But their children will live with the scars of those first months and years for the rest of their lives. The first months and years of a child's life are critical for developing trust, attachment, empathy, and the ability to regulate feelings. The child's limbic system is being shaped during these crucial months, and before a child learns to use language, implicit memories are being encoded directly into the child's amygdala (Siegel, 2003). Implicit memories (Siegel, 2003) operate without reference to time or self and lead to a child's inherent anticipation of what is going to happen next. Thus, a child who was bitten by a cat at age six months will likely react immediately with fear without any reference as to why or where. Similarly, a child who was struck by an adult who glared and cursed may respond to other adults glaring and cursing with an immediate shudder, wincing as though he or she has been hit again. A twelve-month-old who avoids eye contact, withdraws from people, or conversely is indiscriminately clinging has already been damaged. By eighteen months, the same child may agitate and provoke caretakers with repetitive demands and transgressions.

Children have a great deal of resiliency as long as their basic needs for nurture and protection are met. The infant learns whether or not he or she will be relieved of the pain of hunger or being wet. The infant in a home where parents are consumed with their own problems will show signs of deprivation from the first months.

Early childhood is a golden opportunity to shape a child; and early interventions are the most cost-effective. Few would argue that we should "wait and see" when a child is suffering from a disabling disease such as diabetes or a neurological handicap that interferes with his or her development of speech and language abilities.

Attachment disorders can be identified in a child's first years. Signs of neglect and abuse can be detected. Children simply have no time to wait months and years for parents to get their act together when a home is unsafe and children are being neglected. Every month counts.

The Rule of No Marks

This rule of thumb was introduced to limit the size of the stick a man could use under English common law to chastise his wife. Hitting wives was finally outlawed in the late 1800s, but even today, it is legal to hit a child, as long as no significant marks are left. Spanking has been portrayed as "for the child's own good." An estimated 90 percent of American parents reportedly hit toddlers (Straus, 1994). Yet, studies (Straus, 1994) have shown that children who are hit by their parents are significantly more likely to become depressed or suicidal, fight with siblings, hit their own children or spouses, become arrested for violent crimes, develop an alcohol problem, and have trouble keeping a high-level job and income. Parents can learn how to teach respect and self-control without resorting to hitting a child, but many parents never learned effective ways to teach their children right from wrong without resorting to hitting children and have great fears of children being over-indulged and "spoiled rotten."

The Christian proverb, "spare the rod, spoil the child," has sometimes been taken out of context to justify beatings, rather than a message to parents that children need to be raised with consistent discipline and nurture, stressing the love of God (Traynham, Personal Communication, 2002). The "rod" has also been interpreted by some ministers as a symbol of teaching and guidance, rather than any form of physical aggression with a child.

Other ministers have taught that at times a spanking is warranted and necessary with young children, but that when children become older, there are more effective means of discipline that do not require physical enforcement (Traynham, Personal Communications, 2002). Religious and community leaders who advise parents to spank young children within a relationship of love and respect face the risk that many parents, especially parents traumatized by violence in their own lives, may be unable to spank a child without losing control of their own anger and may be unable (or unwilling) to reunite with a child after hitting him or her.

Biblical phrases such as "an eye for an eye . . ." have also been cited as sanctioning hitting a child who hit or hurt another child. "An eye for an eye" represented the ancient Jewish practice of calling for just compensation for the loss incurred by another (the *worth* of an eye for the *worth* of an eye), and was never meant to be taken literally as calling for the poking out of eyes (Shpeen, Personal Communications, 2001). Atonement[3] for an offense in biblical times was expected to include an apology, full restitution for the worth of the damage or loss, and an extra penance defined in the Bible as 20 percent of the value of the offense. This meant an admission of responsibility before the community, acceptance of the need to make full restitution, and carrying out the restitution and atonement.

Spanking does work, but, in just the opposite way that most parents believe. Hitting children in their earliest years often implants rage and aggression at the neurological level. Instead of teaching self-control, children learn to rely on power and externally imposed threats of aggression to control their behavior in the short run. Spankings teach children that parents cannot control their anger and that physical aggression is okay according to the highest standards, Mom and Dad.

Steve pointed to his left cheek. "That's where my dad hit me. It hurt all the way to the top," he added pointing to the top of his head. Steve's father had whacked him on the face and belted him on his rear. Then, without a word, Steve's father turned, walked out of the bedroom, and slammed the door behind him. A day later, Steve was brought to the crisis residence, his second placement for aggressive behavior.

"I was bad again," Steve said as he drew a picture of himself. He selected a bright red marker and added a jagged mark down the left side of his face, the side where his father had struck him. "So I had to go away."

No visible marks were noticed when Steve entered the crisis residence. Accordingly, under the state's child protective laws, the case was not "indicated." Steve, however, had learned some important lessons. The raw pain of a blow lingers on, long after being hit by a parent. Inflicting pain can be justified by parents and adult authorities. And, the worst pain comes when the door slams, when children are left all alone, and need to go away.

When spanking is coupled with neglect, children feel demeaned, abandoned, and worthless. When hitting involves objects such as sticks or cords, children learn that their bodies will be violated. Children have described to me how beatings opened up their bodies to the blood and guts. Beatings teach our children the ways of the tyrant and the slave master.

Children raised with corporal punishment, cursing, and neglect learn to use violence as the primary solution to problems. Whippings and beatings teach them that might makes right and that extreme anger justifies violent revenge by whatever means possible. In a country with easy access to guns, this is a prescription for disaster.

Austria, Denmark, Finland, Norway, and Sweden have banned corporal punishment of children. In the United States, the old "rule of thumb" has been transformed into a "rule of no visible marks" when it comes to hitting children. Children who fear for their safety and dread upsetting their parents are very likely to wait before finally summoning the courage to tell a friend or teacher. By then, even major bruises may be gone. Parents have bragged to me about being able to hit children without leaving marks that could be seen. Other parents have recalled painfully how they or a sibling tried to get help and were severely beaten once authorities left their home. I have seen older adolescents with scars all over their bodies, hidden for years by their clothing. They never felt safe enough to tell anyone.

The "rule of no marks" gives children the message that authorities condone hitting children. In many countries, parents are allowed, and sometimes encouraged or expected, to intentionally cause pain, the definition of corporal punishment. Parents often feel pressured by relatives or neighbors to "teach a child a lesson" when a child misbehaves.

Discipline is an educational approach to teaching a child self-control and how to use rules and skills so that a child can succeed. The meaning of discipline has, however, often been constricted to mean *punishment*. And, punishment has been equated with hitting. When this happens, an escalating cycle develops in which children's misbehavior leads to corporal punishment that, in turn, incites accelerated transgressions by them. As the cycle continues, parents and children become further estranged and the positive, loving parts of their relationships become lost.

"Lock 'em Up!"

Children and adolescents are brought into the criminal justice system typically as PINS when they become too big and too defiant to control at school or at home. The authority of the court is often invoked to control boys, often as young as seven or eight. These youths typically have been skipping school, disobeying their parents, talking back to teachers, and spending their time with peers, often older youths or young adults.

In homes with domestic violence, children often learn to fight parents or parents' partners as a way to protect a parent, siblings, or themselves. Cursing and fighting are often learned responses to conflict and stress. Parents or schools may petition the court to order a defiant youth to obey rules or live for a period of time in a supervised group care facility. This often begins with a thirty-day placement in a detention center. Youths see this as a punishment, a sentence to serve time for their transgressions, usually followed by a warning. Judges are asked to provide the discipline and structure that the children have not received. The youths hear from the court that one more time and they may be placed for eighteen months in an institution.

Youths typically leave court bearing the responsibility for their actions and the implicit power to leave home by committing transgressions "one more time." Worse, many experience placements in detention facilities as terrifying. They feel abandoned by parents and thrust into an environment where they may be beaten or threatened by larger and intimidating youths. Children and adolescents in this context learn to fight harder and more viciously in order to survive. Aggression becomes equated with survival, and many youths become more skilled in evading adult authority, authority which they come to see as inherently unfair.

Often, PINS cases are really cases of educational neglect. I have met many adolescents placed in group homes who felt they had to stay home from school to help take care of younger siblings. Other youths felt that they had to stay home to keep a sibling or a parent safe from harm. Others felt no one really cared whether they went to school. In many cases, schools offer only minimal help to children with learning disabilities or gaps in their learning caused by years of needing to watch out for violence, drugs, or harm in their homes.

A child who does not go to school is telling teachers and parents that something is wrong. Similarly, a youth who steals candy at the grocery store or underwear in a department store is sending a message. The child may start out showing, "I can't get what I need at home." Later this becomes, "I don't care any more." Looking closer, we see that these are youths who have lived for years with neglect and have given up on their families. By age thirteen or fourteen, they are physically large enough and smart enough to see that they do not have to take the hitting, demeaning, or lack of care in their homes. Peers become very powerful and provide an alternate source for affection and identity, places to sleep, and a new chance to get love.

Youths defined as PINS are not lost. Unfortunately, courts typically focus on outward behaviors and issue orders or services to force children to behave. The underlying neglect and lack of positive relationships in a family are often ignored. The power of the court may work for a while, but soon youths will find ways to get around curfews and probation officers. The excitement of older boyfriends, chasing girls, drinking, drugs, etc., is hard to beat, when the core issues of emptiness and disrespect remain in their homes. When this happens, courts feel compelled to order even more severe forms of restriction, sending youths away to institutions that can force them to go to school. Youths have described to me years of doing what they saw as "jail time" for petty offenses. The core issues of youths in trouble often remained unresolved; and once their sentences have been served, they are typically returned to the same problems in their homes and communities.

The most violent adolescents do need to be locked up in order to protect their communities. These are typically children who grew up without attachments from their earliest days and learned at a young age to turn the pain of severe physical and sexual abuse into hatred for other people. For most youths in trouble, however, community and family-based interventions can have a powerful effect. Successful programs typically include mandated family therapy, home-based interventions, mentors, education geared to a youth's needs and strengths, after-school programs, and supervision. Caring and effective parenting can often be restored if a parent and youth's desire for a family can be mobilized and supported through predictable crises.

Youths need to make an appropriate form of restitution for transgressions and acts that have hurt other people. I am amazed at how often youths adjudicated as "delinquent" are never asked to replace the value of stolen items or make up for the damage they caused. Instead, courts often punish youths by sending them to detention centers, often transporting them in shackles. In my community, we have a small locked detention center just behind the county jail for adults. I've visited twelve-year-olds locked within cinder block walls and fences topped by coils of razor wire. Children call it the "little jail" behind the "big jail." But, just as with the "big jail," the community is only kept safe for the limited time, usually just the few weeks that the youth stays behind the barbed wire. Healing and protection for the child *and* the community are replaced by temporary controls.

PINS youths certainly needs supervision. What is too often missed, however, is that these are youths who come from "families in need." If we dropped the "S" in PINS, courts could be empowered to mobilize the guidance, nurture, and opportunities youths need to reach their potential, as well as to challenge them to develop more appropriate behaviors.

"There's No Place Like Home"

Mark grew up amidst his father's drinking and marijuana use, the fights between his parents, and his older brother trying to beat him up or molest his younger sister. One older brother, Bill, served an eighteen-month placement for sex abuse and delinquency but never admitted responsibility for his behavior. Bill did well in his institution and was sent home before Mark. A few months later, Bill was arrested again after assaulting a peer. This time he was tried as an adult and sent to prison.

After three years of living in temporary foster homes, five years of family counseling and substance abuse services offered to his parents, and a lifetime of watching his parents and four older brothers continue the same old ways, Mark told his mother he did not want to come home. She cast a burning look directly into Mark's eyes. She left the room, stopped calling, visiting, or writing and forbid the other children to talk to Mark.

Mark had nightmares of his mother coming to steal him away in the middle of the night. A court hearing was coming up in which the judge would rule on whether to extend Mark's placement in foster care or summarily send him home to his mother. Mark met with his law guardian to prepare for the hearing and tried to say how scared he felt and how nothing had changed in his mother's home. His dad was once again in an alcohol treatment facility, but Mark knew his mother would soon take him back. She always needed his money. And, he would be drinking once again. Then, the hitting would start again, as it did so many times before.

Mark's new law guardian introduced himself and immediately got down to business.

"Children should live with their parents. Don't you want to go home?" the lawyer asked.

Mark felt pressured to go home, hated by his family, and no other option but to return there. His nightmares increased. He could not sleep. Mark began to defy his foster mother and accidentally hit her in an argument. He worried about sexual feelings he had toward a younger child in the foster home, especially when she climbed onto his lap. Mark could not stand it. He knew he was going to become like his father and his brothers. A week after meeting with his law guardian, Mark barricaded himself in his room at his foster family's home, threatened to kill himself, and was admitted to a psychiatric hospital.

Mark's story is common and has led to a series of laws including New York's Child Welfare Reform Act (1979) and more recently the federal Adoption and Safe Families Act (1997), which limit the time parents have to make their homes safe for their children. However, beliefs in prioritizing the rights of parents and treating children as property have often prevailed over the needs of children. Decisions on a child's placement ultimately rest in the hands of judges. Some have refused to sever a parent's rights even in the worst cases of continued abuse and neglect. In other cases, judges have ruled that a child had suffered permanent neglect, as defined by the state's statutes, but suspended judgment with an order that the county provide another year of services to reunite the child and his or her family. When a child such as Mark experiences such an order, it is often a sentence of doom. "Another year" means a lifetime to a child who has already spent years waiting in temporary homes. Another year often means taking away hope to find another family.

It is hard to face the reality of a parent continuing to drink, abuse drugs, whip children, or beat a spouse. We have been raised to believe that "blood" relationships take priority. Unfortunately, not all parents can or will provide the care, consistency, safety, and bonding a child needs. Good parenting has to be learned. Some simply cannot manage the day-to-day demands of raising a child. Parents may be certified by one branch of government as so disabled that they cannot be expected to work at a menial job, even under supervision, because of their emotional instability, irrational thinking, rages, and diagnoses of mental illness or personality disorders; and yet, at the same time, a family court judge may feel compelled to order that a child be returned to the same parent's care, to be raised without any supervision or change in the parent's diagnosis. These messages reinforce myths that biological parents are always the best choice for children and that raising children is somehow less difficult and less important to our society than working at the most menial job under an employer's close supervision. Children learn that the adult world of business and property is given a higher value than their rights.

To ignore very real mental disabilities in parents means leaving children subject to inadequate care or harm. The best interests of children are too often placed beneath parents' wishes to raise them. Authorities, judges, legislators, and CPS workers can help both parents and children by honestly facing the dilemma and pain. It helps to ask ourselves, Would we feel safe sleeping in this parent's home? If not, What would be needed to make the home nurturing and safe? This does not mean giving up on parents, only to help parents address what is needed to care for their children.

Impairment of a parent's abilities to develop secure attachments often develops from the parent's inability to resolve his or her own traumatic experiences as a child. Children's facial looks, gestures, and behaviors at different ages may trigger parents' own trauma responses. If a parent is easily induced into trauma behaviors, the parent may not be capable of utilizing reasoning or self-modulation in managing day-to-day problems (Siegel, 2003). Similarly, a traumatized parent may very likely be unable to effectively process complex information from a child, will not recognize a child's distress, and will not be able to help a child modulate the child's own feelings (Siegel, 2003). Instead, the child may experience his or her parent showing frightened or frightening behavior at times of even minimal stress. Traumatized parents may inadvertently evoke fear in their children stemming from their own experiences (Hesse et al., 2003). Such parents can often work effectively in trauma therapy and help their children by recognizing their own reactions and changing their responses to their children.

We need to respect a parent's right and responsibility to say in words and actions that "I can't" or "I won't" provide the care my child needs. In many cases, mentally disabled adults will need another adult to act as the child's primary caretaker unless the parent can overcome his or her disability. This is painful to admit, and often, contrary to what a parent may wish. The parent can still love the child and provide support, but more in the role of a loving aunt or uncle.

"He's Just Playing a Game"

Even the most well-meaning of parents may have inappropriate expectations of children at a given stage of development. Little children are often assumed to be thinking the same way that adults do. With this logic, parents come to believe that children are deliberately provoking them. Parents may frame a child's misbehavior as a battle and believe they must come down hard to assert their authority.

Creative and flexible options that keep a parent calm, effective, and in charge may be cast aside under the dictum that the child is a budding miscreant, deliberately attacking the parent's status. The parent feels hurt, and may respond in anger with tighter rules and greater punishments. This incites a child's anxiety and agitation, as he or she sees and feels a parent's wrath, and sees no solution. The child's worst fears are ignited, often leading to increasingly wild behavior and arbitrary and inflexible rules by the parent. Unless the battle is stopped, an escalating cycle of misbehavior and ever harsher forms of punishment may ensue.

The fact is that children are children. Behaviors such as biting, hitting, taking things, throwing food, etc., are natural for infants and toddlers and need to be reshaped by parents. The calmer the parent, the more effective he or she can be in teaching his or her child how to behave. When war is declared, everyone loses.

Raising children is particularly difficult when only one parent is managing the responsibility of child care. Parents need support, breaks, financial resources, a home, and a safe neighborhood. An understanding of children, child care skills, sensitivity to children, an ability to manage their own feelings, and a sense of humor are also essential. Two parents with support from extended family, employers, and a community have many more resources than a single parent who feels estranged from family, friends, employers, colleagues, and community organizations.

When a child has neurological conditions or learning disabilities, we need to adapt forms of guidance to match his or her capacity. For instance, a child with a short attention span or poor memory cannot be expected to complete a list of chores verbalized by a parent rushing out the door. The child can be coached to succeed with simple instructions, visual reminders, and very limited requests, often just one task at a time. This takes time and an effort by the parent to learn a different way that will work with his or her child.

It is hard for parents and teachers to validate learning disabilities with a child who physically looks normal but who perceives, learns, and thinks in a different way. Just as with physical disabilities, we need to assess how the child is functioning and then work with him or her to build on his or her strengths and minimize risks. Most parents seek expert guidance for managing sick children and would welcome medical assistance on a daily or weekly basis. Similarly, parents can utilize guidance from experts on raising children with cognitive and learning disabilities, as well as direct forms of daily or weekly support through schools, after-school programs, tutoring, and home-visiting programs.

"This Is Your New Daddy"

When parents *re*marry and tell their children to immediately begin calling a new spouse Mom or Dad, it means asking them to be disloyal to missing parents. It also means teaching children that family members are interchangeable. Adults who ask children to quickly trust new parents are often seen by children as phony or invalidating. Remarriage does not earn a child's love for the new adult as Dad or Mom. The new parent will have to earn this through care, commitment, and perseverance over an extended time.

Similarly, if the last two "Daddy's (or Mommy's)" were violent, it only makes sense that children will expect a new "Daddy" to act just the same way, even if they present as kind or charming at first. Children will likely test new parents to see if they act in ways the children have become accustomed to expect. New parents need to understand that children will very naturally react with trauma behaviors to subtle reminders of past violence, e.g., a stepfather winking or a stepmother combing her hair in a certain way. Trust may take months or years to win based on the child's age and how long he or she had to live with past abuse.

"Children Are a Blank Slate"

Court decisions regarding permanent neglect are based on significant evidence of a parent's failure to plan and make necessary changes to care for a child over at least fifteen months of a child's placement despite services provided to help them reunite. The child's best interests have little bearing in these hearings with the presumption that he or she can (and must) move back to a parent unless the parent fails to make necessary changes. The Adoption and Safe Families Act was designed to set a time limit for parents to make significant progress and reunite with their children. However, with crowded court calendars, overloaded and often poorly trained caseworkers, a shortage of county lawyers and law guardians, lack of funding for assessments and family therapy, and rapid turnover of caseworkers, petitions establishing neglect, violations, or permanent neglect may be delayed for months and years, or sometimes even forgotten. A judge may be torn between giving a parent another chance and a child whose security rests with the bonds he or she has formed with his or her foster parents or guardians. However, the prioritization of parental rights forces courts to effectively ignore a child's lack of attachment or longstanding experiences of trauma with a parent. Children who have been raised from birth by foster parents with whom they have bonded or children who have found sanctuaries and built trust over several years in their foster homes, may be sent back to biological parents who are effectively strangers in their lives or who had neglected and abused them for most of their lives, but made some change before a long-delayed court hearing.

"Leave me alone," Katie (age three) screamed, as she followed her foster mother around the house. Katie began screaming in a high-pitched voice in the middle of the night and would kick, hit, and bite her foster mother in the days following resumption of unsupervised visits with her birth mother. Katie had been an animated, vivacious little girl who looked to the foster parents who had raised her from birth for care and comfort and responded well to their guidance. After her birth mother relapsed and failed to make progress in managing her anger, violence, and emotional problems during Katie's first two years, her foster parents were advised that the county would seek to terminate her birth mother's rights. However, filing petitions were repeatedly delayed as Katie was *re*assigned through five different caseworkers. By the time a judge reviewed the case, Katie was two-and-a-half years old and a permanent neglect petition remained unfiled. Katie's birth mother continued to receive services and eventually completed a second drug treatment program and attended domestic violence and anger management classes. Extended unsupervised visits were ordered by the court with a plan for Katie to return to her birth mother's care within a few months. Katie's foster parents were ordered by county officials to transport Katie to her birth mother's apartment for visits each week despite her crying out to them that she did not want to go, that she was afraid of her mother, and that her mother spanked her. Katie learned that her foster parents could not be trusted. She sat stiffly with a stone-like face in her birth mother's apartment and raged at her foster mother after her visits were over.

Treating children as blank slates also takes place when prospective foster or adoptive parents are encouraged to believe that neglected and traumatized children *just* need a loving home. Advertisements pull on our desire to help and to believe that simply placing a child into a caring family will heal his or her wounds. Many foster or adoptive parents may also want to believe that a child can move on with a safe home, good meals, stimulating activities, and the blessings of his or her new family's support and resources. Similarly, it is easy to assume that a child is ready to grieve lost parents and rebuild attachments just because a biological parent has signed a legal document, giving up parental rights to his or her child, or a judge has terminated a parent's rights.

In the real world, children need a past as well as a future. Food, clothing, a roof overhead, a good school, and a safe neighborhoods are crucial but insufficient to help them master past traumas or to heal from losses. Grief work is almost always necessary. Paradoxically, children can only begin to grieve within a safe and secure relationship, therefore the painful work of facing losses, confronting their anger, moving past denial, giving up on fantasies of reunion, and moving past detachment and depression usually must take place after they enter a new home. Unfortunately, this has been the very time when social services policies have terminated services to biological families reuniting with children who were in placement or adoptive families who provide a new home for children.

"Not in My Town"

It is convenient to think that children are not being abused or neglected in our own neighborhoods, but we know it is not true.

Poverty clearly exacerbates the difficulty and risks involved in raising children. Lead poisoning, lack of maternal and child health care, and lack of appropriate preschool and older-child education leads directly to physical and mental handicaps. In the United States, children represent the poorest segment of the population, particularly children growing up in single-parent families without a father taking an active role in raising them. However, children in affluent homes can suffer a greater impoverishment, emotionally and spiritually, if parents are unavailable, cold, or rejecting. Drug use by poor *or* wealthy parents affects children from conception as chemicals pass into the child in utero and continues to damage them after birth through neglect and inconsistent or abusive parenting. The greatest poverty of all is the lack of a bond to someone a child can depend on.

"Someone Is to Blame"

I believe individuals must be held responsible for their actions, but I also have seen how thinking and reactions are shaped over a lifetime. Parents who lose their jobs in a corporate takeover may turn to drinking and suddenly lose control and smack a rebellious adolescent. This does not mean that a parent is uncaring or chronically abusive. Poverty, politics, economics, and family breakdown are all interwoven.

Natural disasters (e.g., hurricanes) are more readily accepted as requiring community and national aid. Man-made disasters (e.g., the shooting of children at a community center, wars, or hate crimes) also generate traumas in parents and children. Psychological traumas lie beneath the skin, but the signs and symptoms are clear. Indications of posttraumatic stress include hypervigilance; hypersensitivity to sights and sounds; recurrent nightmares; intrusive thoughts and memories; agitation, fears, and rage stimulated by sights and sounds similar to what happened; impulses to strike out; difficulty sustaining attention; difficulty concentrating; and losing track of time.

Going after a "bad guy" is exciting. We can watch on TV the pursuit of the crazed killer, but this is not enough to help children and parents who have lived with neglect and trauma. Looking for one person to blame is simplistic. Worse, it limits our vision of resources that can help children and families.

Similarly, beliefs that *only* men are violent or that *only* men are sex abusers can act as blinders to the way violence cycles in and out of everyone's lives. I have seen county authorities refuse to ask battered women to take responsibility for their drinking, threatening, hitting, or sexually molesting their children. The children were often told by their mothers they would be coming home to them, even though the mothers continued to welcome an abusive father, or refused to admit how they had hurt their children physically, sexually, or emotionally. The silence of the authorities left the children unprotected. As the months and years went by with no change in their mothers, these children became more and more hopeless with escalating tantrums, suicide attempts, and psychiatric hospitalizations.

"It Is Nobody's Business"

None of us are perfect. My children can document scores of my mistakes and omissions on a monthly basis. We get through with help. Asking for assistance violates norms many of us are taught and beliefs that we must be perfect or that heroes never make mistakes. We all need pride, but we also need support from family and friends. Doing it alone may seem heroic but it is also risky. Parents who act as martyrs may not realize the burden they place on their children. Parenting with no supports is similar to walking a tight-rope. Even the best parents need a safety net sometimes.

When bad things happen to people, it is especially important to get help. Keeping traumas a secret may work temporarily for adults who are otherwise fairly secure. They can bury their pain temporarily in their work or a new relationship. However, children pressed to keep traumas a secret often grow up feeling unsafe with their wounds intact. Energy for learning and developing skills becomes diverted to keeping the secret and always remaining on guard for the next trauma to occur.

OBSTACLES TO REBUILDING ATTACHMENTS

"Melting Pot Interventions"

A one-size-fits-all service or protocol may appeal to authorities in a state capital striving to streamline services and cut expenses, but such services make little sense when it comes to serving a wide range of children and families from rural farmlands to inner cities. Crisis-oriented services often miss the strengths in a child's family and his or her ethnic heritage. With professional services limited to short, typically fifty-minute sessions for a few weeks or months, it becomes even more important to quickly find aunts and uncles, grandparents, clergy, and mentors who can support changes in families. Yet, the richness of a family's history in overcoming adversity is often lost when practitioners are constrained to putting out immediate fires and ensuring quick discharges with previously set lengths of service. Similarly, the richness and resources in churches, synagogues, mosques, community centers, and neighborhood organizations are often left untapped by mental health providers because reimbursable time is limited to face-to-face client contact hours. Clinics and agencies typically cannot afford to allow practitioners time to engage community resources or extended-family members or to develop and implement integrated service plans that build on available resources.

"Managed Care Is the Answer"

Helping children and families who have experienced years of abuse and neglect is a high risk and arduous task requiring sensitive, highly skilled practitioners to help clients overcome traumas and build (or rebuild) attachments over time. In the last decade, both government and private insurers have turned to managed-care models of service delivery to cut costs of mental health and child and family services. HMOs (health maintenance organizations) have slashed reimbursements to psychologists and social workers, limited family and individual therapy to five to twenty sessions, required escalating co-payments by clients after the first few sessions, and mandated filing detailed applications that must be approved *in advance* by HMO managers before services can begin.

State departments of mental health, child and family services, and youth criminal justice programs have also cut funding for child and family services in many states. For children and parents whose problems often center on a lack of relationships, state-funded programs often mandate that families seek services from multiple providers in multiple settings. Children and parents are asked to tell their life stories to a series of social workers, psychologists, or psychiatrists, each with only a short time allotted to assess needs and provide services. Thorough assessments have been cut down to brief interviews, and time for bringing in extended-family members, community leaders, and other service providers has been eliminated or severely reduced by the lack of funding and increased caseloads. Intensive family-preservation programs found to be effective with small caseloads have often been institutionalized with caseloads doubled and a reduction of supportive services. Children and parents soon feel like objects forced to move through an uncaring system that neither respects them nor understands their problems. Conscientious, caring, and skilled practitioners leave child and family services frustrated and exhausted with turnover skyrocketing to 50 percent or more each year in some cities. The higher the turnover, of course, the greater the burden on remaining staff and the less parents and children can trust practitioners to provide any form of sustained help.

Managed care has meant moving from providing services that match clients' needs *to* providing what is in the contract. With agencies required to bid against each other for contracts, services have become more and more restricted to meeting the listed demands of the funding source, rather than striving to provide the highest quality of services. Assessment of strengths and needs, engagement of children, parents, extended-family members, and others to work together on setting goals, building enduring relationships, and evaluation of progress have been shown to lead to successful outcomes but require time and skilled practitioners. Regulations and rules limit expenditures but often miss what children and parents need. Priority has to be placed on completing forms, "treating the chart," in order to obtain reduced levels of funding and avoid fiscal sanctions on agencies and practitioners. Effective interventions have been undermined by mandates to drastically cut sessions and hire staff without the necessary training.

Overcoming attachment problems is a lifelong challenge. Effective therapeutic services involve therapists who can build a predictable and continuous relationship. The best services offer children and families the opportunity to come back to therapists as needed with therapists providing a concrete symbol of permanency, caring, and guidance. Therapists can play a significant role in validating children's social and emotional development, promoting attachments, and helping parents predict and prepare for developmental challenges. Ideally, this would involve annual checkups (e.g., going for well-baby visits or dental checkups) with children who have experienced major losses (Sorosky and Pannor, 1978).

Managed care promotes an assembly line model of services that has been successful in hospitals to pare down costs. Unfortunately, moving children from one practitioner to another reinforces attachment disorders. Children traumatized by losses, separations, and abandonment come to see service providers as repeating the pain they experienced in their families.

In New York State, the Office of Mental Health, similar to mental health services in many other states, has achieved notoriety by closing institutions, restricting care in hospitals and crisis residences to short fixed periods of times, mandating a focus on individual mental illness, and limiting provision of community-based services far below the actual need. Funding for crisis residences and home- and community-based programs often excluded psychological evaluations of children's attachments and family functioning. The block-grant funding imposed by New York's legislature and Governor George Pataki in 1995, reduced expenditures for foster care and child protective and family preservation services by 25 percent to help meet the governor's pledge to reduce taxes. After newspaper accounts of children's deaths, this funding was increased by 18 percent in the next year's budget over the reduced level, in effect maintaining a sharp cutback in what were already overtaxed and inadequate services. Four years later, the state legislature found that New York's most vulnerable children were being lost in a dysfunctional and underfunded bureaucracy (Green and Parment, 1999). In New York City, for instance, 43 percent of children who remained with their families after abuse was identified were found to be mistreated again, despite child protective supervision. Only 60 percent of families listed as needing preventive services were actually provided with help. Forty-eight percent of children in group care settings lacked needed medical, dental, and mental health services.

METHODS OF REBUILDING ATTACHMENTS

Strengthening Families

American politics and media have often worked against parents. Messages from advertisements, movies, television, and video games glamorize violence and sex as the answer to life's problems. Lobbyists have successfully stalled efforts to register all guns and rifles, eliminate assault weapons, prevent gun sales to minors, and require licensing of gun owners. In a culture with pervasive and powerful messages that foster materialism, promiscuity, and quests for power, children need even stronger messages at home from parents about how to become caring men and women. The strongest message for any child is the feeling of being loved as someone special by his or her parents, grandparents, and other family members.

Fostering the feeling that children are special works like an "inoculation" (Schimmer, Personal Communications, 1999) protects them against the inevitable adversities and hardships they will face in life. A home can be a sanctuary for children *and* parents. The warmth of decorations, the roots and ties portrayed by family photographs, and the comfort of furnishings change a house or apartment into a home.

Violent music, posters, and computer or television images destroy the sanctity of our homes and the shelter we want for our children. Music and television shows played in a home help define how we interact. Harsh sounds and violent lyrics teach children to be aggressive and to stay on edge, ready to fight everywhere. Calm, soothing music, family-oriented movies and television shows, and stories or games can teach children to be caring toward each other and their parents. Cooking meals, baking cookies, feeding and grooming pets, and helping neighbors teaches children that homes are for caring.

Parents can restrict a young child from forms of violence in the media, especially visual images in movies, television, and Web sites that generate fears and expectations that the world is unrealistically dangerous. Television, movies, and computer or video games need to be carefully limited. More than an hour of television shows or video games a day constrict a child's creativity and development.

We also need to protect our children from the names and labels used, often by well-meaning teachers and medical personnel. Labels can foster constriction and shame, eroding a child's strength and potential. Labels of disorders within the child are often seen by the child as confirmation of how bad he or she is. I have met many youths discharged from psychiatric hospitals who arrived at my agency reciting their diagnosis. "I am a borderline." Diagnoses may help us match children to clusters of behaviors, and may be necessary for funding, but children often hear such labels as messages of blame, damage, and hopelessness. Children feel unheard and often come to see otherwise caring adults as enemies.

We can take a term used to describe a child and reframe it to accentuate his or her strengths and opportunities to succeed. For instance, "chutzpah" in the Jewish tradition refers to daring and boldness that can be used to cause trouble or to triumph over adversity where others have failed. Parents can build up either side. Similarly, when a child has gotten used to being punished for his or her attitude or being bold, it helps to frame a child's choice in using the energy and strength in this attitude or boldness for good or bad. Pop heroes have attitude. Daniel Boone, a pioneer legend, was bold. Harriet Tubman utilized her boldness to rescue slaves through the underground railroad. Reframing labels such as attitude and boldness helps parents to step back, recognize the positive qualities of persistence and energy in their children, and figure out ways they can shape their attitude into a strength that can help the children succeed in life and contribute to their families.

The Rule of Three

The stronger a child's sense of roots and security within the family, the better able the child will be to face crises in life. We can protect children against hard times and crises by modeling and fostering a sense of courage and power. The child's breadth of vision and competence grows within relationships to adults who care enough to fight for the child. We need to become heroes and heroines for our children. This means owning and overcoming our own demons.

I have learned from children in crisis how each of us needs to feel valued and to have people we can trust enough to allow us to share our deepest feelings and beliefs. Children need adults who care enough to put their best interests ahead of other pressures, adults who are strong enough to help them own, understand, and share their life experiences in a way that makes sense, and to raise, or help raise, children to maturity. A child can get by with one solid link, one strong attachment, but two is twice is strong, and three forms a solid foundation.

Many of the homeless children and young adults I have met had at an earlier age felt loved by a grandmother or an aunt, until something happened. The child may have enjoyed a special relationship with a single parent. "You and me against the world." However, with just one link, children are extremely vulnerable to any change in the lives of the parents or relatives who are attached to them. The child's stability crumbles if the key person in his or her life becomes overwhelmed with work problems, the burden of caring for an ailing grandparent, or if a parent begins to lose a battle with a debilitating disease.

It helps to aim for *at least* three solid connections for every child. Three people who will guide a child into adulthood. It takes at least three legs to support a simple chair and a family begins with a father, a mother, and a child. Three connections may not seem necessary when things are going well, but these connections provide the grounding we all need when it is time to make a transition in life and when times get tough.

It may not be possible to build three strong connections in the short run, but the work of building relationships creates hope. The more links to caring people, the stronger each of us becomes. Children gain pride and power from each close relationship with an adult who recognizes how they are special, sees their talents, and recognizes their moments of success at home, at school, in after-school programs, at community centers, within a religious institution, at summer camp, or in the neighborhood. Coaches, mentors, and religious leaders can play a powerful role in shaping a youth's future.

The power of a community comes from teaching a child that his or her life has meaning. Children learn this through strong ties to real people who help them develop a positive identity within their communities. Boys need father figures, and girls need mother figures. Adults who take on mentor roles with children become their heroes.

Parenting As Commitment

With movies, television, and magazines promoting images of casual sex, it has become much harder to reinforce the importance of parenting as a lifetime commitment by both parents. Lonely girls may look to pregnancy as the answer to the emptiness felt inside, ignoring the lessons shared by older teenage mothers who have borne the burden of raising children alone, often after a boyfriend leaves them. Young mothers are suddenly faced with twenty-four-hour-a-day responsibilities, and friends and television shows remind them of the fun they are missing.

Young unwed mothers are often provided with a great deal of support during their pregnancies and in the first few months of an infant's life. Then the young mother typically sets out on her own, searching to establish herself as independent, and thinking she can manage. The difficulty of parenting soon escalates as an infant turns into a toddler moving around, testing the limits, and screaming "No" to a young parent who feels alone, unwanted by her own family, and abandoned by the baby's father.

Single-parent families have all the odds stacked against them for economic, social, and emotional hardship and the impoverishment of children. Teenage mothers are often abandoned by older boyfriends, legal adults, who evade the responsibility of caring for and providing support for their children.

Socializing boys to care for and protect children is critical for any society. Caring fathers are essential and often neglected, even by social services professionals. As a young girl in foster care told me, fathers need to "love children . . . keep me safe . . ." Government cannot replace fathers but government can promote boys learning to care, young men finding a way to gain respect as parents and providers, and men taking responsibility for protecting and nurturing their children.

We require our teenagers to learn about American government, often in high school classes that include participation in town or state government activities. Similarly, adolescents should be required to pass at least a semester's curriculum on child development and parenting skills with volunteer time spent in local preschool or maternity health care programs.

Communities also need to enforce fathers' as well as mothers' responsibilities for child support. Communities can enforce values by penalizing all forms of physical and sexual assaults on children through legislation, police protection, and criminal prosecution. This needs to include prosecution of adult men for statutory rape of adolescent girls.

CONCLUSION

Statistics show that three American children will probably be murdered on the day you read this page. Newspapers flash the latest horror stories: "Infant Killed; Mother's Boyfriend Held for Questioning" or "Mother Sentenced for Shaking Her Baby and Causing Massive Brain Damage." Most of us hope that the dangers are out there, somewhere else, not in our neighborhoods; but the sad reality is that violence spreads outward and touches everyone. The unloved toddler scrapping for food with his or her siblings grows up to menace his or her classmates and community.

Today's victims of abuse and neglect can grow up to become tomorrow's perpetrators of the same violence with their own children, at their jobs, or in their communities. Research has shown that violence is largely learned and tied to experiences of child abuse, witnessing battering of parents or siblings, alcohol and drug abuse by parents, and criminal activity in the family.

Despite the headlines, teen violence and drug use is not rampant in the United States and far less a problem than adult crime and drug addiction. Adults commit eleven out of twelve homicides, and drug death rates fell 66 percent among teenagers from 1970 to 1996 but increased by 113 percent among parents (Males, 1998). Teenage violence shocks us because we see children transformed into perpetrators within the space of a few years.

For many children, the roots of dangerous behaviors may never be addressed. These children learn to give up hope, to stop caring about others, and to increasingly act out the violence they have experienced. It is easy to shun such children or their families, to label them as deviant or sick, and to ignore their distress and their seemingly endless tragedies. But soon, neighbors and communities feel the child's unanswered terror. No one feels safe.

Concerned and committed parents, grandparents, and foster and adoptive parents have taken on the challenge of rebuilding hope and trust with hurt and troubled children in their homes. Psychologists, social workers, physicians, CPS workers, family-support workers, child care workers, nurses, teachers, mentors, CASA volunteers, law guardians, judges, and community leaders can help biological and foster and adoptive families overcome trauma and rebuild hope. These heroes are cutting through the prickers and vines that surround hurt and hurting children. They hear the inner voices of wounded children and parents. They can see past the prickers and vines to the angels inside.

Caring adults can take away the power of toxic secrets and beliefs. In fairy tales, a magic kiss cuts through a century of prickers and vines. In real life, the challenge of helping a lost youth is much harder. The next chapters outline a process for biological, foster, and adoptive parents to work together with practitioners, mentors, and teachers to restore hope and rebuild attachments.

Chapter 5

Restoring Hope and Safety

> Reconciliation does not come easy. Believing it does will ensure that it will never be. We have to work and look the beast firmly in the eyes. . . .
>
> Archbishop Desmond Tutu

INTRODUCTION

The Unsaid

Rebuilding hope means facing the truth about the forces that shaped a child's life, the love a child received *and* the traumas, neglect, and losses that may be driving his or her dangerous behaviors. Rebuilding hope also means dealing with the truth of a parent's choices to act as a responsible parent *or* continue to deny problems and leave a child without a secure attachment.

If they ignore the truth, parents, relatives, and caring adults are teaching children that they must hide from the truth. For boys such as Tommy in Chapter 2, this means continuing to deny the pain of real wounds, and worse, the sting of feeling rejected. It means continuing to hold the pain inside and often to live with the nightmares of family violence.

Hiding the truth means leaving things unsaid. Painful incidents become defined as secrets. This adds power to the painful side of traumas and enforces beliefs that no one can deal with what was experienced. We can close our eyes and ignore what is going on, hide ourselves, and leave these children with their nightmares. For children such as Tommy, the nightmares live on. Over time, the child's rage grows and consumes the parts of him or her looking for love and affection, the parts of every child yearning to be praised for success and to have a parent, a relative, or a teacher value what he or she has done.

Toxic secrets also rob power from family members, caretakers, and other adults who the child suspects know the secret but do nothing to make things better. If all the adults act too frightened to face what happened, how can a young child be strong enough to succeed?

We can help children master the truth, but it means facing the fears we all carry inside. Deep down, we all dread the nightmares experienced by these children. We know the same things could happen to any of us.

Following the Clues

Working as a detective can help. First, we need to open our eyes, our ears, and our feelings. We need to hold ourselves back from rushing headfirst with solutions that may not fit Tommy's family or situation. Instead, we can uncover the strengths within Tommy, his family, his cultural background, and his community. We need to study what each child is showing us. Most of the time, children hit us over and over with the same message. Little kids show us very clearly what is needed.

Four-year-old Jared came to his Head Start class every day with a sad look. Every five minutes, he stretched out his hands looking up at the nearest adult. Sweet, affectionate, and demanding, Jared was looking for love and sending a message that anyone would do.

Four-year-old Justin came to nursery school every day, clenched his little fist, and slugged every child who came near him. Then Justin would glare up at his teacher, a wordless challenge: *I'm hitting. What are you going to do about it?*

Both boys were living temporarily in foster homes, and both showed the neglect they had experienced. Jared was a needy waif, desperate for reassurance. Justin was trying to take control of an out-of-control world and used the tools he witnessed family members or other adults use to get what they needed.

Adults often show the same basic needs and behaviors as these two boys. It is pretty easy to spot the big guys wearing business suits or denim overalls who deep down see the world as cruel and expect others to try to hit or hurt them if they do not hit or strike out first. Their aggressive stance goes back to their own days when they were in day care or preschool, watching and learning to live with their parents, siblings, relatives, and neighbors. Each of them needed the same thing as today's problem child in nursery school.

Young children present us with clear messages and a window of opportunity to intervene. However, they quickly learn to hold back and disguise what is going on. Still, with a few tools, we can move from shock to insight to change. We can summon the courage to look beyond overt behaviors into the rich world of a child's life that shapes his or her behavior.

Parents and teachers too often only see the child's actions functioning with the present place and time, a microcosm of his or her experience. A child's behaviors may be castigated as violations of rules or challenges to authority. This perspective locks us into a losing battle in which we waste our efforts and all too often end up exhausted, struggling in the dark with forces we do not understand.

Both Jared and Justin could do well if they found someone who would care for them, love them, and guide them into adulthood, freeing them from neglect. That would mean working with the biological parents to make changes, or if necessary, to make another plan for who would raise each boy. If the four-year-old desperate for hugs thinks he is going back to neglect, he will remain just as needy and gradually give up. If the four-year-old slugger sees that adults in his family are still fighting and unsafe, his own aggression will become ingrained.

If we take off our blinders, we can open up new perspectives and new solutions. Using the child's actions as guideposts, we can move from marker to marker. We can travel through time to discover the forces that led to violence. We can feel the power of a child's experience with parents and guardians and utilize the strengths of people around the child who care. If we listen closely, we can hear the inner voice of the child pointing the way to what is needed.

INVESTIGATING CHILD ABUSE AND NEGLECT

Bring Out the Bloodhounds

Children leave a trail of clues for us to follow to discover both the traumas in their lives and possible resources that can help these children and their families to heal. I ask myself the following series of questions in order to learn what shaped a child's struggle, the problems and the resources in his or her life.

How old is a child acting?

I look at a child's thoughts, beliefs, actions, and my own reactions. Biting means a year or less. Tantrums such as hitting, stomping, throwing things, and screaming are normal for toddlers (ages one-and-a-half to two-and-a-half). Do I feel as if I am dealing with a toddler, a child ready for kindergarten, an eight-year-old, or a teenager? When did the child first act in a dangerous way?

Tommy became increasingly angry and irritable in the last months of his mother's pregnancy. By the time his baby brother was born, Tommy's nursery school teachers were sending daily reports home about his behavior problems. Marie was told that Tommy had to start behaving or he would have to leave.

What happened at the developmental age that the child shows in his or her behavior?

What hardships, separations, losses, or traumas led to the child's first dangerous behaviors? I try to understand the child's experience at that age in his or her family, extended family, and community. In this way, we can travel through time to the focal point of a child's dilemma, the age when he or she experienced some disruption, loss, or trauma, which the child could not overcome.

Tommy survived the loss of his father and became his mom's special protector, her "little man." He loved being so needed and tried hard to be everything his mom needed. After his father left, Tommy would sit by Marie when she cried. He even tried to hold her hand. Marie would smile and nod, gently stroking his hair.

That was before she found Clyde, before she "fell in love," and before she became pregnant. After that, everything got worse. Marie and Clyde started arguing. Tommy watched from a corner, a three-and-a-half-year-old who did not know what to do. When the arguing became fighting, Tommy began to cry. He charged into his mother's boyfriend, swinging his fists. But, it did no good. Tommy was pushed away.

"Go to your room!" Marie yelled at Tommy.

Tommy backed off, but kept watching from around the corner.

"Get out! I mean it!" his mom ordered. She did not want Tommy to see, but Tommy heard her angry voice and words. He believed his mother was angry at him. He must have done something wrong.

Tommy climbed slowly up the stairs and fell onto his bed. His gut ached. He wanted to ask for medicine but he did not dare. Tommy buried his face on his blanket and pulled a pillow over his head. He tried to drown out the yelling but it did not work. The voices of his mom and Clyde just got louder and louder.

They were cursing now, words Tommy had never been allowed to use. Then Tommy heard a crash, something breaking. Then more cursing, even louder. Tommy could not stand it. He crept quietly to the top of the stairs and peeked down.

"Get out!" Marie screamed at Clyde. Tommy saw Clyde backing toward the front door. Clyde was clutching the side of his face. His eyes were wild, darting all around. Tommy shivered, afraid he would be seen at the top of the stairs, but Clyde's eyes narrowed and locked onto Marie as she came toward him.

"Get out, you goddamn fuckin' asshole! Go back to your tramp!" Marie screamed. Suddenly, Clyde grabbed Marie by the shoulders. "Fuck you!" he roared. Clyde slapped Marie hard on the face and she fell backward.

"Fuck you!" Clyde roared again and shoved Marie into the brick wall by the fireplace. He turned, yanked open the door, and stormed out. The door slammed backward into the wall and swung wildly back and forth, never closing.

Marie crumpled to the floor. Tommy froze. He felt his body stiffen. He could not move. *What if she was dead?* The thought sent a shiver up his spine. Then, Tommy saw her chest move. He heard a sigh, a little cry, then a sob.

Tommy ran down the stairs as fast as he could, stumbling on the last step, but he kept running. Nothing could stop him. Tommy reached out and touched his mother's shoulder. He wanted so much to hug her, to hold her, to tell her it would be okay. He would get the bandages, clean her up, and get her a new shirt.

"I'll take care of you," Tommy whispered. He looked down on his mom. Marie's chest heaved and she sighed. She buried her face behind her arm. *I just want to die,* Marie thought to herself.

Tommy saw the tears dripping down her face. He sat still, then reached out, touching his mom's shoulder again.

"Ouch!" Marie screamed. She did not mean to yell but Tommy heard the same raging voice Marie had used when she screamed at Clyde.

"Leave me alone!" Marie yelled. She just wanted to be alone. It was over with Clyde, and she was pregnant again. Same old thing. *Bastards, all of them,* she thought to herself.

Tommy reached out again. This time touching his mom's knee.

"Go away!" Marie shrieked. She lifted her head. "My knee hurts. My shoulder hurts. You're making it worse!" Tommy shuddered, then froze. He saw the blood running from a cut along Marie's cheek.

"Just leave me alone!" Marie shrieked again. She hid her head and cried. Without thinking, Tommy's hand reached up toward his mother's cheek.

"Just go!" Marie ordered again, not even looking. "Leave me alone!"

Tommy pulled himself up. He trudged back up the stairs. His body felt as though it weighed a thousand pounds.

What is going on in the child's family, school, or neighborhood that may be spurring the child to get in trouble now?

I look for any actions and words that upset the child in the past and which he or she is experiencing again in the present time, reminders of painful experiences from the past which lead the child to think, feel, and act the way he or she had to at a younger age. These typically represent the traumas that the child and his or her family must overcome, the central crises in the story.

Tommy never asked again about what happened, and Marie never talked about Clyde, the fight, or much of anything else after that. She just focused on her job and getting ready for the baby. Clyde was history. She would have to go on, on her own, by herself, just as always. She buried the hurt in her work, but the anger remained.

Tommy saw the difference. His mom never had time any more to cuddle. She stopped telling him about her dreams, how they would make a wonderful life, even without his father.

Tommy heard his mother curse to herself as she was cooking, when she was cleaning, outside, inside, everywhere it seemed. "Clean up your mess!" Marie snapped. "Can't you help for a change?"

Tommy missed his old mom. He remembered the hugs. He tried to show Marie some of the craft work he made at his nursery school. She would look quickly. "That's nice," she would say, but she did not smile. She did not look him in the eyes, and, she would just turn away. So much to do.

As time went by, Tommy knew he had failed, failed to protect his mom from Clyde, and now failed day after day to help her. He still wished he could. He did try to help. One night, when she looked especially tired, Tommy put some peanut butter on a piece of bread, spooned on a little jelly, placed it all on a plate, and silently carried it to her in the living room. But, instead of a smile, Marie just looked at him and pursed her lips.

"Don't you go and make a mess again in here." It was his mom's angry voice, the voice Tommy always associated now with his mother's angry side, such as when she fought with Clyde.

"Get that out of here. Eat in the kitchen like you're supposed to. I'm not running no home for slobs, that's for sure!"

Tommy saw his brother's baby bottle and a spoon from his baby cereal sitting on the living room table. His mother started to fold the baby's clothes again, nodding her head as though she was talking to herself.

Tommy turned and ran into the kitchen. *She hates me.* Tommy thought to himself. He ran out the back door. Tommy grabbed his bike. He was not his mama's little boy any more.

Who could help (e.g., fathers, siblings, grandparents, friends, community organizations, or authorities)? Who is missing?

I look for the people who have believed and nurtured a child and who cared enough to protect and raise a child. Were there sequential losses, a *countdown* in critical relationships that led up to a child's violent outbursts? If so, who would the child like to become close to again? Are there people in the child's world who value him or her enough to help the child learn and grow? Who could provide the child with a safe, nurturing home? I look for the heroes and heroines who could fill a child's story with renewed hope.

Sometimes, caring adults have come to feel blamed by both authorities and family members, and so, tend to stay away when a child is placed. We often need to reach out to possible resources, rather than waiting to see if they will come looking for a child. As I learn a child and family's story, I want to validate how family members have helped and how our role as practitioners is not to blame.

Tommy still saw his father on holidays and birthdays. His father was settling down now, starting a new family, a new life. He figured Tommy was doing okay with his mother. Anyway, he was busy. He had a job to manage, more mouths to feed. He saw Tommy when he could, best he could do. Tommy would have to unferstand. A man's got to work. He was not like those bums Marie hung out with, like Clyde, her last boyfriend. What a loser!

Tommy liked his Uncle Todd, his mother's sister's husband. They lived in the next town. Tommy wondered why they did not see them much anymore. Todd worked a lot. But, he always gave Tommy a special grin and a tap on the back. Sort of a special sign, Tommy thought. He thought Uncle Todd was pretty cool and secretly wished sometimes that he could be Uncle Todd's son.

Answering the Child in Crisis

It is easy to get lost in a sea of problems with children in crisis,[1] especially when the risks include children getting hurt or hurting others. As Tommy zoomed into traffic, he was challenging his family and neighbors to keep him safe *or* risk his dying.

We can easily lose our perspective when faced with the very real risks children such as Tommy pose for serious injury or death. We very naturally start to feel that one small misstep, one missed clue, and Tommy could die. Children such as Tommy make us shudder and recoil, just as the woman who almost hit Tommy with her car did.

Therapists working with abuse and neglect often experience the nightmare of waking up in the middle of the night wondering, *Did I do enough? Did I miss something?* It is enough to drive caring practitioners to a less risky field of work. Self-care means learning to take the time to allow ourselves to feel and handle questions during work hours. Our fears typically highlight the central crises in each child's life story and point to what a child and parent needs to make their lives better.

If I am left with a disturbing feeling after a session, I ask myself what is missing and what messages from parents or children went unanswered. What can I do now to answer covert or lingering messages, rather than taking my concerns or fears home with me?

A fifteen-year-old youth in a crisis shelter at another agency glared at his mother, made a slashing gesture at his throat, and insisted that no one talk about what Dad did. He later mumbled, "I want to kill myself," but adamantly denied being suicidal. Fortunately, I was able to coordinate supervision and referral for treatment with the shelter director, rather than relying on this youth and his depressed mother.

Children are flirting with death when they set fires in their rooms, run alone at night through dangerous neighborhoods, try unknown drugs, and engage in promiscuous sex in the age of AIDS. These children and adolescents push the limits with risky behaviors that seem to say, "I don't care. No one cares."

I keep myself centered by remembering crucial messages that children send through their behaviors, the questions children need answered so that they can grow year by year into successful adults. Over and over, children have shown me that this begins by answering a few basic questions. And these questions, in turn, can serve as the framework for rewriting each child's story.

Who will care for the child now and in the future?

All children need a primary parent(s) who will care for them through good times and bad and guide them into adulthood.[2] Ideally, this is two parents, a mother and a father, who may or may not be the biological parents.

Tommy wanted his mom above all others. His story could change if she changed, if she reached out to him, if she would become the mother he had lost. If not, perhaps his father would answer his call. Typically, fathers are ignored, left out, and assumed to not care.

Bob, Tommy's father, separated from Marie when Tommy was just a baby. He and Marie loved each other at first, but got married too young, Bob thought. They were just kids really. He was eighteen, Marie seventeen. He knew she wanted to get out of her family. Bob figured he was her ticket out. She moved into his apartment and was soon pregnant. They never really got along. Just different, Bob figured. He did not like Marie's temper, how she would criticize him.

They tried to make it work for a year after Tommy was born. Bob worked two jobs, tried to provide for his family, but it just did not feel right. He was gone most of the time, at his job, with his buddies. He had more fun with them. Home became like another job, a job he really was not good at. Bob was not surprised when Marie asked for a divorce. She said she wanted someone who really cared about her. He could have as many visits as he wanted. She had a good job at the time, and did not want much child support. Bob suspected there was another man, but by that time, he really did not care.

Bob thought it was for the best. He promised to take Tommy every other weekend, but as the months went by, he got a better job in another city and met someone else. He called to cancel visits. "Got to work this weekend . . . Going with Rhonda (his new girlfriend) to meet her parents . . . I'll call when I can make it again."

Bob had never been that close to his parents or family and none of them kept in contact. They just sort of drifted apart. He always planned to be a different kind of father. But, by Tommy's second birthday, Dad had become a guy he saw once or twice a year, when he happened to be in town, someone who sent a birthday and a Christmas present.

"I've got to manage a crisis at work," he would say to Tommy. Promises of next month became "next summer, next year," and evaporated into a haze.

Bob most likely did not know about the fight with Clyde, the blood, or the change in Marie. If he knew and cared, he would have to slowly, over time, build a different relationship with his son, a new relationship based on Bob's commitment to raise his son.

Bob would have to join with Tommy, knowing that Tommy had learned to not trust his father to come through on visits, on promises, on being there. Tommy had lost his father for three years. It could easily take three years in Bob's home, three years of steady caring, guidance, and determination, before Tommy would learn to trust Bob and respect him as a parent.

Uncle Todd could be another backup, someone who might care enough. But, as Tommy would insist, his mother needed a chance.

Who will keep the child safe?

Most children who act in dangerous ways to themselves or others have experienced trauma, neglect, and emotional, physical, or sexual abuse. Children need to see that their experience has been heard and believed by people who care enough about them enough to protect them, set limits, implement safety plans, and keep violent people from the past away.

When we recognize a child's fears of the violent people in his or her life, we begin to repair frayed bonds damaged by hardship or trauma. A child and a parent strengthen each other by sharing their fears *and* their courage.

Children need to learn that it is natural to feel scared, angry, confused, or helpless when bad things happen. Validation keeps a child connected to caring adults. Family members, foster parents, child care workers, therapists, clergy, and teachers can "witness" the child's experience, and make it "real," by experiencing the child's emotional pain and grief (Mary Purdy, Personal Communication, 2001). Conversely, running away from problems leaves both parent and child isolated and weak.

Secrets keep the nightmares alive. Reaching out to each other and facing the truth takes away the power of the monsters in a child's life.

The longer it takes parents, children, grandparents, and practitioners to talk about the secrets that lead to disruption or placement, the harder it becomes to talk about what happened and what can be done to overcome past problems.

Parents and children watch especially carefully to see if practitioners are able to talk in the first sessions about disclosures of past abuse and neglect. The practitioner is tested to see if he or she has the courage to address painful issues and the understanding and empathy to avoid further shaming of the family. Avoiding toxic secrets tells family members that these are too difficult to talk about, and thus, too difficult to overcome with this practitioner or agency. "Both/and" messages (Auerswald, 1983; Papp, 1983) can validate strengths as well as serious concerns. Practitioners can engage families by work in the first sessions to identify split messages driving family crises and to validate conflicting messages within a permanency-based approach.[3]

Safety is not a passive goal but an active process. Secure attachments are based on children's repeated experiences that caring adults will soothe and protect them when they are distressed. Safety means monitoring and intervening in a predictable manner. Over time, children learn whether caring adults who voice commitment and caring can truly be counted on to really act.

Adults validate children and reestablish safety by taking concrete actions. Safety plans cannot become viable until secrets about the abuse and neglect are shared. Children need to see that adults are changing the factors that led to past traumas. Parents may need to divorce a violent spouse, take out an order of protection, change the locks, bring in a child-oriented guard dog, install an alarm system, show children how they are locking up windows or doors every night, set up supervision for children with people who can be trusted, give children cell phone numbers to reach parents *and* other protective adults at *any* time of day or night, and practice taking safety steps with children.

Safety plans need to include identification of triggers and indicators leading to past crises, strategies prepared in advance to help adults and children stay in control, what each adult and child can do to prevent another cycle of violence, and demonstrations that safety plans will be implemented. Development of safety plans may need to begin with help to parents and children on developing awareness of different feelings and identification of behaviors that signal an impending crisis.

To check on whether a safety plan has been developed, we can ask if everyone, from children to parents, grandparents, other critical family members, school officials, and authorities can share what will be done to keep children (and adults) safe from further neglect and abuse at home, in their neighborhoods, and at school:

- Who will do what?
- What will signal that a crisis cycle is starting again?
- Who can serve as protectors from outside the nuclear family to guard against any further abuse or neglect?
- Who is committed to protecting the children, even if it means confronting parents or calling CPS?
- How can CPS be contacted? Do children have their phone numbers?
- Who will check on children as frequently as necessary to maintain safety?

Adults may need to build skills for self-soothing, affect management, safe relationships, parenting, and conflict management. These can be fostered through combinations of support groups, classes on parenting, anger management, and prevention of domestic violence, and work in *individualized* therapy to develop and implement *personal* safety plans. Completing a class helps provide vital information, but is not sufficient. Children, parents, and authorities need to share, understand, and experience over time that safety and relapse-prevention plans are being implemented.

Children cannot simply begin trusting a parent who was not able, or was unwilling to stop neglect or violence. And, trust is impossible when parents remain locked into denial of how their children were harmed, or worse, continue to threaten children to not talk, or even to recant, in order to regain their parents' love. If children were hurt by physical or sexual abuse and threatened with violence to enforce secrets, they very likely will never be able to trust that parent again and may also never be able to fully rely on a nonabusive parent who failed to keep them safe. Non-family protectors, orders of protection, alarm systems, and guard dogs may be necessary for these children to feel safe enough to grow.

In my experience, a parent will need to prove that the child is safe for approximately the same amount of time that the abuse and neglect was allowed to continue. So, if a parent was too overwhelmed to protect a child for a year, it will usually take another year of validation and testing to rebuild the trust that was lost. Families can celebrate passing the anniversary dates of past traumas as a way to demonstrate how much they have changed and how children no longer have to be afraid.

In the interim, other caring adults need to be involved in a child's life and show the child that they will watch for signs of the violence or neglect cycle starting again and take action if this happens. Bringing in strong caring adults becomes a key part of safety plans for children to reunite safely with parents and families where neglect or violence took place.

For some children, threats of harm from perpetrators remain very real with offenders free and living nearby. Children may need orders of protection and can benefit from meeting with community police officers to develop safety plans for home, school, and neighborhood. Principals and teachers need to be part of safety plans. The child may need to be escorted to and from school every day. Home security devices are very important and children should learn how they operate. In some cases, the most significant step in trauma therapy may be arranging for children to have a guard dog with them in their homes.

To help Tommy and his mother change Tommy's story, we can learn a lot from what works with children. And, just as in many children's stories, a little magic could help, magic to break the curse.

Billy's mother (see Chapter 2) used magic to help Billy recover from his injury, magic kisses, magic hugs, and magic superpower bandages, the magic of a parent's love for her child. When Billy's mother held him close she showed Billy that she would be with him, even when he had broken her rules and thought he was going to die. She would not run away. She would not teach him to hide the truth, the reality of his pain. Her touch made him feel whole because Billy knew that the most important person in his world recognized that his pain was real.

Cindy's arms encircled Billy, holding him up when he was about to crumble to the floor. Cindy was teaching her son that, "We can handle the worst" and "You matter." It was a lesson on overcoming crises. Billy emerged with a hurt knee, but stronger. He knew he was still loved and still able to succeed.

Marie would need to prove that she could see and feel Tommy's pain. She would need to show Tommy that he could become once again the son she loved and that she was not afraid to deal with the worst times in their lives, even the memories of her last days with Clyde.

Marie would have to become stronger than her fears, the part of her that drove her to run away from her feelings and bury herself in her work. Marie would have to face her own nightmares, so she could slow down and hear her son. A good friend would help and time-out on a regular basis, the daily and weekly respite that all parents need. She needed a decent job and good child care for her children.

If she could not provide the empathy, loving care, supervision, and protection Tommy needed, Marie could still save him by finding someone else to become his primary parent. Marie would always be his mother, but perhaps she would have to be a mother at a distance, more like a loving aunt or the grandmother Tommy really did not have.

In many ways, Marie had already detached herself from Tommy and taken on a new role. Tommy still needed a close bond to a parent for many years to come, but he had learned to look to himself to get what he needed. Tommy was learning to treat all adults as objects to manipulate to get what he wanted. He could smile in a very appealing way, threaten peers, run away, or get into fights. It really did not matter. The longer Tommy went without a secure attachment to a parent (or substitute parent), the more he cared only about getting whatever he wanted at the moment. Tommy learned that relationships were temporary and tentative. Teachers came and went, just as his relatives did. No one really cared. So, Tommy did not care. He would look out for himself.

How long will a child keep sending a message of distress?

I am often asked as a psychologist to determine the level of care a child needs to stop dangerous behaviors within a range of treatment programs and facilities from psychiatric hospitals to home-based family-preservation counseling and wraparound services to help parents and children. Level of care typically means the intensity of supervision and interventions a child needs to be safe, from round the clock, one-to-one supervision by a skilled mental health worker to once-a-week visits to a family's home by a family therapist.

When a child is actively threatening to hurt himself or herself or others, the child is showing us that continual supervision is needed in order to keep him or her safe. This is similar to caring for a toddler. The child cannot be left alone without somebody listening in or watching through a video camera to ensure the child is not doing something dangerous to himself or herself or someone else. Dangerous objects need to be removed from rooms, just as parents do with young children.

If the child is able to keep himself or herself safe, less-restrictive services can suffice. The level of supervision needs to match the developmental level of the child. A child acting appropriately as an eight-year-old does not need the level of supervision that a three-year-old requires.

"Just tell us the level of care needed," a case manager may insist. It is a ticket to funding for services needed to keep a child safe, at least for the time being. Funding in social services, mental health, and juvenile justice programs often does not allow for assessments to explore family resources or the powerful factors shaping a child's behavior.

The forces for healing and change are often harder to identify than negative and self-damaging behavior patterns. Assessments limited by funding sources to an individual evaluation of a child's agitation at a given time in a given situation, such as in the child's home after a fight between parents or in a psychiatric hospital, often miss the crucial impact of other family members and the community including what important people in a child's life are able or willing to do to help him or her. Conversely, assessments limited to family sessions often miss the child's perspective about what is happening and the fears and traumas that frame his or her beliefs and spur dangerous behaviors. A child is not likely to share the deepest fears about a powerful adult in the family when that adult is looking at the child or when the child has been identified as a behavior problem needing medical treatment.

The level of care usually depends on what family members, practitioners, and community services are willing and able to provide. Parents and family members have rights and choices to make. Even for suicidal behaviors, a family can choose between watching a child twenty-four hours a day or sending a child to a hospital where professionals will watch him or her. The hospital typically will only keep a child for one to three weeks. Afterward, the family will need to take over or give up custody.

Change in a traumatized child's dangerous behaviors requires difficult and painful work that can begin within a hospital or crisis residence. The hardest work often comes after the child is discharged, and often when needed family and individual therapy and family supports are not available. The length of time a child acts in dangerous ways is directly related to the time it takes for parents, relatives, practitioners, and community authorities to prove to the child that they can tell the whole story, the truth about what happened in the child's life *and* work together to implement realistic safety plans.

In family after family, I have seen that when this happens, a child will change dangerous behaviors very quickly. When it does not happen, a child is likely to continue his or her dangerous behaviors and to require even more restrictive placements and more expensive treatment programs. Until the child sees that caring adults are facing the truth, including toxic secrets, he or she knows that everything being said or done is really "just pretend" and not to be trusted. The secrets "burn inside" and soon drive even more dangerous behaviors.

For Tommy, this would mean his mother and other caring adults dealing with what happened with Clyde and taking steps to institute the rules and safeguards Tommy needed to be safe in the home. Tommy needed to see what his mother, other family members, and counselors were going to do if anyone became worried again about someone hitting or threatening to hurt someone. Tommy also needed to see that the limits for a child his age would be enforced.

"This is how we're going to keep safe," Marie could tell Tommy. "No one is going to hit me or anyone else again. If you get worried, even the littlest bit, that someone is going to hit again, I want you to tell me or tell Uncle Todd or tell Mrs. Jones, our neighbor, or tell Mrs. Frank, our family therapist. Uncle Todd is going to be coming over every weekend or we're going to stop by his house on Saturdays, so you and he can do something together. And, that's not all. No more riding your bike by yourself until you can show me you won't go past the sidewalk in front where I can see you."

How can children make sense out of their lives?

Children need to learn from their primary-parent figures how they fit into the world. They need help to understand their own life stories within the experience of their families and communities. Each child needs to develop a sense of his or her life based on mastery and hope, a life story that includes what the child saw, felt, heard, thought, and did over time.

Tommy needed a parent who could feel his pain and make his world safe. Attunement means feeling at a gut level where a child is at, not where we, as adults, would like the child to be, but the reality of how he or she feels. This is especially hard when a child secretly feels as though he or she is garbage, unwanted, unloved, and despised. The dirty child with ripped jeans, stained shirt, and strong odor is challenging us to recognize how he or she feels inside: torn, hopelessly stained beyond the reach of any laundry product, and smelling bad. Streaks of blood and old scars mark the most obvious wounds, but the smell and stains show us the child's shame.

Children who have been sexually violated may smear their own feces around their rooms, beds, and clothing. They feel like "shit" and they show it, often by living and acting like a skunk. When violence is combined with sex abuse and they grow up with no one to trust, the skunks may turn into tigers. Hurting animals and other children, urinating on themselves, their belongings, and their bedrooms, and setting fires mark children at the highest risk, children who are exploding out of control. These are often children who have become entranced in a quest for the power to destroy a world that has consistently hurt them.

Tommy, as with a lot of hurt children, learned to glower, to curse, and to rage. These are messages that tell us to "stay away!" These are also messages that protect the child from being rejected again. If no one comes near him or her, the child will never end up betrayed again, nor will he or she have to worry about someone he or she loves becoming hurt, dying, or ever again rejecting the child.

Tommy needed to be raised up again from the time he lost his mother, that horrible night when he saw the cut on her face. Marie would have to become strong enough to answer the little boy who looked down from the top of the stairs, the little boy who drifted away from her when she shrieked at him.

Marie, very naturally, in the face of repeated losses and betrayals had pulled within herself, constricting her own resources in order to survive the pain of the moment. Her anger guarded the pain and emptiness she felt inside. She needed help from someone she could trust to rebuild her confidence and expand her vision. With the help of a therapist, friends, and hopefully family members, she could face her pain and get past her sense of depression.

To keep Tommy safe, Marie would have to show him she could overcome her own pain and had become strong enough to see his. That is why Tommy's cut knee could have become a blessing. Marie would have to prove to Tommy that she could validate his pain.

It was not too late. Marie could begin by noticing the scab growing on Tommy's knee and apologizing for not helping him. She could reach out and pull her son close, cleanse his wound, comfort him, and rekindle the love that had nourished both of them before things got bad.

How can each child become a winner?

Children in crisis need to learn and practice what they can do to be successful, to help themselves *and* others, and to replace behaviors that got them into trouble.

Tommy loved baseball. His mother, Uncle Todd, a family friend, or a Big Brother could take Tommy to see his favorite team and teach him how to play. Together, they could identify Tommy's favorite players and follow their careers. Talking about sports, reading about it, and practicing could form the basis for Tommy to learn about how boys and men can become winners. Within a one-to-one relationship, Tommy could learn how to prepare himself, how to practice managing frustrations, and how to deal with both winning and losing.

Back at home, Marie could show Tommy how to ask for help without slamming his body into her. "Just tell me. I'll listen." Then, Marie could "catch him being good" to show she was watching and cared. When Tommy predictably slipped back into body slamming and cursing, Marie could firmly remind him that that was not allowed to do that any more. He could change or take a simple consequence, something she planned and rehearsed with her family therapist. It would be his choice. Either way, Marie would love him and remain in charge. She would understand that Tommy was driven by the same forces that had made her feel so angry and depressed. Change would take time but no man or possession could ever be more important than her children.

Tommy would test his mother, test her hard for the long year he lived without feeling her love. It would take at least another year to win back his trust. But, Tommy would give his mother other chances, a momentary hurt look, a whimper, a complaint. He would watch to see if she cut him off, sent him away without checking to see if he was really hurt. And, there would be times when Tommy surprised her by helping clean up his brother's mess, by cleaning up in the kitchen without being asked, by offering to help her fix the stroller, or take his brother for a walk.

Marie would have to see behind his angry look to the hurt boy underneath, the boy who needed to be in her arms. Marie could learn to notice these signals. First, of course, she would have to calm herself and slow down her life, so she could listen again and see the messages her son was sending.

Marie could show Tommy that things had changed by taking breaks for herself, going to see friends or family members, and taking unplanned times to do something special with Tommy. Taking Tommy to the doctor for physicals, to the dentist for a checkup, to the grocery for a special treat, and day-to-day caring would show Tommy that she had changed. Best of all, Marie could give Tommy his own time every day with her, a time when he could once again be the two- or three-year-old he once was, cuddling with his mother, or become the "big boy" learning to be a professional baseball player. This would be a special time free from everything that happened and whether or not Tommy had behaved.

Marie would see that the more Tommy misbehaved, the more he was showing her that he needed to *re*learn the love he had lost as a younger boy. Tommy's misbehavior meant missing what worked and showed Marie that Tommy needed more time to be like the little boy he felt inside and to feel her hold him close, cuddle him, and show him that he could not drive her away.

Later, with help, she could help Tommy understand what happened when he was three, four, and five years old. Tommy would need to hear over and over that he was not to blame for not protecting his mother from Clyde, that he could be a child and his mother would survive. She was stronger now. "Feel my muscles. Look at my face." Marie could tell him. "Just try to test me!"

Tommy had learned that children were to blame and adults could not keep themselves or their children safe. He needed help to learn that none of them had to live in fear of his mother being beaten again, and, most of all, that he would not have to live with the shame of failing his mother. Even if she yelled at him for messing up the living room, he would need to be reassured that she loved him, inside and out. It was just the mess she was yelling at, not Tommy.

Marie could play out stories of how she and other strong adults would keep any men or women who acted like monsters away, forever. "No one's gonna hurt us again" could become a mantra or the start of a family song, a song to sing out loudly whenever anyone was frightened. This could be a song about how Marie and other adults stopped the hurting, healed the wounds, and made a new life.

Tommy would see the magic in his mother's voice, her arms, and how they made the story true day by day, night by night, even if Clyde came back knocking on the door, promising in his kindest voice to be good. Every adventure could become a new chapter in their story or a new verse in their song, a special song for Marie and Tommy.

DEVELOPING SERVICE PLANS FOR TRAUMATIZED CHILDREN IN PLACEMENT

Children cannot wait long periods of time to find out if the adults in their lives (moms and dads, grandmas and grandpas, teachers, child protective workers, law guardians, and judges), will give them a safe, secure home and foster the bonded relationship children need to grow and thrive. Permanency work means shifting the anxiety and pain experienced by children in limbo (Finkelstein, 1991) to parents, family members, and authorities (Schlosberg, 1989).

Time limits set by state and federal legislation, such as the Adoption and Safe Families Act,[4] can be used to generate anxiety and press for change (Kagan and Schlosberg, 1989). Effective permanency work includes *a back-up plan* for children, if biological parents cannot succeed in reuniting, and working to press for needed changes within a time span that children can manage. Permanency review conferences scheduled every four to six weeks help to keep this process on track and focus of all work on reestablishing a bonded relationship for children.

When necessary, foster care can be used as a catalyst for trauma and attachment therapy. Treatment foster care models have been shown to be effective alternatives to residential treatment and group care for many youths (Chamberlain, 2000) Treatment foster care typically incorporates recruitment, training, and support for foster parents, public-school placements, no more than two children in a family, family therapy with birth parents, and aftercare resources for a child.

Children in placement need to hear messages at admission and in review conferences about:

- what needs to happen to restore safety and caring in their families,
- what will be done to help their parents,
- what their parents are doing to work on reuniting,
- a back-up plan if parents fail,
- who will keep children safe in the interim, and
- what children need to do (their job) as they wait.

Children cannot hasten their parents' accomplishments; instead, children need to see and hear that their parents, relatives, and practitioners expect that they will work on learning to master school tasks, develop skills for sports or arts, and learn social skills including taking on responsibilities appropriate for their age.

The outline of questions in this chapter can be used as a guide to developing service plans. Permanency meetings should ideally begin within a day or two, minimally within the first week, after placement. Psychological assessments of children's attachments[5] and development of back-up plans are very important to foster hope and focus work on rebuilding families. Assessments are most efficient if they begin with children and work outward to parents, siblings, and extended-family members. Ideally, potential protective adults from the extended family and community should be involved in permanency work by the third session.

Children can be asked who they would want to live with if their parents do not succeed in doing what is necessary to reunite. Identifying family strengths and working to help family members succeed shows children that practitioners and foster parents respect their feelings of loyalty. Developing a back-up plan shows children that they will not be left hanging with no one to care for them if their parents fail.

Visits with family members become crucial parts of the work to reunite. Rather than times for play or shopping, visits should be focused on times for family members to work on building or rebuilding attachments, implementing safety plans, and proving to children that family members will keep them safe and prevent the problems that led to placement from recurring. Consistent work in visits helps show children that parents are working to change. Birth parents can be offered support and guidance as they work to repair attachments, and must help their children and themselves get through the pain in each visit of saying "good-bye" until the next visit (Haight et al., 2001).

Children need to hear and see how their parents are doing in accomplishing specific tasks needed to reunite (e.g., finding a home, overcoming drug addiction or depression, implementing an order of protection, or ending a violent relationship). Showing up for visits is one message to children that parents care. Conversely, when parents do not come for visits or family therapy sessions, or drop out of drug treatment programs, children feel another loss of their parents. This is part of the grief process. Children need to be helped to face the reality of their parents' successes and failures. Children can be empowered to write, call, send audio- or videotapes, or e-mail their parents, relatives, law guardians, CPS workers, and judges to share their needs and concerns. Children need to see that family members, practitioners, foster parents, and authorities are listening and that everything possible is being done to help achieve permanency goals.

Fostering backup plans and other positive relationships with extended-family members, teachers, coaches, clergy, child care workers, and foster parents can help children feel safe enough to grieve when parents fail to work on reuniting or are unable to make their homes or lives safe enough for them to be the primary guardians of their children. Grief work means dealing with the natural process of denial, anger, detachment, and depression along the way to eventual reattachment. Foster parents and practitioners need to be prepared and available to help children with grief, just as they can help children to celebrate their parents' successes in working to make their homes safe and rebuild attachments to their children.

In permanency work, foster parents are challenged to take an often hurting child into their home, to serve as a mentor and support to birth parents working to reunite, and to be open to playing a permanent role in the child's life as part of a back-up plan if the child's parents are unable or unwilling to reunite. Practitioners help foster parents manage the ordeal of permanency work including predictable crises. Foster parents need to be involved in the therapeutic work as part of permanency planning and review conferences along with birth parents, service providers, educators, and community resources. Review conferences should be scheduled frequently, usually every four to six weeks when a child is placed away from home, and need to include updates on the progress of birth parents and children to resolve the problems that necessitated placement.

Recruiting potential adoptive parents is a key component of models of concurrent planning (Katz, Spoonemore, and Robinson, 1994; Lutz, 2000). "Legal risk" foster parents tell a child that he or she will return home if his or her parents make necessary changes or, if necessary, the child can remain with the foster parents. This keeps a child from feeling he or she has no hope, except to wish and wait as long as necessary for his or her birth parents to change.

Community partnerships between families, neighborhoods, private agencies, public agencies, and community organizations can promote recruitment, training, and support of foster and kinship families within a child's community. Involvement of birth parents, foster parents, and community members in service planning and outcome-based decision making are effective strategies for reducing lengths of stay in out-of-home placements, the number of moves of children in care, increasing capabilities of foster family programs to serve children who would otherwise have been sent into institutional or group care, and reductions in the number of children served outside their own families (Casey Foundation, 2002). Permanency work involves the entire community and works best with a focus on attachment-based interventions (Hartman, 1987; Kagan and Schlosberg, 1989), beginning with the crisis of placement and continuing through reunification or placement into an adoptive family. Follow-up services are essential to foster and maintain attachments, monitor safety plans, and provide resources for predictable crises.

Chapter 6

*Re*parenting the Hurt Child

He drew a circle to shut me out.
Heretic rebel, a thing to flout.
But love and I had the wit to win.
We drew a circle that took him in.

Edwin Markham

INTRODUCTION

Rebuilding attachments is similar to taking a long hike up an eastern mountain in the United States. Unlike higher mountain ranges, it may take hours, or even a full day, to reach an opening where the hiker is rewarded with a panoramic view. The first views may be limited to a glimpse through the trees from a narrow ledge. Trails may be narrow and muddy. This is hiking for the patient and steadfast. There are no safe shortcuts to the top.

Hikers learn from experience that trails typically become narrower, steeper, and more difficult the closer you get to the summit. The weather can quickly change from warm and muggy to wintry storms. Preparation is essential: maps, guidebooks, consulting with experienced hikers or guides, and checking on forecasts. Packing the right equipment, the support of fellow hikers, a guide for rough terrain, and the availability of emergency services can make the difference between an enriching adventure and a harmful ordeal.

It helps to keep in mind that far above the tree line the world opens up. Along the way, hikers learn to value the beauty and mystery of the forest, the sound of streams bubbling over the rocks, wildlife, and the rich foliage that surrounds the long trail up to the top. In much the same way, we can view rebuilding attachments as a journey that can be facilitated by experienced guides, preparation, resources, curiosity, and an appreciation of children, their joy, their distress, and how they challenge us to struggle to win their trust.

TOOLS FOR PARENTING TRAUMATIZED CHILDREN

Community Support

Parents need support for themselves, safe homes, safe neighborhoods, safe and stimulating schools, nurturing child care, qualified medical care, and sufficient financial resources. Social services agencies can help parents gain an understanding of the needs and behaviors of children with attachment problems and coach parents in developing skills in raising children.[1] Family practitioners can foster parents' confidence and security and help them to be sensitive to their children's strengths and areas of difficulty. Parents also need regularly scheduled breaks, a chance to relax, to vent, and to get relief from the strains and stresses of bringing hurt (and hurting) children into their homes.

Children placed into adoptive homes, or returning to families after placements, frequently have developmental delays along with serious emotional problems resulting from trauma, physical abuse, sexual abuse, neglect, malnutrition, and alcohol or drug exposure. As these children accelerate behaviors that disturb family members, family friends, relatives, schools, and organizations, parents often find themselves increasingly isolated.

Most community programs do not train staff to understand the impact of losses, separations, and traumas on children; the impact of placement; the challenge of reuniting families; or the essential elements of adoption for a child. Teachers and practitioners may implicitly blame the parents who have taken on the challenge of rebuilding attachments with these children. Unfortunately, few mental-health and special-education practitioners have been trained to understand how children's experiences of losses and traumas from the past often lead to problems within their new families. Families can end up feeling overwhelmed, abandoned, and financially devastated.

Preparation and support are key factors in preventing disruptions when children return to families or move into adoptive homes. Specific factors linked with disruption include: insufficient assessments of children and families, insufficient preparation of families taking a child, inappropriate matching of a child's needs and experiences with adoptive families, inadequate postplacement services to support families, multiple severe behavior problems of children, parents' lack of unity or marital problems, lack of attention to the impact on siblings of bringing a traumatized child into an adoptive home, and lack of parents' flexibility and effectiveness in meeting a child's special needs. Successful adoptive placements (Moss, 1997) have been linked to the willingness of parents to seek help in a crisis, open communication in a marriage, tolerance of negative behaviors, a sense of humor, a willingness to take time away from children, and knowledge of child development and attachment problems.

Parents need to see that they are not alone, that practitioners and other parents understand what they are going through, and that they have a team to call upon when the going gets tough. A two-parent approach works best, but single parents can succeed by sharing responsibilities with a close relative or with the ongoing support of a friend or family support worker. Difficult times should be expected and normalized to prevent parents and children from blaming themselves and to promote preparation and support. Participation in activities and meetings with other parents reinforces the message that parents are not alone and that the fears and anger that parents of attachment-disturbed children experience is predictable. Parents and relatives have benefited from providing and receiving support through parent associations, school-based organizations, and community centers.

Agencies help biological and adoptive families prevent disruptions by providing

- respite services with availability of home-based work on a temporary basis;
- emergency hotline services with skilled practitioners;
- information, referral, and consultation services including a directory of skilled practitioners with training in adoption and available to assist adoptive families;
- family-centered mental health services including therapeutic interventions for attachment problems, trauma, grief work, and impact on siblings, parents, and family development;
- case-management services and assistance in accessing specialized services for developmental disabilities, medical problems, and understanding the medical history of children and their biological parents;
- assistance with adopted children's desire to search and renew (or continue) contact with biological parents;
- hosting support groups for families with similar interests and problems;
- providing normalizing activities for families such as family trips, days at the ballpark, picnics, or cultural events; and
- lobbying and advocacy services.

Commitment

Rebuilding attachments depends on strong and caring adults committed to raising a child in crisis. The child's biological parents, or if necessary, adoptive parents, develop the courage to help the child confront and overcome traumas that have blocked his or her development. To help a child, parents must develop the strength to face their own demons and protect a child from having to relive the neglect or abuse of the past.

The adults lead the way and show the child that it is possible to *re*-member, to recover the good parts, to look terror in the face (Monahon, 1993), and to master the bad. The child can only do this *within* the security of relationships with caring *and* committed adults. Temporary relationships cannot provide the antidote a child needs when attachment breaks down. Respite placements may be necessary, but the core work needs to take place between the child and adults committed to long-term relationships.

The child needs to see that his or her parents have the capacity to deal with stress and to demonstrate self-control, before he or she can risk rebuilding or creating an attachment. Effective parenting means staying calm "in the eye of the storm"; remaining in control emotionally when the child is out of control (Levy and Orlans, 1998).

Practitioners can help parents step back, appreciate the "dance" of their child, and maintain a sense of humor. Crying is healthy. Asking for help leads to support and encouragement. Validation is essential. Only a parent awakened several times a night, night after night, by a ten-year-old shrieking "No! No! No!" at the top of his or her lungs, can truly appreciate the impact of trauma on a child and how this affects family members. Only a parent facing a glaring youth holding a bat, a large pot, or a knife, can appreciate what "domestic violence" means to families.

Parents need validation, respect, and concrete resources in order to re-parent traumatized children. Family-support workers, parenting classes, and training in advocacy (Rojano, 1998) can empower parents, with a focus accessing or creating the services needed by their children. "Time-outs" for parents, opportunities to call for help, availability of respite and crisis workers, and having someone trustworthy to call are essential components of both adoption and reunification plans. Support from relatives, friends, practitioners, and community leaders strengthens parents. With back-up services in place, parents can step back and work with practitioners to expand possibilities and develop creative responses to their child's behavior.

STEPS AND TOOLS FOR REBUILDING ATTACHMENT

Countertransference

A neglected and abused child typically rekindles painful feelings in biological parents seeking to reassert their authority, or substitute parents trying to bring a child into their home. The child has learned that attachment-related behaviors provoked his or her parents or previous caretakers to become disoriented, to reject or abandon the child, or to act in a frightened or frightening manner. A child's new parents, or parents working to reunite, need to be strong enough to validate his or her past experiences and help him or her find a new way to feel safe from the pain.

The hurt child's simultaneous need *and* fear of closeness naturally triggers parents' *own* memories of loss, rejection, or abuse. Parents need to master their *own* losses and any conflict with attachment figures in their lives (Main and Hesse, 1990), at least to a level at which they can manage the child's reminders of what happened in the parents' own lives. Parents who have faced and overcome their own experiences of losses, neglect, or violence become far stronger in the eyes of hurt children than adults who have never faced, or faced but not addressed, these problems. Hurt children have developed, by necessity, a way to tell whether an adult's courage and commitment are "just pretend" or authentic.

Parents often see their children's behaviors as personal threats or provocations. It helps to understand that traumatized children typically reenact their past with any parental figure who tries to change their lives and especially with adults who appear similar in age, sex, or mannerisms with previous caretakers who have hurt the child. This is an essential part of children's testing whether their homes (new or old) are really different than in the past.

When we stop and listen to a child's repeated behaviors, we can almost always find patterns that make sense in terms of his or her experiences. For instance, a child who lived with a series of violent men, may repeatedly provoke men, and father figures in particular, to lose their tempers. If the child provokes a man to lose his temper, the child gains a sense of predictability. The child's expectations have been confirmed. Repetitions of the past can paradoxically serve as *re*assuring rituals to calm a child's fears of change and to fill the voids in his or her life. A child who experienced a series of placements lasting nine to twelve months will often begin getting into trouble as he or she approaches the nine-month point in a new home. Once we see a child's behaviors as part of old patterns that fit with the child's experiences, his or her behaviors tend to fall into fairly predictable patterns. Behaviors may be annoying or obnoxious, but they begin to make sense. With this understanding, parents can pull back and prepare for the next predictable outburst.

Parents can work with practitioners to detoxify these patterns by making the covert, overt (Papp, 1983). At this point, a child's behaviors may still be upsetting but at the same time, can become far less powerful, redundant, and *even* boring. Parents can remind themselves that their job is to maintain a calm demeanor, as much as possible, and understand that their child is pushing them to do the painful *and* essential work of rebuilding (or building) attachments. *Re*parenting the hurt child is a test of parents' courage, understanding, and strength.

Every "crisis" generated by the child, thus, becomes a call *and* an opportunity to demonstrate that the child's new home is *different* from his or her past. Parents need to develop and utilize support from friends, family members, and practitioners to stay calm, to stay in control, and to affirm their commitment to raising the child. The child's stability grows in conjunction with the parents' increasing empowerment *and* renewed dedication to the child.

From a diagnostic perspective, a child's provocative behavior can be both expected and welcomed as indicators of what the child and his or her family need to address in efforts to reunite, or if necessary, what losses must be grieved and what past hardships must be overcome with new parents. Crises test the truth of parents' commitment and provide crucial steps in the process of reattachment.

Mis*behavior*

*Mis*behavior literally means behavior that misses; it does not work. Neglected and abused children need to learn another way to succeed. They need to *un*learn habitual behaviors that may been essential or effective in the past to protect them from dangerous relationships.

Caring adults can restrain themselves from reacting immediately to a child's behavior, calm themselves, or even take a few minutes in another room. This is the first step in breaking the child's patterns of *mis*behavior, patterns of interactions that depend on parents responding in an impulsive and predictable way that confirms a child's expectations that parents are weak and untrustworthy, and that, in the end, he or she will be, once again, identified as bad, blamed, abused, or cast out. Instead, parents can block a child's efforts to be in control by changing the rules he or she has learned from the past about how parents and children behave.

Interactional cycles of abuse and neglect work similar to a board game in which children always end up losing what is needed most, their parents' love. In these games, children can feel momentarily in control by provoking the worst outcomes. So, they pull the "go to jail" card by pushing parents to play out how "bad boys get beat" or girls get locked away behind bars in the "bad girl's home."

Parents can stay in control by learning and then avoiding these accustomed games. Parents can listen to their child's message, then form a response that prevents them from becoming locked into "no-win" battles of control. Instead, parents can convey over and over to a child that their home is centered on love, acceptance, and safety for everyone, a home where it is safe enough to learn new ways of living.

A thirteen-year-old boy secretly kept a pocketknife under his pillow. When his foster mother[2] discovered the knife, the boy insisted that he could not sleep without it. Instead of grabbing the knife, lecturing the boy on the need to give up all weapons, or chastising him for feeling scared and disrespecting the family's rules, his foster mother replied that she understood. She knew that the boy had lived a lifetime with physical and sexual violence, especially at nighttime. He had no reason to trust anyone. She asked the boy if he would please, for her sake, keep a whistle under his pillow instead of the knife. She promised him that she and her husband would respond to the whistle and protect him at any hour of the night. She also urged him to test this out, to see if he could trust.

Using respect and validation, this foster mother answered the boy's need for safety. He gave up his knife for the whistle, tested whether it worked, and gradually learned that there were some people in the world he could trust.

Attachment is learned in times of pain. Efforts to rebuild attachment will be tested in times of pain. *Mis*behavior is often a mandatory element in a child's testing of whether closeness is possible with a parent. The challenge to caregivers is to keep focusing on the central test of the child. *Will this be a parent who is brave enough to face the shame, the fears, and the rage the child carries inside?* This is the "transference" of the child's unbearable pain to a would-be parent.

A therapist skilled in both trauma and attachment therapy can help parents understand a child's behaviors in the context of the child's life experiences, rather than as personal attacks on the parents. Learning from other parents is very valuable through parent support groups, associations, and practice guides.[3]

*Mis*behavior is a necessary component in a child's work to *re*learn attachment. Violating rules and getting into trouble lead to reprimands, limits, "no" messages, and essentially a breaking of the attunement between parents and child. Typically, a toddler will respond by hanging his or her head, looking down, and becoming quiet. Children who have experienced violence and broken attachments may immediately react to reprimands by accelerating crisis behaviors. For a traumatized child, a parent raising his or her voice may signal the start to the next skirmish in a lifetime of war. The child moves into battle mode, adrenalin pumping, lips pursed, and arms swinging. Behaviorally, the child may suddenly act as a toddler having a temper tantrum.

The parents' challenge is to help a traumatized child learn a different way of testing and to show him or her that they will repair the bond and help both themselves and the child *re*attune, even after *mis*behavior. Behavior problems provide opportunities to show a child that connections will not be disrupted between parents and children. These are teaching moments (Hage, 1995).

Developing Trust

Practitioners can help parents repair the discipline cycle by reframing *mis*behavior as signals for parents to help children learn to trust parents and caregivers. Suggestions include:

- Remain calm, take a deep breath, and take care of themselves first, just as the airlines tell adults to pull down the oxygen mask first for themselves before helping children. In the struggle to rebuild attachment, if parents lose control, their children are also lost.
- Remind themselves of how their children's behaviors are usually testing very real expectations based on past experiences. Parents can remind themselves that whatever they do, it is important not to give children the message that parents are going to evict them or repeat past abuses.
- Expand arbitrary constrictions. More time may be needed. Parents may need to take a short break, review a note kept in their pockets summarizing plans for dealing with predictable *mis*behavior, call in a supportive friend, call a hotline for support of parents, or call practitioners working with the family.
- Reaffirm family rules, reprimand the child, and impose logical consequences for the child's behavior that keep a parent in charge and match a child's developmental age. The child may need to take time to consider how he or she can improve, or to *re*do a task. The old rule of a minute for every year of age is useful to keep in mind when developing consequences as learning opportunities and as a means of avoiding parents and children becoming locked into harsh or unenforceable consequences.
- *Re*attune with the child and repair the relationship after a reprimand.

The parent's predominant message needs to focus on commitment and safety within the relationship. Any scolding or criticism should be brief and limited to less than a minute (Hughes, 1997). It is important to avoid sarcasm, angry outbursts, threats, food deprivation, or any form of hitting; all of these responses would take away a child's hope that the parent will be different than parents in the child's past and would likely engender further negative behavior. The parent's goal is to use the child's *mis*behavior to teach the child that he or she cannot push the parent into the old cycles of crises and rejection. Instead, the parent can reassert his or her authority with messages that briefly shame a child, *re*establish limits, and lead to *re*attunement.

Without *re*attunement, the child will feel once again isolated, to blame, "no good," and very likely will move into more severe levels of depression, hypervigilance, irritability, and impulsive responses. Traditional time-outs often backfire with attachment-impaired children. After being sent into a distant room, often with the door closed, they may become more agitated, "shut down," or periodically rage in a dissociative manner that makes little sense, except as a declaration to anyone listening that their current placement is just the same as their past experiences of abandonment, rejection, or violence. When these children are left alone in their rooms, they may start destroying toys, photos, or other symbols of their "home," or react with self-destructive behaviors. It helps to keep young children close and older children within eye contact, as they are taught to contain their impulses. "Sit in that chair (a minute for every year) where I can keep my eye on you." Using a "thinking chair" (d'Aversa, Personal Communication, 2002) in the kitchen or living room keeps children connected to parents and avoids isolation and reminders of abandonment.

By looking at the developmental age of the child's *mis*behavior and reaction (e.g., a tantrum), we can develop effective responses to obnoxious and irritating behaviors. Once caring adults recognize how the child's behaviors reflect where his or her social and emotional development stopped, the current minicrisis becomes an opportunity for *re*learning and healing.

Children often need help in learning to become aware of feelings before they react, to attach words to feelings, and to begin to substitute words for tantrums. When children start to misbehave, parents can gently ask them, "How are you feeling, right now?" This redirects children to become aware of bodily signs and to attach words to behavior. Neurologically, the parent is helping the child link the left prefrontal cortex with its language and reasoning abilities to the child's perceptions of feeling states centered in the limbic system and right hemisphere. If children cannot verbalize a feeling, parents may need to help them initially in this process by attaching words to their behaviors (Hughes, 1997), which describe what a child is doing. For example, "You're angry because I wouldn't let you go outside and you're stomping your feet." This helps children reflect and also helps parents provide messages that answer children's implicit testing and habitual patterns of *mis*behavior (e.g., "Sit on the time-out chair and think about how you could have told me this without stomping your feet and banging the chair.")

*Mis*behavior often signals a child's greatest fears, and becomes powerful when a child transfers his or her own anxiety and rage to parents without ever saying the words tied to the child's past experiences and current distress. A previously abused child may repeatedly provoke a parent to become so angry that the parent feels close to hitting the child. It is often important to help a child *voice* fears that the parent will become similar to parents of the past and abuse a child, or allow abuse of the child. Similarly, if a child has experienced repeated rejections or losses of past parents, it will often be important to help a child to express his or her fears of losing new parents.

Therapists can help children work methodically, such as a detective or a scientist would act, to find out if their worries will come true and to show that they really care. We can help children to plan and practice how to change their old behaviors, to make positive choices, and to succeed. Therapists can also help children develop lists of ways they can show parents that they love them (Hughes, 1997), and to try out new and different ideas for having fun with parents, doing things they all can enjoy.

With children who have lived in foster family, residential treatment, juvenile justice, or psychiatric hospital placements, it is important that biological and foster/adoptive parents prepare for these behaviors *before* the children return to family living. Research has shown that parental participation in residential treatment is associated with better outcomes (Jenson and Whitaker, 1989; Lyman and Campbell, 1996; Taylor and Alpert, 1973), and that the efficacy of residential treatment programs is increased by providing intensive family work, comprehensive aftercare services, and help to youths in developing problem-solving and life skills to succeed in their communities (Maluccio and Marlow, 1972; Whitaker and Pecora, 1984; Curry, 1991; Casey Family Programs, 2001). Strategies can be practiced during sessions in the program and in progressively longer visits, so that parents are coached and supported in recognizing children's behaviors as part of children's work to test whether traumas will recur and whether attachments or *re*attachments will lead to new losses or rejections.

Parents can then begin a placement of a child in their home by asserting rules from day one that make their home different than the past. A traumatized child should not be treated as fragile (Hughes, 1997). Parents need to be firm and stay in charge with preparation, support, and planned strategies to deal with predictable misbehavior. The hardest work in rebuilding attachments takes place after a child moves into his or her new home, or returns to biological parents who have worked to reunite. This is when practitioner support and intervention is most essential.

Directions

Preschool children rely on external guidance to follow rules, and traumatized children often need adults to model and teach them how to use words to guide behavior. When a child begins to become hyperactive, a parent can use a reminder command with a gentle, reassuring, and soothing drawn out voice, "S-L-O-W D-O-W-N" or "It's time to practice patience." Over time, as a child develops security and cognitive ability, he or she can practice verbalizing self-control directions out loud, and later to himself or herself.

Clear, simple directions work best with children. As one foster parent told me, it is important to say "by when," with every directive, especially with adolescents. If you do not, most children and almost all adolescents will put off the request, and parents may feel that the youths are being defiant. The youths, however, are simply responding to their own understanding of the parents' message. Traumatized children, in particular, act with little sense of time and may misunderstand the time frame an adult thinks he or she is communicating through a gesture or emphatic look, which the child perceives as annoyance, anger, or even rejection.

Directives work best when parents, teachers, and practitioners:

- use a calm, firm voice;
- ensure that a child is listening when giving directions by asking for eye contact and preventing distractions from other youths and by muting radios, television, computers, games, etc.;
- offer choices (e.g., pick up your room now *or* after supper), sitting quietly in a chair in the kitchen watching a parent, reading in a quiet place, *or* performing ten jumping jacks;
- state what the child *needs* to do, rather than dwelling on what *not* to do;
- have a logical, attainable, and enforceable consequence ready for a child who misses the mark;
- post important family rules with attractive pictures, humorous caricatures, or bright-colored pictures as visual reminders; and
- match directives to a child's capacity for memory and attention. Children with ADHD (attention deficit hyperactivity disorder) and PTSD typically can handle only one or two simple directions. More complicated tasks can be broken down into simpler steps. Visual reminders, lists, posters, or taped instructions may be necessary along with frequent supervision and reminders to return to tasks. (Adapted in part from Barkley, Edwards, and Robin, 1999)

Respect is a two-way street. It is important that children hear that therapy is work time to make things better and for him or her to become stronger. A child may be aloof, hesitant, or quick to say "no" to requests. I want children to see me as respecting how they protect themselves, and at the same time, establish from the onset that I expect respect in return. That includes common greetings, requirements for polite behavior (e.g., saying "please" before requests), and building a relationship based on mutual respect.

Choices and Consequences

Day by day, parents can model appropriate ways to share feelings and encourage children to share their own feelings. Children can then be guided to consider choices for what they do with their feelings. Choices lead to consequences. Parents have the power to "choose their battles," but ignoring deliberately disrespectful behaviors only makes things worse. Parents can be reminded that when children will eventually test their true commitment when they see their parents feeling tired and worn-out. This is where the trail has become steep and difficult. The summit remains nowhere in sight and deep down, children expect their parents to falter and give up.

A parent may need to create a diversion to avoid falling into the child's expectation of driving a parent crazy. "Whoops. Sorry, honey. I know this is important, and I'll be right back." The parent may need to take a break, call in some help, or go into another room and close the door. He or she can disrupt the child's expected cycle of behavior problems in a family, do whatever is necessary to regain composure, and return to respond with a reaffirmation of composure, self-control, and consistent consequences tied to a child's behaviors. In this way, the parent models care for himself or herself and controls the pace and duration of the child's struggle to test his or her commitment. For example, a mother working to adopt a child who was accelerating his defiance and oppositional behavior set aside a week in her schedule and declared that she and the boy would be spending the week home, together, in "boot camp" (Blanchard, Personal Communication, 2002). This mother determined her own program and schedule using the model of military initiation to demonstrate her commitment *and* have some fun at the same time. Practitioners can help a parent use an understanding of the child's behaviors to surprise him or her and remain in charge.

A child's privileges can be tied to the developmental level shown by his or her behavior. Is he or she acting like a fifteen-year-old or a four-year-old? Four-year-olds require close supervision and help in carrying out basic tasks. Fifteen-year-olds can manage routines pretty much on their own, asking for help when needed. Consequences teach lessons and reinforce the child's responsibility for *choosing* behaviors and *facing* predictable consequences.

The key to success revolves around helping parents and teachers to model remaining calm and centered with expectations geared toward children's abilities. For first mistakes, a reminder may suffice. For a second mistake, a reminder including an expected consequence that involves *re*learning can be repeated. For a third mistake, it is time to implement a *pre*planned natural and logical consequence (Dreikurs, 1964) designed to help the child relearn how to succeed in the task.

Parents can give children limited choices that keep the parents in charge and out of endless battles, and help children to develop self-control. For example, a four year old can be told to go to the time-out corner for four minutes *or* until he or she is *calm* enough to behave. If a child continues to rebel, he or she can be given the choice of spending twenty minutes screaming and yelling, or ten minutes thinking of how he or she could make things better (Hughes, 1997).[4] According to Hughes (1997), either way is okay. This forced-choice situation helps parents to keep themselves calm and in control, and gives children opportunities to succeed.

Parents can stay in charge by listening to their own feelings of becoming overwhelmed and using their own internal cues to signal that it is once again time to help their children break out of their accustomed cycles of battling (and eventually losing) with parents. When parents feel the tension rising, it is helpful to remember that children need parents to remain in charge, no matter how hard they try to assert control.

From a child's perspective, *mis*behavior can explode into reenactments of life-or-death struggles. This makes defiance very powerful. Traumatized children have learned a lot of short-term tricks to get what they want, or feel they need, to survive in an out-of-control world. Parents are challenged to the extremes of these past traumas, and parents and children both need and deserve all the help they can get.

Parents have a great deal of underutilized power, because they often do not allow themselves to take advantage of their resources and limit their options with beliefs (see Chapter 4) that they have to do everything alone, that all children need is the right mix of love and discipline, etc. Parents can alternate between being coaches, nurturers, teachers, and umpires and utilize much higher levels of thinking and creative options to guide children toward self-control, and have some fun in the process. As with all teachers, parents may need time to go to the "teacher's lounge," consult with veteran colleagues, bring in some expert advice, and get help.

When things get tough, parents can blow a whistle, change the tune, or simply move the entire family to a new activity. When things become too tiresome, Deborah Hage (2000) teaches parents to declare "Mom time." Parents can issue a proclamation, "We're out of here!", pack up the kids in the car, and head off to the park, the beach, the local museum, grandma's house, the library, or an adventure in the seafood section of the grocery store. In this way, parents stay in charge, and show children that tiresome, annoying behaviors, are simply just tiresome and annoying. Most important, "Mom time" shows a child that parents can break the cycle.

Many children who lived with neglect do not feel safe having fun. Any pleasure times may have been associated with sequences of affection, often associated with alcohol or drugs, that led unpredictably into fights and someone getting sick or hurt. Learning that a parent can have fun without losing control may be a new experience and a powerful lesson. Experiencing a parent turn a battle into an opportunity for a hug, an outing by the parent's rules, and later, a good chuckle can shatter a traumatized child's assumptions of parents as uptight, constricted, and inflexible.

Parents can also help children move out of old battles by keeping them off guard. Parents can utilize paradoxical messages and responses to show children that they can stay above the fray and avoid falling into children's expectations to repeat the old battles. For example, a child who screams can be asked to practice screaming with the parent (Hughes, 1997), or invited to work harder with coaching, as needed, on his or her tonality, modulation, intensity, and duration of screams, because you never know when a good scream will be important.

Paradoxical responses take the power away from a child's behaviors and can help him or her to change from *mis*behavior to winning behavior. The bottom-line message, however, is that the parent cares, remains committed to the child, and cannot be hemmed into any narrowly defined boxes of *expected* parental behavior. This keeps the child in a bit of suspense, and helps the parent avoid becoming identified as really not changing, in adoption, as being the same as previous parents.

A parent can also challenge a child's behaviors by showing that he or she knows another side of the child. For example, one foster parent responded to a child's outbursts by asking, "Would the 'Real Billy' please come forward?" Children who *mis*behave can have the option of missing out on an activity in order to continue their *mis*behavior, or instead, choosing to gain a desired activity by acting at their age level. Positive images can be stressed (e.g., a "big boy," a sixth grader, a model for younger children, or a mentor to help younger children resolve the problems an older youth has faced). A youth's aspirations can be facilitated with mentoring, lessons, summer camp programs, and practice with parents to help them achieve a desired goal.

Understanding that children carry different attitudes and beliefs helps us to keep in mind that the provocative behavior of today can be replaced by the loving, affectionate parts of children hidden under their fears and distrust. The challenge to a parent is to respect the importance of all the different parts of a child, his or her fears, rage, desire for closeness, wish to be accepted, love, and expectation of rejection. Each part represents both a truth of the child's experience and pathway to building his or her potential.

Discipline from this perspective becomes a matter of skill development and mastery, winning versus losing, and gradually step by step, earning the rights and privileges of a child's chronological age. The parent's goal is to avoid power struggles that reinforce a child's *mis*behavior and to help a child replace old behavior patterns with more effective words and actions. Keeping our eyes open for small signs of children trying out new behaviors helps parents to stay the course. A polite request, saying "please," a sullen look in place of the usual tantrum, or a mumbled "whatever" instead of a curse, each tiny change signals a child's growth and can help caring adults to remember his or her potential.

Remaining focused on developing strengths also helps parents avoid interpreting a child's positive behaviors as proof that *mis*behaviors are manipulations. Labeling a child as manipulative or provocative focuses the parent's attention on the child's *mis*behaviors and sets the stage for battles and power struggles. The parents can be much more effective by focusing on a child's need to develop a new understandings of what works, learn new skills, and practice these skills over and over in different situations. The child's challenge is to try out new ways, and to learn that he or she can succeed without his or her old habitual ways of coping, habits that are maladaptive in their new homes.

Change begins by testing parents. Change for a child who lived with neglect and beatings means learning to trust a parent to protect him or her from the harsh world of the past. If the child can make a parent so enraged that the parent (or teacher, child-care worker, practitioner, etc.) curses, screams, gestures menacingly, or runs away, then the adult has lost his or her authority. Similarly, if a parent asks a child if he or she really wants to stay in his or her home, the traumatized child will often understand the parent as saying that the parent does not really want the child and is looking for a way out. The child once again experiences an out-of-control adult world and the power of his or her *mis*behavior. Focusing on skill-building helps a caring adult to depersonalize a child's behaviors and prevent emotional reactions that inadvertently reinforce a child's sense of being in control of the adult.

Life Skills

Strength-based treatment models move beyond a focus on deficits and work to increase competence (Masten and Curtis, 2000), as well as reducing stressors and risk factors and boosting stress protection (Wyman et al., 2000). Traumatized children typically need to learn basic skills of attention, emotional regulation, and communication that can easily be taken for granted by teachers and parents accustomed to working with other children of similar ages. A twelve-year-old who lost his or her biological parents as a four-year-old may continue to think and act very similar to a preschooler needing to take charge and care for an ailing mother and somehow fend off siblings. Youths seen as deliberately acting defiant, may, in fact, be repeating the thinking and behavior patterns they have utilized for years. Often, neglected or abused children need to learn how to

- focus attention on what a teacher or parent is saying;
- utilize memory aides to manage assignments and instructions;
- manage frustrations and distress by calming themselves, asking for help, and refocusing themselves as they wait;
- think out choices and consequences in the future to resolve problems; and
- manage conflicts with peers, siblings, parents, and adults in authority without overreacting.

Children may have learned that such skills made things worse in their homes. Paying attention to subtle clues of danger and overreacting may have been a necessity for survival; and no one may have responded when the children did ask for help. Once caring adults have restored safety, children need to work to develop each of these skills. This is the child's job and a critical part of growing stronger and mastering trauma.

Many traumatized children have attention-deficit problems, and it is very important for parents, coaches, and teachers to limit instructions, use visual reminders for daily tasks, and design assignments for children to succeed.[5] Simply learning how to listen can be a challenge for many traumatized children. It helps if they can sit close to their teachers and if adults ask them to look at their faces and eyes when instructions are being given, instead of checking all around the room as sentries guarding the classroom or home. Often, children may only be handle one instruction at a time. Even sending a child to get something in the garage may require asking him or her to write the name of the object down or draw a picture of it. A teenager asked to change the oil in a lawn mower may need to draw pictures and symbols for the steps in the exact order and then remember to bring the instructions (or post them) near the work site.

School is a child's job and succeeding at school is an important part of a child's treatment plan. Often, traumatized children have not mastered basic study and learning strategies. Practitioners can help parents and teachers *re*-structure the learning process to foster success. Effective guidelines include

- daily (or minimally weekly) communication between parents and teachers;
- using an assignment book that uses visual reminders children can understand;
- using tape recorders for assignments for some youths;
- providing mentors and tutors before children fall behind;

- pacing the day to match the attention span of children in the class based on their abilities with regular and frequent periods of physical exercise and breaks from instruction;
- avoiding timed tests, and allowing distractible youths to take tests alone in quiet rooms;
- seating youths away from very active or provocative peers;
- using visual modalities for instruction;
- *pre*arranging and practicing ways children can ask for help, ask for breaks, and have someone they can go to talk to at school (e.g., a guidance counselor) if they become stressed;
- arranging a quiet study space and time at home free from distractions; and
- teaching children to reward themselves after accomplishing small tasks along the way to larger goals. (Adapted in part from Barkley, Edwards, and Robin, 1999)

Schools can make a crucial difference for traumatized children by providing an environment where positive behaviors are reinforced and every child is helped to succeed through learning and mastery of both academics and skills in extracurricular areas (e.g., art, music, debate, sports, peer support, volunteer work, etc.) that establish each student as someone special.

Affect Management

Most traumatized youths need instruction, support, and practice to develop affect-management skills. Viewing affect management as a mastery challenge can help parents, teachers, and practitioners move away from focusing on deficits and categorizations of children as bad or good. Affect skills can be developed in groups or with individual work. Eggert (1994) provides an excellent guide to developing groups, contracting, teaching children an understanding of how their anger works, and a detailed curriculum for group or individual work on anger-control problems. Ford, Mahoney, and Russo (2003) have developed detailed manuals to help children understand how trauma works, recognize and learn to use their emotions, understand how stress acts as the body's warning system, and gain "FREEDOM" through skill building: Focusing, Recognizing triggers (understanding), Emotions, Evaluating thoughts, Defining goals (immediate versus the youth's true goal), (considering) Options, and Making a contribution. Skill-building curricula have also been developed to help with specific problem areas. For example:

- Self-soothing and mindfulness, e.g., helping youths differentiate their "emotion mind" from their "reasonable mind" (Miller et al., 1995; Miller, Rathus, and Linehan, in press)
- Managing reminders of stress and guides to help children understand the linkage between thoughts and feelings (Layne et al., 1999; Layne, Saltzman, and Pynoos, 2003; Saltzman, Layne, and Pynoos, 2003)
- Skill building with children in kindergarten through elementary and early middle school who have experienced a trauma or disaster (Gurwitch and Messenbaugh, unpublished manuscript)
- Attention-deficit problems (Nadeau and Dixon, 1997)
- Managing stress (Moser, 1988; Sanders and Turner, 1983)
- Anger problems (Whitehouse and Pudney, 1996; Eggert, 1994)
- Impulse-control problems (including sexual abuse) (Cavanaugh-Johnson, undated)
- Abused children (Karp and Butler, 1996; Gil, 1986)
- Sexual-behavior problems with children (Cavanaugh Johnson, 1998)
- Sexually abused teenagers (Munson and Riskin, 1995)
- Divorce and remarriage (Evans, 1986)

Traumatized children often have a difficult time learning to "stop, calm, and think before acting." They need to learn how to soothe themselves at home, at school, and in the neighborhood. They also need to remind themselves to use their skills, often, in the same way young children rehearse with parents to stop and look both ways before crossing a street. It takes practice and supervision.

Children can learn to relax and calm themselves utilizing all five senses. Since trauma activates the more primitive parts of the brain and often constricts verbal processing in the frontal cortex, effective self-soothing rituals built on touch and smell are especially powerful. Caring adults can help calm children with gentle warm embraces, even if just for a second. Children can learn to help themselves relax with a warm bubble bath after a hard day, or in class, by stroking a small stuffed animal given to them by someone who cares (e.g., a tiny elf invested with magical powers such as strength and wisdom).

Children can carry with them special objects with scents that remind them of a special time or place, such as a scented candle, a ring symbolizing the power of the family, or the emblem of a team, drama club, etc. Symbols of their ethnic heritage can be powerful reminders of the wisdom and legacies they carry from generations over time. Charms, rings, necklaces with special symbols, and special stones to carry in a pocket can be very useful to help children stop a crisis cycle, and calm down. It helps for many children to have permission to pull out and squeeze (not throw) a small, soft object, to work on a small craft project, such as knitting, or to continue a detailed drawing. Others may need to ask permission to take a break, in which they can walk outside, sit quietly in a time-out corner of the room, or visit the school nurse.

Touch can help children break out of trauma cycles (e.g., a tickle, a gentle wrestling match, or a foot massage). At the same time, they can be warmed with the taste of freshly baked breads or cookies. Chicken soup has truly magical properties when prepared by a loving parent. The smell of dinner cooking pervades every room. Children can utilize smell and taste during the day if parents pack special treats in a lunch box, or other surprises to brighten their day.

Imagery is another powerful modality to reach children and help them learn to relax. It often helps for children to carry with them copies of photographs or drawings of themselves with a special person during a special time or at a special place. Special drawings and photos of positive memories can be carefully matted, framed, and mounted in their rooms. Mounting pictures drawn by children or photos of them in family living spaces helps show that this is their home, just as teachers often post work by children around the classroom for everyone, including parents to see.

Words and meaning can be added to the pictures, the objects, and the food used to help children relax. Caring adults extend their love throughout a child's day with a little note inserted in the lunch box, a smiley face on a lunch bag, a joke or riddle for the day, or a poem. All are messages that tell children how special they are. Families can develop mottoes, mantras, logos, or recite prayers that affirm strength, determination, and unity.

Many children can benefit from practice in learning deep muscle relaxation, meditation, yoga, or activities that foster discipline and self-control (e.g., karate classes). Singing and dance lessons can help a child build skills that can be used to manage frustrations. Encouragement to write diaries and poetry can also help many youths find an outlet.

Affect-management skills take patience, practice, and courage to develop. As with riding a bike, it may seem impossible at first, especially if children grew up living with adults and children often acting out of control. If children see that parents, siblings, and peers can master these skills, they can be helped to steadily develop essential skills for managing stresses and frustrations that otherwise would continue to propel them into crisis behaviors. Practitioners can help by taking on the stance of coaches, beginning at a child's developmental level and working with a plan in mind for skill development, step by step with fun activities, practice assignments, and reinforcement of success.

In general, effective skill-building curricula begin with education of parents, teachers, and caring adults on how trauma impacts children at different ages. Understanding how trauma works can help adults step back and depersonalize children's behaviors, thus avoiding their own emotional reactions. Skill-building curricula help caring adults understand how antecedents (beliefs from the past) trigger immediate emotional reactions (fear, anger, panic, etc.) and lead to repetitive cycles of escalating behaviors. Practitioners can help caring adults understand anger and other reactions as energy that can be utilized to foster change, rather than definitions of a child as bad or sick. Skill building usually entails the following steps involving both adults and children to work for effective change.

Understanding Emotional Reactivity

- How stress or trauma primes our brains to react as a means of coping and how these responses can become ingrained and often immediate responses
- How "triggers" work
- Emotional reactions: how they work, practice in identifying feelings from pictures and role-plays with other children and adults acting out different feelings, and promoting permission to try out and share feelings in a safe way
- Analyzing behavior: antecedents-behaviors-consequences
- How thinking is dominated by old feelings
- How anger/fear reactions increase with repeated traumas
- Patterns of attack/withdrawal/submission
- Invitations to change: choices, repeat or change, setting positive goals
- Working on mastery, not just stopping a behavior
- Contracting with children for work on changes

Thoughts and Feelings

- Recognizing and expressing feelings
- The power of beliefs
- Identifying thoughts about themselves and others and understanding how these developed
- How have these thoughts helped in the past and present?
- How have these thoughts led to trouble?
- Winning beliefs

Relaxation/Self-Soothing

- Using the muscles—deep muscle relaxation
- Using the imagination—visual imagery
- Using concentration—self-trance work
- Using dreams—changing the story so the child becomes safe
- Using music—playing, listening, letting both sides of the brain work
- "Safe-place" imagery
- Practice daily with coaching and warm, gentle sounds, within safe relationships

Self-Monitoring

- What gets each person going? Identify "triggers."
- Daily tracking sheets
- Rank easy to difficult situations
- How does each person respond (assertive versus withdraw/rage/submission)?
- What is working well? What is not?

Change the Game Plan

- Time to revise the plan (such as a football team, in the locker room at half-time)
- For each "trigger," develop new plan with coach/mentor/therapist, recognizing initial feelings by scanning your body from head to toes, recognizing first thoughts, thinking about what message your body is giving you, especially impulses to run away, fight, or freeze, try out different reactions, e.g., to squeeze a stress ball or talk to a school counselor (after Ford, Mahoney, and Russo, 2003). Then

  1. Practice step by step
  2. Role-play
  3. Test it out
  4. Make it harder (the Zen of affect management)
  5. Keep practicing

Safety First

Safety always comes first with traumatized children. Children need reassurance that specific safety plans (see Chapter 5) have been set up to protect them. To check whether a safety plan is really in place, a child can be asked who will do what, when, where, and how. A safety plan begins with identification of the adults who will act as the child's protectors at home, at school, and in the community. Safety plans require details a child can understand, such as the rules of a game. And, as with playing a game, the rules only work if the people in charge take the responsibility to implement them with everyone, including parents, siblings, and extended-family members. An order of protection barring Uncle Will from being in a home should not be violated, just because he looks good one day, Mom is tired, or a family therapist is finally feeling accepted by a parent in a home visit and hates to ask who the sleeping man on the family room couch might be.

Children may allude to fears of being kidnapped at school, or may have actually experienced attempts by an angry parent to meet them on the playground at recess. It helps to involve the child with school officials, and other responsible adults, so the child can hear that authorities are aware and will protect the child from any unauthorized contact.

One eight-year-old was terrified of monsters in his closet. His foster parent wisely called in the family dog and together with the child, they asked the dog to check in the closet and under the bed, something the dog was excited to do. The child was asked to guide the dog to check in every corner. When the dog finished sniffing and pawing carefully everywhere in the room, the dog was directed to jump on the child's bed and the boy stroked the dog. With other children, taking the time to lock windows and turn on security systems may become an important nighttime ritual. In one family, a boy and girl were terrified that their mother's previous boyfriend, a violent sex abuser, would come to terrorize and take them away. The man was not arrested and had threatened the children. In this case, the children very realistically needed to have a guard dog with them at night, as well as a security system, orders of protection, and visits to discuss safety with community police.

Gurwitch and Messenbaugh (unpublished manuscript) illustrate use of dream catchers based on Native American lore to help children deal with bad dreams. Children learn that the elders believed that if a bad dream somehow made it through the dream catcher, then this meant that the person should share what was learned in the dream with someone important and work together with that person to develop a solution for the problem represented in the dream. In this way, a child's private nightmare can be transformed into a collaborative effort enlisting the power of adults in the community.

Safety also means preventing unsafe behaviors by children. Parents, teachers, and program directors need to have the support and stamina necessary to implement supervision, learning, and consequences that keep children safe. Bluffing never works with children who have lived through violence and rejections. These children quickly find out what is real and appear almost driven to point out an adult's weaknesses and pretenses. Falsehoods are simply too dangerous to endure for a traumatized child. And, these children often become very skilled at discovering and dramatizing to everyone the truth of what is real and what is not. When a child threatens to break down the rules and safety plans, our response needs to focus on his or her central test and demonstrate concretely that the parent and other caring adults are going to keep the child and themselves safe, no matter what.

Safety plans include helping children avoid impulsively going back to their old ways that got them into trouble. Safety plans need to include contracts for managing children's own behaviors including identification of triggers, stop signals, reframing beliefs that lead to trouble, development of safety responses when stressed, and practice in implementing safety plans.[6] Children need to learn and practice, step by step, the skills necessary for avoiding impulsive acts that have led to behavior problems. Learning new ways of handling frustration means taking risks; children typically have become accustomed to the predictable results of their old ways of responding including tantrums, hitting, or isolating themselves.

Effective approaches to teaching children to overcome impulse-control problems include reminders with posters and signs to children of the early warning signs of getting into trouble, step-by-step ways that children can break away from problems, outlining the consequences of continuing with unsafe behavior, and practicing winning behaviors with enactments, storytelling (see Chapter 8), or game therapy (see Chapter 11).

Matching Children and Families

Some children who have experienced multiple traumas at the hands of adults *and* siblings may only be able to tolerate a home with no other children, or no children of the same sex and age of perpetrators from their previous families. When children have learned to abuse younger siblings, they may have great difficulty avoiding repeating this abuse with younger children in their new homes and should be placed only with older children.

Matching children in placement to families should include the child's preferences and best chances for overcoming traumas with parents who are prepared and willing to address the child's past experiences and behaviors. Preparation of foster parents should include training in understanding and working with attachment and trauma disorders. Preparation also needs to include work with the biological children of foster/adoptive parents. With careful assessments of children and preparation of families, most disruptions can be avoided.

It helps to ask children what they look for in a family, ages of parents, interests, activities, sex and ages of siblings, and rural versus city versus suburban. When temporary placements are needed, children should be told honestly that this will be a short-term stay. Although we cannot promise children to find their ideal family, we can show children that we respect their wishes and will try to find the best possible family. Weekly, or at least bi-weekly, visits by supervising caseworkers including one-to-one private times with children are essential to show children in placement that they are not lost and that someone cares. Frequent contacts also help to prevent children from the risk of being neglected or abused in their new homes.

Reality-Based Expectations

Children need perceptual, language, fine and gross motor coordination, auditory and visual memory, concentration, persistence, and many other skills in order to succeed at school. We can help them develop skills and avoid unnecessary conflicts with parents and teachers by accepting their genetic and trauma-induced abilities as a starting point, the way they are. Every child and adult varies in every ability. Some of us are great at basketball or art, but cannot read. Others can read well, but cannot do arithmetic in their head.

A child's development may be impaired from conception by stress, hardships for the parent, abuse of the mother, or drug and alcohol abuse. Caretakers of impaired children need support and assistance from service providers to understand and recognize real limitations and match expectations to a child's abilities and neurological functioning with assistance in securing specialized services from birth through adulthood (Streissguth and O'Malley, 2000). Frustration and disruption of placements is likely when parents are left to manage children alone without comprehensive assessments, and the high likelihood of unrealistic expectations or a lack of critical educational, therapeutic, and support services.

Neurological Conditions

Fetal alcohol syndrome (FAS) has been linked to cognitive impairments of abstract thinking, planning and organization, information processing, and problem solving (National Institute on Alcohol Abuse and Alcoholism, 2000). Although ADHD children have trouble maintaining attention, FAS children typically have trouble shifting attention from one task to another, or moving from one problem-solving pattern to another in a flexible, efficient manner. Learning spatial relationships and visual memory has also been found to be reduced in FAS children and language development is often impaired. FAS children have difficulty encoding new information, the initial stages of memory that hinders learning. Perseveration in thinking patterns and coping are often seen along with distractibility and impulsivity (National Institute on Alcohol Abuse and Alcoholism, 2000). Children with FAS often have prenatal and postnatal growth retardation, cranial anomalies, malformation of major organ systems, symptoms of neurological disorders, seizures, ADHD, and hyperactivity with mental health problems that often develop by adolescence (Mitchell, 2001).

Understanding neurological conditions helps parents to understand how children perceive their world and helps parents understand children's behaviors as fitting patterns of neurological disorders, rather than as provocative attacks on a parent. Practitioners can help parents understand and differentiate different neurologically based disorders. Levy and Orlans (1998) outlined differences between ADHD,[7] bipolar disorder, and reactive attachment disorder (RAD). Children with ADHD have difficulty focusing attention and are often impulsive as a product of their generalized inattention. They are often genuinely friendly and show regret after impulsive acts. In contrast, children with bipolar disorder tend to display an attention span based on their interest and motivation, and may be highly impulsive but in a more accentuated driven, thrill-seeking manner, with little regret shown for their behaviors and often attitudes toward others that are unpredictable, mood-centered, and often negative. A nine-year-old child with bipolar disorder cited by Papolos and Papolos (1999) urged caring adults to hold children until they calmed down, stopped wanting to kill themselves, and felt part of "this world."

Compared to ADHD and bipolar children, children with RAD can demonstrate extended attention as part of their hypervigilence and focus on control (Levy and Orlans, 1998). Impulsive behaviors with these children are usually tied to planned actions with a lack of consideration of consequences (cause-effect thinking) and no remorse. Children with RAD are often charming on a superficial level but distrustful and emotionally removed.

Although children with ADHD may break things carelessly in a non-aggressive manner, bipolar children often break things as part of tantrums and extended anger outbursts. Children with RAD, on the other hand, often break things in a planned manner. In tantrums, these three groupings of children also tend to be different. Children with ADHD often calm down from a tantrum in twenty to thirty minutes, children with bipolar disorder may rage for hours, and children with RAD vary considerably in the length of tantrums tied to the situation and the impact on caregivers; children with RAD may carry out transgressions at a later time out of revenge (Becker-Weidman, 2002).

Levine (1987) helped children look at a range of abilities as the instruments of a pilot's cockpit, with each meter ranging from too high to too low. Levine's concentration cockpit included: mood control, motor/verbal control, behavior control (thinking before doing), sensory filtration control (tuning out unimportant sounds and sights), appetite control, memory control, arousal control, tempo control, and consistency control. From this perspective, each of us can take advantage of the best medical, environmental, and technological tools available to help us do the best we can.

Medications may help one child focus attention. Bringing a small tape recorder or palm pilot may help another child remember important tasks to accomplish. Distractable children may need to sit close to a teacher within a smaller, quieter classroom. Visual instructions and reminders may be essential for children with auditory processing problems or poor auditory attention. Sensory-impaired children may need to have a quiet, secluded place available in their classrooms and homes, so they can physically block out too much stimulation. Other children may need to be held by a parent or trusted adult for the first minutes when they enter every new environment in order to settle in and calm down their natural agitation responses to unfamiliar sights, sounds, and smells.

Psychotropic Medications

Neurological abilities are shaped by genetics and the child's experiences including the impact of drugs, alcohol, and stress especially during a child's earliest years, beginning in utero. Behavior patterns may reflect biologically based syndromes such as FAS[8] or attention-deficit disorders. Many children benefit from medications that help them modulate environmental stimuli, focus attention, calm impulsive responses, and overcome neurological problems.

Psychotropic medications provide an important adjunct to attachment and trauma therapy. Sometimes, however, medications are used to calm or even to subdue a child, and chronic, precipitating stressors are left intact. Medications can help a child succeed; but medications alone are insufficient to repair the breakdown of attachments and the beliefs, expectations, and emotional reactions following a child's experiences of trauma.

Children need to hear in words they can understand how medications can help and the possible side effects. When children lack an understanding of how medications help, they often believe that something is wrong with them, something they cannot fix, something that is their fault and all they, their parents, and their teachers can do is to depend on the medications to "calm me down," or modulate their behaviors. It is easy for children to come to see themselves as little monsters, especially if they are failing both at home and at school.

It is important to help children and parents to understand that taking a medication does not mean children are defective, damaged goods, responsible for their own neurological functioning, or worth less than other children. Instead, diagnoses and medications can be presented from a strength-based perspective, recognizing abilities and weaknesses, and emphasizing what can help a child to succeed. A diabetic child may need insulin and help from adults to maintain his or her diet and monitor his or her sugar. This does not mean the diabetic was bad, or shameful in some way. Similarly, a child who experienced cocaine and alcohol in utero may need to take a medication and receive instructions in school in a way that matches his or her attention span and concentration ability.

CONCLUSION

Children learn the most important lessons during times of stress, the hard times when parents feel they are at their wit's end. That is when parents, grandparents, therapists, and teachers are tested to see if they really are committed to provide the caring that they have professed. To pass these tests, they have to free themselves and those they love from the constricted beliefs and vision learned in the midst of trauma. Parenting hurt children means cutting through the prickers and vines that hide vulnerability and teaching children to move beyond fears, rage, and shame.

Chapter 7

Permanency

> Do or do not. There is no try.
>
> Yoda, *Return of the Jedi*

INTRODUCTION

Permanency work is an intensive therapeutic effort to reclaim lost and hurt children and to rebuild families. It means working with pain and fighting to overcome neglect in our communities. Permanency means providing each child with a safe, nurturing home and a bonded relationship with a parent (biological or adoptive) who is committed to raising the child into the future (Kagan and Schlosberg, 1989).

Therapists can prepare and coach parents, organize supportive services, and work with children and families to overcome traumas; but the real challenge is faced in the middle of the night or after several months of provocative and irritating behavior. Traumatized children have to find out if their life stories are really changing. Spoken words mean very little to hurt children whose lives have been filled with broken promises. Legal documents do not mean you will keep your parents. Even young children have learned that adults divorce. Children test parents to see if they can stay the course.

Permanency from a child's point of view is built on actions, not treatment plans or court adjudications. It is the look on a parent's face when a child does something right, and how a parent disciplines *and then* reconnects when a child does something wrong. It is proving to a child that the parent is brave enough to listen to the child's experiences, no matter how frightening, and to protect the child from any more harm. It is a parent who can connect with a child's innermost needs and show that it is okay, for instance, for a teenager to still want to play with dolls or to snuggle with mom reading a book.

Permanency means responding to children's experiences and everything children carry with them. Rebuilding attachments means beginning where a child's development stopped and providing the commitment a child needs to move ahead.

ACTIVITIES THAT FOSTER ATTACHMENT

Permanence

Babies learn that objects and people remain constant by playing games beginning with dropping food or objects and having parents pick them up. As a baby develops, he or she learns that objects remain present, even when they cannot be seen. Beloved storybooks, such as *Goodnight Moon* (Brown, 1947), gently remind toddlers that everything around them will remain constant, even when they go to sleep. Games that highlight making things appear and then disappear are great fun. Toddlers cry out "all gone," dropping food to the floor, and delight in impressing themselves and their parents by finding their toes or uncovering a stuffed animal hidden under a blanket. Parents celebrate *re*discovering a toddler's toes and chant, "This Little Piggy . . .". Ritualized rhymes and songs when children are dressing or undressing remind them that body parts remain, even when they are covered by clothes.

Games such as "peek a boo," "find me," and later, "hide and seek," help to teach toddlers that moms and dads and other important people remain, even if they cannot see them. Parents can enjoy how their children move through the stages of object permanency (Mahler, Pine, and Bergman, 1975), first believing they are hidden just by covering their eyes, then by covering parts of their bodies and eventually their whole selves. These games work best when parents give a child a big hug when he or she is "found" (Lansky, 1993). Each search thus ends with a reunion, suspense giving way to affection, and each *re*enactment reinforcing the lesson that children can trust parents to return.

Van Gulden (2001) has found that some adopted children in therapy, and even some adults, have never fully integrated object permanency. Children may intellectually understand that objects and people remain, even when not directly perceived, and yet, deep down, may remain convinced that in the end, the most important people and objects will be truly "all gone." Abandonment can become a predominant metaphor for a child's perceptions and understanding of life. When parents repeatedly fail to *re*appear, or cannot be found, children eventually give up.

Traumatized children may need to repeat early childhood games with parents and practitioners to *re*master what they could not learn before. We can utilize playful enactments of childhood games such as hide and seek, or searching for missing characters in books (e.g., *Find Waldo* books) (Handford, 1988). Older children may enjoy using a variety of magic tricks to make objects appear and disappear. These games and tricks, performed for attentive parents, may help children to practice and demonstrate mastery of object permanence in their lives. Practitioners can also use magic to empower parents (see Chapter 9).

Some children (or adults) may be scared by magic because it raises doubts and confusion about what is real. By mastering magic tricks with support from caring adults, children can build the courage to look behind the curtains and learn the truths of what has happened in their lives and what was real. The child's mother or father may have said that he or she cared and promised to come back, leaving the child with an illusion of caring and permanency. Magic tricks can help a child to master illusions and see that behind each feat of magic lies the truth of the trick, the mathematical logic, the sleight of hand, and the secret of how it worked. Magic can also be used as a means of helping attachment-impaired children to develop cause-effect reasoning skills within a format that appeals to their desire for control.

R*eattunement*

We promote bonding[1] between a parent and a child through touch, eye-to-eye contact, and special time set aside for parents and children to be together. Even if a child stiffens up, parents need to persist and demonstrate over time that they care and will not be scared away. Nurture should be noncontingent. Minute by minute, day by day, children and parents work on rebuilding trust with hugs, tickles, smiles, and persistence.

Change is slow, with ups and downs. Practitioners can help parents to notice the small signs, the sighs, the furtive looks back, the gentle touch, the demand for a bedtime story, which reveal a child's tentative desire for closeness. A child may only be able to look at a parent for a fraction of a second today, two seconds after a month. Noticing the little changes helps keep parents on track. It helps to remind them that trust takes a long time to rebuild, often as long as the child lived without a secure and safe relationship. Fast fixes are fantasies. *Re*parenting means going for the long haul.

To attune to a child, it helps to pay attention to the rhythm of his or her behavior and the tones, tempo, and feeling of his or her sounds. Imagine each child singing his or her own melody, as shown in how he or she talks, moves, and gestures, or the songs he or she chooses to sing. Learning a child's favorite songs helps to capture his or her hopes, passions, and fears.

Children's language and behaviors give us essential clues to their social-developmental age.[2] It also helps become aware of how we react, in turn, to their behaviors. Are we pulled to hold and cradle tearful children? Have they mastered playing by the rules of games, or barely begun to enjoy parallel play? Our sense of a child's developmental age can help in selecting approaches to engage a child.

For older children, who did not experience warmth or caring, it is often necessary to *re*do the caring and positive discipline that the child missed as an infant or toddler. This may mean bringing out a baby bottle for an eight-year-old or building with blocks with a twelve-year-old. A fifteen-year-old traumatized youth may need a special time every day to be a six-year-old once again, and work at his or her own pace to overcome the memories of what happened at that age.

Safe touch and holding are critical parts of *re*attachment. Holding a child on a parent's lap, rocking gently, play wrestling, reading stories, sitting side by side, an arm around the child's shoulder, or a tap on the back can help a child learn to safely touch again. Working with messy materials can also be helpful with children who have trouble with touch. Clay, finger paints, human figure play in sandboxes, cutting, pasting, and making Popsicle stick houses are just a few activities. Silly games can be used to have fun, such as counting toes with playful teasing. "Let's see how many toes you have. '10, 9, 8, 7, 6' plus five more makes 11. Hmm, *very* interesting!"[3]

Playing physical games such as Twister and falling down on a parent, may be a challenge for a hurt child, but gradually something that he or she can enjoy and that can allow him or her to experience safe touching with an adult. Learning how to hold a bat or to shoot pool provides other opportunities for a parent to gently guide a child with a steady hand.

Showing affection is important, even when a child responds by stiffening up. A parent may only be able to touch a child for only a moment in the beginning—a quick hug, a warm smile, and away. It helps again to remember that a child's resistance to being touched is often his or her way of showing adults where he or she is stuck, that secrets exist about what happened to the child, and that this is an area where the child needs help.

Reciprocal and joint activities are invaluable (e.g., holding a song sheet and jointly singing songs or reciting nursery rhymes from a book, working together on puzzles or drawings, and alternately reading paragraphs from a book). Board games are very helpful to show children how parents handle ups and downs (e.g., Chutes and Ladders®, Aggravation®, Sorry!®, or Monopoly®). Children learn through games and sports how to win with grace, acknowledge their opponents competence, and how to lose with pride, knowing they will have another chance to win at this game or another.

Working together on putting things away and household cleaning are important, daily activities that can be used to foster reciprocal interactions. Raking leaves, washing dishes, folding laundry, the mundane chores of daily life, also provide natural opportunities to work together sharing frustrations and accomplishments and adding words and strategies to tasks to foster shared values and build skills. Making tasks fun or silly helps, so that children and parents can have opportunities to laugh together. Tasks given to children should be selected to enable them to succeed and gain their parents' approval with opportunities for help along the way.

Brief messages of praise with smiles, hugs, taps on the shoulder, and other gestures become very powerful when tied to specific accomplishments that a child can feel good about. General statements (e.g., "You're a great boy"), usually are not believed and often lead to negative behavior by the child to show that he or she has another side.

Negative responses by a child after praise or successes may surprise a caring parent. It helps to anticipate that a child with attachment problems will very likely behave poorly, or regress, after being praised for successes. It is as if the child needs to remind everyone that deep inside the shame remains. The child may feel that he or she can never be good enough. Parents and practitioners can help the child learn that despite his or her success today, no one is expecting him or her to be perfect or to always succeed.

Children with attachment problems often oscillate between shame and the need for perfection. We can help them stay balanced by keeping praise focused on small actions, and surprising children with special gifts or activities that simply affirm parents' caring and are not contingent on anything. For children who like sports, it often helps to point out how a batting average of .333, getting on base one out of three times at bat, is an excellent record for a major league baseball player. Even basketball stars miss shots at the hoop.

Children listen very carefully to what adults say about them to other adults, especially their tone of voice, facial looks, and gestures. Talking within earshot of children thus provides powerful moments for parents to send a message of validation of children's achievements and struggles and to emphasize the parents' commitment.

Showing Children They Are Special

Children's security and self-esteem are strengthened when significant adults nurture and value children over time. Successes and appreciation prepare children to face the inevitable taunts, criticism, mistakes, and rejections of childhood. Hurt children are especially sensitive to whether parents, teachers, or other adults are genuine. False or superficial praise carries little value, and will be quickly understood by traumatized children as temporary and not to trusted. Children look for consistency in parental response, tone of voice, what adults say to each other about children, and the spontaneous looks on an adult's face.

Therapists can help parents develop, or *re*develop, children's self-esteem with a wide range of interactions that show children that they are an integral part of their families. Many traumatized children have not experienced positive interactions with adults, or have learned that fun and intimacy is followed by violence or separations.

Activities should match a child's ability to handle interactions, a little at a time, building gradually over time to an age-appropriate level. Therapists can help parents to "pace" (d'Aversa, Personal Communication, 2001) children to slowly develop competencies and simply learn to have fun. Too much attention and closeness can scare away hurt children. Parents can be coached to build attachments a little at a time, recognizing that children need to develop trust that they can allow themselves to have even a little fun with parents without rekindling fears of then losing parents they have begun to love.

Activities and crafts can be employed to foster children's sense of belonging and value. Conjoint projects naturally lead to parents sharing with each other something wonderful the children have done, such as fathers helping young children making a clay jewelry case for Mom on Mother's Day.

Adults in a frenetic world need to allow time just to "be" with children, time that allows creativity and spontaneity. Daily routines that allow slow and gentle care (e.g., hair grooming completed with a kiss), help send children off to school with a self-esteem boost. Special snacks ready for children after school and dinner times with both parents and children sharing what was good and exciting in their days, the best and the worst (Zweibel and Nelson, 1999). Rainy days, birthdays, holidays, and anniversary dates can become opportunities to reinforce how children are important to their families. They help to give children special roles to play during holidays, religious observances, and family reunions. Taking children shopping for clothes and inviting their preferences for colors, styles, and comfort help to show children acceptance (Fahlberg, 1979a). Sick days home provide unique opportunities for parents to care for children (Fahlberg, 1979a), and to comfort them with chicken soup, storytelling, chamomile tea, and other home remedies and family traditions for managing sickness.

Children can be invited to play both at their developmental age and at their chronological age. This validates their desire to grow up and the preoccupation with mastering earlier stages. Developmentally delayed adolescents may relish time each day to work with LEGOs. Children traumatized in infancy may flourish after *re*playing being fed a bottle. Teenagers may need time to play board games and learn beginning skills, opportunities missed during latency years filled with domestic violence.

Gardening is a great way to teach children about patience, care, and nurture needed for living things to thrive with opportunities for them to take on responsibilities and succeed. Gardening takes time, means thinking ahead in terms of months and seasons, and teaches the importance of responsibility and persistence. Rebuilding the roots of a hurt plant is also a wonderful metaphor for helping rebuild connections for children who have lost parts of their families.

Hundreds of fun and silly preschool activities can be used to foster the trust children may lack and help set children's new and permanent homes apart from past placements. Fun time is teaching time for children to learn about reciprocity between parents and children, playing by the rules, and that fun time is a time for affection and playful touching.

The possibilities for fun activities are only limited by the imaginations of parents and children, and of course, the availability of resources. Fortunately, some of the most creative activities that promote bonding cost very little, except, of course, in a parent's time and patience. This is the most powerful resource that can be offered to hurt children.

Adventure-based programs and activities offer natural opportunities for parents and children to build shared memories of overcoming challenges together. Rebuilding attachments means "doing with," in good times and hard times. Parents can take advantage of school, community, or religious activities and trips to create special times. Activities are great ways of breaking out of routine parent-child dialogues (e.g., "make your bed"), and to promote mastery over challenges with some risk (within safe limits). Parents and youths can take on challenges of learning together to ski or take on double-diamond trails, to kayak or canoe, to hike a mountain, to surmount a ropes course, to survive a white-water rafting trip, to master Italian cooking, to improve their basketball game, or to take up a new sport, just for the fun of it.

Activities are especially powerful when children are not expecting parents to have time. Meaningful activities include crafts and recipes passed on from generation to generation, such as a treasured holiday pie from great grandma, a family collection of favorite recipes, or a tradition of honoring mothers on Valentine's Day. Time-honored family activities can be expanded with popular books on fun activities that parents can employ to show children that they are valued and belong in their families. Caring adults can help children to succeed by promoting development of skills fostering children's own competence and lead to recognition of how they are contributing art, gifts, music, etc., to their families. Activities should be fun and rewarding for both parents and children. This is an opportunity to enjoy children, to enhance pride in accomplishments. The how and where crafts are hung up by mom or dad adds immeasurably to children's sense of pride.

The following list of activities was adapted for traumatized children from Vicki Lansky's (1991) wonderful book, classic preschool and early childhood activities, and some of my personal favorites.

- Make hand prints in plaster of paris of child and parent, and place together.
- Make a family coat of arms with symbols of family strengths (e.g., skills, faith, significant people, heirlooms, awards) contributed by child and parent, or illustrations of family members vanquishing past problems.
- Honor the cultural background of a child coming into the family from another country or ethnic background with magazines, artwork, and foods, and participate and learn about that culture through camp programs or cultural organizations.
- Outline child and parent's body, color, and hang them up.
- Plant shrubs, trees, perennials and give them special meanings in honor of a child's accomplishments (e.g., graduating preschool), an important family event, or as an annual tradition tied in with a religious, cultural, or made-up holiday (e.g., a spring festival to celebrate growth and renewal).
- Create a home theater beginning with acting, such as elephants going to a party, dogs going to school, monkeys singing songs, or kangaroos on a playground and add sounds, gestures, and looks to show different feelings.
- Compose sounds and melodies just for fun or to entertain Mom or Dad, with pianos, keyboards, children's xylophones, guitars, karaoke, or homemade instruments; hold preschool children on your lap as you compose.
- Draw a funny face and a special message on a child's lunch bag to take to school or day care every day; this can be a single word that reminds a child of something fun to look forward to such as spaghetti for dinner, a planned trip, or simply a heart and kisses.
- Sneak up on a child with the attack of the "hug monster" or "tickle bees"; and a reminder, "I'll be back."
- Initiate rides on Mom or Dad geared to a child's age (e.g., up and down on a parent's legs, flying through the air as super girl or boy, pony rides, or bucking broncos in a swimming pool); these fantasy trips can be expanded into adventure stories of the child flying through the air over the neighborhood, zooming through school or day care centers, or flying over mysterious lands.
- Go to the library to get a library card in the child's name, similar to mom's or dad's.
- Do face painting to surprise the other parent at the end of the day.
- Ask a child to name a pet, a car, or a tree and family members use this name.

- Call a special party in honor of a made-up holiday and invite a child's friends.
- Create a family newspaper with a child's personal column.
- Help a child write his or her own suspense story, make printed copies for grandparents, and a special laminated edition for the family room bookcase.
- Create home videos, include made-up adventure stories or simply capture "a day in the life" of the child.
- Read and *re*read baby books and share photo albums chronicling a child's life in the family.
- Take part in togetherness activities such as riding a bike for two, swinging side by side, swimming, hiking, fishing, or boating.
- Dance together, beginning with toddlers in socks or barefoot standing on a parent's feet.
- Mark each child's growth and parents' heights on a family height chart placed on a mounted board or backing that can be moved with the family.
- Save headline pages from a child's birthday each year.
- Celebrate birthdays with invitations to family members and children's friends, even if that means two parties; take photographs of the child with family members and friends; and write a private letter or note to the child chronicling some of his or her accomplishments during the past year.
- For families celebrating Christmas, add an ornament each year to symbolize a special event or accomplishment for each family member (Johnston, Personal Communication, 1999).
- Create secret recipes including "special" ingredients chosen by a child from suggestions by a parent (e.g., adding white chocolate, a little vanilla, or butterscotch to a cookie or brownie recipe).
- Explore hobbies such as foreign money collections, shell collections.
- Compete to see who can blow the biggest bubbles in the world, hop around the yard, or make it through an obstacle course on the sidewalk or driveway.
- Make up mazes and crossword puzzles for a child using figures and words that are special to him or her, such as a child's favorite activities, a teacher's name, the child's birthday, etc.
- Take special adventures, such as going to the airport to watch planes taking off, going to an overlook to see trains at a rail yard, checking out cars at an antique auto show, and all manner of museums, including adult-oriented museums with parents helping a child imagine how it would be like to sleep in a 1700s bed with three other children, life

in a log cabin, or imagining magic in an abstract painting and then making personal artwork to rival the masters.

- Go on a bus, subway, or train ride around town or to explore another part of a city, sampling favorite foods along the way.
- Make up a special vocabulary together with funny-sounding words, such as "super-dee-duper."
- Make a family month-by-month calendar with photographs of the child and other family members.
- Follow a child's interests (e.g., in fish), and take the child to pet stores, bookstores, museums, and libraries to learn more, cut out articles in magazines, videotape special shows, go fishing, or imagine and investigate with a child what could living in a nearby river or pond.
- Share special stories from a parent's childhood from photo albums or trophies, crafts, jewelry, etc.
- Give each other back rubs and foot massages, just "because . . ."
- Decorate a child's room and rearrange the furniture with the child's help.
- Cut a child's name out of cardboard or with a jigsaw, paint the pieces, cut out a frame, and create a homemade puzzle the child can assemble, or that can be mounted or placed on a bookshelf.
- When parents travel, collect special objects tied to a child's interests (e.g., foreign currency, rocks, basketball team shirts).
- Use your computer or hand design special note cards, writing pads, or positive messages with the child's name.
- Arrange for your child to visit you at work and show him or her off to colleagues.
- Find positive ways that a child is similar to parents (birth or adoptive), such as interests, skills, laughs, etc.
- Make up stories with stuffed animals, puzzle people, or favorite characters.
- Create family sculptures with doll collections.
- Print a family cookbook including favorite recipes from each family member.
- Mount family photographs, showing how children grow up from year to year.
- Make a house out of cardboard or blocks, and create family figures out of paper, cardboard, or clay to enact family stories.
- Build a doll house.
- Put on a puppet show.

- Lip synch a favorite band or create a parent-child dance to go with a favorite song.
- Create a homemade movie.
- Send special work, school papers, news articles, citations, poetry published in a school journal, and annual photos to relatives.
- Invite the child to add a sentence to a letter or e-mail to a relative.
- Learn something fun together, such as jump roping, roller blading, or cross-country skiing.
- Attend special events for the child: assemblies when the child is honored, T-ball games, soccer matches, school shows, etc., photograph or videotape the event as well as the child with family members, especially visiting relatives, with dinner out at a child's favorite restaurant or an ice cream treat afterward.
- Teach older children skills in camping, canoeing, reading a compass, setting up a tent, even if it is just in the backyard and going on adventures, carefully planned together (e.g., to climb a mountain, bike a trail in a state park, or take a *multi*day hiking or bike trip).

Special times for each child make all the difference. In busy homes, it may be necessary to let the answering machine handle calls, and ask a spouse, relative, babysitter, respite worker, or friend to supervise the other children. Each child needs one-on-one moments. It is the special quality of the activity that counts for a child (e.g., cooking a special food that a child loves), helping a child build a collection of what is special to him or her, or setting aside a time every weekend, or for younger children, every day, to work with a child on a special project (e.g., building a model or adding a new chapter to a story played out with dolls or stuffed animals and recorded in a book, on an audiotape, of filmed with a video camera).

Expensive vacations can be wonderful but the most important message children need to receive is that parents want to take children with them to important family events, events that define a family and mark their heritage. Over time, these activities change the definition of a hurt child's identify from "I am alone," to "I have someone who cares."

Taking a child to a funeral of a relative is more powerful than a trip to Disney World. Real love and caring in the midst of grief has much more impact than the temporary pleasures of any cruise ship. Children want to see that they are included and know that it is easy to have fun at a resort that offers organized activities, cooks all the meals, and cleans up everyone's messes. The real tests of inclusion versus exclusion come during the hard times a family faces.

Sharing Feelings

Many traumatized children lack awareness of their own or others' feelings and have learned that it is not safe to show, or even to feel, in different ways. Activities can be used to teach them that it is safe to have and share feelings in their families. For example:

- Draw or take photographs of parents and children with funny faces, sad faces, angry faces, or scared faces, and put them together on a poster to construct a personalized feeling chart.
- Take feelings such as being scared, break these apart to show children how adults and children naturally feel their stomachs tighten or how they take in a breath of air and look around etc., when startled. Redefine fear from a negative "bad" or "weak" feeling to a natural warning adults and children can use to deal with whatever is happening. Change the connotation of being scared from dread with little sense of self-control to challenges parents and children can prepare for, understand, and master, such as the feeling riding upward at the start of a roller coaster ride, the beginning of an obstacle course, the kick-off at a football game with the ball on its way, beginning to make a speech, or the first pitch when the child is up to bat. Adults can help children recognize and utilize the energy of fear to take the first and most difficult step in an adventure, a competition, or a performance recognizing that it gets easier with each additional step.
- Conduct "exclusive" radio interviews, including making up stories that are happy, sad, scary, angry, worried, or proud, and sharing with other family members.
- Practice showing feelings by making faces together in a mirror, capturing looks with an instant or digital camera, compiling a feeling photograph book, painting small pumpkins with different feelings, making different sounds, or through puppet shows with hand-held animals or characters from stories. Because traumatized children often misperceive visual cues, it is helpful to accentuate shifts in feelings (after Ford, Mahoney, and Russo, 2003). For example, a parent can ask a child to notice when his or her face changes from mad to sad.
- Practice special, parent-modeled words or appropriate phrases from a child's favorite television, movie, or story characters to verbalize feelings, even silly responses such as barking like a dog to show friendship, to warn away a trespasser, or to relieve stress.

Day by Day, Establishing the Rhythm of a Home

Rituals from morning until nighttime differentiate a new home from the past. Breakfast with Dad or Mom, lunch in a bag with a smiley face and a note, homework time, play time, dinner together at a set time, and a story before bed, develop a rhythm. Each activity can be used to show that a parent cares and that a child will be kept safe.

Mealtimes are critical times for sharing the best in the day amidst the natural nurture of home cooking and the discipline required by family members to plan, cook, and clean up. As a child becomes old enough to help, mealtimes provide an opportunity to give back. Cooking favorite foods is often a wonderful way to nurture a child and teach lessons about caring for others. Helping to bake brownies for the family is a wonderful way for a child to become part of the nurture cycle in the home, not just a recipient but someone who pitches in and helps. Participation in breakfast, lunch, dinner, and holiday cooking demonstrates that a child will be cared for and is expected to contribute as part of the family.

Cooking is also a great way to demonstrate to children how we can balance out bitterness by adding sweeteners and learn to appreciate both. Making a marinara or stir-fry sauce can become an adventure in combining different vegetables and spices (e.g., balancing red pepper with corn syrup or sugar).

Bedtime is an especially important time to establish a nurturing ritual through reading, singing, or special prayers shared by parents and children. Reading (or singing) a bedtime story (Minnear, Personal Communication, 2001) of the children's lives is a great way of *re*connecting with children every night before bed. Cuddling and stroking the "guard dog," bedtime kisses, laying out clothes for the morning, and talking about something special for the next day can be part of ending each day and preparing for a good tomorrow. Each ritual shows children that this is how we keep safe, this is how we stay warm, this is how have fun, and most important, this is how important they are to their parents.

Rituals also provide a healthy antidote to predictable stressors when anniversary dates or times recur. If a child lived with violence frequently occurring around dinner time, it may be necessary to enact special prayers, hugs, or other ritualized acts to remind everyone that this home is different. Holidays or birthdays may often remind a child of past losses or traumas, such as when his or her mom or dad became drunk and got into a fight. When these holidays come up, it helps to ritualize reminders of how the child and parents will be kept safe. This may need to include explicit safety guidelines addressing the precursors to violence from the child's past, even if these seem unnecessary to foster/adoptive families, or relatives taking custody of a child. For example, the child could be reminded that in his or her new family, parents make sure no one gets drunk at holiday meals because Dad and Mom limit any alcoholic drinks and no one drives drunk.

Anniversary dates of times when children lost a family member due to illness, accidents, addiction, violence, or death are important times to help them grieve with appropriate rituals tied to a family's religion and ethnic heritage. Trips to cemeteries, prayers at churches, mosques, or synagogues, and taking time to remember, are important ways for parents to help children face losses together. Respecting their losses and showing children they have permission to mourn helps them to stop hiding the love and sadness they feel. When children witness their parents' grief for losses, they learn by example that it is possible to feel and endure the pain of loss.

Anniversaries of the dates when children returned to their families or moved into new families are times to be honored and celebrated. Children need to see that parents want to make these dates special and choose activities that everyone in the family can enjoy to mark the occasion. In contrast, ignoring or trying to forget these dates can imbue them with a sense of shame, rather than an opportunity to reinforce messages of thankfulness regarding their entry or return to the family.

Although daily and seasonal rituals promote a sense of consistency and structure, parents can enhance their impact with unexpected gifts, hugs, kisses, and touches (Hughes, 1998a; Delaney, 1997, 1998a,b). It is the day-by-day adventure of living that marks the truth for children. Children and parents build attachments through shared moments of joining together for fun, for relief from pain, and for the necessities of life from morning to night.

RIGHTS AND RESPONSIBILITIES WITHIN FAMILIES

Parents connect by laughing, crying, and playing with children, and showing over and over that parents and children can work *together* to clean, repair, and make their house a home.

Children also need responsibilities. Chores should match their age and ability. A ten-year-old with attention or memory problems may only be able to do one task at a time, but that task then becomes that much more important and valued. All of us, children and adults alike, feel better about ourselves when we are helping others and contributing to our families and communities.

Each act of helping becomes a positive moment parents can capture and enlarge with meaning. Hugs, kisses, a touch on the shoulder, a look in children's eyes, and a quick word of praise are especially powerful ways to show children that their contributions are noticed and appreciated. These are special moments that parents can use to foster children's courage to be part of the family and to begin to trust that parents really do care. Watching for these moments takes both patience, sensitivity, and faith in the loving capacity of children.

At the same time, parents teach responsibility and safety with limits appropriate for the age shown by children and adolescents. Privileges go hand in hand with the level of responsibility a youth demonstrates. A fifteen-year-old who acts similar to a six-year-old earns the rights and freedoms appropriate for a six-year-old. Natural and logical consequences (Dreikurs, 1964) work when parents make the effort to find out what is really happening and tailor consequences to fit a youth's behavior. Rigid and arbitrary limits or extensive restrictions, such as grounding a youth for a month, rarely make sense and are easily defied by adolescents. Instead, we can take an incident in which a youth violates a rule and create a consequence that requires the youth to acknowledge his or her mistake, to make up for what he or she did wrong, and to learn why a rule is important.

Re*claiming Lost Children*

Children become part of new families, or *re*built families, when their heritage, the good and the bad, is valued. Parents and practitioners strengthen children by helping them develop a positive sense of their own worth and establishing through action how children are part of their families with a past, a present, and a future. Photo albums and time lines are very helpful to frame children's and families' experience in terms of mastery and competence. Remembering important events and marking anniversary dates with rituals is an important way to validate children's experiences and to show children that they do not have to feel alone any more.

*Re*claiming children also means helping them learn to lower their guard and mourn what they have lost. Many traumatized children have learned never to cry. It helps to share interviews from sports stars, true stories from adventurers, and most important, to let children see their parents cry. Cutting onions forms a perfect opportunity to show how tears are natural and lead into a discussion of how some people cry when they are happy and how crying helps adults, even 300-pound football players, and children to heal.

Parents show children that this is their home by hanging their photographs in prominent places, placing awards and drawings all over the refrigerator and kitchen, marking events for children on the family calendar, and telling friends and relatives about children's successes. Attachment means parents claiming children and children claiming parents (Levy and Orlans, 2000).

Small day-to-day accomplishments such as a good grade on a spelling test, an award for a drawing, the child's first time speaking in front of a class, building a picnic table with Uncle Ted, or teaching Grandma to use the family computer are important times to honor a child with a special dessert, a trip to the store, going out together to a movie, or the gift of a book—any way family members can show support for the child and a belief in his or her potential. Awards, special dinners, certificates, and trophies can mark the occasion and give children something positive to remind them of the good times. Photographs stored in albums and videos can preserve the occasion and be shared later as a way for everyone in the family to enjoy and reinforce the child's successes.

*Re*claiming children also means saying "no." The art of parenting is to match a child's developmental needs and balance attunement with discipline. Pushing a young child too early to be independent promotes detachment or clinging. To coddle a child and give in to all his or her whims promotes narcissism and expectations that the world owes the child everything. As a general guideline, just as in early childhood education, it helps to aim for a 90 percent success rate in family living. It is a matter of balance within an evolving relationship.

Children may not like a parent's decisions. Parents can give a child choices (Hughes, 1997; Levy and Orlans, 1998), and keep themselves in control (see Chapter 6). A child who acts out-of-control may need to take a break, and learn how to calm down and stay in control. He or she can be given a choice on taking a time-out calmly or, to continue screaming, etc., in a time-out for twice as long. A youth who skips a class could be required to work after school with the teacher of that class or another staff person to catch up on what he or she missed and even read ahead of the class to prepare for the next day. A disruptive youth can be asked to find a way to give something back to the class or school to make up for the aggravation and disruption he or she caused. Ideally, this would be something that builds on a youth's interests and talents (Brooks, 1991). For example, constructing something out of wood for a youth with carpentry skills, or for other youths, artwork, baking, or teaching another youth to use a word-processing program might provide a way for them to contribute and develop a positive identity (Brooks, 1991).

Stealing or hurting someone requires an apology, restitution, and demonstration to the person hurt how this will not happen again. Consequences that incorporate the family's heritage, religion, and values can be used to shape an appropriate mode to help a youth atone, or make up for his or her transgression. The consequence should provide a way for the youth to essentially repair the harm done to relationships and to win back the trust of the people hurt. The point of discipline within this framework is to help a youth gain respect in a positive way and to guide a youth into a positive and important role *within* his or her family, school, and neighborhood.

Parents need to know who their children are spending time with, including contacts over the Internet. School officials need to call parents whenever youths are not where they are supposed to be. Caring for children and adolescents means watching over them. The older the youth, the more parents need support from friends, teachers, clergy, and authorities.

Parents create a sense of community by helping neighbors keep an eye on each others' children and taking the time to organize and contribute to community sports leagues, art and music programs, and community centers for children and adolescents. Calling and meeting with parents of children's friends (Fein and Fein, Personal Communication, 1997) creates a reality to the old parental saying that they have eyes everywhere. Teenagers very naturally push their parents to give them space and appear shocked when parents try to build links to the parents of their friends. But, this is exactly what parents need to do in order to create a safety net for their teenagers. We need to build and rebuild a community of caring adults who will watch out for one another's children and adolescents.

Parents set boundaries that define a child's inclusion in a family. Inclusion is understood by a child through acts of caring and limits, the day-to-day decisions by parents that show the child what is real. These are often difficult choices. Parents may be tempted to allow everyone to eat at different times, just because it fits a busy family schedule better. Or, a parent may feel compelled to give into a child's wish to spend an important holiday with a friend's family going to Disney World. Each decision teaches a child what is most important in his or her family.

Invitations to spend holidays with a long-lost aunt, or a previous family that suddenly calls pose special problems. Old fantasies of caring may be rekindled, compelling the child to test again if people from the past have changed or really care. These wishes and fantasies can be addressed in other ways (e.g., through carefully structured visits, sessions involving the child's therapist, or invitations to renew contacts beginning at the child's new home). A child may be initially happy if a parent agrees with requests for holiday visits with old families instead of a child's "permanent" family to please the child, avoid a fight, or prevent conflicts with relatives. But, at the same time, the child may very likely conclude that parents really do not want him or her that much. Or, that the current family is really more like a boarding home, nice in many ways, but not a place that either parents or the child define as "home."

Raising a child has been compared to a melody (Kagan, 1998). Over time, parenting children can evolve into a symphony or a ballet with parent and child accompanying each other in rhythm and tone. When a child cries out in anger or fear, often the parent-child relationship has drifted out of balance. This is a natural part in every child and family's development; a stage of development that challenges parents and children. If we think of the child's voice as an instrument that sounds out of tune, we can step back as a conductor, hear the energy in the child's discordant tone, and help the child to use that voice in a way that will enrich the child and the larger symphony. Of course, just as a child's taste in music changes over the years, parents need to *re*attune to the changes in their child and help him or her adjust the key and tempo to keep the child's development balanced and in tune. With each transition, the family symphony evolves and becomes enriched.

SKILL-BUILDING ACTIVITIES

Schools and organizations provide vital resources for skill development and inclusion of children into communities. Providing children and adolescents with after-school activities is crucial to provide adult monitoring and opportunities for developing skills and finding ways to bring out a youth's talents in music, art, sports, drama, social action, and other areas. Schools and after-school programs work best when they are small enough to promote individual and ongoing contacts between youths and teachers, counselors, mentors, and administrators. A good test for any school is whether teachers, principals, and guidance staff know the children's names and care enough to reach out to them, say "hello" with children's names, and check on how they are doing. Mentors committed to working with children over a period of years can become powerful resources.

Parents, teachers, and therapists can help identify a child's creative spark and talents that can be enriched to help a child succeed. Psychological evaluations often help to identify hidden talents and interests. Children need to have one or two special activities that allow them to excel and earn recognition for their achievements. Involvement in crafts, music, arts, drama, dance, auto mechanics, carpentry, 4-H clubs, religious groups, camping, fishing, or sports are important ingredients in a service plan for strengthening traumatized children.

Activities work best as add-ons, and not substitutes, for family life. Too many activities can make a home more like a sports camp than a place of nurture; and moms and dads can become more like chauffeurs and coaches than parents. Traumatized children also need extra help and guidance to avoid seeing every time at bat or every art project as a measure of their worth. Parents, coaches, and mentors can help by setting realistic goals for every youth and by noticing, and helping children to notice, the small, but steady signs of their growth and progress. Organized activities provide opportunities for children to excel, but should not take away from time to have fun and to simply spend time with family members.

Ideally, children will act out attachment problems in therapy sessions and with parents, leaving school and after-school programs as opportunities to succeed. However, many traumatized children need specialized help in order to succeed at school. For many, this needs to include guidance in *re*learning basic social skills such as how to ask for help with school work, how to wait in lines, how to take a time-out to "cool down," how to make friends, how to handle teasing, how to handle bullies, etc. School-based therapists can work with children on impulse control skills and normalizing reactions to losses and family problems through involvement in groups that allow children to become aware that they are not alone.

Traumatized children may look to other hurt (or hurting) children for their primary relationships, rather than risking rejection again from adults. Involvement with positive, achievement-oriented peers in structured classes and after-school activities can help children learn that they can succeed in developing skills reinforced by adults at home and at school. The goal for every child, especially traumatized children, should be to foster a positive link to some area of interest or talent at school and in after-school activities and organizations, ideally working with a mentor or instructor over many years. Fostering skills in art, music, and theater are especially helpful to promote healing with traumatized children.

Avoiding shaming is very important as well as helping teachers to avoid triggers that remind children of past traumas. With traumatized children, it is important for practitioners and parents to work with teachers on understanding children's "early warning signs," and to help them implement safety plans for times when children become stressed. Safety plans should include identification of special people the child likes and can get permission to see when stressed, during school or program hours (e.g., school psychologists, guidance counselors, social workers, coaches, or administrators, someone who values the child and understands how disruptive or dissociative behaviors reflect a child's struggles). Communication between activity leaders and parents may need to begin on a daily basis, or at least allow for immediate contact, in order to show children that the adult umbrella of caring and guidance extends through their day.

SIGNS OF ATTACHMENT

The Power of Words

Children develop constricted beliefs and behaviors in order to cope with difficult times when they felt frightened, helpless, or unwanted. An adolescent who lost his or her biological parents as a four-year-old may continue to think and act very similar to a preschooler. Moving a child to a relative's home, a foster family, or a residential center may be necessary but almost always means that he or she feels ripped apart. The child's sense of permanency is lost. Often, his or her pain reflects struggles passed on by parents and grandparents, a legacy of broken ties and shattered dreams.

Messages such as "for now," "for as long as you are good," or "for as long as your mom and dad need a break," teach children that love and security are impermanent, uncertain, and, at best, temporary. Messages of commitment based on children's behavior put them in charge, in with adult-level responsibilities that are far too much for children to handle. These messages inadvertently give children power over parents. Messages of temporary commitments also teach children that only the present moment matters and that it only pays to think of what can be gained or lost in the present, or as long as the reinforcing authority is watching.

For children in foster families where reuniting with parents or adoption is uncertain, it helps to give children as strong a message of commitment as is possible (e.g., "We know you are and your parents are working to reunite and want you to know that you can be part of our family for as long as you need"). Substitute families can be described as second homes, to show respect to a child's previous families and recognition that a child will naturally feel loyalty to previous parents, relatives, and family members, even if he or she grows up and becomes attached to a new family.

Children become strong when parents and caring adults teach them that they can link strengths from the past with the competence within themselves and their families to accomplish their goals in the future. Healing comes from pulling out the power of real family members, remembering the pride of their ethnic and cultural heritage, reaching out to family and friends, and summoning the courage to *re*master the nightmares of the past.

Trauma breaks hearts and rips apart children's identities if it is allowed to fester. Caring adults can reweave children's split parts into a whole. Eye to eye, face to face, caring adults help children to heal by showing children that they are safe to cry and to grieve without fear of being abandoned.

Accentuating Attachment

Building an attachment with a hurt child is a test of courage, conviction, and understanding. Parents succeed by mobilizing support for themselves from family members, friends, therapists, and community organizations. The rewards come step by step, along the path to permanency. As therapists, we can highlight signs of a child building an attachment when

- a sick child looks to a parent for comfort;
- a child's furtive look shows she or he expects the parent to be watching what she or he is doing;
- a child can almost feel a parent's look from behind;
- a child becomes accustomed to seeing a parent's face and hearing the parent's voice before going to bed and every morning before going to school;
- a child knows that parents will somehow, some way find out whatever the child did, and then deal with it, no matter what;
- even when a best friend turns away, a child counts on a parent to care;
- a child can look at a parent's smile, nod, or feel the parent's touch, and hold this memory as he or she goes off to school;
- a child takes a symbol of support from the parent (a necklace, a special stone, a photograph of the parent and child together) and carries it with him or her; and
- a child spontaneously burrows his or her head into a parent, begins sitting close, and can fall asleep resting on a parent for support.

We can see children's trust grow when they begin to share spontaneous, seemingly offhand comments that reveal fragments of memories. Later, they share more complete stories of good times and bad. With greater trust children begin to share fragments of shame held deep inside, knowing that the parents caring for them will not make them feel worse and shame them further for what they did, said, or did not do during traumas of the past.

Permanency is a package deal. Children look to their parents to see if their heritage will be accepted and if their parents will accept them with all their feelings of love and hate, fear and courage. Building attachments means helping a child and a parent to uncover the best and the worst from the past, and then to work together to build a new future.

Magic Kisses

Raising a hurt child is never simple and there are no panaceas. It helps me to keep in mind the lessons I have learned from children such as Billy and

Tommy in Chapter 2. The embrace, the validation, and the magic kisses are powerful forces that shape a child's love. I have seen how the caring of parents can emerge and envelop their hurt and hurting child. Foster and adoptive parents have shown me how love, determination, and commitment can work when a biological family is not able or willing to make the commitments a child needs. Mentors willing to work with a child year by year can also make a real difference.

Caring and believing in a child does work when it is coupled with the strength to help a child face his or her greatest fears. Was the child to blame for a sibling being hurt, a mother's addiction, or a father running away? Who has the strength to look a child in the eye and tell him or her when he or she is wrong, when he or she has broken the rules, and to teach him or her the difference between right and wrong?

I have faith that people can change, but none of us can do it alone. Our capacity is shaped by the family members and the friends who we can truly count on and by our employers, educators, religious organizations, our heritage, and our communities.

Hour by hour, day by day, parents, grandparents, aunts, and uncles show children whether or not adults within the family can be trusted. Day by day, teachers, neighbors, family friends, authorities, and religious leaders show children whether or not adults outside the community really care. We all live with the consequences of these choices. If the answer is "yes," the child will learn to live like Billy, with the love a child needs to succeed and become a responsible adult, the kind of neighbor we all want. If the answer is "no," the child will be living out Tommy's experience, a childhood marred by trauma, blame, and neglect.

CONCLUSION

Healing the World One Child at a Time

Practitioners and parents can help children by fostering understanding and support for children's services as advocates and ambassadors to legislators, policymakers, and community leaders. Helping each traumatized child is similar to a suspense novel that raises hard questions and moral dilemmas for anyone who cares. To recognize wounded children means acknowledging our own vulnerability. To allow ourselves to feel their pain awakens our own responsibility. To open our eyes to what shapes children's behavior guides our efforts to make a difference.

Authorities may try to label and blame, lock up, or medicate away our problem children. But, the Tommys of the world keep coming back. We can build gates and walls around our homes, but we still have to drive out at night. We still have pass through those unguarded neighborhoods and walk by Tommy at age four, twelve, sixteen, and as a young man. And, our children will be going to school, to work, to shop, and to live with Tommy nearby.

We can reclaim hurt children by combining rules, safeguards, and supervision with the nurture and attunement children crave. It helps me stay focused by remembering the healing power of a caring parent's outstretched arms. The parent's right arm supports the child's back and forms a solid link that shows a child without words, "I am here for you. I won't let you go." The parent's left arm completes the circle around the child, providing the limits a child needs to stay safe. Soothing and guidance united in the circle of a parent's embrace.

We cradle and rock a baby. The motion itself helps the infant calm down. With older children, a parent's arms provide the same support and calming effect, reducing natural "fight-or-flight" reactions and activating higher levels of thinking and processing. The parent's connection to the child by touch, by looking into the child's eyes, by tone of voice, invokes a positive trance to counter stresses and pain. With the parent's presence reaffirmed, the child can learn how to cope with the hard times we all must face.

We can find the angel inside every child by listening to the feelings they stir within us, the fears, the anger, the despair, and the yearning to be valued and loved. These feelings mark the child's search for connection and meaning. By answering the child's call, parents and practitioners become the heroes children need to help them save themselves. By becoming heroes to these children, we become heroes in our own lives as well. In this way, Tommy's story becomes our story. Each Tommy that we save makes our world a little bit brighter.

PART III: THE MAKING OF A HERO

Chapter 8

Telling the Story

Since then at an uncertain hour,
That agony returns
And 'til my ghostly tale is told,
This heart within me burns.

Samuel Coleridge

INTRODUCTION

When neglect is punctuated by violent episodes, children learn to live on edge, their senses on guard, their bodies ready to move, similar to taut rubber bands. They may appear agitated and irritable, and often provoke others. From a strength-based perspective, annoying and challenging behaviors reflect energy and an effort to cope. Problems keep children interacting with adults; however, over time, their energy and potential becomes strained by the effort to protect themselves and the people they love from further harm. Without change, hope fades and children may give up on adults and peers.

Many children become clinically depressed, their bodies and minds literally worn down from synapses firing off alerts. Many depressed children have earnestly tried, but failed, to make their families safe, and learned that nothing helps. They may become withdrawn and passive, or learn to strike out against others and operate solely for their own purposes. Often, the greatest harm in violent families is the breakdown of trust between a caring adult and a child, the trust a child depends upon to grow and thrive, the trust that fosters a child's resilience and provides the foundation for empathy and respect for others.

Even if the overt violence ends, children may never regain the trust that was lost with a parent. A parent may put an end to battering by pressing charges against a partner. Another parent may finally stop decades of drinking. A fragile peace may ensue. The violent partner may be let back into the house. To avoid relapse, parents may adopt strict rules for all aspects of family life and adopt restrictive practices to support their new way of life. Often, the pain and fear of the past will be locked away, hidden from children's eyes and ears, and appear to children as something too dangerous to address. The traumas of the past become unspoken terrors (van der Kolk, 1996) that live on inside family members, gathering their own form of power through constricted conversations, blocked efforts at change, and an imperative to avoid upsetting other family members.

Grief

Grief leads to healing and reconnecting, but children must first feel safe enough to let go of their fears and rage. Grief requires strength from inside oneself and support from family, friends, and community. Families need to grieve the lost years, the broken promises, and the damage. This painful work is often delayed by parents in order to manage day-to-day life, especially in families struggling to pay the rent, fearing the next visit by the landlord, or expecting any day to be laid off from work again. You cannot grieve as you are fighting a battle. Today's struggle to get by can often lead into tomorrow's battle, creating a life marked by serial crises.

If the adults in children's lives are unwilling, or unable, to face past and present dangers, children will very naturally cling to the hope that somehow, in some magical way, the past reality will disappear like a nightmare, and their wishes for the idealized parent will come true.

Three little girls were placed into foster care after living for months with their mother who passed out night after night, sometimes lying in her own vomit. The oldest, a six-year-old, would hold her mother's head, gently wipe her face, and struggle to get her into bed. The next morning, all the girls would try as hard as they could to not believe it really happened.

A boy struggled hard not to accept disclosures by his older brother and sister that their stepfather had beaten and sexually abused them.

An eight-year-old in foster care for the third time, clung to her mom's promises that the whole family would move to a land of sunshine and endless beaches and everything would be fine.

Before children can grieve, they have to have someone in their lives who validates their experience and helps them muster the courage to feel the reality of their losses. Ideally, this will be a parent, but, if this is not possible, grandparents, aunts, uncles, or foster/adoptive parents can help children to become strong enough to mourn.

Kinship or foster/adoptive parents cannot erase the pain of a child's lost dreams of the original family healing, and any effort to lessen a child's love for lost parents is tantamount to invalidation, typically sparking defiance to new caretakers. Biological parents are not replaceable like a broken toy. New parents win a child's trust by respecting a child's wishes and fantasies about lost parents or relatives, and the memories of affection and nurture a child carries from the past. A child's love for former parents reflects his or her capacity to love again. With support and love, a child can gain a second family, if necessary, and within this family, the child can grieve, build on the past, and grow once again.

TRAUMA THERAPY

Practitioners can help children feel safe enough to remember the hard times and reduce the toxicity of what has happened. Restoring safety from a psychological perspective requires repairing the trust that was broken. To rebuild this trust, means recognizing what happened, sharing unspoken memories, and where possible, fostering remorse and making amends by the individuals responsible. No one can change the past, but within a caring relationship, children can learn how they can become safe and outgrow their nightmares.

Figley (1989) developed the following five-stage model for helping families overcome traumas:

1. Build on the commitment of family members to overcome trauma, including helping family members see they are safe from harm, identifying stressors, normalizing PTSD symptoms, and conveying confidence in change.
2. Frame the problem in terms of memory management, promoting new rules of communication that will allow parents and children to tell their experiences, fostering understanding and acceptance by family members, and overcoming fears of victims being blamed or victims needing to disappear or minimize problems.
3. Reframe therapy as the challenge of telling the story.
4. Develop a healing theory that corrects distorted beliefs, feelings, or perceptions and clarifies insights into what happened.
5. Establish closure and prepare to protect the family from future traumas including learning social skills, establishing family rules that promote safety, creating supports for family members, and developing ways to self-reinforce changes by family members.

Figley's healing theory required that family members find a way to answer five crucial questions: (1) What happened? (2) Why did it happen?

(3) Why did we act as we did during the trauma? (4) Why have we reacted as we have since the trauma? (5) What will be done if this happens again? This process allows children and parents to tell what they did that helped, what they did that did not help, and what kept them from doing what they wanted to do.

A healing story can help children and parents see themselves as heroes with the strength to act. Life and love can go on after trauma. A healing story reframes what led up to traumatic events, including placements or what each child did. Children learn to let go of shaming messages from family members, peers, other adults, and themselves, and to adopt an understanding of why children could not stop the trauma in order to forgive themselves. Instead of looking at behaviors as bad and children as damaged, we can respect what children were pressured to do based on what was happening, each child's capabilities at that age, the risks for the child and family members, and the powerful forces that blocked help for the family.

This often requires breaking down common myths, such as those described in Chapter 4. Cognitive distortions can be challenged by dramatizing a youth's beliefs, for instance, a thirteen-year-old who holds himself or herself responsible for sex abuse at age three can be taken to a nursery school to work with three-year-olds, and later to consider whether those children should be held responsible for an adult's violence. Thirteen-year-olds can also be asked what they would do for their own children if the children were sexually abused.

Traumatized youths may see catastrophes in every event, or search out and obsess over the negative possibilities in every situation. For these children, each cup is not only *half* full, but probably poisoned. Moreover, they may come to believe that they are alone in their misery and helpless to change. Children can be challenged to give up negative assumptions, to remind themselves of what is good in their lives, and to work toward the beliefs that they would like to have about themselves. Challenging and reframing beliefs is a core part of cognitive behavioral approaches (e.g., Lazarus, 1971; Beck, 1976) that have been found to be effective in helping children to overcome depression. Cognitive behavioral therapies for traumatized children and adolescents typically include: normative education on the effects of trauma, sharing experiences of trauma, developing and implementing steps to prevent reoccurrence of traumatic events and relapse of symptoms, and developing ties to significant people (March et al., 1998; Cohen, Mannarino, et al., 2000). The toxicity of trauma is reduced when victims learn that they are not alone and have opportunities to share experiences and coping strategies with other survivors in group therapy (Salloum, Avery, and McClain, 2001).

Cognitive behavioral treatment (CBT) manuals have been developed for work with sexually abused children and *non*offending parents (Deblinger and Heflin, 1996), and also for traumatic bereavement (Cohen, Greenberg, et al., 2001). These CBT models typically involve at least five phases of therapy, the first three typically with a therapist alone and the final stages with a *non*offending, supportive parent:

1. Development of affect-management skills
   - Accepting and normalizing feelings after a traumatic event
   - Identification of feelings or learning to identify feelings
   - Deep-breathing exercises
   - Deep muscle relaxation exercises
   - Thought stopping and replacement of traumatic thoughts with images of safe places and happy times
   - Learning to focus on positives in one's life
   - Focus on safety: who keeps child safe, who child can count on
2. Development of cognitive skills
   - Use of beliefs and thoughts to control how we feel
   - Understanding of how trauma and reminders of trauma lead to feelings
   - Use of thoughts and actions to reduce painful feelings and reactions; take control of how child feels next, and what each person can do to make things better
3. Graduated exposure and cognitive reprocessing
   - Use of stress management and cognitive thoughts to express through narrative what happened, beginning with least disturbing events, first perceptions, and then thoughts and feelings child had during events child described, building to most painful memories with details and pictures
   - Expression of child's fantasies of how he or she would change the past, if possible
   - Recognition that child cannot change past but can change his or her reactions in the present and future
   - Challenging dysfunctional beliefs (e.g., child blaming self for not protecting parent or allowing sex abuse)
   - Normalizing trauma responses
   - Redefinition from blaming and deserving harm to understanding that "bad things happen to good people" (Kushner, 1981)
   - Role-plays with love and support to reframe images and beliefs about traumatic events and reduce toxicity of memories
   - Practicing alternative, more positive responses
   - Preparation for "triggers," reminders of trauma

  - Acceptance of ambivalent feelings about lost people or perpetrators
4. Sharing with parent
   - Preparation of parent to support child, accept his or her memories, and respond with caring and validation
   - Parent skill building for dealing with trauma behaviors
   - Parent affect and cognitive behavioral skill development
   - Developing support for parents with family members, friends, community groups, etc.
   - Assurance to child that memories can be shared without harming parent
5. Mourning and building new relationships
   - Grieving lost people and time: positives and negatives
   - Adding meaning to losses
   - Developing new relationships

Specialized trauma therapies such as eye movement desensitization and reprocessing (EMDR) (Shapiro, 1995, 2001) combine cognitive behavioral approaches with visual and kinesthetic modalities to help an individual reintegrate bodily reactions, beliefs, and perceptions after trauma. Learning how to self-soothe and calm with visual imagery, muscle relaxation, meditations, and developing trust with a therapist helps build the basic security necessary for children to begin to tell their stories and find ways to cope with their nightmares. EMDR and other trauma therapies can help a child feel relaxed and safe enough to put emotional and somatic images in mind while simultaneously promoting language-based cognitions, moving from negative to preferred beliefs about oneself.

A healing story integrates feelings, needs, and beliefs within the context of children's reality. Negatives dominate their self-image. Accepting the positive is hard, because the painful memories loom so large and in many families, children heard messages from parents or relatives, or authorities, that the children were to blame. Research studies (Brewin, Yule, and Williams, 1991, 1993) have found that traumatized individuals do better when shaming is avoided and problems can be externalized rather than blamed primarily on oneself. Traumatized children can forgive themselves when they experience that significant adults acknowledge what they did *without* labeling them as bad or sick. Healing from traumas is also aided when victims find a way to help others as a benefit of their own suffering (Affleck and Tennen, 1996).

Caring adults help children to heal by showing children that they can tell their stories and remain loved. Children are natural storytellers and can use stories to share the goodness and hope they carry inside. Within the embrace of a caring adult, a child's story very naturally unfolds, and with each story, a child learns to voice what had been to frightening to say out loud. Telling the story helps a child to learn how to use words, to understand what happened, to consider alternatives, and to develop a new story of empowerment.

Use of Self

The therapeutic relationship is more important than any methodology and accounts for half of any treatment effects (Schore, 2003b). Therapists begin to help families overcome traumas by showing that they can hear and share the pain of the past. Trauma therapy means making it safe enough to get real. This is not therapy for the timid. Trauma therapy means building a relationship quickly and working with intensity, eye to eye, witnessing bottled-up pain, fear, and anger. We have to recognize our own limits,[1] protect ourselves from taking on responsibility for what has happened, ensure that family members and authorities take responsibility for safety, and accept that traumatized children and their families carry intense pain that is not going to magically go away overnight. Our challenge is to mobilize key family members, or if necessary, substitute parents, who can stay with a child, to talk, feel, and experience again over a lifetime. Most of the work will be done over months and years outside a therapist's office. We may be only able to help a child and a parent move through one or a few of the challenges along their journey to build or rebuild attachments. In some cases, we may be able to provide periodic interventions over the years, maintaining ourselves as a resource available over time and carrying with us an understanding of the child and the family's history.

Trauma therapy requires building a relationship based on respect, honesty, and courage. I ask open-ended questions, inquiring about what happened, not to obsess over the past, but to learn what has helped family members to survive and cope and to show family members that I am not afraid to help them deal with unresolved problems. I want to learn from each child, parent, and grandparent about the richness in their family, the Sunday dinners Grandma used to make, fishing with Uncle Bill, Mom's blueberry pancakes, and how Dad made up bedtime stories for the children. I want to hear how they had fun. I want to show family members that I respect the love that was real and the love they wanted to show during good times and bad. My questions and comments are always intended to respect the elements of a family and to find ways to repair splitting messages with connections and commitment.[2] My goal is to show that I can listen to each family member and that I will not shame them or run away when they share their experience.

Speaking directly about traumas shows children and parents that we are not afraid to hear what happened, and that we have confidence that they have the capacity to heal and grow. It is important not to treat traumatized individuals as too fragile to change. Traumatized children may have literally "dodged bullets," and are not likely to be afraid of a therapist (Benamati, Personal Communication, 2001). Fearing to work on overcoming traumas reinforces beliefs that it is too frightening or dangerous to talk about what happened. This does not mean pushing children or parents to tell all the details of what happened, but rather, to show that we can recognize their pain, how much it hurts, and can listen when they are ready.

When a child has been placed away from home, I often begin a session by noting the caring and concern I have seen or heard about. I want to accentuate the little signs of caring, a mother's outstretched arm, a father's message to a child to not blame himself or herself, a grandfather driving a hundred miles to see a child. I will often share my belief that placement is similar to breaking a child's heart, as if the child was ripped apart inside. The child is pulled to be with family and at the same time needing to be away. And, when parents and grandparents (or other relatives) care about a child, the feeling of being ripped or torn is not just felt by the child, but by other family members as well.[3] I want to engage the family from the first session to work with respect for love and losses, and to begin the grief process necessary for healing.

I have found that the fastest and most effective way to help families grieve and overcome traumas is to begin with a careful assessment of children alone, focusing on their affection, wishes, fears, and ties to family members. An attachment-focused assessment of children[4] guides subsequent assessments and permanency work with parents, relatives, other practitioners, and community leaders. Careful assessments of attachment lead to service plans based on family strengths and what is needed to rebuild children's trust in parents, and to succeed in their communities. Careful assessments save months, and often years, of foster family, residential treatment, and psychiatric hospital care by helping family members, practitioners, and case managers begin vital work from the first sessions and keep services focused on necessary grief and trauma work. Delaying assessments often leads children (and parents) to view shelters, crisis residences, or psychiatric hospitals as punishments, "time-outs," or worse, as "lock-ups." In contrast, focusing from the beginning of therapy on assessing and building attachments shows children and parents that we will work on healing broken bonds and the breakdown of trust that is often hidden by a child's or a parent's dangerous behaviors leading to placements.

Courage

Children can be challenged to be as brave as the special adults in their lives and their heroes from sports, arts, or special characters from movies or books. A child's strength can be fostered with support, training, practice, and permission to take risks. We can elicit a child's courage by helping parents and caretakers to show they can acknowledge *their own* fears, *their own* mistakes, and press on. When this happens, I have seen sullen, agitated, hyper, or "shut down" children burst forth with memories after months or years of silence. Parents, grandparents, and children cry and hug. It is an intoxicating feeling, almost magical. The "magic" comes from the courage of parents and caring adults. When parents and other caring adults acknowledge what they did, apologize, and stop blaming, minimizing, or denying problems, even sullen or "shut down" children will share their memories. Families begin to grieve and heal.

"I am so sorry," sobbed a grandmother. She pulled her twelve-year-old granddaughter close to her as her two grandsons watched. "I should have listened to you when you tried to tell me about the beatings."

"It was my fault," Rena, her granddaughter, insisted. When Rena's grandparents were confronted by CPS with bruises on the children, they had initially demanded of Rena, "Why didn't you tell us?" Deep inside, Rena had always accepted responsibility for the beatings. She was the oldest child and always had been asked by her mother and others to watch over her siblings.

"I was bad," Rena stammered.

"Don't say that," her grandmother replied. "No one should ever have gone through what you did."

The children's grandfather moved over to sit between his two grandsons. With a sigh, he put his arms gently around each of the boys, then turned to look at each one. "I'm never going to let this happen, again. I'm sorry. Do you hear me?"

"Look at me," he said looking at each boy's eyes. "You can tell me. Grandma and I are never going to let you be hurt again."

Rena cried softly in her grandmother's arms, sobbing and shuddering, starting to speak, then, just as quickly, lowering her head, muffling her own voice. Robbie, her younger brother, a rambunctious six-year-old, who never talked about his mother, or the children's' experiences, suddenly leaned forward, his mouth open and unstoppable.

"Mom put duct tape on our mouths . . . Aunt Grace listened at the door to keep us from talking . . ." He began to tell his story, safe for the first time in his life, with his grandfather's arms around his shoulders and his grandmother gently crying. Robbie believed that someone was finally listening, someone who would make things better.

We can help families elicit courage by remembering and sharing stories of how Grandma was able to feed the family during the Great Depression, how Grandpa helped pilots in World War II, or how Mom stopped the beatings. We can also use activities, such as trust exercises and ropes courses, or fantasy exercises to help parents rebuild trust and courage. Parents can be asked to help children deal with challenges such as balancing on a beam, hiking up a mountain, crossing a river, or navigating across a city to a museum using the subway. Summoning the courage to tell the story is often the most difficult and most important trust exercise.

Retelling a Story of Trauma

I have found young children can be engaged to use simple arts and crafts to begin to share their experiences. Early elementary-age children often enjoy making simple stand-up figures of important people in their lives, including themselves. I ask children to draw themselves, then family members, and other important people in their lives. Together, we cut out the figures, then tape them to folded strips of cardboard, about two inches wide and just long enough (usually about six inches) to support the child's figures. The folded cardboard holds up the figures, and within a few minutes, we can create an assemblage representing the most important people in a child's life.

In assessments, I ask a child to enact family stories about day-to-day life from dealing with a hungry child to going to bed. If a child has shared information on what he or she experienced in the past or fears of the future, these can be enacted as well. In assessments, I allow the child to generate material, working to avoid any specific prompts and instead following the child's lead and using the child's words so that the story remains based on his or her perceptions. For assessments, I often continue this work by engaging children to make up other stories using family puzzle people or family doll sets[5] and with more traditional projective evaluations such as the Roberts Apperception Test (Roberts, 1986) and Projective Storytelling Cards (Casebeer Art Productions, 1989). Using different materials helps to assess how obsessed a child is with a traumatic memory, and each medium generates possibilities for the child to present different solutions that can be incorporated into service planning.

I later check out with parents how they would handle the same situations presented by their children. I want to bring parents into therapy sessions to answer children's concerns and confirm how their new homes will be different. Therapists can help children understand safety and permanency plans with parents who have made significant changes to protect children, or, if necessary, with their new parents. In play therapy, therapists can work with children to enact changes in stories by bringing in figures representing positive, protective adults to demonstrate how they will protect children. In this way, children rewrite painful moments in play and often generate solutions that protective adults can utilize to rebuild trust.

As part of trauma therapy, children should practice safety plans (see Chapter 5) with their parents and other protectors. Parents can dramatize how they would protect children from abusers of the past. This can be done in puppet shows with figures representing family members, with family dolls, with videotaped movies created by the child and therapist, or in role-plays with therapists. Hughes (1997) will leave the room, put on a wig or some other piece of clothing to signify that he is pretending to be the child's abuser, and return to repeat some of the toxic messages a child received (e.g., "You're bad!"). The child's parent can then help the child to counter these messages and to resist overtures by the therapist enacting a former abusive parent to join in blaming the child. Parents in role-plays can physically embrace children and enact warding off the former abuser. With children in adoptive families, the child can also be urged by the therapist in these role plays to not trust a new parent or to expect to be sent back to the old parent no matter what. This helps to make overt a child's latent fears and provides opportunities for family members to address safety issues directly.

Prior to enactments, a child needs to receive validation for natural feelings of affection, loyalty, fears, and anger. These enactments build upon the respect and safety a therapist builds with family members and authorities who realistically can and will keep a child safe. The therapist can then help children to enact the story of what happened, what was missing in their lives, what they thought, and what they said.

Healing Rituals

Cultures around the world have developed rituals to help people overcome hardships. Perry (cited by Tinker and Wilson, 1999) found that healing rituals typically included four components: (1) an interactional process that may involve a dyad, part of a community, or the entire community; (2) belief systems; (3) a narrative account; and (4) patterned, repetitive stimulation. Perry believed that the patterned repetitive movements and stimulation (auditory, touch, motion, visual, and auditory) may open up primitive areas of the brain and allow for new learning.

When a family grieves, it is common for friends and relatives to reunite, to remember the deceased, and to support and strengthen bonds to the living. Jewish families sit shivah, a process that requires stopping work, with visits by family and friends, sharing memories (good and bad), prayer, and a reaffirmation of faith. Funeral services commonly include different people sharing stories about the deceased. Burial rituals and family gatherings reaffirm support and family connections, reaffirmed at anniversaries of deaths, with unveilings of headstones, and with visits to cemeteries.

Isolation and cut-offs weaken individuals. Activities that bring people together strengthen. Rituals can affirm unity and provide the support we need to grieve and rebuild. Holidays and rituals also reaffirm legacies passed on through generations by family members and heroes from a family's ethnic group. Autobiographies and legends teach new generations the power of courage and transformation, as well as critical skills and the possibility of redemption.

Parents help children to grieve and heal by incorporating daily rituals that involve touch, movement, and repetition. When children and parents engage together in chanting, drumming, meditation, dancing, singing, or prayer, each person can feel part of a family or a larger community. We feel ourselves united and thus stronger.

Parents and caring adults can create healing rituals by marking out time as special. Turning off the phone, shutting the door, getting down on the floor, kneeling in prayer, cuddling in bed, or singing the special good-night song that speaks of courage and safety or a favorite bedtime rhyme. I have always liked "Tender Shepherd" from the musical *Peter Pan*. Mother Goose rhymes can be used to elicit hope (e.g., "Twinkle, twinkle, little star" or "Star light, star bright, first star, I see tonight, wish I may, wish I might, have the wish, I wish tonight"), which can be sung with a sweet melody. Other simple tunes can be made into personalized songs chronicling a child's growth in the family (e.g., "Oh, once I had a little boy, as smart as he could be,[6] at three years old, he counted to ten, and learned his ABCs . . .") and each month (or year) add some key events in the child's life (e.g., "At five, he learned to ride a bike, and we traveled across the sea"). Rhymes can be very simple. Singing the song after a few favorite stories makes a beautiful bedtime ritual.

A colleague and adoptive parent (Minnear, Personal Communication, 2001) told me that not a week went by when her ten-year-old son was not trying to figure everything out about his adoption as an infant. This is a natural process. My colleague helped her son become able to ask questions and understand by beginning to create a bedtime story about what she and her husband did to bring him to this country, how he came, and what happened month by month, building the story of his life. Although it may have seemed strange to some, for an adoptive parent of an infant to begin telling his life story, this process enabled both parent and child to be able to say the important words from the beginning of their union.

Holding is very important during these rituals, being careful to keep touch to a level that a child can handle and differentiating safe, positive touch from a child's past experiences of abuse. If a child has been sexually abused by a man, it may be necessary for a father to have a woman or other children present during these rituals. Similarly, if a child has been abused by a woman, it may be necessary to have a man present. Over time and with implementation of safety plans and trauma therapy, a child will become more secure with both sexes.

Rituals mark dates of important events and show a child that the family remembers what happened, can still feel the joy, the sadness, and the pain involved, and that the family will go on together. Celebrations of important events show a child that everyone in the family has a past and a future honored by family members. Important events to remember include: dates of return from placement to a biological family, dates of arrival into an adoptive home, dates of legalization of adoption, and the holidays celebrated by families, including holidays honored by an adopted child's biological family. Celebrating customs of a child's native culture with food, music, and communal observances is very important in *inter*cultural adoptions. My agency hosts a Korean Culture Camp every summer for children, siblings, and parents of children adopted from Korea.[7]

Families can build creatively on a child's primary issues by creating unique holidays that celebrate a child's mastery of major challenge (e.g., "Bike Day" to honor a child who learned with difficulty to ride a bike). Earning a certificate for swimming may be a very special event for a ten-year-old who had never learned to swim. For another child, earning a first "A" in spelling could be a time for mom or dad to take the whole family for a special treat, dinner out, or a trip to the bookstore to buy a paperback book in honor of the child.

Therapeutically, we can build on metaphors and meaning with rituals that mark overcoming traumas. For a frightened six-year-old, this may mean learning to sleep alone. For a defiant teenager, learning to stay calm with a frustrated teacher or an angry parent may be a major accomplishment. By honoring achievements, we can help youths to own problems and develop solutions[8] to long-standing problems. Celebrations accentuate successful resolutions, reinforcing a child's courage to take risks and try out more adaptive behavior.

Books and Movies

We can promote mastery of trauma by reading to children and encouraging older children to read books about children similar to themselves who master difficult situations. Children have always used play and stories to master their worst fears and often identify with characters grappling with their own issues, including abandonment, loss, grief, nightmares, or day-to-day challenges such as going to the doctor or the dentist.

Strong characters model transformation and courage. I try to find books and characters that tie into a child's areas for interest. For children who are interested in nature and animals, books to consider include Margaret Wise Brown's (1991) *The Runaway Bunny,* and for older elementary school children, G. Paulson's (1987) *Hatchet* (a boy who crash lands and must learn to survive in the wilderness). For adolescents grappling with their parents strengths and mistakes, Anna Quindlen's (1991) *Object Lessons* may be useful. For children who like fantasy, the Harry Potter series (Rowling, 1997) are wonderful adventures about a youth overcoming loss of his parents and neglect by his relatives that teaches children about friends helping friends, the importance of consistent adults as teachers and mentors, summoning courage to face terror, and a strong female hero (Hermione Granger).

Heroes from books model how to cope, instill values, and foster learning. Stories of children as heroes often open up possibilities for children of *re*doing attachment experiences. I especially like Maurice Sendak's *Where the Wild Things Are* (1963), about a defiant child's dream that incorporates becoming like monsters, starting a voyage (courage), and returning to the smell of a hot meal prepared by his mother (reunification). Mercer Mayer's *There's a Nightmare in My Closet* (1968) is a great example of a child mastering his fears. *Love You Forever* (Munsch, 1986) captures a mother's devotion to her son. *Horton Hatches the Egg* by Dr. Seuss (1940) teaches the meaning of parenting. *Goodnight Moon* (Brown, 1947) uses attention to details in a ritualized manner to create a feeling of safety at bedtime. *The Little Engine That Could* (Piper, 1961) models determination. *An Elephant in the Living Room* (Hastings and Typpo, 1994) demonstrates overcoming secrecy supporting addictions. *Alexander and the Terrible, Horrible, No Good, Very Bad Day* (Viorst, 1972) is an engaging story of frustration with the lesson that some days are just like that. For much more secure children,[9] *Holes* (Sachar, 1999), and for adolescents, Maya Angelou's *I Know Why the Caged Bird Sings* (1969) or *A Child Named It* (Peltzer, 1995) and its sequel, *A Man Named Dave* (Peltzer, 1999), can be helpful to expand a youth's understanding and perspective of how people survive and grow despite neglect, violence, or abuse.

Youths who like science fiction can find core principles of trauma therapy in the original *Star Wars* movies in which the orphaned hero, Luke, is guided by his mentor, Obi-Wan, to calm, center himself, develop his skills, and elicit his powers to help others. Obi-Wan's messages can be used with *Star Wars* fans as a trance-like induction to invoke courage and strength and to help youths see themselves as heroes who can utilize positive energy and guidance to succeed. Obi-Wan's intonation of "Luke" before he destroys the Death Star elicits an image of being a hero and not alone. "Use the Force," reminds youths of the positive energy around them. "Stretch out your feelings," is an antidote for the constriction of trauma and opens up perception and solutions. Luke's mentors teach him to give up his assumptions, experience how hatred leads to the "Dark Side," respect his fears, master his angry impulses, and learn to trust again. Yoda's instruction to "Do or do not. There is no *try*," models the conviction and commitment hero needs to prevail and a readiness to accept failures as part of life.

Star Wars is just one example of books and movies that teach different ways of coping with trauma and encourage youths to expand their perspectives, to look for guidance from mentors, and to practice step by step to develop skills and succeed. Youths can also model courage from real heroes including pioneers such as Daniel Boone, leaders of the underground railroad (e.g., Harriet Tubman), war heroes from a child's family or community, famous presidents who wrote about courage (e.g., John F. Kennedy), or medical researchers who saved millions of lives (e.g., Jonas Salk).

Storytelling As a Model for Healing

Books about heroes offer children solutions for resolving their own crises. Fantasy questions can empower children to share how they feel about significant adults in their lives, eliciting critical information about who they can trust, who they fear, and unresolved traumas regarding people in their lives. I ask children about their favorite books and movies and invite them to utilize their favorite characters in fantasy exercises utilizing their favorite formats for storytelling, picture books, comic books (especially for *non*-readers), adventure stories, music, movies, TV talk shows, radio interviews, etc. The formats can be used to empower children. For example, interviewing a child on a tape recorder after a dramatic introduction of the child and an invitation for the child to use this "radio interview" to share his or her stories with the radio audience.

With collectors of Pokémon cards, I invite children to make up brief stories about what they would do in different situations if they had the power of their favorite character (e.g., Charizard, with his 120 HP of power. "What would you do if you saw your mother (father, grandmother, etc.) coming down the hall and you had the power of Charizard?") Similarly, for a Harry Potter fan, I may ask, "What would you do if you had the magic of Harry Potter and there was a knock on the door and it was your uncle?"

I invited a sixteen-year-old fan of *The Jerry Springer Show* to make up a show in which she had Jerry and his bodyguard/bouncer ask the questions she was afraid to ask. She was able to identify the resources Jerry used to give him courage, the big microphone, the bodyguard, selection of who was on stage, walking in the audience at a distance, and could then develop a format for her own show that would give her support and protection. She placed her mother, father, and a supportive relative on her imaginary stage and had herself and Jerry walking through the audience holding their big microphones and asking the girl's mother what led up to her kicking her father out, obsession with a female friend, and neglect of her daughter.

Storytelling has been used in psychotherapy to help children resolve seemingly insurmountable problems and to change repetitive trauma stories in which people are hurt (or lose) into stories in which people can succeed. Richard Gardner (1975, 1986, 1993) developed the mutual storytelling technique and pioneered use of storytelling and storytelling games in assessments and psychotherapy. Gardner elicited stories from children and helped them to develop positive endings. I adapted this approach (Kagan, 1982, 1986, 2000) to help children create stories and games that reflected how they were coping with family crises, to explore use of different beliefs, perspectives, and actions leading to different outcomes in their stories and games, and to challenge children to make choices in their lives that could help rebuild connections.

Together with the child, we can create a story tied to the metaphor and explore different ways to master the dilemma expressed in a metaphor. A child's affect, actions, and perspectives are matched to a character in a story. Stories can address the challenge of mastering problems and resolving a child's impasse at a developmental stage (e.g., feeling shame versus developing autonomy). Using a typical framework (beginning, middle, and end), we can help a child develop his or her own resources for managing overwhelming and terrifying situations and resolving unmet needs for support, safety, and hope. Storytelling provides a creative modality for opening up possibilities and developing solutions, a powerful means of combating the constriction and disempowerment after traumas.

Young children are easily engaged to make up stories when this is presented as a special and fun activity. It is sometimes more productive to invite them to develop stories with animals. For example, "If I was a (pick a favorite animal), and my parents were (pick animals) and my grandparents were (pick animals), this would be my story." The child can be helped to develop a beginning, a middle, and an end, with a lesson for other children. With older children, I like to build on any interest in fantasy or science fiction in developing stories.

I have worked with children to create "My Game," their own personal game (Kagan, 1986, 2000), representing their primary conflicts and goals (e.g., to move into an adoptive family). The task of creating a child's own game can be used to develop beliefs and feelings with predictable events in a child's life leading to different outcomes along the path of the game. Games can be used to practice cause and effect thinking with children who have learned to expect chaotic and disorganized relationships and who operate with little sense of consequences. Belief and feeling cards provide a wonderful way to introduce and practice more constructive beliefs and affect regulation (see Chapter 11).

Narrative therapies deconstruct problem stories of victimization, label and externalize problem narratives, expand preferred stories of strength, and empower individuals to share solutions with others (White, 1989, 1995;

White and Epston, 1990; Freedman and Combs, 1996). "[T]he narrative metaphor proposes that persons live their lives by stories—that these stories are shaping of life, and that they have real, not imagined, effects—and that these stories provide the structure of life" (White, 1993, p. 36). White and Epston (1990) showed how stories of individuals, families, communities, tribes, etc., can be compared to an archeological dig. Roberts (1994) outlined models for helping clients to "reauthor" stories that have been told and have not been working, to overcome restrictions imposed by intertwined stories, secrets, rigid boundaries, brevity, and interruptions, to "coher" fragmented events and information into integrated stories, and to invent new stories involving fantasy, animals, fictional characters, and future scenarios in order to overcome problems. Narrative therapies work with stories, beliefs, and key words to generate more constructive meanings and potential solutions.

LIFE STORIES: FROM SHAME TO STRENGTH

Life stories have been used in foster care and older-child adoptions for several decades (Fahlberg, 1991; Jewett, 1978; Kagan, 1996; Kliman and Zelman, 1996; MacKinnon, 1998; Wheeler, 1978) as a way of helping children to grieve losses, to remember their past, and to share their experiences with adoptive families. Kliman (1996) found that life story work can significantly decrease disruptions in foster family care. If children are asked to write their life stories, many will initially balk or outright refuse. For many children in placement or at risk of placement, life-story work appears dangerous. They fear opening up painful memories, losing control, generating problems in their homes, or violate their loyalty to family members. A child may simply not be safe or secure enough yet to do this work; and practitioners may find it necessary to continue work on basic safety issues (see Chapter 5).

Practitioners may be tempted to write a life story for a child; however, the child will likely see it as invalid, since the practitioner could never fully capture the child's real experiences or perspective. Many life stories written by therapists have ended up being sparse accounts dominated by a child's losses and tragedies in the family with little explanation of what led up to placements and what was done by family members to try to make things better. In other cases, life stories have glossed over traumatic events or failures by parents to protect or care for children.

Children in many cases have learned to see their life stories as bad or shameful. Many children have heard messages from family members or even foster parents that they were placed because they were bad or evil, and not allowed to return because they did not change. Children with these messages and beliefs may rip up their life stories or "accidentally" lose them, with a wish to start all over again and to deny any disclosures of past abuse or neglect.

In life-story work, as in other trauma therapies, the therapist, family, and authorities must first help children overcome barriers to telling the story. Threats to enforce secrets and mandates to remain loyal to mandates of an abusive or neglectful parent need to be identified and safety plans implemented (see Chapter 5) by judges, police, CPS, legal guardians, CASA workers, teachers, etc. Therapists can help children to overcome typical barriers to storytelling, including

- thinking only in the present,
- needing to do everything alone,
- working only with words,
- restricting life-story work to an office,
- avoiding relatives in keeping with mandates from parents or others,
- sharing disclosures with violent parents,
- limiting a child's hopes to one parent,
- minimizing positive memories,
- blaming by family members,
- labeling the child as bad or damaged,
- beliefs that children or parents must be perfect, or
- fears of upsetting a new parent by honoring love for another parent.

With support from caring adults and authorities, therapists can help a child (and parents) to master the challenges (traumatic events) in a story by recognizing skills in coping and eliciting a child's creativity and natural drive to heal. Life stories can illuminate protective factors in an individual's ecosystem (Waller, 2001). By working with a caring adult, problem-centered narratives can be transformed into openings for building attachments.

Retelling the Story with a Past and a Future

Traumatized children typically think and act in terms of only the present. From a neuropsychological perspective, they appear to rely on "implicit memory" functions carried out by the amygdala, limbic, and basil ganglia systems. The ability to tie memories to self-experience and utilize a perspective of time is typically developed in a child's preschool years, beginning after age eighteen months (Siegel, 2003). Children who experience chronic traumas in their first years appear often to lack the capacity to work with an understanding of themselves functioning in time. Children who experience traumas after their preschool years may have learned that the past is too hard or dangerous to face. Parental injunctions, threats, and observations of distress in parents, siblings, and relatives can also teach children that painful events cannot be put into words. The child and family go on as if the problems and traumas did not exist. Without a past, there is no future; without a future, there is no hope. Time simply revolves, around and around, without any meaningful change.

Children learn to value themselves by fostering images, feelings, and beliefs about how important people in their lives have valued them. Stories of how children were helped in the past by family members, relatives, friends, teachers, clergy, and other caring adults rekindle warm feelings and help children to feel good about themselves. Remembering who helped in the past also helps children recognize who could help in the future and how they can keep themselves safe with the help of people who care.

Life stories can help build a strong sense of family and cultural heritage including legends, philosophies of life, religious beliefs, insights, cooking, home building, community practices, historical events, and traditional skills (cooking, crafts, industry, etc.). The richness of a child's heritage can help replace the fears and shame a child may have learned to associate with people in his or her nuclear family, ethnic group (Azibo, 1989), or neighborhood. Malgady, Rogle, and Costantino (1990), for example, used stories of Puerto Rican heroes and heroines to connect adolescents with successful role models and bridge generational and bicultural gaps. As part of work with the Real Life Heroes model, practitioners are encouraged to develop a library of storybooks including biographies and autobiographies of positive role models representing each of the ethnic groups served by a clinic or agency.

Beliefs centered on feelings of helplessness and weakness can be replaced by perceptions of how real people from a child's own family coped with wars, famine, emigration, slavery, and other hardships in order to build better lives for themselves, their children, and their children's children. Stories about family members including grandparents, great-grandparents, aunts, and uncles succeeding are especially important for children and parents who have experienced disruptions, losses of family members, or traumas. In this way, the past can be opened up from the perspective of strengths and wisdom shown by extended-family members, even if a child's parents have abandoned or abused the child and made no significant changes to help the child recover.

Children can be encouraged to interview relatives with guidance from practitioners, and, of course, avoiding contact with any violent family members. Children can be helped to develop and practice interview questions that pull out strengths, for example:

- What do relatives remember about the child as an infant?
- What did they like?
- What did they wish for the child as he or she grew up?
- Who helped care for the child?
- What did they like best about the child at different ages?
- How did the child help others?
- What were some of the hard times the relatives faced and how did they overcome them?
- What can they teach the child about lessons in their lives, wisdom and strengths from their ethnic heritage?
- What do they remember about the child's parents: their lives, their successes, what was important to them, and what happened?

Practitioners can also practice with children how to handle any anticipated injunctions, rejections, or destructive messages based on what relatives have said in the past.

Use of tools that provide a sense of power and detachment can be helpful (e.g., cameras, video, e-mail). Collecting photographs and organizing them into a life-story album with captions can be very helpful. These can include photographs of the child and the person interviewed, with captions written by the child. Use of special pens or markers, colored or high-quality cotton paper, or other special tools can be useful to help engage and empower children.

Life stories can be developed to highlight both the reality of losses and stories of strength, "preferred stories" from a narrative therapy model (White and Epston, 1990). The life-story approach helps children to capture stories of kindness, caring, and courage. Hard times can be understood within the broader context of how extended-family members (or other caring adults) acted to overcome adversity. And, this learning can then be used to open new perspectives on the future. Children learn how each of us makes a difference in our lives and in the lives of our families and communities. In this way, life-story work can help children develop connections, confidence, and self-respect.

Transition Stories

For children in foster or adoptive homes, life stories chronicle difficult transitions including expectations, fears, and what happened from the first moments a foster/adoptive parent learned of a child. What attracted them to the child? What they learned? What they liked best? How the child tested their love and commitment.

Life stories also provide a structured means for foster and adoptive parents to honor biological family members by documenting and preserving customs from their family. Family rituals, celebrations, custom, hairstyles, and personal histories of family members can be included when available from records or, optimally, through discussions with biological parents or relatives. Foster parents can help children develop their story of transition from the crisis of placement, back to their biological families or into adoptive homes. The child's parents can contribute information on the past and changes made to bring the child back home and overcome traumas. Whether a child is returning home or moving toward adoption, his or her parents (biological or adoptive) can use life stories to provide a message of commitment into the future.

It is important that foster parents and practitioners do not give children constricted or problem-laden messages. By working on a life story with foster parents, practitioners can hear and confront negative messages. I have heard foster parents tell children that their behavior problems would prevent their biological parents from reuniting with them, thus reinforcing blaming of children who were already ambivalent about returning to their parents because of past addictions and neglect. In some residential treatment programs, children have been blocked from visits with parents because of the children's disruptive behaviors or lack of progress in the institution. In either case, children are given both power and responsibility for work on reuniting that needs to be shared by parents, relatives, children, and authorities. Necessary work on facing family problems becomes diverted by focusing on the children's behaviors, and foster parents or child care workers may take over parents' responsibilities to guide and discipline children. It is not surprising in these situations to see children begin to lash out at their substitute parent-figures with all the rage they cannot share with their biological parents.

Life stories also provide a way to chronicle back-up plans for where children could live if parents are unable to bring them home. Practitioners can check on whether children are only hearing one possible permanency plan, for instance, return to one parent, with the other parent or relatives not considered as possible resources.

Chronicling a life story with the help of foster/adoptive parents provides a way for practitioners to help foster or adoptive parents to respect and manage children's love for biological parents and predictable patterns of testing. Children need permission to feel attracted to both families, and both biological and foster parents may need help in managing predictable periods of defiance as children swing from love to defiance, in an effort to manage feelings of conflict.

If a parent decides to surrender rights, the parent may be willing to provide photographs and special mementos to help the child remember his or her former home. It is helpful to complete life stories as much as possible before legalization of an adoption when records are sealed, as required by law in most states. Children may be able to keep their own life stories, but documents listing information about parents will become unavailable. Where possible, open adoptions provide opportunities for children to continue to receive support from biological parents and to be able to ask questions about their heritage.

I have encouraged parents considering "surrender" of a child to write out, tape record, or videotape a message to their child about their life, their struggles, their values, and what they wish for the child. This can be a message to the child at different age levels, forming a partial legacy, extending positive lessons and values into the future, and helping to keep the memory of the parent alive for a child. It is also important to help biological parents understand that their actions leading up to reuniting or a "surrender" shape how their child will remember them into the future. Parents who rage at authorities, castigate their children, or threaten to hurt themselves or others are writing a frightening life story to pass on to their children.

I ask parents what they would like to say to their child at the child's present age, as a young teenager, and as an eighteen-year-old. It helps for biological parents struggling with a decision to make an adoption plan to meet with prospective adoptive parents and find out how the biological parents' memory would be respected and maintained as the child grows up. Birth parents can also be encouraged to list themselves in adoption reunion registries (Fischer, 2002).

Detoxifying the Story

Trauma therapy means detoxifying the painful events in a child's life, so that a child can recall the story, without becoming overwhelmed by terror. In many cases, caseworkers, practitioners, parents (birth or adoptive), or relatives know at least parts of what a child experienced in his or her earliest years, but may be afraid of upsetting a child, or even disrupting a placement, by telling what they know. Children in adoptive families may grow up feeling that something is missing in their understanding of what happened, or that they are simply *crazy* because of how they react emotionally and physically at times and cannot understand why. For example, a teenage boy in an adoptive family may feel his fists clench, his heart pound, and an impulse to slam a youth he hears cursing a girl or a mother with words, gestures, or angry tones, not knowing that these were the same words, gestures, and rage he experienced as a very young child.

Children need to learn what happened in their lives, even the hard stuff (e.g., sexual abuse, violence, deaths, missing siblings, etc.). Most adopted children will want to know what their parents were like, how they felt when they gave up their parental rights, and how they may be feeling, even now, about their children. These are healthy responses to the losses a child has experienced. In contrast, by age ten, not asking is a warning sign with a child who has experienced significant losses or other traumas.

Parents and practitioners teach children to face painful events and to move on in their lives. It is important to help parents to avoid minimizing past traumas. The key is honesty and timing, sharing messages with children in a way that the children can manage safely at each developmental stage. By age eight, children need to hear difficult information (van Gulden and Bartels-Rabb, 1995) that they might not be aware of from their early childhood experiences. Practitioners and parents model strength by sharing what happened in a calm and honest manner, without over- or underemphasizing what happened. Details should be shared in a way that children can handle at their level of development without overloading them with negatives or frightening imagery. In general, the old axiom applies, "If they are old enough to ask, they are old enough to know" (van Gulden and Bartels-Rabb, 1995). By age twelve, children should have heard a comprehensive account, including major facts and avoiding either exaggerations or minimization. Keeping secrets usually leads children to develop greater fears, to believe that whatever happened is too hard for their parents or themselves to face, and to lose trust in parents and other family members to manage adversity. Worse, youths may come to see caring adults as deceiving them.

Young children can be given simple answers. This can begin with their adoption story (e.g., "Your birth parents couldn't raise you and decided you would be better off in another family. So, you have two sets of parents, your birth mommy and daddy, who gave you life, and your 'forever and ever' parents, your mom and me (dad) who are taking care of you.") All children want to find out how they came to be. For adopted children, this is a critical question that goes beyond common childhood books about how babies are made. Starting an adoption message in the earliest years normalizes children's experiences and helps them prepare them for later questions from peers and adults about their "real" parents, etc. When children have experienced painful events, it helps to include general references to how "things were hard," for children and birth parents before they were moved to another home on a temporary or permanent basis. This helps open the door for more complete information when children get older (Blechner, 2002), including learning about birth parents who were neglectful, incarcerated for assaults or murder, mentally ill, retarded, addicted, or who kept other siblings. Here again, the parent leads the way, by finding out, recording, and accessing help in dealing with what happened in a child's life, even before moving into the new family.

The emphasis in telling a child about traumatic events should be on how adults made choices and that the child remains inherently "good" (van Gulden and Bartels-Rabb, 1995). Diminishing the pain of past events does not help a child. Parents can share how remembering or learning about what happened makes them want to cry or scream, but it is still important to talk about it. This helps a child to feel that he or she is not alone anymore and how important the child is to the parents. Parents can emphasize how they wish they could have been present when terrible things happened so they could have protected the child (Hughes, 1998b; Becker-Weidman, 2002).

When talking to children about the hard things in their lives, it helps for parents to work out in advance what they want to say.[10] Parents may even want to practice messages with practitioners and set up the best way to ensure that children listen. Parents can choose how, when, and where to give these messages. Blechner recommends (2002) a quiet time, preferably with a dessert, the phone unplugged, and no one else around. Driving in a car provides privacy and helps avoid any fears about others listening in or seeing a child's reaction. It is important for parents to set the stage for these communications by sitting close enough to touch and support a child and using eye contact, unless this is contrary to a family's traditions. Parents can introduce these discussions by saying that they have something important to share. When parents have held on to secrets for many years, it helps to preface these talks by honestly saying how they had not been ready and may not have understood that the child was old enough to hear about these things until this time.

Parents can be coached by practitioners to anticipate and prepare for their child's reactions including becoming angry, slamming doors, crying, etc. Practitioners can help parents see how this typically leads to the child coming back and asking for more information. Parents may want to give children the choice of hearing about what the parent knows at this time, or later (Blechner, 2002). Either way, parents show their children that they are able and willing to help them deal with what happened, the good and the bad.

Adding Protectors and Time

A child who has experienced years of inconsistent care and lack of protection cannot quickly learn to trust a parent to do the right thing. In families with addictions to alcohol, drugs, or dangerous behaviors, promises do not offer protection, and in fact, can be dangerous. Promises of Disney World and trips to toy stores, or the new bike for your birthday may have been dashed when Dad or Mom passed out, flew into a rage, or disappeared on the promised day and then lamely apologized "Next year!" By age twelve, many children have given up on their parents and turned to peers for their primary support. Yet, the wish for parents to take responsibility remains.

"No adults can help," one sixteen-year old told me; and yet, her words included an implicit challenge and appeal. Would her adoptive father, caring but detached and long divorced from her adoptive mother, actually provide her with a home, his love, and the firm guidance she needed?

"I want to be innocent again," a seventeen-year-old homeless girl confided to me, three years after running away into a world of alcohol and drugs to escape her stepfather's abuse and her mother's neglect. "I feel like I never got to be a child."

If neglect and/or violence has gone on for some time in the family, a parent may change but it will take a concerted effort of the parent and significant others to prove to the child that the change will last. Healing means finding powerful people in his or her life (parents, teachers, mentors, foster parents, CPS workers, group care workers, family therapists, psychologists, psychiatrists, law guardians, and judges) who can make it safe enough to tell the child's story. New and more adaptive meanings are constructed *with* other people (Roth and Chasin, 1994). A traumatized child needs to rework his or her life story and can only do this with the help of real people who care enough and who are strong enough to face the nightmares of a child's past and continue on to help a child build a new future.

This takes time, often longer than the length of time the child experienced living with a parent who periodically became violent or abandoned the child. If children experienced violence between a parent and his or her paramour for two years, getting past the next two years without a violent incident will be crucial. Children have a built-in time clock. In substance abusing families, I always ask what was the longest Mom or Dad went before a relapse. If a parent had stayed clean for fifteen months before relapsing, the child will not begin to trust a parent until after his or her parent has gone beyond the fifteen-month point. Going past the fifteen-month point and remaining sober makes for a wonderful opportunity to celebrate how family members have changed. In this way, hidden fears of relapse can become milestones for accomplishment.

DETOXIFYING TRAUMAS

Practitioners can help parents understand children's learned expectations and physiological reactions to reminders of past traumas, building on the finding of recent research. van der Kolk (2003), for instance, studied neural activity when individuals read a script describing their personal traumas and found that the ability to verbalize (left hemisphere) is closed down during a flashback, while activity in the visual cortex of the right hemisphere increases. Flooding of verbal memories impedes ability to create a verbal narrative. Practitioners can help parents and other caring adults understand normal human reactions to trauma and prepare interventions to help children manage these reactions. Effective therapeutic interventions promote affective regulation skills before a child is asked to *re*experience traumatic memories (Ford, Mahoney, and Russo, 2003; Schore, 2001; van der Kolk, McFarlane, and Weisaeth, 1996; van der Kolk, 2003).

*Re*exposing children to memories of victimization without developing necessary safety and affect management skills can lead to *re*stimulation of overwhelming pain, perceptions of helplessness, and dissociative reactions (Pitman et al., 1991). Too much arousal sensitizes children and associates therapy with pain, confirming the power of the trauma.

*Re*exposure to past traumas can facilitate healing when a child experiences how trauma stimuli lead to a very different result than in the past when a child may have felt vulnerable, isolated, and trapped. Trauma therapies appear to work by helping clients to *re*experience parts of traumatic memories while at the same time activating activities, perceptions, and meaning that reroute or block patterned trauma responses (Rothbaum and Foa, 1996). New interactions developed and practiced in therapy sessions become at first an option to old trauma patterns and then, over time, a child's preferred responses with practice, "homework," reminders, and reinforcement.

Children develop *auto*regulatory skills by working with an emotionally available parent figure and therapist. This means overcoming the obstacles that blocked the child's developmental progress, the loneliness, vulnerability, and fears of violence or abandonment. The key to effective trauma work revolves around promoting safety so that children, parents (biological or adoptive), and therapists can reciprocally manage affects that in the past could not be addressed. In this way, practitioners can work with parents, relatives, and other caring adults to detoxify often unspoken fears and show children how to get out of their nightmares.

Trauma therapy is not focused on a child exposing painful feelings, but rather a means to help him or her learn how to tell the story of what happened without reliving, day after day, the traumas of the past. By working together on life stories, therapists and parents show a child that they can accept and deal with whatever a child experienced, the good times and the bad. Parents and children learn to say forbidden secrets out loud and to rebuild trust that parents care enough to protect children and themselves. Working together, practitioners and parents can open up lessons from the past and possibilities for the future. In this way, life-story work provides a means for caring adults to help children overcome the traumas in their lives.

Chapter 9

Real Life Heroes

Great deeds are usually wrought at great risk.

Herodotus

The *Real Life Heroes* workbook was designed to promote the understanding and commitment children need to surmount trauma. The intent is not to simply tell a child's life story, but rather, to rebuild a story of people who care for a child based on strength, courage, and belonging. The heroes in this work are real people, the women and men, who define what it means for a child to live in a family, to overcome real crises, and to live in a community with adults who care about children.

LIFE-STORY WORK

A Bonding Tool

Working on a structured life-story workbook *with* a child provides a way for practitioners, parents, and other caring adults to show that we care enough to join with a child, to face the hard times, and to keep on going. The child's life story becomes a vehicle to mobilize courage. Our courage as parents and practitioners is passed on to the child as we share together ways we can overcome adversity and get beyond a sense of being helpless victims. Shared work by caring adults and children make life stories a wonderful way to help a child to master difficult moments in his or her life and to foster positive values and a sense of pride in a child's successes.

We help children overcome a natural reluctance to tell their stories by showing that we want to learn about their experiences. Children may share their experiences through art, drama, dance, music, or other creative modalities. The workbook can be used as a framework for addressing critical topics in trauma therapy, and allow practitioners and parents to work creatively with children as unique individuals. Our task as practitioners and parents is to show children that we respect each child's perspective, and will protect them when they share the truth of their experiences: their love, their fears, their anger, their losses, and their hopes.

Discovering and recording real stories of caring from a child's life provides an antidote to unspoken terrors from the past, feelings of loneliness, and the self-blame and self-hatred that often accompanies feeling unloved, rejected, or abandoned. The child's completed life book represents a testament to the courage of the child *and* the adults who worked with the child to maintain (or rekindle) hope. Life-story work can help children rebuild trust in themselves and the adults who care enough to help them heal the rips and tears in their lives.

Redefining the Truths of Life

Practitioners and parents face the challenge of helping traumatized children move beyond old beliefs and *mis*behaviors that may have helped children survive in the past. When children grow up with repeated neglect and abuse, they learn that the world is dangerous and no one is safe. They learn the secrets of survival, the truths of life in an out of control world. Trauma therapy becomes, in many ways, a heroic quest.

From a child's perspective:

Monsters are very real.

No matter what parents, grandparents, or teachers might say, abused and neglected children know that people can act like monsters.

Monsters hurt you deep inside.

It is not the sex or the beatings as much as the degradation, the loss of control, and the betrayal of trust when family members and adults in authority positions act as monsters. It is not the whack, as much as the impact of the words "You are no good," "You're just like your father," or "I can't stand you."

Monsters make you keep secrets.

Children often keep secrets because they care about family members, even adults who have abused them. Many children have also learned that it is too dangerous to talk and have been threatened that if they what happened, they will be seen as traitors to the family, somebody will be hurt, or worse, the abuser may abandon them or commit suicide. "I will never love you. You will never see me again." Threats keep secrets locked up, secrets that burn inside and keep children up at night.

Monsters take away your home.

Abandonment is real for children living with abuse and neglect. Parents disappear, become incarcerated, or send children away. Children learn they are going to "the bad girls' home," often see placements as "lock-ups," and may be told they cannot return until *they* change and obey all the family rules, no matter what that means. Until then, the family will go on without them.

Believe what you see, not what they say.

When adults lie, no one can be trusted. Children learn to say what they need to say to get what they need. Testing adults becomes crucial to determine what is real, and the truth may be something they will never know.

In a dangerous world, children must be in charge.

If adults are out of control, children try to take charge, care for parents, and become a "little man" or a "little mommy" to guard their homes and care for younger siblings.

Look to peers for love and identity.

When children give up on adults, peers provide hope and a sense of family. Children living with abuse and neglect will often be attracted by early adolescence to youths who challenge adults, especially authorities.

One answer to monsters when you are all alone is to become a monster.

Children naturally want to become the biggest, the scariest, the worst-ever monster, in order to gain the power to fight off adults who act as monsters, typically by using the same techniques of power modeled by adults.

Violence often yields power.

When aggression succeeds, children learn that violence gives them power over other people. This is the power of the "dark side," of *mis*behavior. Abused children may see their own fear in the eyes of peers, and later with adults. Bullying and defiance may work to give youths power over siblings or classmates. Peers may cringe and adults may become upset and allow them to disrupt homes or classrooms. Arbitrary consequences may reinforce their sense of power. Children may saunter off to the principal's office once again, relishing for a moment the reputation of being "bad" and getting away from a difficult work assignment or a problem with a peer. Suspensions reinforce children's "bad" reputation and often increase their perception of their power to disturb others when they return, and reduce their ability to succeed with classwork they have missed. Instead of running from their own nightmares, children may learn to bring their nightmares to others.

From Monsters to Moms and Dads

Children need adults to keep them safe, parents and caring adults who are brave enough to go where the monsters are, to look into the dark places, and to help children change their life stories from stories of trauma and harm to stories of survival and mastery. Caring adults and parents can become heroes for children in distress. The adults make it safe to heal by validating children's experiences, developing and implementing realistic safety plans, and grieving with children for their losses. Working together on sharing memories provides a medium for caring adults to make it safe for children to share pain, to grieve lost family members, lost months or years as children, and their own innocence. The stories carried by children can be changed from powerful monsters and terror to *real* people in the past who made choices leading to neglect. Sharing memories with loving and strong adults helps children move from a life of victimization to a future in which they can master their demons.

The goal of this approach is to make children into heroes by modeling persistence and commitment, by developing positive expectations, and by helping children learn life skills to succeed. Child by child, caring committed adults make a difference. This is the difference between therapy with traumatized children and crisis "stabilization." Healing the wounds of abandonment and rejection means showing up week after week. It is very tempting to prioritize crises and rush to face the day's emergencies; but it is the consistency of meeting with a child and a family over weeks and *often* months that pays off. It takes time and administrative support to focus on attachments and the importance of sustained relationships.

*Re*parenting hurt children means taking risks. Parents will very likely experience wounds from the child's past. It helps to remind parents that this is a positive sign, and not a sign that the parent is failing or the child is "bad." When we feel the pain, we know we are doing the work that is needed (d'Aversa, Personal Communication, 2000). Pain spurs parents and other caring adults to work on finding solutions to buried traumas.

Wounded children almost inevitably sense and evoke similar wounds in the people around them. Caring adults often need to rework their own attachment and trauma experiences. When children have been traumatized in their families, parents must often first develop their own abilities to manage stress without losing control, and work in therapy themselves to move past blocks in their own development. Overcoming parents' own traumas can be presented as a critical part of the challenge of changing *multi*generational cycles of trauma and a way for parents to empower themselves and show their children how to stop the nightmares of the past.

Proving Oneself

Just as in fairy tales, heroes must pass critical tests and symbolically cut through prickers and vines to find the entranced princess or battle fearsome dragons that haunt a boy's dreams. It takes real people to become children's heroes, real people with strength, skill, and staying power. Children test us to see if we care enough to go the distance.

Every time Tiffany, age seven, came to see me, she would shut off the lights in the stairwell, walk up the stairs in the dark, and sit quietly for a moment in a darkened room listening for ghost sounds. It was a ritual test she gave to every foster parent, child care worker, or therapist. Afterward, she would begin to tell her story.

Children find out who really cares at 3 a.m. when their throat burns or 1:30 p.m. on a busy workday when they get in trouble in art class and the principal calls their parent. Children watch carefully when the hot water heater leaks, the car breaks down, and the parents' boss demands extra work. For traumatized children, bad days mean bad things happen. Wounded children listen through doors and heating vents to find out if a parent or caretaker's commitment wavers or breaks. The heroes children need do not give up in the middle of the night. Do Mom or Dad leave the home for hours (or days) when things get tough, just as they (or former parents) used to do before a child's placement? Does a *pre*adoptive parent bring the child along to a funeral when a parent's beloved aunt suddenly dies? How is a child introduced to Great Grandma and Uncle Bill? And, if a cousin teases the child for being placed away from home, what does the parent do?

Children dare caring adults to succeed. They want them to succeed but the tests are hard. Practitioners can help parents prepare for typical challenges from abused or neglected children.

A list of Top-Ten Dares would include the following:

1. *Dare to see.* Will we notice the flashes of caring on a child's face, the glistening of the tiniest teardrop before a youth turns his or her head away, or follow a child's gaze as he or she watches a parent leave?
2. *Dare to feel.* Can we allow ourselves to feel a child's message with the hair on our scalp, the prickles on skin, the ache in our hearts, and the cramp in our guts? Can we feel a child's highs and lows, using our selves as a guide and resource to the child while keeping ourselves safe with intense feelings?
3. *Dare to listen to a child's unspoken message.* Can we step back and struggle with what a child is showing us and look at behavior as an interactional message, a message and a challenge to family members, practitioners, and other caring adults? If we move quickly to judgmental words, assumptions, or arbitrary reactions, we miss the child's message and miss the child.
4. *Dare to question.* Can we invite a child in words, with a comforting arm, and with gentle questions to share what they remember? Who they want to see? Who can keep them safe? Can we offer to help a child to discover, as detectives, the missing information that led up to traumas, to search out and find the information necessary to help develop realistic safety plans and to help a child let go of fantasies about what happened?
5. *Dare to face the trauma the child cannot bear.* Can we show a child that whatever happened, whatever was done to him or her anywhere on his or her body, whatever was imprinted in his or her mind, and whatever he or she did, we will not be scared away?
6. *Dare to care.* Can we show a child we care, knowing children coming from neglect cannot trust until they have tested us with the power of their nightmares?
7. *Dare to stand up for a child in distress.* Will we stand up for a child in court, with other service providers, with teachers or authorities, with relatives the child fears?
8. *Dare to discipline.* Will we be frightened by a child's defiance or worn out and stop caring enough to teach a child right from wrong and how to succeed?
9. *Dare to give up myths about ourselves.* Will we shun children when they expose our weaknesses, our failures, and the little excuses we use to comfort ourselves? Can we accept that we make mistakes? Children know that every Pokémon character has a weakness, even Charizard, with his 120 HP can inadvertently cause forest fires. Real Life Problems require Real Life Heroes. Vulnerabilities lead to con-

nection. Without any weaknesses, heroes would be one dimensional, plastic, and of little enduring interest. Superman had to beware of kryptonite; Luke Skywalker in *Star Wars* was impulsive and his enemy, the emperor, played upon his fondness for his friends; Spiderman was in love with girl next door. Caring adults can use these stories to teach children that we all have weaknesses but we can still act as heroes.

10. *Dare to love the real me.* The biggest dare of all is often a child's challenge to adults that "No one can love me." Children from violent homes have often learned that it is safer to become "the monster," than to live in fear of someone else in the family becoming a monster. After months and years of getting in trouble, children may believe deep inside that if you really got to know me, you'd see that I am "no good," "evil," "stupid," "trash."

THE REAL LIFE HEROES *WORKBOOK*

A Practice Model

Real Life Heroes can be used as a framework for mental health, child protective, and PINS/JD (juvenile delinquency) services based on attachment and trauma research and the principles outlined in Chapters 5 through 8.

1. All children need a primary parent(s) who will care for them through good times and bad, protect and guide them now and into adulthood, and help them to own a life story based on mastery and hope, a life story that includes what they saw, felt, heard, thought, and did over time.
2. Children referred for child and family services have often experienced trauma, neglect, domestic violence, addictions, emotional abuse, physical abuse, or sexual abuse. Traumatized children need to see that their experience has been heard and believed by people who care enough about them enough to protect them, set limits, implement safety plans, and keep the "monsters" of the past away. A supportive group of people (parents, guardians, relatives, foster/adoptive parents, therapists, teachers, and community leaders) can help children give up dangerous behaviors by proving to them that they are safe enough to share toxic secrets and that responsible adults will implement realistic safety plans.
3. Children in crisis need to learn and practice what they can do to become successful, to overcome their fears, to test whether they can trust

adults in their homes and schools, and to replace behaviors that have led to trouble with behaviors that help themselves and others.

Practitioners can help children and caring adults to *re*write a story of trauma, violence, and depression and uncover the hero often hidden deep inside troubled and troubling children.

To answer children in distress, we can keep in mind ways to answer each of the challenges of children struggling to rebuild attachments.

- *Listen to children's messages.* Show children that we will listen for the love, the caring, the fears, the anger, and the sadness they carry inside.
- *Find heroes for each child.* Show children that we respect attachments and will use assessments of attachments, strengths, and risks to help locate and foster connections with family members, relatives, or other caring adults who could help children. Show children that services will work to replace the monsters of their nightmares with the greatest heroes of all: moms and dads working twenty-four hours a day, seven days a week.
- *Support heroes.* Biological, kinship, and adoptive families face a high risk of disruption after children have been in placement. Providing supportive services after placement is essential.
- *Pass children's tests.* Understanding testing as necessary, we can prepare ourselves and invite children to test us with supportive services in place.
- *Demystify trauma behaviors.* Parents need to understand patterns of family interactions and the neuropsychology of trauma and attachment disorders to take away the power of children's negative powers.
- Re*mystify the power of parents.* Practitioners can enhance parents' strengths by adding a little magic.
- *Help children rise above the trauma.* Trauma work requires taking risks. Children's heroes make it safe to risk by developing realistic safety plans, practicing skills, desensitizing toxic reminders of traumas, and challenging children to overcome their nightmares.
- *Bring out the hero in each child.* Use activities to foster growth and pride in sports, arts, music, drama, wall climbing, hiking, camping, etc. Model and guide children to face and succeed in overcoming adversities and difficulties with others.

Discovering the Magic in the Child's Message

When working to help children, it helps to use a little magic to fight fears of monsters and demons. Therapists can help parents develop crystal balls of their own. Adults can utilize the wisdom of experience and the courage to learn a child's history in order to help a child change his or her future.

Adults know that storms will end, the sun will shine again, and another storm will come in time. Adults can also learn to predict a child's behaviors by watching and listening carefully. Traumatized children typically revolve in fairly predictable patterns of crises. If we learn about a child's experiences and watch him or her in action, we can see these revolving patterns play out with a rather boring regularity. Act I, Scene 1, followed by Act I, Scene 2 . . .

Five-year-old Bobbie sees a toy his little sister (or another child at school) is enjoying and wants it. When she moves on to the next toy, he grabs it. His sister (or classmate) screams. Bobbie clutches the toy and looks up. When he sees his parent (or teacher) begin to scowl, lips forming a reprimand, Bobbie slams the toy onto the floor, lurches forward, and he is off into a full-scale tantrum, stomping, throwing himself on to the floor, hitting his head against a wall.

For a parent or teacher, Bobbie looks wild and crazy. He likely disrupts everyone around him, or may even be seen as threatening if he is large or menacing enough as he swings toys or chairs.

Children such as Bobbie are often repeating traumatized behavior, reenactments of violence experienced when children were in their "terrible two's," a time when children normally use tantrums to cope. When children regress into traumatized behavior, caring adults can pull out their crystal balls, their ability to learn what sets a child off, to understand the pattern of the behavior, to appreciate the impact (e.g., disruption), and then to change the course of the behavior. It is rather like magic.

A parent or adult can disrupt the child's usual pattern and change the script of the play. Understanding the pattern helps us to remind ourselves that, for instance, Bobbie is doing his trauma show. It is time to calm ourselves and to *re*orient the moment into an opportunity, presented by Bobbie, for parents or teachers to use their repertoire of interventions.

Practitioners can help caring adults prepare for each of their children's repeated behavior patterns (see Chapter 5). We can change our behavior from the expected angry look (or threatening gesture that signaled violence time in the child's past) to new words and gestures that show a child that the old behaviors no longer have the effect the child expected. Later, we can challenge a child to show a tantrum. "Show me your angriest look!" "I don't think you think I can handle it. So, let's see it." A child may be asked to practice his or her favorite tantrum, to bring it to perfection and show it to the parent again at a later time, as long as it is not destructive or self-injurious.

We can also dare a child to move beyond constricted behaviors. For example, a child who can only handle a one-second hug may have had good reason in the past to fear closeness or being held. With a shared understanding of what happened before and assurances of the safety a child needs, a parent could gently challenge the child to move up to a three-second hug. The parent could end a gentle embrace with a smile and another challenge. "Not bad, for today. Maybe we'll get to five seconds next week." A parent could dare a child to trust, just a little, by closing his or her eyes and falling backward into a parent's waiting arms. Trust exercises can end with a quick hug and a tickle.

Life-story work enables practitioners and parents to stay a step ahead of children by learning to understand their messages and developing strategies to take away the power of their negative behaviors. We can learn from their experiences to add words that redefine their *mis*behavior as a message about life in the old days, or an invitation to their new, or *re*formed families, to participate in the old script. Adding new words shows children that together, we can think this out and move on.

Breaking the Curse

Traumatized children act as if they are in a trance, a spell from the people of the past who hurt, trapped, threatened, *dis*empowered, and *dis*couraged. Children learned to *dis*trust and to *dis*respect. Traumatic entrancement leads children to lose vision and perspective and over time to give up hope.

Just as in a fairy tale, it takes a hero to break the curse. Our challenge as practitioners is to open up possibilities for heroes to *re*enter a child's life. We can rekindle hope by encouraging children to give caring adults in their lives another chance to be the parents and guardians children need.

I have asked children living in foster care what a hero is to them. "It's a person who will save you," one boy told me. Other boys and girls have told me how important it is to have people who care enough to tell the truth. A hero is "someone who you can look up to, someone you can depend on, someone who can help you," a teenage boy told me.

The Myth of Perfection

Many children believe that heroes need to be perfect. The *Merriam-Webster's Collegiate Dictionary* (2002) defines a hero as someone who is the main character in a story, someone admired for their achievements and qualities. A hero can be a legendary figure known for great strength, courage, and daring. The standard definitions of heroism do not help children grapple with the inconsistencies and flaws of real people.

"The only heroes are those you can't know much about," one seventeen-year-old told me. Children know from an early age that even adults in leadership positions are far from perfect. The flaws and failings of presidents, sports stars, and pop singers are covered in vivid detail on the front page of newspapers, broadcast with powerful images on the evening news, and *re*-played over and over on cable news networks. Children watch hockey players brawl, listen to baseball players curse, read about the relapses of baseball stars and movie stars, and see television reports on the sex lives of political leaders.

Children growing up with neglect are especially prone to crave perfection. They may idealize people they know little about or, as adolescents, move from one idealized romantic partner to another, staying in a relationship just long enough to fall "in love," sometimes taking risks with pregnancy or sexually transmitted diseases, before becoming disillusioned once again. I met a severely anxious and obsessive fourteen-year-old girl who compared herself and everyone else around her on a Gwyneth Paltrow scale, based on the Academy Award-winning actress. From this girl's perspective, she was a "negative 100" on the scale. Gwyneth was perfect, and no one could compare. In this context, everyday moms and dads, teachers, and coaches seem to have little chance.

Practitioners can promote a broader definition of heroism to open the door for caring adults to become the heroes children need. We can accentuate how heroes rise above problems in their homes, communities, and weaknesses in themselves. We all have weaknesses, and we all have strengths. Even mythological or legendary heroes had problems.

Traumatized children need to be reminded frequently that we all make mistakes, including parents and practitioners. No one is perfect; and we learn from our errors. Parents, especially "certified" foster parents, often need to be reminded that it is okay to make mistakes. It helps to recognize our mistakes and to go back to children (or parents), acknowledge what we have done, apologize, and give a more constructive message. This is especially important when we as practitioners or parents realize that we have been emotionally triggered and have responded to a child with a false, misleading message or implied cutting off or rejection of the child or child's perspective. Just as a carpenter can repair a mistake, or a famous painter will make multiple sketches, parents can be helped to repair their messages.

The power of a parent's message lies in the courage to *re*pair by telling the truth. Lies create distance and keep traumas alive. *Re*pair work takes courage and fosters strength in children and adults.

Stories from biographies of superstars can be helpful. Michael Jordan, the legendary basketball star, shared[1] how as a young adolescent he became aware of racism, the damage to African Americans, how he became angry, acted out his anger on others, and was pulled back by his mother and father who taught him that "yes" bad things such as racism happen, but people can rise above anger and racism to succeed. Michael Jordan's parents helped him to believe in himself and work harder to succeed, even when he did not make the cut for a school team.

It helps to elicit the personal heroes of parents and to help them denote what made these people inspiring. I have been inspired by the image of Abraham Lincoln writing the Gettysburg Address as he sat alone on a train riding to the battlefield during the Civil War. Many parents can tell you what they were doing when they heard about J.F.K. being shot. Grandparents remember Pearl Harbor. Young adults know what happened on September 11th. It helps to enlarge these memories by sharing the personal meaning of events and special heroes with children and grandchildren.

It is often difficult for family members to share their own stories, but these can be hidden treasures for children. I remember my grandmother's story of how her parents smuggled her and her siblings in the dark of night across the border of Russia to escape the murders, assaults, and destruction of the pogroms. My dad tried to rescue pilots downed in the English Channel in World War II. My family blessed me with support and stability, even after experiencing serial deaths.

Difficult childbirths, natural disasters, wars, economic problems, near-fatal accidents, and other real life crises usually involve very real acts of heroism. But, many people have learned to keep up a stiff upper lip and carry on after hard times, as though there was nothing to talk about. Children may grow up never knowing about the critical steps and the risks, small or large, that moms and dads or other relatives took to save their families. Family stories can invest children with a heritage of strength and resilience.

REDEFINING HEROES FOR CHILDREN

Young people are not likely to identify significant people as heroes, per se, but it is clear when I talk to youths who are succeeding in life that they have key people in their lives who have made a real difference. A young man I admire told me that after years in foster care, "I have no heroes. But, I have people I look up to. They're smart. They're caring . . . I can have a hassle with them one day, and the next day, they're still there. It's like we just start over." This youth emerged from years of oppositional, defiant, and disruptive behavior with the support of his new parents, their extended family, a coach he met while in group care, and a minister in his new community. In my mind, each of these people were heroes for this young man.

Adults become heroes for children by the little things they do, the special chicken dinner made just for the child, baking the child's favorite dessert, teaching a child to hit a ball or ride a bike, or giving a youth a chance for a college education. The heroes for children show they care by making the time and going to the trouble to be there week after week. Child care workers show up for work at group care agencies[2] week after week, teaching children critical life skills, reaching out to children when they are distressed, keeping children safe, and touching children's lives by showing they care. CASA volunteers[3] listen to children, report to judges on the best interests of children, help children speak up for what they need, and conduct follow-up visits. Law guardians take time from their practices to meet with children, to answer phone calls, and to prepare children for court hearings. Teachers and principals ensure that children have the support they need to succeed at school and develop programs that allow youths opportunities to build relationships with mentors and develop special skills in areas of strength and interest from drama to art, or literary magazines to volunteer programs for younger children.

Real heroes fail at times, but keep trying. Traumatized children know that real people fail. Often, what they need to learn, is that, caring adults keep their promises. Perhaps the greatest measure of a hero is the courage to be honest about mistakes, even relapses into old, negative patterns, and to take steps to protect other people, especially children. Heroes are strong enough to share their own stories of struggling to succeed, their triumphs and setbacks, and their family's stories of combating prejudice, poverty, war, and other problems.

Heroes show courage with persistence. Our natural reaction to danger is to fight or run away. Heroes make sacrifices beyond their own personal self-interest. Parents who give up addictions can become heroes to their children. At the same time, parents who make an adoption plan for their children because they know they cannot overcome addictions, are also heroes. Adoptive parents are typically unheralded heroes who save children and communities by taking troubled children into their homes and accepting that these children bring loyalties and unresolved traumas from the past.

I have met boys and girls, moms and dads, grandparents, foster parents, teachers, and many others who have been *real* heroes, people you could depend on to help, even if it meant taking great risks, even if they did not always succeed. Heroes to me are people who keep on caring for others and helping others, even when they feel hurt, scared, lonely, or so mad they cannot think straight. It takes courage, the courage to do the right thing.

FINDING HEROES

Our challenge as practitioners working with children in crisis is to quickly find heroes for children and begin the work of repairing broken connections where possible, or rebuilding new bonds. Fortunately, children show us the way.

> Teddy, an eight-year-old boy, would play over and over a story in a sandbox about an older woman and himself. Teddy had been in residential treatment for three years and reported to have been abandoned by his mother with no known father. I took Teddy to the county department of social services to check records for any clues about who the woman in his stories could be. We met past CPS workers who remembered Teddy. One remembered picking Teddy up from a babysitter, a woman who had cared for Teddy for months at a time when his mother would disappear. We were able to contact this woman and I visited her at her home, asking if she would be willing to see Teddy again. This led to visits, weekends, and a connection for Teddy who's behaviors improved enough to move out of residential treatment.

We can expedite children's recovery from trauma by providing careful and comprehensive assessments of a child's attachments and working quickly to bring these people together for a child or youth. With children referred for dangerous behaviors or crisis placements, I work to bring in protective and positive adults, by the second or third session, moving outward quickly from nuclear families in order to bring in additional protective adults to support for children, adolescents, and parents. This may surprise children and parents accustomed to believing that individuals need to make changes on their own, and that psychotherapy involves, at most, custodial parents and diagnosed children, but not siblings, relatives, mentors, clergy, special teachers, or friends.

Permanency work is not just for children. Effective programs work to engage youths with significant adults from their families and communities (Casey Family Programs, 2001). Critical components of foster care work with adolescents (Charles and Nelson, 2000) include assessing relationships with peers, family members, and adults; teaching youths how to have a relationship; developing lasting relationships with child welfare workers including regular visits; developing peer support groups, enhancing family ties wherever possible; involving youths in service planning and policy development; helping youths in care to decrease conflicts with birth families; life-story work; and keeping adoption open as a viable option. This includes working with older adolescents in group care and independent living programs. I ask every prospective applicant about the adults in their lives they would like to involve in contracting and review conferences, who they could call in the middle of the night if they became distressed, and who they would like to find or try, with help from staff, to build a better relationship. Seventeen- and eighteen-year-olds are often surprised, but usually impressed when my colleagues and I invite them to bring in sponsors, supportive friends, grandparents, and other family members.

Psychological evaluations are very important to help staff quickly uncover primary attachments, a child's hopes, and a child's experiences with key family members. Storytelling with human figures and projective tests (see Chapter 8) are very effective tools. Variations on traditional projective questions such as "If you had all the powers of the universe, and could change the past, the present, and the future, what three wishes would you make come true?" "If you won a million dollars, (or, for younger children, found three bags full of money at their door with their name on it), what would you do?" If the child mentions buying a house or a car, I ask him or her who he or she would have live in the house, who could visit, and with the car, who could come with him or her and where would they go.

Other traditional projective questions can help elicit the names of significant family members. "If you were to go to a magical island for a year (with everything the child needs and loves to do), would you go alone or take someone with you?" Similarly, "If you won a vacation trip and $3,000, where would you go? Would you take anyone with you? Who would you take?" And, more direct questions, "Who do you like the most? Who can you count on to help you in a crisis? Who can you count on to tell you when you are wrong and give you advice when you need it? Would will listen to you?"

I look for a child's reactions (facial looks, gestures, actions, affect, concentration, compliance/defiance) before, during, and after visits with parents and other family members. I ask foster parents and child care workers how a child talks about family members (affect, wishes, frequency, desire to see). During the course of an assessment, I ask a child in placement how often, and for how long, the child would like to see a parent if it was up to them, and whether they would want anyone else with them during the visit.

I also frame interview questions to elicit how a child would react with different family members.

- If there was a knock on the door and it was your brother (mother, father, grandmother, other significant person) what would you do?
- Would you let him or her in?
- What would you say to him or her?
- What would he or she say to you?
- What would you do with him or her?

I try to elicit memories from children of people who cared for them in the past.

- When you were sick or got hurt (ear infection, a scraped knee), who did you go to?
- Who comforted you?
- Who helped you when you had trouble with schoolwork?
- Who made you feel better if you had a nightmare when you were very little?
- Who saw the best in you?
- Who believed you could achieve goals, dreams?
- Who gave you hugs when you needed them?
- Who did you want to see on holidays or your birthday?

Appendix A provides a brief survey to assist in assessing attachments. This survey can be used as part of an interview or given to older children and adolescents as part of assessment evaluations to complete in writing. The last part of the survey is useful for pre-post evaluations for programs working to foster attachments and self-esteem. Assessments can include how parents would answer the same questions to elicit resources to help parents, or as possible, supports for children. For children in placement, I ask later in the session who they would want to live with if they could not go back to a birth parent. If a judge is making a custody ruling, I ask children what they would tell the judge about what could make things better in their families and where they and their siblings would do best.

By the end of an assessment, I would like to be able to identify a child's strongest attachments and understand how much of a child's stated hopes are based on real experiences versus wishes and fantasies. My focus is always on *who* could parent the child to maturity and who has shown by their actions that they are committed to parenting the child.

To keep myself focused on attachments, I utilize an attachment-centered ecogram.[4] (Please see Appendix B.) The attachment ecogram highlights significant connections for a child with adults at three different levels: (1) adult provides tentative or partial support; (2) adult believes in the child, nurtures, and protects the child and protects child in the present; and (3) adult is committed to nurturing, protecting, and guiding child to maturity. The Attachment Ecogram incorporates a genogram, ecogram, time line, metaphors, reasons for referral, parent and child goals, and both family strengths and problems.

Mapping family resources highlights who could help family members, who is helping, and who should be helping.

- Who can each family member go to for help in a crisis?
- Who will listen to each family member and validate his or her experience?
- What community organizations are involved?
- Who needs to share responsibility (judges, county attorneys, probation officers, school officials, CPS workers, group care staff, foster parents, family therapists)?
- Who cares enough to check up on the child regularly, signal alarms, bring in help, confront the parent if necessary?
- Who believes child (or children) and the parents can change?
- What could help foster/adoptive family, extended family, community resources, and practitioners develop safety plans?

Time lines are very important for identifying when things have worked well and what was different at that time. They can help practitioners identify past and possibly future resources. Who helped? Who was there in the good times? Who was missing when things got bad?

Mapping attachments and outlining time lines leads directly into answering key questions for service planning. These include permanency questions, factors that drive behavior problems, work needed to build/rebuild attachments, safety plans to prevent retraumatization, alcohol/substance abuse services, developing community support, trauma therapy, life-skills development, individualized education, medical/health care, and legal work.

SUPPORTING HEROES

Heroes do not work alone. Even the Lone Ranger depended on Tonto. The military provides multiple support staff and intelligence officers for every front-line soldier. The truth is that heroes need a lot of support to succeed. Practitioners play a vital role in preparation, skill development, provision of resources, allotment of time, protection, relief, and healing from wounds and wear.

Before embarking on life-story work, it is helpful to review services that are in place, to acknowledge what is missing, and to work with family members, community, and religious leaders, and other service providers to fill in the gaps. Pulling caring adults and service providers together builds the strength to overcome the "monsters" children carry with them.

Heroes for children in crisis need tools, a plan of action, and integrated, supportive services. Working to help children gain heroes and develop a sense of themselves as heroes means focusing on *enduring* versus *temporary* connections, and *real* parenting versus *wishes* by children, relatives, or other adults. Long-term relationships with caring parents, relatives, clergy, advocates, and mentors makes this process work.

Skilled therapists can address real dangers, children's fears, and the fears we all carry in ourselves; however, the intensity of this work is often too much for solo practitioners. The most effective programs foster enduring relationships and address real needs over time with integrated services including supportive teams of practitioners, parents and caretakers that build on strengths, offer services in children's homes, schools, and neighborhoods, and provide assistance before, during, and after any needed placements or hospitalizations of children.

Unfortunately, adequate services are difficult to arrange with current managed care health insurance programs and the regulations that govern child and family services in most states. Insufficient funding for children's services has resulted in truncated programs with limited effectiveness. Agencies face a critical shortage of skilled practitioners willing to work with traumatized children and adolescents. Recruitment and retention have become national crises due to the tremendous risks involved, low pay, insufficient staffing, and resulting cutbacks in time available for practitioners to work with children and families (Waldfogel, 2000). Funding adequately trained and staffed programs has been hampered by news reports, television shows, and movies that highlight tragedies in child welfare services or present practitioners as incompetent or as workers who seem to do little more than take children away from their homes (Malm et al., 2001). Regulations and funding sources often require labeling children and parents with diagnoses or citations of abuse that emphasize problems and identification of someone or some condition to blame. Systems of care can all too often generate adversarial relationships by focusing narrowly on specific problems and ignoring strengths.

Children in child welfare and mental health programs commonly experience transfers from one practitioner to another, especially with high turnover rates and a shortage of staff. It is not uncommon to see children who have experienced a series of partial assessments by several different providers, none of whom had the time to work with children and parents on putting together the whole story, and no one who could work with children and families over the months and often years it takes to prove to a child that their family has really changed. Moving children from agency to agency and from practitioner to practitioner is similar to placing children on an assembly line where different service providers intervene. An assembly line model of services teaches children that they are being treated as something less than human. Inadvertently, the service system can foster attachment disorders with vulnerable children, by functioning as if caregivers and practitioners are dispensable, or that a child's love and security is transferable from caregiver to caregiver.

Crisis residential programs with two- or three-week time limits may offer temporary refuges and supervision of children, but often have little or no capacity to assess, and help family members change chronic problems that have led to dangerous behaviors. Children, all too often, describe group-care placements as "serving time." Children who succeed in group-care programs often find that they lose the support they have valued from counselors and youth workers after they are discharged. Home-based family preservation programs may be asked to help children cope with periodic violence in "families" with chaotic, disorganized attachments and no CPS monitoring, a dangerous proposition. Some mental health sponsored "wrap-around" programs have empowered parents and provided funding for parent advocates and concrete services, but, at the cost of labeling children as mentally ill or ignoring lack of attachment to parents and lack of safety in the home.

All of these programs provide partial services that can help different children. Practitioners and families often have to piece together the services children need. It is important that the responsibility for services be shared, rather than one parent, child, or practitioner trying to take on challenges that could easily lead to exhaustion and disruption of a child's home.

Appendix C outlines key components of an attachment-based model for engagement, assessment, and service planning for children and adolescents in crisis (adapted from Kagan, 1996, Chapters 4-6).[5] Practitioners are often invited or pressured by referral or funding sources to focus on a specific target, and key elements of permanency-based work are omitted or put on the "back-burner." When I am feeling stuck or see a child not making progress, it helps me to review this outline to check for what may be missing in assessment, engagement, and service planning.

PROTECTING HEROES

Working with traumatized children and families in crisis means working on painful issues with children at risk of serious harm to themselves or others. To succeed, we need to be sensitive to what children and parents are feeling. But, this means exposing ourselves to the family's pain.

Stress has been defined as high risk and low control, the essence of work in child and family services. It is easy to get caught up in crises. Crisis work can be seductive; it is nice to be "needed." But, crises can also become rather addicting. We feel a "rush" of adrenaline and later a downside of exhaustion. It is natural for caring adults to try to rescue a hurt child, but in a few days, weeks, or months, the same practitioner or parent, previously so full of energy and determination, may feel overwhelmed, confused, or deeply wounded. Caring adults may find themselves waking up worrying about dangers not sufficiently addressed. Practitioners can become irritable, demanding, abusive to colleagues or loved ones, or simply depressed. Idealistic therapists can start to see every glass as not only "half empty" or "unfillable," but also that there is nothing around to fill the long line of glasses waiting to be served.

Amongst practitioners, this is recognized as "secondary post-traumatic stress disorder" or "burnout." Real heroes differentiate themselves (Campbell, 1990) by setting their own goals, making choices, and saying "no" as well as "yes." No one can do it all. Practitioners and parents who start out believing "I can do everything," often end up leaving or rejecting a child, creating another broken attachment for a hurt (and hurting) child. Real heroes acknowledge the need to care for themselves in order to keep going.

To protect heroes for children, we need to provide real forms of support and protection. This means time, daily and weekly, for parents to get a break with help from relatives, friends, respite workers, after-school programs, camps, religious, and community organizations. Funding is needed for post-discharge services in order to prevent disruptions when a child returns home or moves into an adoptive family. Access to trauma and attachment therapists, hotlines, emergency services, classes, and short-term respite services can make the difference between success and failure of a placement.

Practitioners can help parents and other caring adults to set limits for themselves. We can remind them of the airline safety message. In the midst of a crisis, caring adults need to take the oxygen for themselves first. If a child sees a parent weakening, the child becomes even more out of control. Caring adults need to know, to practice, and to take advantage of ways to relax, even if that means, calling Grandma, Dad, or a friend to watch the children and taking a break. Yoga, meditation, deep muscle relaxation, music, art, whatever works for a parent, it is important to have forms of relaxation and relief in place before predictable crises occur.

It helps to share stories of success (White and Epston, 1990). Parent support groups can be helpful. Activity-based networks that support family outings can build natural connections. Parents can be encouraged to review the good moments in each day. By paying attention to the little things children do, we can see their tentative efforts to reach out and remind ourselves of the work we are doing together to build or rebuild attachments.

An often defiant boy climbed into his foster mother's lap and cuddled up close every evening as she read him a story.

An often oppositional six-year-old, would hold on to her *pre*adoptive mother's little finger and recite her lines from her favorite book. "I am your baby. I will always be your baby."

As a practitioner, I try to remember the high points of my day before going home. What helped? What were the magic moments that I was privileged to witness? I remind myself that I cannot expect to know everything or catch every problem. Children keep me learning. Children also keep me humble, showing me day by day how little power I have as a practitioner; and yet, at the same time, revealing for me how little acts of kindness and validation are often just enough to help a child to blossom and change.

THE HERO'S CHALLENGE

When we feel a child's traumas within ourselves, it helps to remember that this is what rebuilding attachments and trauma therapy is all about. As annoyed or exasperated as we may become, we can remember that children are doing their jobs, testing us where it hurts the most, and highlighting their wounds and our own. Healing means facing real pain and not shutting down.

This is the hero's challenge. To face the monsters a child carries inside. To go above and beyond the expectations of a child. To prove to a child, that there is another way out from the "rock and the hard place," and that a mom or dad, with the help of a team of caring adults, can outwit the monsters of a child's nightmares.

Chapter 10

The Magic of Parents

Memory is the way past events affect future function.

Donald Siegel

UNDERSTANDING AND TREATING TRAUMA AND ATTACHMENT DISORDERS

Practitioners can help parents *de*mystify and *dis*empower a child's behaviors, and, at the same time, *re*mystify and magnify the capacity of caring, committed parents. This works by empowering parents to become stronger and smarter than their children's worst nightmares.

De*mystifying Trauma and Attachment Disorders*

Parents and teachers can develop effective interventions with an understanding of how trauma and chronic stress affects neural functioning. Neurobiologists (Siegel, 1999, 2003; Schore, 2001, 2003a,b; Amen, 1998; van der Kolk, McFarlane, and Weisaeth, 1996) have stressed how brain development is experience-dependent. Experiences shape what information is filtered into the brain and how the mind develops capacity to process this information. Interpersonal-relationship experiences influence regulation of bodily states, organization of memory, ability for communication to others, and development of meaning.

When children experience severe and repeated trauma, stress hormones and long-standing patterns of amygdala excitement and discharge may limit hippocampal functioning, block encoding of memory, or lead in cases of repeated stress to damage to the hippocampus (Siegel, 1999). Traumatized children also have been found to show an asymmetry in their neural functioning with impairment of the corpus callosum, the connecting tissue that provides for transfer of information between the right and left hemispheres (Teicher et al., 1997). Lack of integration in the brain has been found to be associated with impaired ability to understand and share life stories that allow emotionally significant events to be placed into a consolidated permanent memory. Instead, traumatic memories may remain in a state of activation that intrude into an individual's current experiences and relationships (Siegel, 1999).

The psychologist/physician Donald Hebb taught that "Neurons which fire together, wire together" (Siegel, 2003, p. 5, based on Hebb, 1949). This presents both a challenge and an opportunity. A child's brain continues to develop over time and even small changes can help him or her to learn critical skills. Practitioners can help parents and teachers to recognize the power of repeated patterns of neural processing in children and how children's brains have been shaped to focus attention on potentially dangerous stimuli, to rekindle memories of frightening events, and to trigger emotional responses based on experiences of the past. Dyadic interactions between adults and children can then be used to *re*shape patterns of neural activity through repeated interventions, skill building, and guided practice (Siegel, 1999; Schore, 2001; Amen, 1998; van der kolk, McFarlane, and Weisaeth, 1996).

Practitioners can help parents understand how traumatized children function in critical dimensions: attention, memory, affect regulation, sense of time, beliefs, and *re*enactments. Understanding how each of these abilities represents critical skills that traumatized children often need help to master (see Chapter 6) helps parents and teachers to get past labeling children as bad versus good, or healthy versus damaged. Practitioners can then help parents and teachers to help children learn new ways of functioning.

Utilizing Attachment Patterns

By understanding children's history of attachment patterns and their current attachment behavior, parents can match guidance, directions, and their reactions to children's neurologically based patterns of perceiving, thinking, and processing information. Attachment patterns reflect the organization of children's minds (Siegel, 1999). Secure attachments lead to flexible thinking, emotional resilience, affect modulation, and openness to new learning. When parents are unavailable due to their own level of stress, dissociation, avoidance, or intoxication, children learn that there will be no repairing and no healing. Unresolved losses lead to constriction and fragility. Repeated experiences of parents acting frightening, or frightened and unavailable, leads to disorganized patterns of perception, reasoning, and behavior.

Children who experience parents repeatedly dismissing or avoiding them may learn to shut down their own affective processing and restrict their perceptions of the world and processing to their left brain (Siegel, 1999). In *avoidant* attachment patterns (Ainsworth et al., 1978), children learn to block out input from others in order to prevent *re*experiencing rejection and abandonment. By adolescence, they may have learned to trust no one, to block caring for others, and simply do what it takes to get what they want or need. In *anxious* attachments, children may have stored traumatic memories in the amygdala in the right hemisphere (see Schore, 2001). Memories of harsh screaming are largely stored in the right brain (Siegel, 1999). Perceptions of renewed traumas can generate floods of anxiety that children may try to suppress with obsessive rituals, running away, or isolation.

Parents and therapists can help these children by promoting skills in relinking their right and left brain capacities through guided imagery, free association with images, or creative arts combining clay, painting, and writing. Traumatized children can be gently guided by parents, mentors, and teachers to *re*learn how to link their visual, kinesthetic, and verbal abilities. In these guided activities, children can learn to tolerate mild levels of distress within a validating relationship with an adult who understands that *re*linking sensory, movements, and verbal learning and memory is a significant step toward healing. Learning to develop empathy for others begins with helping children learn that it is safe to feel again and that they can become more successful by combining the strengths of their left brain aptitude for verbal reasoning, logic, and organization with the untapped creativity of their right brain.

Music provides a natural mechanism for stimulating reintegration since it involves both the left brain (duration, sequencing, rhythm) and the right brain (tonal memory, melody recognition, intensity). Accordingly, learning to play instruments and sing positive songs may promote restoration of blocked linkages between left and right prefrontal cortex.

When children have experienced their parents caring and then rejecting or neglecting them, children naturally become hypersensitive to words, tone of voice, and subtle behaviors of their parents and other adults who take on parenting role. Subtle signs of distress, anxiety, or anger in adults may trigger the limbic system to flood the children with anxiety and disrupt their fragile reasoning and verbal processes. A frown on a teacher's face may be enough for such children to act as if their teacher had expelled them forever. Such children often learn to shame themselves. Children growing up with *ambivalent* attachment patterns (Ainsworth et al., 1978) typically anticipate adults changing from being detached and neglectful to overly intrusive. These children often cope by disconnecting themselves from others at the first signs of parents, teachers, or other important adults acting in either a rejecting or overly engaging manner.

Neborsky (2003) argued that psychological defenses represent the "disintegration" of genuine, innate preconscious processes. A child who grew up with rejection or emotional neglect learns to avoid consciously feeling longings for closeness that might become unbearable. This helps the child cope with attachment problems in childhood but, at the same time, restricts the child's ability to manage future stressful situations in relationships. Such children may have a limited ability to genuinely experience themselves or to form and maintain intimate relationships with others.

Children's reactions become even more disturbed when they have experienced *chaotic, disorganized* attachments (Main and Solomon, 1986, 1990). Their brains may quickly resort to *dis*associating different perceptions and memories in order to cope with anticipated trauma. Children living with unpredictable violence and repeated abandonment often develop patterns of neural connections characterized by emotional flooding that blocks verbal processing and modulation (Siegel, 1999). Children growing up with repeated abuse and neglect often are unable to organize a coherent response to events in their lives and instead act in response to scattered patterns of neural activation (Siegel, 1999). These children learn to cope with perceptions of life-threatening events and their own helplessness with restricted processing of what is happening around them. Reasoning may become limited to isolated patterns of responses involving different centers of the brain in what appears to be disorganized patterns (Siegel, 1999) that match their experiences of relationships to adults.

Therapists can help parents and children to respect how early experiences of ambivalent and chaotic disorganized attachments have led to hypersensitivity as an effective coping strategy. The child's neurons are working in patterns that were necessary in the past for preservation in the face of anticipated rejection or overly intrusive parenting. Trauma experiences in early childhood create patterns for the release of stress hormones in stressful situations and trigger patterns of neural connections in response to daily life experiences (Siegel, 1999; Schore, 2001; van der kolk, McFarlane, and Weisaeth, 1996). Rather than fighting (or hating) themselves, it is helpful for the child (and parents) to learn how the child's memory center, deep in his or her limbic system, has learned to protect the child from harm. With an understanding of the impact of trauma on a child's developing mind, the child's neural patterns can be accepted and valued. It helps to counter typical shame reactions, often taught to children by adults, by teaching children to thank themselves for brain patterns that served them well in the past. Children can practice recognizing signs of stress in their bodies, and saying to themselves, "thank you" to their own memory. "My inner brain is working." "That's my mind helping me." "That's what I needed to feel and do to survive the bad times."

Teaching a child relaxation skills with imagery, meditation, and deep muscle relaxation can form the foundation for changing self-statements when a child begins to feel anxiety (or anger) mounting and "fright-or-flight" responses taking over. Parents can help children to see and feel how their lives are different now and to practice affirmations that remind themselves that they do not need their old tense-up, run away, or fight reactions any more. Children can practice self-assertions (e.g., "I'm twelve-years old now. I have a parent who cares, a teachers who smiles, a guidance counselor down the hall. I'm bigger, stronger, and smarter now than the monsters of the past . . .")

Recalling images of comforting scenes with a loving parent, safe places, pulling out photographs, or drawings of people who cared about the child, or touching symbols of love, connection, and strength can help to redirect right brain and limbic system anxiety into new and more effective patterns of responding. Children can practice refocusing their attention and redirecting (utilizing) the energy inherent in their emotional reactions.

Parenting children with ambivalent and chaotic, disorganized attachment patterns requires intensive, ongoing support from an integrated team of parents, extended-family members, therapists, mentors, family support workers, and teachers. From a neurological perspective, the most effective interventions would occur during the child's first eighteen months to three years when the right hemisphere is dominant. At this time the right hemisphere is differentiating and most plastic (Schore, 2001). Programs that foster positive parent-child relationships and secure attachments provide powerful modes for developing a child's adaptive skills that will have a long-term impact on his or her abilities and functioning.

With older children, attachment and trauma therapies can function as a "growth-facilitating environment" for the experience-dependent development of right orbitofrontal neural systems (Schore, 1994, 1997, 2001). MRI research (Hariri, Bookheimer, and Mazziotta, 2000) has found that the right prefrontal cortex operates to modulate emotional responses associated with all parts of the brain and therapeutic approaches may work by "modulating emotional experience through interpreting and labeling emotional expressions" (Hariri, Bookheimer, and Mazziotta, 2000, p. 47). Developing an understanding of trauma through an organized narrative or healing theory (Figley, 1989), facilitates transfer of affective experiences stored in the right orbitofrontal brain to the left orbitofrontal region (Schore, 2001). The child learns through this process to utilize verbal reasoning to solve problems and discover solutions to previously hopeless conflicts.

Acceptance

Traumatized children are often handicapped by learning disabilities, developmental delays, and neurological and medical problems. It is important that every child have a full medical, psychological, and developmental evaluation, so that parents and teachers can set appropriate expectations and utilize the most appropriate approaches to encourage success. In most states, it is also important for adoptive parents to conduct these assessments before legalization in order to access appropriate subsidies and arrange for continuation of essential services.

Acceptance of a child as a total person means recognizing the impact of what happened to him or her. Parents often have to give up fantasized expectations for their child. Love, caring, and a nurturing home can do a lot, but neurological effects of fetal alcohol exposure or serial traumas will likely remain. Parents may need help to grieve the child they wanted. Bringing a hurt child back home or adopting a child means changing the family. The whole family has to *re*balance. Acceptance and grief work are critical first steps in this process.

Practitioners can help to make sure that appropriate assessments are conducted and that parents and teachers are not over or underemphasizing problems. Often, parents may not understand a child's developmental abilities and inadvertently push a child to be similar to other family members. Here, again, it is important to grieve what has been lost, to accept abilities as they are, to build on a child's strengths, and to recognize that we all have strengths and weaknesses.

A Little Magic

Validating the reality of a child's past experiences and current neural processing does not mean that caring adults have to be limited in their capacity to help the child heal. Healing from trauma means pushing past the limits of constricted thinking and discovering new opportunities for learning and mastery.

Children love magic because they can learn to dazzle adults and find ways to overcome what appears impossible. By practicing a "little magic" in sessions, practitioners can reaffirm the power of adults and show children that these are special places and special times to get unstuck.

Practitioners can help parents to use magic and to encourage children to learn tricks from their parents and other adults. Magic provides an opportunity for caring adults to become mentors and teachers in fun activities that help children expand their perspectives, understanding, and powers.

Parents can utilize simple, even silly, tricks matched to both the chronological and psychological age of their children. With young children learning to count and add, parents can ask, "How many toes do you have? Let's see: ten, nine, eight, seven, six; that's the first foot, plus five from the second, makes eleven, eleven toes!"[1] With five-to six-year-olds, parents can magically turn the picture of George Washington on a dollar bill upside down.[2] Begin by holding a dollar bill facing the child with picture of George Washington forward and make up a little story. For example:

> One day George Washington got tired out from all his work founding a country, so he went and covered his *head.* (Fold dollar horizontally up from the bottom.) So off he went to *bed.* (Pinch dollar in center, creating two halves, left and right, and fold left half back.)
>
> "Come back George," his wife, Martha, called *out.* (Pull front folded portion open to the left.)
>
> "It's time to be up and *about.*" (Unfold top horizontally upward to uncover face of George Washington, again facing child.)
>
> "Oh dear!" Martha said. "Poor George is upside *down.*"
>
> "Back to bed you go," she said. "Time to lie *down.*" (Fold dollar horizontally up from the bottom, covering his face again.)
>
> "Then turn yourself *around.*" (Pinch dollar in center, creating two halves, left and right, and fold left half back.)
>
> "Count up to *ten.*" (Count out loud, and pull front folded portion open to the left.)
>
> "And get your head on right *again.*" (Unfold top horizontally upward to uncover face of George Washington, again facing child.)
>
> And that's how Martha Washington saved our first president.

This story could be changed to teach other lessons. For example, how George became tired of learning not to tell a lie and how his mother taught him to get his head on straight.

Some of my favorite brainteasers from children's activity books include:

1. Drawing a large letter T about two inches wide, cutting it into different pieces (see Figure 10.1), and asking the child to reassemble it.
2. Asking children and adults to find all meaningful ways to work with "710." After the child generates different permutations, the numbers "710" can be turned upside down, symbolizing the word oil.
3. Challenging children and adults to connect nine dots with four consecutive straight lines, not lifting their pencils (see Figure 10.2). The answer (Figure 10.3) has been used in psychotherapy and management for many years to accentuate the need to move out of the boxes that constrict our ability to solve problems.

If we feel boxed in, we are probably only seeing the box. Einstein said, "It is the theory that determines what we may observe." If you are living in cycles of trauma, it is hard to see beyond the present crisis. A rabbinic saying advises, "To a worm in horseradish, the whole world is horseradish." The questions we ask lead to the answers available. Our task with children and families at impasse is often to take off our blinders, challenge harmful rules, promote curiosity, and expand perspectives.

"What if?" games can be both fun and provocative. For example, a parent can offer a child magic beans, using mild wasabi flavored soybeans, often available in health foods stores, or a spicy candy, to dare a child to test something different and to imagine what could happen if these were really as powerful as they taste. Growing perennial ryegrass or small plants from seeds is magical for young children and demonstrates how the child's patience, diligence (regular watering), and the right nutrients works. Growing a sweet potato plant can lead to imagining "what if" the potato plant spread outward to a magical land where a child's wishes can come true.

Children can be challenged to solve problems that promote moving beyond a sense of themselves as alone and unable to accept or count on help. For example, I ask a child, "What if you had to lift a five-hundred-pound barbell. What could you do?" This challenge can be dramatized to bring out the difficulty, or to incorporate hints, if needed, for example, "Who can lift five hundred pounds? Maybe seventy-five pounds, or one hundred pounds . . . Dad could lift one hundred for sure, what do you think?" Children will typically come up with innovative solutions, typically breaking down the artificial barrier of needing to do it alone. For example, "Why can't I have five people or twenty kids or a giant forklift?" Every solution counts in the battle against trauma and distrust.

I invite children to contribute their favorite riddles or card tricks, to try them on parents, and to compile them in books or boxes that can be shared with others. In this way, children help adults to push back boundaries, open

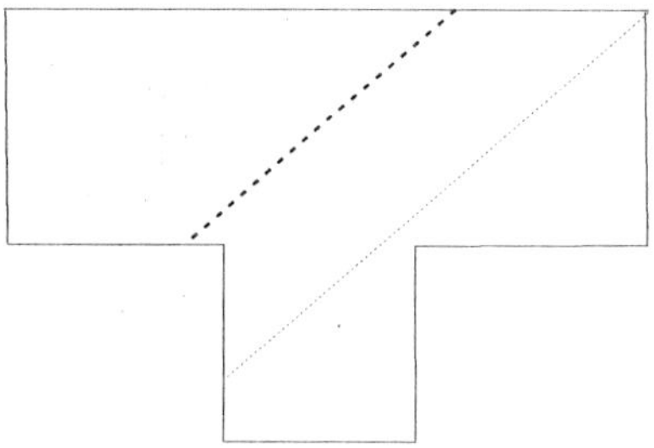

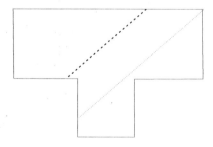

FIGURE 10.1. T Puzzle

Instructions: Connect all dots with four connecting lines.

FIGURE 10.2. Breaking Free of Constraints

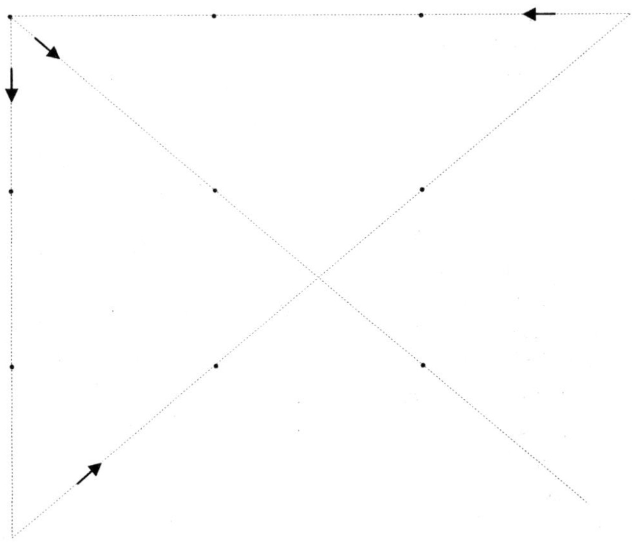

FIGURE 10.3. Out of the Box

up solutions, help other children, and learn how to take pride in their successes.

Magic tricks work to demonstrate that there is more than one way to work out a problem and that frequently solutions lie outside the boxes in which we have been trained by life experiences to think. With each magic trick, we build a little more hope that a child and a family can get out from between the proverbial "rock and the hard place." Each solution is similar to a little miracle. As Einstein said, "There are two ways to live your life. One is as though nothing is a miracle. The other is as though everything is a miracle." When we open our eyes to the magic of attachments, we can see the miracle of parenting traumatized children.

The Power of a Smile

Perhaps the greatest magic is a parent's smile. From Dale Carnegie (1994) to Sam Walton (cited by Mackay, 2001), business leaders have stressed the power of a smile to influence others. A Jewish proverb teaches, "Don't open a shop unless you know how to smile" and "The man who gives little with a smile, gives more than the man who gives much with a frown" (cited by Mackay, 2001, p. C7). These are words of wisdom for parents, as well.

A smile shows a child that parents are still in charge of themselves. The child is not in control. This is a crucial response to a child's provocations. The child needs to see that despite *mis*behavior a parent's temporary reprimand, and even sometimes a temporary separation between a parent and a child, the parent can return to caring and commitment (see Chapter 6). Moreover, the parent can summon the wisdom and resources to stay healthy. It takes only seventeen muscles to smile, but forty-three to frown (Mackay, 2001). Lasting frowns take energy and waste precious time. A continually frowning parent is using up his or her resources. Traumatized children often see a parent's frown as a sign that the parent is wearing down and that rejection, abuse, or abandonment will recur. This, in turn, reinforces a child's negative beliefs about himself or herself and undermines a child's sense of security in his or her home.

Practitioners can help parents to regain their smiles and to stay ahead of children by fostering opportunities for each child to succeed and each parent to smile. A bag of tricks and opportunities for shared activities can help. Win or lose, succeed or fail, the key to bonding is reciprocity and continuity. As Hebb said, "Neurons which fire together, wire together" (cited by Siegel, 2003, p. 5). The power of parenting lies in promoting repeated positive experiences of neural connections over time.

Encouragement

Supervised adventure activities matched carefully to children's abilities and interests can be used to foster the courage of parents and children together. Roller coasters, white-water rafting, ropes courses, and waterslide parks all offer opportunities to push back the frontiers and boundaries, and to give children another area in which to utilize their energy and to excel with parents. Fun activities generate shared moments of pleasure.

In just the same way that a teacher designs a curriculum to foster children's successes, practitioners can work with teachers, coaches, religious leaders, and family members to help generate new opportunities for a child to succeed. A general rule for many service businesses is that you need ten satisfied customer experiences to counter every one negative experience. Negative emotional and behavioral reactions can be replaced over time with repeated positive experiences involving parents and other caring adults.

We can use activities to redefine a child's identity. I want to help parents discover at least one area in which each child shows courage. This could be as simple as going into dark areas, killing bugs in the house, setting mousetraps, downhill skiing, or riding the fastest, scariest roller coaster in the park. Sports, theater arts, and adventure-based activities provide opportunities for caring adults to act as mentors for children and to promote experiences of success in mastering fears.

We can enhance children's acts of courage by finding ways for children and especially adolescents to help family members, classmates, and neighbors (Brooks, 1991). A roller-coaster savvy youth could be asked to coach a younger child or a grandmother on how to survive the ride. Hypervigilant children can watch for rocks while paddling in the bow of a canoe. A child who can assemble LEGO cities or create flourishing metropolises with simulated computer games could help other children master design skills. Good kickers could help with soccer practices; skilled headbutters could become champion goalies. With a strength-based perspective, caring adults enable a child's skills and interests to become a means for the child to help others. Each act of helping works to counter negative voices and denigration from the past. Recording, celebrating, and remembering successes can help replace negative thinking patterns and soothe trauma responses.

The Genies of Invincibility

Practitioners can also invite children and parents to think magically and open up possibilities from fantasy. Fantasy stories with narrative, action figures, or movies can be utilized to break out of the constricted thinking of trauma.

Practitioners can help a child open up a perspective that includes a past, a present, and a future with a fantasy exercise modeled after a little Aladdin, a little Dickens, a little magic from fantasy novels, and the solution-based exercises of Yvonne Dolan (1991). The purpose of this exercise is to elicit connections and strengths in a child and enable him or her to generate in fantasy different ways to overcome problems. I find it works best to say this out loud, dramatizing the story, and putting it into words adapted for a particular child, but it can also be used as a written exercise with a child who responds better to written assignments. The possibilities and solutions generated by children can then be shared with parents who support their growth. Parents can be encouraged to foster their children's creativity and to understand how children use fantasy and creative arts to find solutions.

Fantasy Exercise

Imagine once upon a time, maybe even next week, you wander around the home of someone in your family, far from where anyone is looking. At the end of a long hall, you see one door that is closed. The door seems stuck, so you pull as hard as you can. The door opens. It is totally dark inside. There is no light switch, but with the door open you can see what looks like a small closet.

As you look around, a board in the floor begins to wobble. You step to one side and the board creaks open, just a crack. As you step back, the board closes again. A single rusty nail holds it in place. The head of the nail sticks out just enough for you to grab hold and tug. Slowly, you pull the nail back and the board lifts up.

Under the board you see three bottles standing upright. Carefully, you pick up the one on the left side, a dark dusty violet. The bottle feels warm to the touch. You rub the sides to see what it looks like under the dust and suddenly the top bursts open. Hot, white smoke streams out. The blast knocks you backward onto the floor. You look up and see a tall, purple genie towering above you. Her eyes glow like a cat in the night and her lips are pursed. Her face looks stern, as if she was a teacher about to give a lecture. She looks into your eyes and begins to smile.

"I am the Genie of the Past," she says in a soft voice that somehow warms you from deep inside. "Give me your wish, and I will allow you to visit anyone in your family at any time in the past when this person needed help. You will have the power to help this person in a time of trouble. I will make you invincible as you travel through time and space. Nothing will hurt you. No one will see you."

Where would you go? Who might you visit? What would you want to find out? You could go see what your father looked like when he was twelve years old and having trouble in school or check out whether something you heard about your mother was really true. You could visit your great-great-grandfather, anyone in your family who was having a hard time, and help him or her.

"Now tell me, who do you want to see?" the genie asks, still smiling.

Who would you want to visit?

How old would your relative be?

Another blast of hot white smoke knocks you down. Slowly you open your eyes. Your face feels hot and your eyes sting from the smoke. You look around.

What do you see?

Who else is there?

What is he or she struggling with?

What could help him or her? What would you do?

Imagine you summon the power of the genie to help your relative. Warm, white smoke swirls around you, and then in a flash everything is clear and quiet. The trouble is gone. Your relative is okay. You see his or her face. (If you wish, draw a picture on the back of this page to show how he or she looked.)

"It's time to go," the genie calls out from above. For an instant, you see the smiling face of the genie and then she is gone. In a flash, you are back in the closet. The violet bottle is back on the shelf and covered again with dust and dirt. But something has changed.

What might be different for you and your family if you could help even one relative overcome a time of trouble?

Slowly you reach out and pick up the next bottle on the shelf below. This one is taller than the other first, a deep blue covered with silver specks. Your fingers trace letters on the side. With a deep breath, you blow off the dust and the letters begin to glow red, brighter and brighter.

"Beware, only those with true courage may proceed."

Without thinking, you grip the bottle tighter and tighter. The bottle becomes hot in your hand, glowing now a bright blue. Suddenly, hot, white smoke streams out. The top bursts open and a blast knocks you down. You look up and see a giant red genie towering above you. His eyes glow white and his beard shakes.

"I am the Genie of the Future," the genie roars in a deep voice. His breath pushes you back against the closet wall. "Give me your wish, and I will allow you to visit anyone in your family at any time in the future. I will give you the power to help him or her or anyone else in a time of trouble. I will make you invincible as you travel through time and space. Nothing will hurt you. No one will see you."

You could go see what you look like when you are twenty-five. Or, check on what happens next week. You could visit anyone you think may have a hard time in the future, and help him or her.

"Now tell me, who do you want to see?" roars the genie.

Who would you want to visit?

How far into the future would you go?

Another blast of hot, white smoke knocks you down. Slowly you open your eyes. Your face feels hot and your eyes sting from the smoke. You look around.

What do you see?

Who is there?

What is he or she doing?

What could help him or her?

Imagine you summon the power of the genie to help your relative. Hot, white smoke swirls around you, and then in a flash everything is clear and quiet. The trouble is gone. Your relative is okay. You see his or her face. (If you wish, draw a picture on the back of this page to show how he or she looked.)

"It's time to go," the genie bellows from above. In a flash, you are back to where you began. The blue bottle is back on the shelf and covered again with dust and dirt. But something has changed.

What would be different for you and your family if you knew you could help even one relative overcome a problem in the future?

Slowly you reach out and pick up the last bottle on the shelf. This one is smaller than the other two, a misty green bottle with ripple along the side. Your fingers trace letters on the side. With a deep breath, you blow off the dust and the letters begin to glow yellow, brighter and brighter.

"Hold me and be strong."

The bottle warms in your hand as you stare at the message. Without thinking, you pull the bottle to your chest. The bottle begins to warm against your body. Suddenly, the top bursts open. Hot, white smoke streams out. Again, a blast knocks you down. You look up and see a little genie standing before you. He is no taller than you. His eyes glow a pale blue and seem to dance.

"I am the Genie of the Present," the genie laughs. "Give me your wish, and I will allow you to visit anyone in your family right now, anywhere he or she may be. I will give you the power to help him or her in any way. I will make you invincible as you travel through time and space. Nothing will hurt you. No one will see you."

"Now tell me, who do you want to see?" the genie asks.

Who would you want to visit?

How far into the future would you go?

Another blast of hot, white smoke knocks you down. Slowly you open your eyes. Your face feels hot and your eyes sting from the smoke. You look around.

What do you see?

Who is there?

What is he or she doing?

What could help him or her?

Imagine you summon the power of the genie to help your relative. Hot, white smoke swirls around you, and then in a flash everything is clear and quiet. The trouble is gone. Your relative is okay. You see his or her face. (If you wish, draw a picture on the back of this page to show how he or she looked.)

"It's time to go," the genie cries out from above. In a flash, you are back to where you began. The green bottle is back on the shelf and covered again with dust and dirt. But something has changed.

What would be different in your life if you knew you could help even one relative get over a problem today?

Fantasy exercises can help to identify resources and magic in people, places, and things. Fantasy work can identify people to visit or call, to interview, photograph, or videotape places that inspire a child with hope, and stories from movies and books that promote optimism and creative solutions to seemingly unsolvable problems.

RISING ABOVE TRAUMA

Psychotherapy appears magical when we witness the transformation of children from weakness to strength, from shame to pride, from isolation to bonding. The magic lies in the power of parents and practitioners to work together over time with children to battle monsters and soothe fears, until children begin to trust once again that love, kindness, and family bonds can overcome their nightmares. Behind the magic lies hard, often painful work that succeeds with understanding, support, stamina, and skill.

Effective therapeutic interventions foster

- safety and security with committed adults;
- *re*attunement with contingent, collaborative communication;

- shared interactions that generate positive emotions and decrease negative emotions (right brain to right brain, parent to child, experiences);
- emotional regulation skills within relationships;
- renewed hope and positive expectations for attachment and friendships;
- positive beliefs and self-statements;
- latent strengths and skills;
- successes in relationships, academics, sports, the arts; and
- a sense of mastery of an individual's own life story.

Traumatized children test parents and practitioners in the places where they are most sensitive, the areas of pain that children believe will lead to rejection, abuse, or neglect once again in their lives. Practitioners can help parents pass these crucial tests by understanding children's patterns of behavior and by helping parents develop the strength to persevere.

THE PARENT'S LIFE STORY

Parents lead the way for traumatized children by owning their own lives and by modeling the courage to *re*integrate memories from the past. The parents' ability to flexibly access information about their own childhoods and to coherently tell their own stories may very well be the strongest indicator of parental capacity and effective parenting (Main and Goldwyn, 1998). Moreover, researchers (Main, 1991; Hesse, 1999) have found that a parent's ability to coherently tell his or her own life story was the strongest predictor of a child's attachment to that adult. Parents become powerful by demonstrating how they have been able to integrate their own life histories into a coherent, meaningful story, a story of their own courage in changing their lives, so that a troubled child could return or become part of their home.

Practitioners can help parents contain and manage the darkest fears of both parents and children. By working with therapists on their own traumas and the pain elicited by their children, parents demonstrate that it is possible to overcome problems with understanding and courage. This work begins by helping parents, as well as children, understand how trauma works, thus defusing feelings of shame for what happened in the past. Parents become empowered by demonstrating how to accept themselves and make amends, even when they have done things they regret. When parents have done something that has hurt a child or another family member, the parent can model ways to heal, to apologize for mistakes, to atone for wrongdoing, and to carry out an appropriate form of restitution. By conquering their own trigger monsters, parents can prove to children that it is possible to be imperfect, and yet to persevere, to make mistakes in relationships, and come back and reaffirm their commitment time and again. When this happens, children learn that it is possible to open their own minds, to share their experiences, and to interweave their present and future with the strengths of their parents and other caring and committed adults. It helps to have parents apologize at the beginning of a session and to say out loud to their child what they have done (Minnear, Personal Communication, 2001). The parent models the courage to heal wounds that the parent helped to cause. This demonstrates once again that the parent is leading, rather than the child.

As part of trauma therapy for children, it is important to ask parents to complete the *Real Life Heroes Life Storybook* for themselves or, if they prefer, to write a narrative autobiography or utilize another format to tell their own story. Parents can be encouraged to use their own words and add visual imagery, photographs, videos, music, and documents (e.g., birth certificates). Practitioners can help parents in this effort to address the themes and critical points covered in each chapter of the *Real Life Heroes Life Storybook* as a model for their child.

Telling life stories fosters reciprocal interactions in which caring adults can share what they have learned in their lives with the children they love and work together with children to build a coherent understanding of the past. Strength-based life-story work helps children rebuild a sense of faith that caring adults exist, people have and will care about them, they can overcome hardships, and a future, better than the past, is possible.

Chapter 11

A Hero's Story: Using the *Real Life Heroes* Workbook

Life is not a problem to be solved but a mystery to be lived.

Joseph Campbell

INTRODUCTION

The *Real Life Heroes* workbook helps children (and parents) to rewrite their life stories with a wide range of activities including drawings, photographs, music, dance, videotape, posters, crafts, and narrative. Parents, grandparents, teachers, foster parents, adoptive parents, and mentors can use these stories with psychotherapists to help a child replace a self-image of weakness or victimization with feelings of validation and competence.

Real Life Heroes highlights and preserves moments in which important people in a child's family and community showed they cared, moments in a child's life that signify how the child was valued. Stories of how children were cared for in the past and how children have helped others enable children to feel better about themselves and to put traumas in a more realistic perspective. Children also learn who could help in the future and how they can keep themselves safe with the help of people who care. Parents and caring adults can use this workbook to show children that they can learn from the past, resolve problems in the present, and build a better future.

BEGINNING THE JOURNEY

Life-story work can be introduced as an adventure. By focusing on heroes, anxious and resistant children are often amenable to beginning the hard work needed to overcome old traumas. *Real Life Heroes* is often very useful for children who are not willing or able to work with other forms of trauma therapy. The workbook becomes a quest, a search for meaning, and a means of building up enough trust to enable children to reshape beliefs and behaviors.

Children often respond better to a structured curriculum with a beginning and an end, a format that fits with their experiences at school. I am frequently impressed with how children and especially adolescents may not verbally respond to a therapist's questions, and yet will frequently write (or color) in candid responses to critical questions on a printed sentence-completion test, depression inventory, dissociation survey, or addiction scale, or draw or enact with family figures sensitive issues that have not been previously shared. This only seems to work, however, after a youth has met, tested, and developed an initial level of trust in the therapist. Simply handing youths a questionnaire or workbook rarely yields the critical information therapists need. As in all forms of therapy, the relationship with the therapist is central.

The workbook is recommended for use in the *beginning* of therapy with children who have experienced hardships or who have been placed away from their biological families. Practitioners can use this approach to engage children in therapy by showing children that they are not afraid to deal with even the most frightening parts of their experience, that the therapist will not shame children or parents, and that the therapist respects children's loyalties to parents and other caregivers. The workbook approach is also very helpful in the early stages of therapy as an assessment tool to identify important people for children and thus help develop service plans for family and network interventions.

I believe it takes a hero to make a hero, just as it takes guidance and modeling to learn how to be an effective parent. Children quickly learn whether the adult has the courage and persistence to help them retrace their life story, or whether they can distract the work with problems, oppositional behavior, or complaints. Children may demand that therapists and parents meet their immediate needs and put off day after day, working on their identities or overcoming difficult times with the workbook. It helps to structure every session to include work time on the life storybook. This can be followed by fun time with therapeutic games, shooting baskets, or arts and crafts, all of which can be designed to foster creative approaches to overcoming trauma.

A therapist can serve as a coach to help a biological parent, foster parent, or adoptive parent show a child that he or she can face even the worst experiences and celebrate the child's successes. *Real Life Heroes* provides activities to engage parents and children to work out conflicts and rebuild trust without blaming. The involvement and success of parents in this process can be helpful in assessing attachments, commitment, and the need for additional services. This process can also facilitate evaluation about who can best care for and guide a child, or in some cases, who can best raise a child to maturity.

In cases of abuse and neglect or a parent's mental illness, it may not be possible for a parent to work together with a child. Therapists can work with children and in special sessions, help children to share their work with supportive biological parents, or, if necessary, with foster or adoptive parents. It would be important for children living in foster family or group-care facilities to become safe and secure enough to share their books with their permanent families (biological or *pre*adoptive) including grandparents, aunts, uncles, and older siblings when possible.

An Invitation

Life-story work is an invitation to children to regain power in their lives, to move from a history of victimization to the possibility of seeing themselves as heroes in their own stories, stories with a past, a present, and a future. The journey begins with an invitation to children to use the workbook to look at the important people in their lives, at home, at school, and in their neighborhoods, and to find out who helped, who they could depend on, who told the truth, and who they could look up to as friends and caring adults.

Each life storybook can be shaped into an adventure about one special person. *Real Life Heroes* is designed to become the child's own book. By working on this book, practitioners can encourage children to find the special "qualities" in themselves, in their families, and in the people who care (or cared) about them, the special qualities that have helped them through good times and bad. By exploring courage and accomplishments in their families, children can learn how we can all become heroes in our own stories, the stories of our lives.

Shared Stories

When parents share their experiences and memories, children are *en*couraged to work on their own life stories. Children often listen closely to how parents coped with problems at the same age as children. Shame is reduced when children learn that parents have made mistakes, acted in defiant or stupid ways, and learned lessons in their lives.

Many traumatized children have learned that adults in their lives avoided dealing with traumas and demonstrated that traumas were too frightening to face. Following Main (1991) and Hesse (1999), the most critical part of work with traumatized children may be the effort to help caring adults show that they are (or have become) able to coherently use words and an understanding of time (past, present, and future) to validate what the child and other family members experienced. It is important to help parents understand the impact of trauma and develop skills for managing their own feelings so that they can assure a child that they (and the child) will be safe when the child shares his or her memories. Preparation of parents should include sessions alone with a therapist to work on accepting the parent's own reactions, moving beyond shame and blaming, understanding the impact of trauma on development and behavior, developing support for parents with family members, friends, and community groups, and practicing how to respond to children in order to rebuild trust. Parents and other caring adults can be coached to show acceptance of children's memories and to respond with caring and validation.

By completing their own life story workbooks, parents can teach children that it is safe to talk about the good times and the bad, that both are part of life, and that families can help each other to overcome problems. Parents can use their own life-story work to demonstrate that it is safe for children to share their memories and expectations without fear of their parents becoming upset, out of control, or triggering another cycle of depression, substance abuse, family violence, or abandonment.

CONTENTS OF WORKBOOK

The workbook is organized into eight chapters:

1. A Little About Me
2. Heroes
3. Looking Back
4. People in My Life
5. Good Times
6. Making Things Better
7. Through the Tough Times
8. Into the Future

An introduction for parents and caring adults summarizes guidelines to promote effective use of this workbook, including safety guidelines, promoting creativity, the making of heroes, how to facilitate storytelling, when to bring in a therapist, and a note for practitioners. The importance of validation is stressed and the book begins with a pledge by helping adults to respect the child's perceptions, thoughts, and feelings.

Chapter 1 introduces children to the format of the workbook. The heading at the top of the page directs children to think about doing something fun, and then picture it below with a drawing or a photograph. A question at the bottom of the page directs children to write a brief note about other things they like to do for fun. Questions were designed to build-up their sense of being valued and their sense of competence in different situations. The completed page will typically contain both children's visual memories and a short narrative to add additional details and their understanding of what was most important.

In the first few pages, children are invited to share a little about themselves with the adult who is helping them write this book, and by so doing, to learn from that adult that it is normal to have a wide range of feelings. This is especially important for children who have experienced separations and traumas leading them to become constricted in their feelings, beliefs, and sense of hope. Parents and other adults can use this chapter to show the child how they see the child is special and that they are committed to listening to the child and respecting his or her perspective. Chapter 1 gives adults an opportunity to validate how a child has been successful and to show acceptance of a child's wide range of feelings. Children who feel they can trust the adult who is helping them will be much more willing to move ahead in the book.

Real Life Heroes helps children see how they are special within their families and communities. Chapter 2 builds on the conception of heroes as people who help others and contribute to their families and communities. Helping others is an integral part of building self-esteem and shaping tomorrow's citizens and leaders. This chapter provides a place for children to remember how they have helped others and to envision what they could do in the future. Chapter 2 emphasizes the courage to help others and the making of a hero.

In Chapter 2, children are invited to draw, act out, or write a brief story of someone in their lives who has acted like a hero. By making this a shared activity with a parent, relative, or committed adult, children learn that they are not alone and that important people in their lives can see the importance of caring for one another. At the same time, adults can learn from children what they look for in a hero.

Chapter 3 provides a chronicle for children's moves between different locations or homes. Children can also use this section to develop a time line of good and bad events. Ratings of events from "worst" to "best" can help children to see how forces outside their control have affected their lives and at the same time help to develop a sense of time including a past, a present, and a future. This helps children develop the understanding that they do not have to remain stuck in an uncomfortable position.

Chapter 4 helps children remember people who cared for them from day to day, through sickness and health. Memories of being valued and of positive people are often lost or minimized when children have experienced difficult times in their lives. This chapter provides an opportunity to expand children's awareness of people who have helped, even in small ways, and to highlight resources in their lives including their own talents. Children can also bring in images of heroes from stories, music, movies, fantasy, and real life.

Chapter 5 helps children remember the strengths, skills, and supportive relationships that helped them in "good times." They can then utilize these memories to learn from the "tough times."

After children complete the time line, it is helpful to emphasize how we can learn from the bad times, but it is just as important to learn from the good times. Practitioners can ask children to draw a line connecting each circled number on the right side, then turn the page horizontally so the page number is on the right side. This highlights every year in children's lives when the line went up and can be used as guides to learn more from them about what helped make things better in those years. Who helped in these special times and how did they help themselves?

The time line helps to identify positive events in children's lives. By looking more closely at these important and often neglected times, caring adults can help children learn lessons about who helped them succeed, how they helped themselves, and how they and important people in their lives overcame problems. In this way, successes from the past can expand a child's sense of hope to deal with problems in the present or the future. Chapter 3 also provides a framework to help children to diagram the roots of their family tree, highlighting ties to family members, friends, caring adults, and levels of support.

Chapter 6 helps children make things better in their lives working from magical wishes to things they could do to make up for mistakes they have made. Skills in self-soothing are introduced and children are encouraged to remember and enlist the skills and resources that helped them in the past in order to learn from difficult times in their lives.

In Chapter 7 children are encouraged to remember and enlist the skills and resources that helped them in the past in order to learn from difficult times in their lives. The chapter includes an opportunity for children to think about what they could do to make up for mistakes they have made.

Chapter 8 provides a chance for children to develop images of themselves becoming successful in the future. This can easily lead to planning activities and educational programs to help children achieve their goals.

By the end of this workbook, children should be able to identify people who cared about them in the past and the present, and who they would like to have in their lives in the future. Children should also be able to verbalize, picture, or dramatize what they have learned about themselves and their families.

After completing Chapters 1 through 8 of *Real Life Heroes,* it is often helpful for children to put their memories together into a narrative story of their lives. Children can write their life stories as traditional autobiographies, using the notes section at the end of the workbook, or preferably with a word processor, to allow flexibility and easy revisions. The completed narrative can then be inserted at the end of *Real Life Heroes*. The children can put together a summary of the most important experiences in their lives beginning with how their parents came to be together, their birth, and how family members have coped with good times and bad leading to their achievements. The narrative can emphasize how the child mastered difficult situations and developed skills with help from important people.

Children are invited to create their own title page as the final step in this workbook, a title that reflects how they have mastered "good times and bad." I invite children to remove the title page that came with the workbook as well as the Introduction for adults and insert in their place the child's title sheet. The child may also want to insert a dedication page. Examples of titles include: *My Book About Good Times and Bad, All About Me, My Family and Me, My Life from A to Z,* and *How I Learned to Enjoy My Life.*

OBJECTIVES OF WORKBOOK

After completing the life-story workbook, children should be able to

- identify people who cared about them in the past and the present;
- identify people they would like to visit, call, share holidays with, or possibly live with in the future;
- identify people who could help them with problems in the present or the future;
- share memories and feelings with words, pictures, or action;
- share stories of how they and significant family members overcame hard times;
- understand how their behaviors fit into past relationships and experiences and why they did what they did, a healing story (Figley, 1989);
- choose what behaviors they want to keep and make a list of new skills to learn;
- share memories of how they helped other people; and
- share goals for how they would like to help other people in the future.

By working with children on their life-story workbook, caring adults should be able to:

- identify people who cared for children in the past;
- identify people who will validate children' experiences;
- identify children's primary attachments;
- identify important losses for children and whether they need help to grieve;
- identify children's fears and develop any needed safety plans;
- help children break down destructive beliefs;
- understand how children's behaviors fit into past relationships and experiences; and
- develop opportunities for children to develop skills in communication, relationships with peers, siblings, parents, and authorities, as well as special talents or areas of interest.

Safety First

Before working on life stories, children must be protected by the adults who are raising them and be safe from any threats of violence, emotional abuse, or neglect. Children also need to have developed skills in calming themselves (see Chapter 6, this text).

Children must feel free to be able to signal or say, "Stop. I need to take a break," and then be able to utilize some form of distraction, imagery, tension release, physical exercise, prayer, or meditation that works to soothe themselves. Therapists and teachers using this workbook need to be able to work individually with each child, pace the work to a child's capacity and level of security, and assure confidentiality as appropriate.

Remembering past events can rekindle both happy and painful feelings including sadness, loneliness, or anger. This is a natural part of healing. To make this process more understandable, it is helpful to point out to children that these feelings are normal and that it is natural for them to sometimes remember other events later on. This can be presented as a natural process in developing strength as a person and mastering old problems and a component of trauma therapy (Shapiro, 1995).

The adults involved in this work can help children relax and feel safe. Knowing the children involved is essential. A hug from a trusted family member, a pat on the back, and praise for their courage may be all that is needed. Having a trusted adult sit close is very important. Many children benefit from supportive touch by a parent or therapist, e.g., an arm around their back. Young children may want to sit on the lap of a parent they trust. With therapists of the opposite sex of the child, it may only be possible to sit close to the child and reinforce work with a tap on the child's shoulders or by gently stroking the back or top of their head. Proximity to the child should at all times be based on a child's comfort. With some children, it works best to give them a page to work on while the therapist attends nearby to other work. However, as soon as the child completes a page, it is important for the therapist to quickly move over to the child and help the child to share his or her work (Taboh, Personal Communication, 2003). For other children, practice in relaxation techniques with a therapist will be needed.

Writing this book should be guided by a skilled trauma therapist (licensed psychologists, social workers, or psychiatrists) whenever children have experienced traumas, appear agitated, lose awareness of what is happening around them, or act in ways that put themselves or others at risk of being hurt. Use of the workbook should follow an assessment of the children alone, an assessment of the family, and contracting with children and parents to work in attachment and trauma therapy. Practitioners should have training in attachment and trauma therapy. When children are in foster or adoptive families, it is important that practitioners are also knowledgeable about the experience of placement and critical issues in adoption.

Children showing signs of acute stress often need intensive services including close supervision in order to feel safe at home, at school, or in their neighborhoods. The workbook was not designed for use with schizophrenic children who do not have the capacity to separate fantasy from reality, or for children who cannot deal with the anxiety created.

Formal inventories of dissociation may be necessary to assess children's stability and differentiate dissociation from drug-induced behaviors. Signs of dissociation that warrant caution and safety measures include the following:

- Mumbled, garbled verbalizations
- Repetitive movements
- Lack of awareness of time or place
- Lack of awareness of the practitioner's identity or of self
- Trancelike movements or visual fixations
- Sudden changes in movement that do not fit with the children's stories
- Inability to remember if they really did something or just imagined doing it
- Not being able to remember actions observed by others
- Finding themselves in a place and not knowing how they got there
- Inability to feel parts of their body
- Hearing voices or seeing things that were not really there

Tension or distress in children often reflects very normal reactions to real crises. Their actions, the words they use, and the feelings they show can guide caring adults to old problems that still bother children. Therapists, parents, and other caring adults can then help children to overcome specific fears and memories of events that shaped their lives.

Involving Caring Adults

Real Life Heroes works best as a shared activity guided by a psychologist, social worker, or school counselor along with the primary adults who are working to provide children with safe, nurturing homes, adults who children can trust to believe and protect them. The success of this activity relies largely on the ability of the adults in a child's life to show that he or she will truly be safe to share. For a child, this means that the adults involved will validate the child's experiences and feelings and will help him or her to overcome distressing and shameful problems. This begins with the pledge at the beginning of the book for adults to show that they want the child to share what the child thinks, remembers, and feels. Children need to see that caring adults have the courage and ability to make this pledge a reality and that children do not have to fear losing a parent or any further abuse, neglect, or violence as a result of their disclosures.

Children should be allowed to decide when to invite parents and other important relatives to sign the pledge and become part of life-story work. Ideally, this will occur by the time the child is ready to work on Chapter 3, but in some cases, a child may not feel safe enough to share this work with a parent or relative, or the child may only be able to share portions of their work with special safety steps developed and implemented in advance. Before inviting caring adults to participate in sessions, it is important to be certain that

- A caring adult gives the child support and permission to share what he or she experienced.
- A caring adult has validated the child's experiences, including traumas involving adults.
- A caring adult is committed to protecting the child from anyone, even other family members.
- A caring adult identifies how he or she sees the child as special and part of his or her life.
- A caring adult can manage his or her own reactions to trauma without retraumatizing the child, including being able to face traumatic memories and reminders or reenactments.
- A caring adult demonstrates commitment to protect, provide, and guide (James, 1989).

- A caring adult assures the child that both the adult and the child will be safe when the child shares memories.
- A caring adult writes coherent narrative addressing all key points in the *Real Life Heroes* storybook.
- The child indicates in private to the therapist that he or she feels safe to share with the caring adult present and wants the caring adult in sessions.

Validation

Children cannot be expected to work on life stories if they are being asked to deny their experiences or to return to a home or school marked by violence. Similarly, children can not be expected to utilize life stories for positive growth if the adults around them do not have the courage to speak honestly about what has happened and to take responsibility for their own actions. Children learn to deal with the truth from their parents and significant adults in their lives.

Subtle or covert pressure by adults to say or remember certain events in a certain way will lead to greater constriction in the child and could generate false memories that distort a child's understanding and accelerate behavior problems. If the child shows any signs of feeling pressured to say or remember in a way to please a family member, foster parent, or other significant person, it is essential to have a neutral therapist address this issue first and work with family members to keep the child safe.

More secure children will test adults overtly to see if adults will allow them to share or believe them. More frightened children will often test adults in covert or even sneaky ways, reflecting their experience that sharing has not been safe. Caring adults need to know that the process of testing is both normal and necessary for children to find out if it is safe to open up their feelings and beliefs. Children need to find out if adults will criticize them in a shaming manner or become too stressed to deal with real situations and experiences. Testing can be facilitated by allowing young children to dictate stories to adults. The adult can help by carefully writing down exactly what the child says, using the child's words. The child can then see that the adult is truly hearing the child's story and not trying to change it to fit the adult's perspective or wishes.

Work on the storybook is not intended to be a forced project for the child to work on by himself or herself. However, some children may prefer to do sections by themselves and then share these parts later with their therapist or family members they can trust.

It often works best if the caring adult works on his or her own life story (Mullin, Personal Communications, 2000) at the same time and pace as the child. In this way, the adult can model that it is okay to share both good and bad memories without shame or embarrassment. The adult can also pass on what was learned in his or her own life in a way that matches a child's work in his or her life storybooks. If a parent or a child is too uncomfortable to work together on sharing their experiences, it may be helpful to bring in a trusted relative or a friend. When significant adults work on their own life stories, children see that adults are really not afraid and that life story work is valued.

Threats

If children balk at writing life stories, it is often a sign that they may be living with secrets or unresolved fears. By the end of Chapter 1, children will often know if they can begin to trust the adult(s) who are helping them. Page by page, children will see if this adult validates how the child is successful and will accept the child's wide range of feelings, providing guidance where needed but without shaming or showing fear of the children's real feelings, and pacing the work to show them that completion of the work is possible while respecting their need to take breaks, get help from adults, and test how safe it will be to share experiences.

When children become tense or agitated, they can be encouraged to express their feelings and concerns directly to their parents, guardians, or other significant parent figures through letters, tapes, or in conjoint or subsequent sessions. It this becomes unsafe, a child needs to be given a sense of hope that authorities understand the child's predicament and will work to protect a child from being forced to return to unsafe situations or a dangerous home. Children will know if this is true by how authorities respond to fears about visits. Are children forced to go to visits when they feel unsafe? Have practitioners, law guardians, CPS workers, CASA workers, and judges taken the time to hear a child's story? Have realistic safety precautions been implemented? Are authorities supporting mandates from family members that children return to unsafe situations as "goals." Can authorities voice the experiences and fears children carry from past traumas, or do authorities appear to be placating parents, fearful of lawsuits, and unable or unwilling to say out loud in front of the children what has been reported?

If a child feels threatened by a family member or another person, he or she needs to be assured that disclosures in life-story work will remain confidential within the limits of the law and ethical practice. Practitioners need to acknowledge their responsibilities to bring in authorities if a child was neglected or abused, or if someone is in danger of being harmed. Success in these situations often requires orders of protection, supervision of any contacts with perpetrators, and transfer of custody of the child to someone who can be trusted to protect the child from any threats with monitoring by CPS and reports to family court.

Sharing Feelings

Children are invited at the end of Chapter 1 to share photographs or drawings of themselves showing different feelings. For children who have difficulty recognizing or expressing different feelings, it is frequently necessary to practice identifying and expressing different feelings. Fears, inhibitions, and traumas may lead children to become constricted in their ability to express basic feelings. Use of pictorial charts of different feelings can provide a reference and looking at photographs from magazines can be used to practice understanding other people's expressions.[1] Adults also model how they show different feelings in their faces, tone of voice, words, and actions, and how recognition of feelings helps to strengthen our abilities to cope with problems by enhancing our awareness of what is going on around us, reminding us of what happened in the past, and cueing us to use our resources to solve real or potential problems.

A video camera, digital camera, or instant camera can provide a fun means to practice expressing feelings. Such exercises can be used to show children that it is normal and expected for them to show a wide range of feelings. For children with an aptitude for physical expression, this can be enlarged into activities to enact emotions and messages through movement and dance. For other children, use of colors, shape, and intensity in drawings or crafting clay figures can be useful to develop an awareness and ability to utilize their feelings. Chapter 6 lists activities and protocols (e.g., Ford, Mahoney, and Russo, 2003; Miller et al., 1995; Miller, Rathus, and Linehan, in press; Layne et al., 1999; Layne, Saltzman, and Pynoos, 2003) for developing children's competence in both expressing and identifying emotions.

Creativity

There are no right or wrong stories and no right or wrong ways to share feelings and memories, as long as children are not harming anyone. Some children are better with words. Some prefer visual images, music, or movement to show how they feel and understand situations. Children's creative strengths facilitate resolution of conflicts in ways that would be impossible if they were required to work within one framework, such as verbally telling what happened. Moreover, painful memories are stored at different levels and associated with different senses such as visual images, touch, smell, auditory memory, or feelings.

Beginning in Chapter 1, it is helpful to ask children to utilize a combination of modalities to enhance expression of the child's responses for each page. Children can utilize creative approaches such as drawings, posters, stories, poetry, music, videotapes, collages of pictures cut from magazines or picture books, cartoons, interviews with adults in the format of news shows, dance or movement patterns recorded on videotape, or other creative approaches that tap into a child's special talents. In general, the more modalities used the better. As a general format, children can be asked to do the following:

- draw an image,
- accentuate facial details,
- demonstrate tone of voice accompanying an image,
- tap out a rhythm and intensity to match the image with a "magic wand" or drum stick,
- identify feelings with words, e.g., have child "scan" or touch his or her head, fist, gut, legs, and toes and then share how different parts of their body are feeling,
- highlight positive beliefs stressing strengths and coping with problems, or
- enact with movement, dance, a sports move tied to a task (e.g., "happy" dunk shot in basketball, a "sad" free throw, a "powerful" soccer kick at the goal, or with family dolls or homemade puppets representing family figures.

Practitioners can help children carry this out in different ways using different tools and materials to promote flexible and creative responses. Photographs could also be collected (or copied) from relatives and inserted along with other important documents. It helps to have a camera that can generate immediate print or digital photographs, but an ordinary camera can also work well if photographs can be developed in a timely manner. It also helps to begin this work by giving the child a special deluxe set of markers or colored pencils reserved for life story work.

It is very helpful to involve children in the development of creative arts skills at the same time that they are working on the *Real Life Heroes* workbook. Developing skills in areas of interest, such as singing, playing a musical instrument, painting, dance, or theater arts facilitates a child's ability to share feelings and find creative solutions. Working with a mentor on skill development is very helpful to foster competence and self-esteem. Working with a long-term mentor[2] also provides a youth with a relationship to a supportive adult, a positive sense of identity, and hope for the future.

ADAPTING THE WORKBOOK FOR ADOLESCENTS AND YOUNG CHILDREN

The *Real Life Heroes* workbook was especially written for children between the ages of six and twelve, but this book can easily be adapted for adolescents by using the themes addressed on each page and creative approaches. An adolescent can be invited to try out something written for younger children who went through what they did when they were younger and see if they can enjoy it, even though they are *much* older now. Adolescents can be invited to let themselves go *back in time* and imagine themselves at a younger age, respond to workbook exercises, and then work on the book at their current age. For example, they could be six and fifteen, completing pages the way they *used* to feel and think when things were very hard, and then contemplating how they feel and understand situations from the vantage point of their current age, older and wiser. Adolescents could also be invited to complete the book as a gift for younger siblings or as a way of helping younger children who experienced what they did. At the same time, work on developing special competence in an area of strength or interest, e.g., singing, art, sports, takes on even more significance for adolescents and can lead to mentoring relationships and opportunities for adolescents to help others and, at the same time, boost their own self-esteem.

Adolescents are often more receptive to writing a journal or an autobiography, e.g., "My World, My Way." They can often be engaged to draw, paint, sculpt, make up songs, or choreograph a story addressing issues raised by pages in the *Real Life Heroes* workbook. Youths interested in sports can be invited to develop a move or play that reflects what it would take to deal with a situation. With adolescents, it is also helpful to build on peer orientation, bringing in positive friends and relatives, promoting involvement in positive groups, and utilizing abstract reasoning skills to find new ways to master old problems. Group exercises in learning to understand and overcome trauma, manage feelings (affect regulation), and develop assertive communication and problem-solving skills are very effective with adolescents (Ford, Mahoney, and Russo, 2003; Miller et al., 1995; Miller, Rathus, and Lineham, in press; Layne, Saltzman, and Pynoos, 2003).

Adolescents may be much more receptive to sharing their work in groups, once safety rules have been established. Chapters of the life story book can be used to develop themes to address in group projects emphasizing who helped youths, hero images, recognizing how we all have weaknesses and strengths, learning how to safely recognize, accept, and express feelings, identifying supportive people who can be trusted, and practicing skills in dealing with difficult situations. Adolescents often can become actively engaged in role-playing solutions to stressful situations in their lives, e.g., being insulted by a storekeeper, being accused by a peer of trying to take away their boy- or girlfriend, being pressured to engage in unsafe behavior. Discussions in groups can also promote understanding of sexual, economic, or ethnic victimization and can help to engage older youths to direct their anger into active steps to reassert a sense of personal power and break out of self-shaming. This can lead to active involvement in advocacy groups such as NOW, the NAACP, "take back the night" marches, etc.

The workbook can also be adapted for children with developmental delays or learning disabilities. For some children, narratives may need to be limited to single words, and more verbal children may want to generate full page stories for every topic. Additional guidance is needed for children with cognitive abilities under age six. Therapists or caring adults may need to read the text to children and help them spell words, working carefully to reflect the child's responses without bias.

For younger children, the adult can write out the child's dictated story on notepaper or on a word processor. Then either the adult or the child can insert the story on to the appropriate page of *Real Life Heroes.*

Often, children with limited writing skills do better by dictating answers into a tape recorder that can later by typed. It sometimes helps for therapists to take on the role of a radio or TV show interviewer, or to become a TV host a child admires, and then use the questions on each worksheet as a mock interview taped for later transcription.

Other children may prefer to use word-processing programs to facilitate writing and editing narratives that can be pasted into the book or printed directly on the bottom of pages under pictures. Or, for children who prefer, audio- or videotapes could be made to accompany the pictures, page by page.

FACILITATING STORYTELLING

Children learn to love reading books with a parent, teacher, or another caring person who sits with them, repeats their beloved stories, and later guides them at their pace to start reading themselves. Similarly, story telling is facilitated when practitioners and caring adults work closely with children. Verbal guidance, proximity, supportive touch, and reinforcement should match the child's age emotionally and developmentally. A ten-year-old who feels and acts like a five-year-old may need the same level of nurture and assistance as a five-year-old in order to overcome past traumas.

Storytelling should be a magical time for children. Therapists and parents can set the mood by working with children in a comfortable and quiet setting, minimizing distractions, and serving an herbal tea or hot cocoa and a special kind of cookie, creating an aroma and taste that conveys comfort and support. Allowing children to select a favorite herbal tea each day, reading the label and choosing the taste, smell, and attributes (e.g., calming or invigorating), can help empower and soothe a child from the inside out. Treats in this approach are just part of the work, a way of modeling how we help ourselves to deal with difficult situations, rather than a reward for compliance.

Work on the life storybook can be introduced by saying, "I have a very special book . . ." It helps for practitioners to highlight the "Pledge" and to accentuate both the challenge and the rewards of this work, for example, "Some of this is hard, but it's the kind of hard work that really helps to make the hard things become not 'so hard.' It really helps to write these things down and put them in a special book" (Taboh, Personal Communication, 2003).

Practitioners can help children to develop each story by gently asking them to write or share what they remember and to make up a brief story to go along with the picture. Their stories can be enriched by asking questions geared to their age and abilities. Examples of facilitating questions include:

- Draw a picture in your mind and focus, just for a minute on what was happening.
- Where would you be?
- What is around you?
- Who are you with?
- What do they look like?
- What are they doing? (For example, How are they taking care of you?)
- What are the expressions on their faces? What are they showing in their eyes, their mouths, and their cheeks?
- Focus on your sensations: touch, smell, sight, sounds. What are you feeling?
- What are you doing?
- What happened just before?
- What happened next?
- What would happen in the end?
- What was the most important part of this story for you?

- If you shared this story with another child, what would be the lesson he or she could learn?

For memories of difficult moments, it is helpful to open up possibilities to prevent any future traumas by asking the child to consider questions such as these:

- What could have made it just a little better?
- What could have helped you and (other people in the story)?

If the child balks, working on solutions should not be forced. Rather, a therapist can ask such questions[3] as the following:

- Was this fair?
- Who should have helped (parents, aunts, uncles, grandparents, friends, neighbors, police, teachers, doctors, etc.)?
- Who could help now?

If the child blames himself or herself, the adult can ask the following:

- Do you know any children (at the age of the child during the incident in the story)? Would a ____________ year-old child, like the child you know, be responsible for what happened?

SELF-SOOTHING SKILLS

Pictures and stories in the workbook provide a good starting point for work on developing self-soothing and self-monitoring skills, if this has not already been done. Children need to be able to utilize sufficient self-soothing skills in order to complete this book. For children with high levels of anxiety, it would be important to find ways to reassure them, to help them to relax, and to strengthen their sense of security before completing Chapter 7.

Developing "safe-place" imagery is very important. Each child should be able to bring up relaxing images of a time and place when he or she felt safe. This can be practiced with some form of repetitive stimulation such as tapping, eye movements, or alternating sounds (Shapiro, 1995, 2001). Trauma and traumatic memories activate the brainstem, and patterned repetitive stimulation may "trick" the brainstem into allowing the child to learn new ways to perceive and cope with traumatic events.[4] Healing rituals, such as prayer alongside a comforting adult, drumming, chanting, dance, or singing hymns and reassuring tunes may also be very helpful.

Children can be guided in developing self-soothing skills with exercises (see Munson and Riskin, 1995) in deep muscle relaxation, visual imagery, and meditation. For children who have difficulty managing frustrations and anger, exercises in anger management may be very useful (see Eggert, 1994; Whitehouse and Pudney, 1996). Similarly, children with difficulties focusing attention may benefit from workbooks that provide guidance on slowing down and sustaining attention (see Nadeau and Dixon, 1997).

ATTACHMENT AND TRAUMA THERAPY

Real Life Heroes was designed to foster permanency from a child's point of view and to build a foundation for trauma therapy. Children in foster homes, psychiatric hospitals, or group-care facilities need viable backup plans for where they could live if they cannot return to their biological families, and practitioners need to be well versed in permanency work (see Kagan and Schlosberg, 1989; Kagan, 1996) and legal requirements such as the Adoption and Safe Families Act.[5] The workbook format provides sequential activities that help build (or strengthen) relationships between a child and parents, siblings, foster or adoptive parents, therapists, or caretakers. Worksheets foster empathy and understanding by parents of both connections and gaps in their attachments to children over time.

Use of the workbook provides openings to stories about important areas of a child's life (e.g., holidays, visits, moves). Therapists can then tailor additional work or interventions where needed. For example, a child may benefit from a special meeting with an uncle to learn about what happened to a parent. Another child may show an interest or skill in painting, leading to a mentoring relationship with an art teacher. A child who shows fear about a particular time or family member needs help from protective adults to develop necessary safety plans and to deal with what the child experienced.

Practitioners can adapt the workbook to individual children and select the most relevant pages although the order presented was designed to build a child's skills in a step-by-step manner. The most important exercises are highlighted by a special symbol. Therapists may choose to focus on only certain chapters or selected pages in each chapter, combined with other modalities for attachment and trauma therapy. By combining the structured approach of the life-story workbook with open-ended art, music, dance, or other modalities, the therapist can cover important areas of a child's life and at the same time allow the child to develop creative solutions with fantasy and modalities visual, kinesthetic, auditory modalities.

This is facilitated by inviting children to add feelings, movement, rhythms, tonality, or enactments to go along with pictures.

As a child works on a particular task, a therapist may notice a change in a child's face, the beginnings of a frown, a teardrop forming, or the child's head slumping down with a whispered sigh. The child's reactions can lead practitioners and caring adults to sensitive issues. In the child's face and gestures, we may witness the child's reexperiencing of original traumas. A child's reactions to workbook questions can guide practitioners and family members to memories of events and people that continue to trigger trauma behaviors in a child. These can be addressed in trauma therapy once the child has developed the safety and basic affect regulation skills to avoid flooding or rekindling and strengthening trauma reactions.

Children who are secure enough can be asked to think about a memory and share any feelings, thoughts, or images that come up. This can be done with markers, colors, sounds, or movement. Closing their eyes and letting their fingers draw or tap (on a drum) can be helpful. Opportunities for a physical activity after working on stories can include invitations to use speed, action, and intensity tied to their feelings as they make a basket, hit a ball, or jump on a trampoline. The practitioner or parent can validate this feeling by witnessing children's energy and encourage them to write down, tape record, or remember any other feelings that come up in later days.

Pictures and images drawn by children provide rich focal points for additional work by children who are involved in trauma therapies (see Shapiro, 1995, 2001; van der kolk, McFarlane, and Weisaeth, 1996), including desensitization approaches with certified therapists. Memories and feelings can be encouraged as important work by the child on healing, a natural process that practitioners can incorporate into trauma therapy for the child. Completing *Real Life Heroes* can build up a child's self-esteem to the point where he or she can more easily write out a more traditional narrative life story (see Jewett, 1978; Wheeler, 1978).

A Developmental and Skill-Based Curriculum

Appendix D outlines a phase-oriented curriculum including key points, objectives, strategies, and safety criteria, as well as procedures for involving caring adults in life-story work. Children typically begin the workbook in individual sessions with a therapist. A parent or another caring adult can be brought into sessions after safety criteria have been met, including acceptance of a child's experience without pressuring child in any way. Appendix D also includes steps to take when children resist work or appear stuck.

In use of the life story book, it is important to focus on interactions more than content. Each page completed represents an accomplishment. Each activity also offers another opportunity for protective adults to attune to children and demonstrate their commitment to join with the child to disempower the child's demons. Children and caring adults reconnect as they work to rebuild positive memories and overcome events that may have been too painful to address before in the child's experience. Storybook activities provide opportunities for children and parents to relate to each other with nonverbal acceptance and attunement through touch, facial looks, tone of voice, humor, and having fun.

Throughout this work a child's behaviors can be used as a guide to the balance between pain and resources. Crises in work with traumatized children are predictable, including avoidance by a child (or parent) of work on sensitive issues. Clinicians can use strategies presented in Appendix D to foster development of resources needed to reduce pain and to keep children and caring adults working on rebuilding trust. Appendix D includes criteria to ensure that a child has the necessary resources to address the "tough times" before asking a child to recall difficult memories.

Completion of tasks in the workbook demonstrates that parents, practitioners, caring adults, and children are committed to overcoming trauma and coping, rather than continuing to hide from pain and relive traumas. With each chapter, the hero concept and emphasis on courage can be accentuated to foster collaborative work to conquer the "monsters" of the past.

ADOPTION

Real Life Heroes works very well with children who have been placed into *pre*adoptive homes or with children who have been adopted after experiencing multiple moves in their lives. The workbook allows children to share their past with their new parents and relatives, to get help in answering questions, and to find out if their new family will accept their past experiences, affection, loyalty, grief, and wishes.

Children adopted as infants often grow up with questions, doubts, and at times, deep-seated insecurity, when their past is shrouded in secrecy. Life-story work helps children and parents to transform *non*verbalized feelings of tension, fear, or sadness into pictures and words, providing a means for adoptive parents to connect with a child and help a child grieve. By working with their child on the life-story workbook, adoptive parents can validate typical concerns of children and demonstrate courage and commitment to their child. Parents who adopt can show that they respect a child's natural curiosity and feelings of loyalty by helping a child learn as much as possible about his or her birth parents, or first family (or families).

If adoptive parents tell children that they "chose" to adopt them, the children will naturally want to know why their previous biological or foster parents chose not to keep them. Adoptive parents may be tempted to block out information on lost parents out of anger or fear of losing a child, or as a way of protecting a child from dealing with birth parents' medical problems, criminal actions, addictions, neglect or rejection of a child. Other adoptive parents may feel a need to make up some excuse or justification for what previous parents have done. Neither is helpful for a child (van Gulden and Bartels-Rabb, 1995).

Adoptive parents should be encouraged to provide a balanced view with respect for children, parents, and family members. Dichotomies, such as the "good" versus the "bad" parent may be initially comforting but often lead later on to idealization. Children who learn to think in "black or white" terms often flip back and forth and soon begin responding to their new parents as "good" or "bad," but never "real."

Life-story work is about honesty and courage. Deep inside, children have experienced what really happened. Distortions confuse children and teach them that their parents are afraid to address and overcome what really happened.

COMPLETION OF THE WORKBOOK

Step by step, chapter by chapter, a child can build a stronger identity. Appendix E of this text includes a chart that can be copied and used to help reinforce a child's progress in completing the workbook. Life-story work can help children to see themselves as growing stronger than their problems. At the end of Chapter 7, children can compare their drawing of themselves as a hero with their image of themselves from a "tough time" in the past. Therapists can help children visualize how they can grow, but their problems stay the same size (Rojano, 1998).

Completion of the book can be highlighted with a signing ceremony and a celebration for the child as the author. Certificates can be framed and/or combined with a photograph of the child. The photograph could include the caring adults and therapist who demonstrated that they honored the "Pledge."

Children may also be honored by being asked to share their life stories with younger children or children who have recently experienced some of the same kinds of hard times (after White and Epston, 1990; Freedman and Combs, 1996). With consent from children and guardians, this could include donating a copy to a special library with names and other identifying details changed, allowing a therapist to share their books with other children, or reading their book to younger children.

Given the importance and emotions generated in this work, it is always important to maintain a backup copy in a safe place. The original can be laminated and bound. Keeping two or three copies is highly recommended in order to preserve a child's memories and provide a resource for him or her in later years. After completing and sharing the book, a child may wish to put it aside. A parent can offer to lock the book away in a safe place, to be read again whenever the child wishes.

Chapter 12

Impasse and Beyond

If you want to raise a man from filth and mud, do not think it is enough to keep standing on top and reaching down to offer him a helping hand. You must go down yourself into the mud. Then take hold of him and pull him and yourself out into the light.

Solom ben Meir Halen of Karlin
(1738-1798)

INTRODUCTION

Impasse represents a treacherous and often necessary part of a hero's quest. It's the supreme test of *dis*couragement and often represents the bottom-line question for a traumatized child with broken attachments. Will today's caring adults give up, reject, or abuse, as the adults of the past? When family members and practitioners feel stuck, weary, and on the edge of removing a child somewhere, to somebody else, it often helps to see periods of impasse as reenactments of the child's old life and a test to see if the worst traumas of the past will be repeated. In these difficult days and weeks, parents and practitioners often seem to be *re*living the story of the child's trauma.

As therapists and parents, we feel the impasse in our bodies as tension, pain, fear, or anger. We may feel as though we are walking on eggshells with a child, or afraid to say certain words. We may find ourselves snapping at the child and other family members, or feel we are ready to explode ourselves, reject the child, and leave the child for someone else.

From a strength-based perspective, the experience of impasse means that parents and practitioners have entered the pit of a child's nightmare, the core of a child's conundrum. With courage and commitment, they have gone down into the mud with the child. Now, it is time to find a way out, for the child and caring adults. The hardest work has begun.

GETTING PAST THE IMPOSSIBLE

An old saying goes, "Listen also for what goes unsaid and you'll hear the simple truth." As practitioners and parents, we can listen between the lines and watch the choreography of a child and family's dance. We can use our reactions, our frustration, our rage, our fears, and our understanding of attachment and trauma to break down boundaries that have trapped the child. Covert rules can be made overt (Papp, 1983). The "unsaid" can be discussed out loud (Ausloos, 1985). Practitioners and parents can change the "rules of the game" that define a child's repetitive behaviors.

As in all forms of therapy, nothing is more important than how we use ourselves as we experience the pain and challenges of a child and family in distress. Impasse typically marks a growing divide between parents and children. When pain and stress mount, even the most caring practitioners are pulled to detach. This can include labeling children or parents with diagnoses that make repeated behavioral patterns sound like permanent diseases, labels that can strengthen the power of negative beliefs and engender powerlessness to change.

Practitioners play a crucial role at these points in attachment and trauma work and are often requested or pressured to manage a child's behaviors under threat of eviction. With an understanding of a child's terror of trauma and abandonment ingrained from real life experiences, practitioners can help parents and other caring adults to focus instead on the child's challenge to adults to master the "monsters" of the past. Rather than becoming caught up in the child's *re*enactment of traumas, practitioners can bolster the staying power of parents, relatives, teachers, and other caring adults.

Impasse typically signals the presence of lingering and very likely unknown obstacles to attachment. Practitioners can help parents to understand impasse as part of the therapeutic process and work to unblock healthy forces in a child and parents that will lead to growth.

As a quick guide to impasse, these techniques help:

- Accept feelings activated by a child's behaviors as vital clues to the child's impasse, rather than personal failings or signs of weakness.
- If a child has reactivated old problems in a caring adult, work separately on our own issues, keeping in mind how traumatized children often sense and activate painful issues in the adults they are beginning to trust.
- Learn how a child's behaviors fit with the child's experiences, beliefs, and expectations.

- Identify noxious messages a child received before he or she was freed for adoption, or later, during visits or through contacts with extended-family members (e.g., a birth parent who surrendered rights to a child after years of neglect, and gave the child a message, "We're always here . . . Come back any time (or) Come back when you're eighteen . . . They stole you . . . You were kidnapped" or a former stepfather who calls out to a child from his car, "Your Mom needs help . . . be sure to call her after school before your parents get home . . .").
- Identify hidden dangers (e.g., a child returning home to a parent who is secretly keeping a formerly abusive partner in the home against court orders and pressuring the child to keep this secret, or a child who is surrendered but asked to keep the secret of how a sibling remains in danger of abuse or neglect.)
- Address noxious messages by helping children look at the choices made by parents, their decisions as adults, day by day, hour by hour, during "diligent efforts to reunite" (e.g., Did the parent stop the drinking, fighting, abuse, and provide a home? What help was given to the parent? What did they agree to on the surrender document? What did they write to the child?) It helps to remind a child of all the help that was offered or provided to parents, listing the names of the service providers, parent advocates, parent aides, etc. It also helps to review constructive messages parents who surrendered a child may have given, such as wanting the child to have a family, or the safety and security parents never knew.
- Develop safety plans for previously unrecognized risks including any reminders of old traumas.
- Help children replace destructive beliefs (e.g., "I am no good. . . . I made my dad so mad and my mom run away. . . . I must have done something terrible for my parents to birth parents to place me away. . . . I am deep down a horrible person for what I did [the sex, the hitting, the stealing, etc.]. . . . Somehow I got lost from my parents" [Fahlberg, 1979b]), with reality-based and constructive messages, a healing theory (Figley, 1989).
- Catch the positive side of each child. Identify his or her talents, strengths, passions, and interests, and enable each child to build on strengths, to succeed, and to help others.
- Find the power and strength in a child's *mis*behavior and find ways the child can use this power to succeed (e.g., to use a loud yelling voice to support a favorite team, to use hypervigilance to win at games such as Clue, Concentration, or card games, or to use fears to design the world's best home or business security systems).

- Supervise and discipline to break negative beliefs and constricted thinking by emphasizing a child's choices to earn privileges or face consequences, recognizing that many traumatized children have not learned to think in terms of cause and effect and have trouble believing this makes any sense based on their experiences growing up in chaotic homes.
- Take away the power of negative behavior by depersonalizing the child's behaviors and exposing them as repeating old beliefs from when the child was younger, weaker, and had fewer (or no) alternatives, stressing a child's choices to act at his or her current age or as the little child of the past.
- Empower parents with strategies, support, and understanding of a child's need for permanency.
- Use the impasse as part of a child's story of transformation.

Practitioners' use of self is the greatest tool we have to help families utilize a crisis and generate solutions. Appendix F outlines an exercise that colleagues can use to help each other build on their own transference and countertransference reactions to broaden perspectives and possibilities for solutions.

CALLING A CRISIS

Practitioners can help parents anticipate crisis-generating behaviors by understanding a child's repeated responses to reminders of past traumas and the messages inherent in a child's behavior. There is no reason to wait for a child to "blow." From a neurological perspective, practitioners can help parents and children strengthen the verbal reasoning and planning side of the brain and foster self-soothing before the child, parent, or practitioner become flooded with fears, anger, or impulsive reactions generated by recurring trauma.

Crises can be predicted when a child is down to just one key person whom a child trusts, or when a parent shares wishes to send a child away forever. A severely traumatized child can often overwhelm one caring parent or practitioner. Traumatized children usually sense the fragility of their relationship, even as they seemingly push the person they need the most to the breaking point.

Rather than fearing the child's behavior, signs and signals of an impending crisis can be defined as opportunities for caring adults to demonstrate how the child's world has changed. This is to mobilize caring adults and authorities. Practitioners and parents can advocate for the help that is needed by calling emergency meetings, writing letters, and visiting missing members of a child's team (judges, county attorneys, probation officers, school officials, child protective workers, group-care staff, foster parents, family therapists). We can use our voices, letters, petitions, parent associations, and conferences, to generate legislation, and funding for needed services for children.

Calling a crisis can be a constructive means of empowering parents and bringing covert rules and beliefs out into the open to be shared and confronted by the people responsible for helping a child. Sharing the work shows a child that parents have the support they need to maintain their composure and fight off the demons from a child's nightmares. The remainder of this chapter addresses practical steps we can take to pull ourselves and our clients out of common impasse situations encountered in work to rebuild attachments.

THERAPEUTIC TOOLS FOR BREAKING IMPASSE

Creative Arts

Impasse often means that a parent or practitioner and a child are not connecting. Just as a bad telephone connection or a "coverage hole" with cellular phones, it helps to switch lines of communication. We can utilize different modalities (Bandler and Grinder, 1976) and expand how we reach out to engage children. Often, children (and parents) can use poetry, music, artwork, movement, and sculpture to represent symbolically what they cannot say in words, or even bear to face directly.

Cooking together (see Chapter 7) provides a unique avenue for transforming a daily necessity into a therapeutic opportunity to reach a child. Creating a special marinara sauce, trying out a new recipe from a country associated with a child's ethnic heritage, and, of course, baking brownies, cookies, pies, and cakes, can be wonderful activities to *re*link with a youth outside of chronic areas of conflict.

Life-story work can be geared to make every child feel special by utilizing his or her interests and talents to develop the medium and structure for the story. For some children, it may be possible to assemble a photo history book chronicling every year and important events in their life with an accompanying time line listing both positive and negative events (Suddaby and Landau, 1998) and the people involved. Another child may become excited about developing a videotaped life book (Clegg and Toll, 1996) based on visits to old neighborhoods and homes with interviews of available relatives, neighbors, teachers, child protective workers, and others who might remember a child and a family. Older youths may wish to compile journals or poetry.

Arts and craft materials can facilitate developing a memory and then utilized to develop new solutions. Some children can be engaged to make up songs or dance routines to symbolize an event. Others may wish to make several collages or clay figures. When three-dimensional crafts are created, it often helps to take photographs of the child's creation to help preserve it and to enable the child to incorporate it into a more formal life book with an accompanying verbal narrative at a later date.

For children who appear "shut down," it can be very helpful to help them transform basic actions and feelings into color and form. For example, children can be asked to draw their breath, to pick a color, to choose how dark to make the drawing, and to let their fingers and a marker (preferably non-staining, washable marker), crayon, or paint, reflect their breath. If children can relax enough to close their eyes, they can be encouraged to imagine letting their breath flow onto the paper through their hands and a marker. As children become engaged in drawing, they can be invited to alter their breath in small ways and to changes the color, strength, or tempo of their drawing to reflect this change.

Children can then be asked to draw other feelings or actions. If a child is sighing, he or she could be asked to sketch a "sigh." If a child is looking angry, the child could be asked to sketch anger. This is not intended to be an exercise in ventilation, but rather a way to foster awareness and ownership of feelings, to learn to accept feelings as natural, and to learn how to transform feelings. So, after drawing anger, a child can be asked to draw a state of calmness, and later a picture of one of his or her favorite places where he or she feels safe. After a drawing of anger, children can be invited to draw what could help regulate their anger so their anger works for them, rather than getting them into trouble.

A frightened child could be asked to sketch the worst monsters possible and then to carefully change those monsters from fearsome objects to fearful, or less threatening images: by changing mouths and eyes to show apprehension of a powerful force coming, by adding hearts, flowers, formal dresses, high heels, or funny hats to evoke humor in place of menacing images, by adding soft, funny words, in a balloon, or by locking the whole monster in a vault with huge steel walls. The power of monsters can also be defused by adding a story line to show the "scared" or "silly" monster underneath the fearsome first image.

Children can also be invited to draw themselves "in control" and "out of control," as well as angry, sad, happy, or frightened, and then to rate on a one to ten scale the power and pleasure of each feeling. If being "out of control" is more powerful than being in control, practitioners can help a child boost the strength of being in control through activities, skill development, and by removing constraints or irrational beliefs that have made "in control" appear less effective to a child. Straus (1999) has written a wonderful guide and compendium of activities to engage mute, oppositional, rude, and otherwise "resistant" children in psychotherapy.

Drawings of feelings can lead into drawing strengths, skills, and fun activities. This can be followed by taking the practitioner for a tour of a child's life (Gil, 1988), including drawing former homes. Children can be asked to draw themselves at different ages, year by year, showing a steady growth in size and strength. This will include, of course, the year (or years) in which children were abused, and can be used to accentuate their positive growth, including their visual expectations for how large they will become as adults. The size of their drawing of themselves as teenagers and adults can then be contrasted with their size at the time of trauma to foster a sense of children's developing strength and capability.

Linesch (1993) and James (1989) describe many innovative techniques, including representing family members in clay or drawings as objects, shapes, etc. Parents and children can be asked to draw the family in the best times remembered, in the worst times, in the time just before placement, and how they wish the family to appear in the future. Children can draw how they feel or felt inside, how they think they look to others in the family, and how the family would look/act if, by magic, their problems went away. Drawing what could help a family move from pictures of the current crisis to pictures of the family with problems resolved (Mills and Crowley, 1986) can help family members to identify the resources available to make changes. Practitioners can then work with family members to access people, technology, and services that can help the family make their wishes come true.

Game Therapy

Children enjoy games in which they can master the rules, play with friends and family, and feel rewarded for success. Practitioners can utilize games to help children rebuild connections, develop skills, and overcome traumas. Creative game approaches (Kagan, 1986, 2000) can be designed to help identify important people in children's lives, to highlight adaptive and maladaptive beliefs, to consider alternative solutions to problems, and to help children learn critical skills.

Games can make it easier for children to deal with some of the painful covert issues (e.g., loss, grief, rejections, abuse, etc.), which have contributed to constricted perspectives and negative beliefs about who they are and who they could become. These beliefs can be enacted in game formats leading to behaviors with realistically positive or negative outcomes. Children can then experiment with different choices for themselves as they play these games. Repeating games that involve choices in beliefs, feelings, and behaviors linked to consequences can help children practice and learn cause-effect thinking.

For children in placement, game therapy can facilitate moving on with the terribly difficult task of facing past traumas, creating safety plans to prevent *re*traumatization, and helping children cope with grief (Kagan, 1982). Maladaptive behaviors can be presented as choices, rather than spontaneous actions. This framework can help children and parents try out more adaptive behaviors and take responsibility for their choices.

Games such as "Cast Adrift," and "Heading Home" (Kagan, 1986, 2000) can help prepare children to develop their own personal game. Rather than utilizing a *pre*packaged game, practitioners can engage children to develop their own game based on their experiences, what happened in their lives, what they thought, felt, and did, and what they have learned. Helping children develop "My Game" (Kagan, 1986, 2000) provides a means of joining with individual children and helping them to creatively share difficult experiences and set positive goals. Use of "My Game" can facilitate work with parents and family members on rebuilding broken ties or, if necessary, bonding to a new family.

It is important that a child's own game be relevant to his or her current interpersonal dilemma as well as to his or her internal feelings. For instance, a child coping with the loss of his or her parents will need to work through stages of grief including: denial, rage, anxiety, withdrawal, and *re*attachment. Each of these feelings and behaviors can be connected to interpersonal relationships in the child's life.

Denial and rage maintain a child's distance from both past and potential family relationships as well as from developing bonds to group-care staff, therapists, or foster parents. Experiencing anxiety may allow the beginning of new relationships or the *re*negotiation of bonds to a child's family. Withdrawal reflects a child's need to experience feelings of emptiness and also may serve to protect him or her from the risks involved in renewing attachments or developing new attachments to another family.

The child's personal game can reflect these feelings and interpersonal relationships. By so doing, the game can facilitate expression of painful feelings and thus reduce their intensity. At the same time, key squares on the game board (e.g., corners) can be used to highlight a child's most important goals including returning to a biological family or adoption.

Game therapy can be viewed as a means of expanding possibilities for connecting with children. Some children come into therapy with past experiences playing games with previous therapists and expect to do the same with their new therapist. Appendix G illustrates how practitioners could utilize children's favorite games to develop their own personal game within a cognitive behavioral approach to help children develop and practice more effective self-talk and responses to manage external pressures and internal feelings. Children can be challenged to find a way to win their game in no more than ten turns, by incorporating more positive beliefs, or helping adult cards. Power points on cards can be adjusted to emphasize strengths and master typical trauma sequences. This fosters children's sense of control over what they do and what happens.

A child's own game also can provide significant clues to important attachments (e.g., to past foster parents who may continue to have a great impact on the child's behaviors or expectations derived from parents or family members, or a parent's message that a child should grow up in an institution). Children's personal games typically reveal relationships that are causing them a great deal of trouble and visually dramatize their difficulties in working through feelings of grief and loss.

Games can also be used with adults to illustrate the difficult situation of children "in limbo." This can be very helpful in preparing prospective adoptive parents or in redefining a child's behaviors to his or her biological family so that change can occur. Therapeutic games can also emphasize parents' choices about their own beliefs and their methods of dealing with feelings through overt behaviors.

Family members can use games together to experiment with new models of interpreting their world and as an opportunity to share otherwise hidden feelings and beliefs. Painful conflicts may thus be addressed through a concrete visual format (e.g., the game board). As conflicts are addressed in an overt manner by the family, a child can be freed from his or her role as the "bad" or "crazy" youth. Dysfunctional beliefs and roles (e.g., victims, rescuers, persecutors, etc.), can be highlighted and parents engaged to develop competence in coping with their lives and in managing their children.

From Shaming and Blaming to Restitution and Healing

Disciplinary interventions can augment a youth's estrangement from family members, positive peers, and normal activities. Behavior-management approaches can inadvertently reinforce a youth's power by emphasizing that the child change, without working with him or her in the context of his or her family. The pathologizing of a child may begin from birth with excessive shaming and demeaning, especially when a child is branded with slurs, curses, or identification with a hated parent (e.g., calling a child a "b-itch" or "b-astard," labeling the child as evil or a "devil," or when one parent screams "You're just like your (father/mother)," using the same angry tone of voice and glare the child remembers from the parent's last fight, the time when Mom chased Dad with a knife or Dad pushed Mom into the wall). Later, a child may be suspended from school, falling further behind classmates. These interventions foster a youth's developing identity as a "bad boy or girl," a delinquent, and possibly, a criminal offender. As behavior problems and reputations develop, youths may find themselves increasingly alone, disillusioned about their families, and convinced that no one cares, so why should they? Negative behaviors often increase with threats of placement if youths do not change. By the time youths are placed, they often have little hope left that their families can change and have learned to use the power of the labels put on them by parents and authorities.

Todd's parents had screamed and yelled at each other throughout his life. By age eight, Todd had learned he could provoke his parents to rage at him by cursing and breaking their rules, gaining him both notoriety and attention. His mother rarely followed through on consequences and his father became verbally abusive and detached himself more and more from the family. Todd kept himself at the center of the family's aggravation, learning to expect and manipulate the threats of his parents. Placement came as a surprise, but by then, Todd had given up on his parents changing. He was twelve years old and tired of living with all the screaming.

"You can come home as soon as you stop calling me names and you start talking in family sessions," Todd's mother said after placing Todd away from home for his defiant behavior. "I can't have you home like this." Todd's grandmother shared how Todd at age eight had told her he had a "hurt heart." Still, she added her own punishment, "You can't come to my home for visits until you start respecting your mom."

Todd was respectful and talkative in his foster family, with therapists, child care workers, and peers. However, when he met with his mom and dad, he stopped talking or called them "stupid." His parents wanted therapists to change his behavior, warning Todd that he could not come home if he continued to act as he did, and if he did come home, and started up again, he would be sent out.

Todd left home as the defiant but proud son, using the limited power he held. He listened to his parents and grandmother's threats and resigned himself to living away from home, becoming obstinate and defiant whenever he saw his family. In permanency work, his parents were asked to work in marital and individual mental health therapy to resolve the roots of their own anger, cursing, and verbal abuse, and Todd worked on learning more adaptive ways of coping with family members, peers, and teachers. Todd's parents were asked to make a choice as adults whether they could commit to raising Todd and dealing with his behaviors, with an expectation that he would probably need to test them with his defiance and anger.

For a year, his parents resisted any work on their problems and repeated their demands that Todd change. In permanency review conferences, Todd's parents were reminded about the Adoption and Safe Families Act time limit for work on reuniting. Therapists addressed Todd's "hurt heart" and the "hurt" feelings of other family members. As the Adoption and Safe Families Act time limit approached, Todd's parents began marital therapy. Todd relaxed in family sessions.

Over the next few months, Todd and his parents made changes separately and together leading up to his return home.

Many children at impasse have been unable to forgive themselves for things they have done, often behaviors that they have been unable to share with caring adults. It helps to show children that we all do things we regret and that this is a normal part of life. In their new lives, mistakes can be remedied. Children can be helped to make up for what they done wrong in the past with apologies and restitution.

It helps to reduce shame by working with parents to teach children moral behavior through progressive developmental stages (Cline, 1995; Kohlberg, 1981-1984). Traumatized children may appear to know right from wrong, but only on a superficial basis, such as a preschool child watching to see if anyone is looking as he or she takes a cookie out of the cookie jar. Through personal stories, family rules, and especially modeling, parents can provide crucial lessons to change how children think about violating the rights of others and getting what they want at any cost. Children may need coaching to learn to become sensitive to the feelings of others. Parents can share with children how all of us at times may feel we deserve things that do not come our way, but this does not justify stealing or tricking others into giving us what we want. When we have transgressed or hurt others, we can learn from our mistakes and help to repair the damage we have caused.

Practitioners may need to help parents to understand how wants often assume great power with traumatized children, and lead almost immediately into a powerful urge to fill the want *before* it explodes into a traumatic reminder of emptiness and deprivation. Detoxifying and telling a child's life story helps by adding words and meaning to this reaction. Skill development (see Chapter 6) can foster ways for children to succeed in reaching positive goals in a healthy manner.

The *Real Life Heroes* workbook invites children to consider who they would want to apologize to, if they could, and how they could make up for what they did. In this exercise, it is important to help children find ways to apologize, and make an appropriate form of restitution based on their age and abilities. This could mean writing a letter to (or if possible, meeting with) an aggrieved person and enclosing money earned to replace a broken or stolen object. Working to repair damage may be possible in some cases, or finding a way to provide an equivalent amount of service to the injured party by cleaning, weeding, cooking, etc. When no contact is possible, a child could help out a charity that works in a similar area. A teenager could do volunteer work at a day care center for handicapped children or a senior citizen center. Restitution provides an opportunity for youths to learn positive skills for handling mistakes and reduces shame, a primary factor in recurring problems.

It is important to develop a plan that is do-able, roughly equivalent to the harm a child did, and safe to carry out. Plans for restitution should be guided by a family's religious and cultural teachings on how to show remorse and atone for *mis*deeds. This could include confessions to clergy or ceremonies that bring supportive congregants together as a caring and guiding community for a child.

Given the limitations on children, it often takes assistance from caring adults to help children work out an appropriate form of restitution and avoid punishments that could cause more harm than good. Punishments that remind children of "lock-ups," "serving time," or being sent away should be avoided.

Children should be required and assisted to implement their plan for restitution as soon as possible. This should be given the same level of priority as a medical prescription. Delay leaves shame and guilt to fester and grow in strength. Delay also undermines their courage to own mistakes and do what is right. It is easier in the short run to leave things as they are, but this means leaving children without a way to atone for what they may see as terrible sins. Practitioners and parents can advocate restitution as a crucial component in therapy and essential to teach children that their new homes will be different than the past.

OBSTACLES TO BREAKING IMPASSE

Fantasies of Lost Parents

Parents may fear a child's affection and fantasies about lost biological or psychological parents. Many children fantasize about birth parents coming to get them, even if these parents were abusive, neglectful, or abandoned them. Children may naturally fantasize that deceased parents are really alive somewhere and could return. A child with an "unknown" father may suddenly come across a man at the grocery store who looks just like him, or even, as happened with one sixteen-year-old I know, accidentally meet a man with the name of the father he never knew.

If children experience their primary parent as scared and cutting off the child's interest, the child will often feel invalidated and that somehow his or her primary parent cannot accept the part of the child connected (through genetics or experience) with a lost parent. The more a parent fears a child's curiosity about lost family members, the more powerful this becomes. A child's natural desire to search can over time break apart a parent-child relationship.

On the other hand, parents can welcome and a support a child's desire to learn about his or her previous families. Parents can help a child to find out whatever can be learned. This reduces a child's fear of searching, takes away toxicity connected with a child's pull to previous families, and often solidifies a child's bond to his or her primary parent. The search is a time for a child to learn what happened, to grieve, and to *re*develop his or her own identity, pulling out the best from his or her past and present families.

Fear of Violence

Parents may become increasingly alarmed that youths will become violent, return to past violence, or act similar to relatives who have been violent. Parents' fear of youths' violence may increase if cycles of aggression and trauma are not understood, and changed, especially as youths enter puberty and begin to look like men and women. Practitioners can help parents understand factors associated with violence and develop effective interventions in order to help parents avoid become trapped by their own fears and to ensure that parents get the help and services their children need to succeed.

Research studies on predictors of violence in youths have found multiple factors but no definitive indicators to differentiate who will become a violent perpetrator. Significant correlates of violence (Ewing, 2001) include the following:

- Youth was abused or witnessed violence, typically at home.
- Youth learns not to respect life of self or others.
- Youth sees no future, just more of the same.
- Youth has committed violent acts in the past.
- Stated intentions—almost all warn in advance.
- Alcohol/substance abuse—half of all juveniles who killed were using alcohol or drugs.
- Availability of guns—85 percent of violence by young men involves guns.
- Violence was reinforced by success.
- Perpetrators were young males ages fifteen to twenty-five, although teenage girls are moving up, correlated with cultural portrayals of women as violent.
- Viewing media portrayals of violence as normal part of American life desensitizes youths to violence.
- Being economically disadvantaged is a small predictor associated with both perpetrators and victims, helplessness, hopelessness, lack of opportunities, and economic skill development.
- Presence of psychotic mental illnesses is a small predictor.

Too many youths have experienced violence in their homes, at school, in their neighborhoods, in group-care facilities, and through violent movies and video games. Children exposed to violence as a means of domination may come to believe that intimidation or violence pays off for peers, family members, or other adults in their communities. Or, children may learn that they have to fight adults to protect family members. Children may even be given nicknames reflecting their roles as the substitute "man of the house," guardian, or parent's special friend. Children can grow into these roles and relationships only to find their status and position terminated when their parent brings in a new adult partner.

T.J. and another boy tried to set gas tanks on fire in a parking garage, nearly killing themselves in the process. "I'm my mom's back," eight-year-old T.J. informed me in no uncertain terms, a stern look in his eyes. T.J. and his mother had been very close with T.J. growing up as her protector from several violent boyfriends. He literally learned that he needed to watch his mother's "back." Then his mother fell in love with Randy. T.J. tried to drive Randy away, and instead, his mother sent T.J. to live with an aunt. A few days later, T.J. set the gas tanks on fire.

Fortunately, T.J. and his friend were not injured and T.J. heard clear messages from his mother and authorities that violence would not pay off. T.J.'s explosion brought in help for his family. He was placed into a crisis residence where my colleagues and I were able to engage his mother and T.J. to work on repairing their relationship. His mother was both frightened and angry at what T.J. had done. She recognized the risk and began working with staff to help T.J. get the affection he needed as a boy, rather than needing to be always on guard as his mother's guardian or cast out of his home.

Dr. Lonnie Athens (1992) interviewed several hundred violent criminals and described primary factors associated with children growing up to become violent offenders.

- The child is violently dominated.
- The child witnesses loved ones violently dominated.
- The child is coached that violent responses to provocations are his or her personal responsibility.
- An abused child learns to use violence, often to begin with, in self-defense.
- Violence leads to respect from peers and adults, notoriety, and power.

Shaping beliefs that violence is both justifiable and necessary is a critical component in perpetuating violence. In some families and neighborhoods, becoming a man or becoming part of a substitute family, a group of youths, a mini-gang, or a more formalized gang, may require some act of violence toward others. Children have told me they were ordered by a parent to not let anyone beat them and told not to come home if they were beaten up once more. Other youths have told me how they needed to stay home from school to protect a mother from being abused again by her boyfriend or the children's father.

An eighteen-year-old homeless youth quietly stressed his reputation as a fighter who never sought a fight but if pushed too far, would snap and usually sent his adversaries to the hospital as he coldly walked away. This youth shared with me how he was placed into a detention center at age ten by his mother and stepfather for defiant behavior at home. The youths there were older and larger, and he was terrified. He was beaten, but he learned to fight back and win.

This is a critical step in Dr. Athen's progression. The child learns that violence is necessary for self-preservation and later discovers that violence works. The child finds an answer to vulnerability. When violence is allowed to work for a child, the child may become accustomed to resorting to violence when angered and frustrated. The child sees peers and often adults pull back, wince, or react in an "out-of-control" manner that dramatizes their weakness, yelling, screaming, cursing, or even hitting. The child sees fear in their eyes, the same vulnerability and terror that the child knew so well, growing up with domestic violence. Now, however, with a growing reputation as a fighter, the child's fear is projected onto someone else. The child takes on a fleeting sense of mastery transforming feelings of being hurt to hurting, troubled to troubling, and a sense of power that more than compensates for the usual punishments and restrictions.

The most effective interventions prevent, or stop, children's experiences of violence in their homes. This means not leaving babies to experience violence when an older child has been abused or parents continue to fight. When family members and communities tolerate brutal treatment of children, they learn that violence is acceptable behavior. When children are returned home from placement without the children, parents, grandparents, child protective workers, judges, and other concerned adults understanding and taking responsibility for implementing a viable safety plan, children learn that disclosure does not help and that adults, even authorities, are not committed, or caring enough to stop the violence.

We see children's vulnerability clearest in work with preschool children. Many children learn by age three that they can gain a fleeting sense of power by imitating a violent parent, that boys and girls can become either perpetrators or victims, or that Mommy and Daddy see them as horrible, damaged, or doomed. This is a crucial time to intervene for the sake of children, families, and our communities with bonding programs, parent support and education groups, CPS, domestic-violence prevention programs, and permanency work in which the adults in a child's life take the responsibility for protecting children.

Fostering enduring attachments with protective adults is the greatest deterrent to children becoming violent. Permanency work fosters the nurture, stimulation, and guidance a child needs to continue developing empathy, frustration tolerance, and social skills from childhood and into maturity as an adult. Developing empathy in children means they will have the empathy to parent their own children.

Dr. Athens' research found that the previous factors were usually established before children develop into violent offenders. From a strength-based perspective, parents, teachers, clergy, community leaders, and therapists can prevent violence from becoming a habitual pattern by stopping as many of these key factors as possible and eliminating the correlates of violence. Parents who are fearful of children's past experiences of violence can work with practitioners to institute violence-free homes, avoid children's exposure to television, movies, and video games that glorify and normalize violence, teach children effective skills in managing frustration, and practice day by day, in words and actions, implementing family and school values for *non*violent resolution of problems.

It is very important that parents and schools work together to ensure that youths are never reinforced for violent outbursts with notoriety or that youths or adult perpetrators escape from personal responsibilities. Violent outbursts mean that a youth is acting as a toddler in a temper tantrum and has a lot to learn. A youth can be sent to a special classroom or program to work on developing and practicing social skills and to get individual and family therapy to help change them succeed in school. Out-of-school suspensions should be avoided, except in cases where children are clearly dangerous to themselves or others. In those cases, violent children need to be treated with the level of supervision and treatment afforded to suicidal youths (e.g., around the clock supervision by family members, or, if necessary, professionals, and extended intensive therapy involving family and community members). Sending a child home from school without assessments and family and school interventions often reinforces a traumatized child's sense of abandonment, leads to detachment from respected adults and positive peers, and fosters a belief that even authorities (teachers and principals) cannot manage the child's rage.

Children who demonstrate violent outbursts should be mandated by parents and authorities to work on overcoming their own vulnerability. In other words, violence should be uniformly addressed by adults in the child's world as a sign of weakness and pain that the child can overcome with help. To accomplish this, parents need access to skilled practitioners, neuropsychological evaluations, respite, crisis relief, insurance, and subsidies for adoptions to allow for the intensive supervision, therapy, medications, skill building, and other services needed. Mentors and structured involvement with successful peers in activities is very important. Access to weapons of any kind needs to be prevented.

If drugs and alcohol are involved, effective treatment programs should be mandated. Frequent, ongoing, and random drug testing is essential to catch relapses and demonstrates that parents and authorities are really monitoring and that drug/alcohol use really has to change. Youths need to know that they may be tested on any day of the week, and then again the next day, or the next.

Violent outbursts typically reflect hidden traumas and breakdowns in attachment experienced from a young age. The disrespectful and uncaring child has typically grown up feeling disrespected and uncared for in a crucial way. Rather than focusing on punishments for behaviors, family members, practitioners, and authorities can work with a child to grow stronger than the traumas and to demonstrate this by preventing *re*enactments. The child has a lot of work to do to catch up to peers and learn to succeed by developing age-appropriate social skills including taking responsibility for his or her actions and learning to respect the rights of others. Youths need to experience that they will consistently be restricted to the privileges typical of the age level of the behaviors they demonstrate at home, at school, and in community organizations. Consequences of violent outbursts necessarily mean supervision, just as toddlers must be watched at all times. Practicing age-appropriate skills, respecting the rights of others, and showing responsibility earns age-appropriate privileges.

Children Who Cannot Trust Parents

With most abused and neglected children, trust and attachment can be rebuilt over time with the commitment and courage of parents, practitioners, and family services. Therapists can prepare parents to take advantage of critical moments in children's lives, to look for these moments, and to use these opportunities to comfort children as they face and learn to overcome difficult issues. Therapists can use sessions to demonstrate with parents present and to coach parents on how to help a child feel safer as he or she overcomes painful events from the past. Parents can learn the use of gentle and nurturing forms of contact such as tapping, chanting, humming, back massages, pats on the shoulder, hugs, or rocking on a special chair with an arm around a child, or, if necessary, an arm around just the back of the chair.

A child's ability to manage physical contact with a parent can be gradually built up so that over time, parents can hold him or her gently, and firmly, without any sense of imprisoning or abusing the child. Abused and neglected children can slowly begin to trust enough to allow themselves to feel the warmth and security provided by a caring parent and even to allow that parent to cradle them.

For children with severe attachment problems, more intensive approaches may be necessary than those described in this book. Parenting severely attachment disturbed children often means *re*parenting from infancy, in order to rebuild basic trust. Attachment therapies for children showing symptoms of Reactive Attachment Disorder (see Hughes, 1997, 1998a; Levy and Orlans, 1998) have been developed to help children overcome fear of loving and being loved by a parent (Becker-Weidman, 2001), and to work with children who are not responsive to other interventions because of their intense need to be in control and inability to trust (Levy and Orlans, 1998).

Therapeutic "cradling" can help a child to access emotional wounds. This is an emotionally regressive approach designed to elicit the child's vulnerability and to safely structure corrective healing experiences (Becker-Weidman, 2001). Therapists work to provide children validation, support, and empathy in a *non*punitive manner (Levy and Orlans, 1998). Given the danger of misuse of variations of "holding therapies," it is important that only *non*coercive interventions are utilized, avoiding restraints or punitive approaches of any kind. In this work, a child's adoptive or birth parents who have made major changes in their lives, help a child confront and overcome the pain of past traumas that have blocked the child's ability to trust that parents will provide basic security. Nurture and noncoercive holding by therapists and parents has been successful in some cases to help a child to recognize his or her own feelings, recall emotional memories, describe events including what previous family members did, and express his or her feelings about these events (Becker-Weidman, 2001). As they carefully and safely cradle a child in a nurturing position, new bonds can promoted with parents working closely with specially trained therapists in this process.

Intensive attachment therapy programs typically screen birth or adoptive parents regarding their own attachment experiences, their ability to coherently relate their own life stories, their capacity to manage their child's distress, and their commitment to working in ongoing, or intensive two-week therapy sessions, often involving travel to a certified center for attachment therapy. Intensive treatment programs are typically preceded and followed by long-term therapy with a specialist in attachment disorders who can continue working closely with the family.

Some children and adolescents have experienced so much abuse and so many failed attempts to rebuild bonds that they give up on living with a family. Some of these youths can still do well in families where the parents act more as group-care workers and have arranged for extensive support services. Others can still find guidance and support from several identified staff and volunteers in group care programs. For youths in group care, it is important to maximize contact with staff they can trust and to keep them connected to several staff to ensure continuity should staff leave the agency. Adolescents, in particular, need to be reminded that achieving their goals for education, jobs, wealth, and future families of their own means developing social skills and positive connections.

From the beginning of placement in group care, work should focus on helping these youths develop the strongest possible relationships with caring adults (relatives, friends, sponsors, mentors, youth care workers) who could be available and continue contact with the youths after discharge, adults who they could call for help, guidance, or just someone to talk to in the middle of a lonely night, and adults who would be willing to invite youths to share holidays and celebrate their successes. These connections typically make the difference between success and failure when youths "age-out" of group-care programs and enter "independent living" or transitional living programs.

The key to success in independent-living programs is paradoxically to build up and maintain a high level of support and interdependence with several significant, caring adults. Youths in group care can be challenged to work on building relationships with at least three, and preferably more, adults they could go to in the future for help or assistance, and to develop these relationships before referral to independent or transition living. These should be adults who the youth can trust enough to share their life stories. These individuals could then become part of a youth's support team in an aftercare or independent-living program, and participate in contracting and regularly scheduled review conferences.

BEYOND IMPASSE

Impasse typically reflects a child's vulnerability and expectations that terror or abandonment will recur. The monsters of the past come back to life in the form of the frustration, fear, and rage experienced by the people who care the most for a child. Family members and practitioners feel themselves "walking on eggshells," afraid of upsetting parents or children, and increasingly constricted in their perspective. As stress mounts, impulses to run away, fight, or abandon escalate and core issues once again become obscured by current crises.

Rebuilding trust is the key to resolving impasse. Practitioners can help children rise above traumas by offering them different ways to share and experiment within the safety of a therapeutic relationship. Each of the activities in this chapter was designed to tap into a child's interests and skills, to foster courage, and to reduce trauma experiences from the size of monsters to something manageable, a specific time, a specific relationship, just one small part of a child's life. When one format, such as work on the life-story workbook, seems blocked, practitioners can pause, experience the impasse, and consider how their interventions may be triggering a child's or parents' sensitivities to trauma, or may rely too heavily on areas of weakness rather than strengths. Practitioners can utilize other modalities that may match a child and parents' interests, and capacity better, or which can tap into family, community, or cultural resources to foster a greater sense of security or success.[1] Practitioners can utilize the *Real Life Heroes* workbook as a guide to important components of life-story work and utilize the most effective modalities for children and families to complete each section in their own way.

Practitioners and parents do not have to have all the answers. Creative tools can help, but it is the quest that keeps hope alive. The staying power of parents and other caring adults is the ultimate answer to a child's provocations.

Chapter 13

Into the Future

> History, despite its wrenching pain, cannot be unlived, but, if faced with courage, need not be lived again.
>
> Maya Angelou

Children present a paradox with time. On the one hand, children are blessed with the rest of their lives to make things better. On the other hand, children have no time to wait for the parenting and safety they need. All children who have been placed away from home know that they can lose their parents and family. Every adopted child knows that loss is real and can last a lifetime. *Permanency* defies the reality of change; and yet, fostering children's trust in parents' enduring commitments and attachments is necessary for children to develop their potential. Each day of impermanence or living with the threat of renewed violence, leaves children more and more convinced that no adult can be trusted.

Trauma does not dissipate into the air or fade away with time. Instead, it is as if time stops for children. Children showing symptoms of PTSD often act as though their social and emotional growth, their personal movement through time, has stopped. Behaviors seem to repeat their yearnings to cling to lost parents or to cycles of loss and rejection. It is not so much a purposeful reenactment, but rather a repetition in keeping with traumatic constriction of a child's beliefs and the child's ongoing struggle to both master and yet avoid the pain of what has happened. Repetitions keep a child focused on resolving broken attachments, and yet, without any resolution, the child remains trapped in time.

Traumatized children often act as though there is no past and no future, just the present. And, the present becomes a repetition of what children could not change, often, the script traumatized children came to believe about themselves. "I am unlovable, undeserving, and deep down, bad, damaged, or crazy." Traumatized children often appear to repeat disruptive behaviors that punctuated past rejections or losses. This puts them temporarily in control of time, but in a risky manner.

For youths in crisis, it is as if they have climbed aboard the highest and fastest roller coaster. The gate has shut and they are off. Entreaties, warnings, or commands from adults become irrelevant. The action and excitement of risky behaviors becomes their story, a way of life fostered by neural patterns and repeated reenactments. Unchecked, crises and danger can dominate their lives.

THE QUEST

Violence and rejection wound children, physically, psychologically, and spiritually. Traumatized children act as if they are entranced "by a wicked cursor," as one youth told me. They become lost in time, trapped by curses of neglect, abuse, and abandonment.

Children cannot heal alone, but resilience can be built upon the commitment and support of children by adults who validate their experience (Farber and Egeland, 1987); someone who cares enough to listen to a child and to see all sides of their distress. Committed adults can break the curse and help free a child. Practitioners and family members can *re*open a child's experience of time and join with him or her to become stronger than the traumatic monsters of the past.

The image of a hero matches the enormity of this challenge. Joseph Campbell (1968) wrote of mythic heroes' call to adventure and the hero's courage to enter unknown territory.

> [T]he call to adventure signified that destiny has summoned the hero and transferred his spiritual center of gravity from within the pale of his society to a zone unknown. This fateful region of both treasure and danger may be variously represented . . . but it is always a place of strangely fluid and polymorphous beings, unimaginable torments, superhuman deeds, and impossible delights. (cited by Cousineau, 1990, p. 1)

> Once having traversed the threshold, the hero moves in a dream landscape of curiously fluid, ambiguous forms, where he must survive a succession of trials. (cited by Cousineau, 1990, p. 18)

> [T]he full round, the norm of the mono-myth requires that the hero shall now begin the labor of bringing the runes of wisdom, the Golden fleece, or his sleeping princess, back into the kingdom of humanity, where the boon may redound to the renewing of the community, the

> nation, the planet, or the ten thousand worlds. (cited by Cousineau, 1990, p. 114)

Heroes from legends, biblical tales, and mythology have always represented mankind's effort to move forward, the creative advance (Campbell, 1968), versus the darkness of fears and the powerful forces that maintain oppression. Neglect is the curse of today's children in many lands, regardless of their nation's relative wealth or power. Parents (birth, foster, and adoptive) utilize cunning, experience, and fortitude to overcome oppressive forces harming children. These are real stories of struggle, risk, and transformation, and, as in all hero stories (Campbell, 1968), these heroes bring back lessons. We can learn from their stories about how to vanquish our fears and make all of our lives better.

Parents working to *re*claim a traumatized child experience "unimaginable torments, superhuman deeds, and impossible delights," similar to the heroes of myths and legends. Parents can help a child move beyond trauma and its aftermath, the terror and rage, the desecration of the child's body, the demonization of the self, and the child's adaptation to crises with hypervigilence, impulsivity, and distrust. By so doing, parents become true heroes for troubled (and troubling) children and their communities.

The quest requires parents, children, and their allies to muster the courage and their combined strength to cope with a succession of trials. With each trial, parents, practitioners, and children challenge the power of trauma and work to learn from the past. With each success, the power of a child's nightmares is reduced. Monsters become real again, with weaknesses and vulnerabilities.

"Crisis" from the ancient Greek referred to separation (Vogler, 1998), and in most stories and legends of heroes, crises marks both a time of loss or death of past relationships *and* an ordeal through which the hero of the story becomes transformed and, in essence, reborn (Campbell, 1968; Vogler, 1998). The challenge for parents and therapists is to help children overcome crises of separations, losses, and sometimes violence, through a series of ordeals.

Facing trials, means, in effect, changing the child's present from repetitions of beliefs, feelings, and behaviors that leave him or her mired in the past. A child can be guided to experiment with new ways to cope. The adventure *re*opens possibilities and a child's future. Parents, practitioners, and children can rewrite the meaning of traumas, and over time, transform a child's life story from living *within* a state of trauma to living *with* trauma in the past.

THE THERAPIST'S ROLE

Practitioners are pulled to become a child's heroes, but, in reality, we cannot provide the day-to-day, month-to-month, and year-to-year commitment that traumatized children need in order to rebuild attachments. Even if therapists wanted to become the primary adults in children's lives, each therapist could only emotionally manage a limited number of children (d'Aversa, Personal Communication, 2001). By definition, most therapist's interventions are time-limited and thus not sufficient for helping a child overcome his or her experience of abandonment. In fact, children frequently lose therapists, family support workers, child care workers, and other practitioners because of managed care, caseload requirements, transfers of a child to another "level of care," or staff leaving an agency. If a therapist becomes a child's primary "hero," the child will naturally cling to the therapist. When therapy ends, the child experiences another loss[1] and reaffirmation of the transience of attachments.

Commitment means passing the test of time. Each child in placement or at risk of placement needs to find out who can and will provide the bonded relationship and guidance the child needs to guide him or her to maturity. From the beginning of work, practitioners can focus on building (or *re*building) positive connections to people who will remain committed to a child. Practitioners, as mentors and allies in this quest, play an essential role by engaging, empowering, and supporting the parents or substitute parents who dare to become the primary heroes for a child.

CROSSING THE THRESHOLD

Returning home after placement or entering an adoptive family can mark the beginning of a "new world," a special world that incorporates new possibilities for a traumatized child. In this special world the greatest fears of parents and children are tested through a series of trials and ordeals to determine whether this will only prove to be a variation of past losses or abandonments, or whether, this new *re*formed family will foster a parent-child bond.

When parents (biological, foster, or adoptive) fail to maintain promises and commitments to raise children with love and nurture, children lose part of their internal drive to love and be loved by others. Violence and intimidation can seal away the truths of the past. Abandonment and disruptions destroy possibilities for a future.

Parents face a paradox in their quest to rescue traumatized children. The children, themselves, typically resist parents' overtures and act, in effect, as threshold guardians (Campbell, 1968). Returning biological parents, relatives, or adoptive parents, may face a fiercely resistant child guarding the door to reunification or adoption. Underneath the defiance and stubborn resistance of traumatized children, caring and sensitive adults can find the hurt child. Practitioners can help caring adults persevere with the understanding that the children's bravado often marks their unspoken terror.

The strength of the child's defiance or troubling behavior typically matches the level of the traumas experienced. It is as if the child is warning would-be or returning parents, "Do you dare to enter my world?" The child's behaviors push parents away, but at the same time, challenge parents to face the child's deepest secrets.

This cycle of interaction is most evident when a child tells adoptive parents, "You're not my real parents," or worse, "I don't want to stay with you. I want to go to my 'real' parents." By overtly challenging any adoption plans, wounded children test their assumptions, often proven from multiple past rejections, that "deep down," as one almost-eighteen-year-old told me, "They (her adoptive parents) *want* me to leave." The parent or guardian's responses, day after day, to the youth's challenge can prove their commitment over time or confirm his or her deepest fears.

Real life heroes challenge children and themselves to cross the threshold into a new world, a life in which parents dare to face children's worst nightmares. This may begin with verbalized promises or legal documents, but these mean little to a traumatized child. Truth means facing and passing the tests of fire from a child's traumatized past.

The secrets of success for parents, just as in mythic stories, revolve around learning from each test, and from the threshold guardians (Campbell, 1968). Hurt and hurting children provide the clues to success. Behaviors light a path to unresolved dilemmas and their deepest terrors. Belonging, claiming, and mastery are keys to overcoming the ordeals. Isolation, rejection, and blaming foster obstacles and turmoil.

In this context, threshold guardians include the fears, narrow-mindedness, and hopelessness engendered in families by many sources.

- PTSD makes a child's brain appear as "kindling," ready to ignite with emotional flooding and impulsive, repetitious and often primitive, "fight-or-flight" behaviors.
- Birth parents of children in adoptive homes may give children (and practitioners) messages that they are too fragile to help their children overcome traumas with warnings that they could become dangerous to themselves or others.

- Birth parents may also give children in adoptive homes repeated messages that "I want you back," "I need you with me," "Come back when you are eighteen," "Take care of me," or "I'm your real parent. Don't listen to anyone else." Birth parents' alcohol or mental health therapists may also put a chronically neglectful or abandoning parent first out of concern for the parent's fragility, and insist on not pushing the parent to act as a parent to child, with an implicit request for the child to wait and remain loyal for years.
- Relatives of birth parent may pressure the birth parents to keep children, even when parents are unable to act as parents, and give children commands to "Take care of your mom," a message that "You should be with your mom," or "Don't trust anyone outside of the family."
- Friends and neighbors may ask adopted or foster children, "Who's your real mom?" or "Why didn't your real parents want you?"
- Teachers may inadvertently force a child to pick one family over another, not realizing that the child may have lived in several different homes (e.g., by asking a young child to "pick one family" for his or her "family tree"), or promote feelings of inadequacy by assuming children can access the memories of relatives (e.g., by assigning children to "Write a story about your family when you were born").
- County social services workers may guard secrets from child protective reports about traumas, believing that they must not upset children or foster/adoptive parents and risk disruptions of hard-to-find placements, or simply because they are too overwhelmed with primary safety issues and inordinate caseloads to help with a child's therapy.
- Funding sources may provide for only crisis management, a temporary safe bed, with no comprehensive assessments, no assessments of attachment or trauma or child's developmental level; and funding limited to supportive services, even when these add up to tremendous costs for a community in "per diems" for placements over months and years. Funding sources may also mandate transfers between programs leading to repeated abandonment and teaching children that all adults are temporary, no matter how caring and committed they appear.

Practitioners can serve as mentors to help parents and children learn from these challenges and to keep focused on helping parents become heroes for their children. Practitioners can help parents to understand and detach themselves from children's behaviors, to understand and engage the caring side of family members, service providers, and funding sources, and to empower parents with skills, support, and a little magic in the eyes of their children.

Symbolically, practitioners help parents to *de*mystify children and to add a little magic and power to committed parents.

Practitioners can empower and guide parents to step back, to listen with their hearts, to watch for patterns of behavior, and to welcome a child's challenges as clues to untangle his or her past. Troubling children offer returning or adoptive parents the opportunity to enter their real world, and become real parents by overcoming their worst nightmares. For parents and practitioners, this means strengthening themselves with understanding and support so that they can touch a child's pain and develop an understanding of the perceptions, beliefs, and feelings of the child's world, no matter how frightening, or how close a child's terrors may be to the adult's own experiences in their lives.

By accepting the challenge behind each behavior, practitioners and parents open up solutions to children's fears, fears that typically revolve around key traumas in their past and very real experiences of abandonment and violence. Practitioners can use behavioral messages as keys to the doors that separate the hurting child from the wounded child within. Crises can be utilized as the "calls to adventure" (Campbell, 1968), by which children test the truth of parents' commitment and the reality of parents promises of a different life in their new world.

RECONNECTING

When practitioners, teachers, and parents step into a troubled child's world, they often face the challenge of a youth moving at breakneck speed. Caring adults see and feel the risks generated by the child's behaviors. We also feel the child's affection and drive to heal.

Traumatized children often appear to vacillate between acting as angels or demons, needy babes looking for affection or belligerent avengers. These seemingly opposing personalities often represent real experiences in a child's life of being alternately loved and then hated, rejected, or abandoned. The challenge to caring adults is to help children *re*knit their fractured experience.

Working side by side, practitioners and parents can engage children in motion with therapeutic activities that open up their access to emotions and memories and help children to experience new solutions to their worst nightmares. The courage to remember is built upon tests of a parent or substitute parent's commitment. *Re*membering and rebuilding trust allows traumatized children to grieve lost family members and lost innocence. Committed adults can show children how to get past beliefs that they cannot talk, see, hear, feel, or change. Caring adults can challenge children to develop the courage to learn and understand what happened in their lives by leading the way with their own courage to validate what has happened. Parents and children can overcome feelings of victimization and helplessness by telling their life stories within a safe and supportive relationship.

Discovering and recording real stories of caring from a child's past can provide an antidote to his or her feelings of aloneness and the sting of rejection. Storytelling connects a child's reasoning with the challenge to overcome past traumas and current fears. Story by story, children learn how family members, other children, and adults in their communities have struggled and overcome hard times. Each story teaches a child about facing transitions, rebuilding families after separations, deaths, or other losses, succeeding in school despite learning problems, preventing violence, developing social skills, balancing work and family, overcoming addictions, and how to help without being hurt.

Storytelling also helps pull out a child's natural concern for others.

> In the telling and recreating of the stories there is a sense of the openhandedness of other children. . . . They are not always kind, as we know. They are, however, on the edge of kindness, ready, and waiting for an opening. (Paley, 1999, p. 89)

We can utilize the magic in storytelling to rekindle a child's connection to others.

Storytelling approaches can elicit strengths in a child and begin the process of rebuilding confidence that good things can happen. Through fantasy and creative arts exercises, practitioners and parents can join with a child's innate curiosity and explore new possibilities. In the process, a child's energy can be channeled into solving problems.

We can also use storytelling to help children remember times when they helped others in the past. Their concern for others can also lead into stories about helping others in the future, and these stories, in turn, can be developed into opportunities for children to succeed in developing skills and helping others. These successes can form the outline of new identities. Children can transform images of themselves from victims or demons into helpers and heroes in their own stories.

"The Search"

Children's drive to reconnect with missing birth or psychological parents marks another part of the "hero story" for children and new or reunited parents. Parents who block children's quests are often seen as invalidating them. A fissure develops between parent and child, a tear in their attachment. If children cannot enlist their parents as allies in this often essential step, then, they will frequently turn to their own world, apart from their parents. Over time, as a child's curiosity and drive to *re*connect with lost parents grows, the fissure may grow into a gap, and the gap into a gulf.

Adolescents may run away to reconnect with their "real parents." They may come to think of their new parents as not "real," because they are not able to face the "real" world of the child. They may see their primary, permanent parents as too afraid, or, more likely, as jealous or resentful of past parents or guardians. The refusal by parents to help in "the search," or an effort to block a child's search by withholding or blocking access to information, is often seen by the child as a demand to live an unreal life and disrespectful to the child's quest to be whole. In contrast, when parents welcome a child's desire to learn more about former parents or guardians and help him or her in this effort, the attachment between parent and child grows stronger (d'Aversa, Personal Communication, 2001). Children see that their parents are willing to deal with all parts of their experiences, their "real" world; and by so doing, reunited or adoptive parents become "real parents" and real life heroes to their children.

WORKING WITH TIME

Practitioners can help parents enhance their flexibility and range of solutions by understanding how time works for a traumatized child. It helps to remind ourselves of how a child's length of placement in a new family, or length of time back in his or her previous family, fits with previous lengths of time and experiences in different homes (see Chapter 8). Children's past experiences and the length of past placements with different parents often determine how long they must remain on guard and struggle before they can relax their fears and trust again. Parents can benefit from understanding the child's quest and learning to depersonalize a child's provocative behaviors with an understanding of how those behaviors fit in with a child's often distorted beliefs about what happened and what that meant for a child's identity.

Parents can make time an overt source of power, challenging a youth's efforts to take control and paradoxically comfort the part of each youth looking for a parent to provide care and guidance. Parents can remind a ten-year-old child that "I've got eight years until you're legal." With a six-year-old, "I've got twelve years." "Too bad, this isn't New Zealand. There, you'd be legal at sixteen. That would mean only ten years." Each of these messages reinforces a parent's commitment and challenges a child's expectations of disruptions and *re*placement.

By understanding and using a child's sense of time, parents can break out of seemingly endless battles. Parents can declare "fun time," "work time," "ice cream time," "reading time," "tickle time," "Mom's boot camp time," or "Try to beat Dad in basketball challenge time #545." Taking and making time to be with children makes a big difference. Surprises challenge a child's beliefs about being unworthy or bad because of what he or she has done.

An adoptive parent and colleague raised her children with the axiom that "Tomorrow's a new day." She told her children that no matter how hard a day they were having, they could "start fresh" the next day (Minnear, Personal Communication, 2001).

Parents can demonstrate that a "new day," has begun. The new day may start with baking chocolate chip cookies or a visit to a cemetery with the graves of family members the child or the child's new parents lost. By taking charge of time, parents can break up a child's negative expectations of how time works in the course of a day, a week, or a year.

With older teenagers, it helps to respect their dilemma of not having full legal rights. Adolescents have only limited control over major issues in their lives including where they live, where they go to school, who has authority over them, and what they are required to do during each day. Parents and teachers carry both the authority and obligation in most countries to help adolescents learn how to become successful and contributing members of the community. Parents and teachers promote adolescent's social development by requiring teenagers to earn privileges by taking on responsibilities. For adolescents, this becomes the challenge of learning to become a man or a woman.

By expanding children's and parents' understanding of time, we open up possibilities and solutions as their life stories evolve. A story (cited by Mackay, 2001) tells of an old man who experienced one hardship after another. The man confronted each obstacle in his life with a smile and a positive attitude. He was asked how he managed to remain so cheerful after all his hardships. The old man answered: "Well, the Bible often says, 'And it came to pass,' but never once does it say, 'It came to stay'."

Adoption or reclaiming a child by biological parents does not mean starting over (d'Aversa, Personal Communication, 2001), but rather a middle point along a child's lifeline. Starting fresh does not mean forgetting the past. Simply loving a child and giving him or her a new home is not sufficient to help a child overcome trauma and the breakdown of attachments.

Practitioners can help caring adults to open up time by working with children to reclaim their past and rewrite their future. Practitioners can help children to see old traumas as lasting for a day, months, or several years, but time-limited. The rest of a child and family's life story remains to be written, blank pages of paper waiting for a writer, a block of stone to be carved by a gifted sculptor, or notes on the keyboard ready to be formed into a musical composition. Practitioners can help children and parents use their talents to master time in their life stories.

Successful parents and caring adults are neither perfect, nor infallible. But they do have courage, the strength and the support to persevere, to own their mistakes, to apologize and make up for what they done wrong, and to *re*pair after life's inevitable crises. Perhaps, the greatest strength caring adults can bring to a troubled child is the wisdom to understand time, the vision to see past his or her limitations, and the persistence to shepherd a family through crises and into the future.

ADVOCACY FOR PARENTS

The challenge of adopting or reuniting with a traumatized child always becomes personal for the "would-be" parent. Accepting the quest means opening oneself to the child's pain and bringing a child's struggles into one's home. I admire the courage of these parents; they are truly heroes who "serve and protect."[2]

Prospective parents take enormous risks, especially when government authorities withhold support and respond to legalization of adoptions or custody by terminating services, often just when a child's struggles are about to peak. Practitioners help parents to approach this challenge with honesty, with realistic messages about the difficulties of this quest, by careful screening of prospective foster, kinship, and adoptive parents, and with preparation for the struggles ahead.

Part of the quest for heroes in this work is to engage legislative leaders, county authorities, and judges to mandate and fund essential services. Parents need allies to succeed. Children's dangerous behaviors mark the call to adults who care about their communities to provide the answers to children's challenges through prevention of placement and *post*placement services that meet real needs and match the level of risks presented.

Support and advocacy groups can counter the despair of children and parents who feel isolated and unwanted. Practitioners, parents, and older children who have overcome traumas can work together in agency-based, state-wide, or national organizations to help other children in need. With each ally, children and parents become stronger.

THE MAKING OF A HERO

Many children have learned to look for perfection, and at the same time have grown up with the flaws of leaders in government, the arts, sports, and communities graphically exposed every day in newspapers and televised in the nightly news. It is not surprising that many children in our fast-moving contemporary societies have no heroes.

Lies, deception, and detachment leave children vulnerable. Practitioners and parents promote resilience by opening up possibilities for children to succeed with the truth of their experiences, the good and the bad. By accepting flaws in ourselves, we can help children reconnect to the positive parts of their families. We can help redefine heroes from impossible images of perfection to real people who make a difference in all of our lives.

I have met boys and girls, moms and dads, grandparents, foster parents, social workers, teachers, psychologists, physicians, lawyers, and many others who have been *real* heroes, people who could be counted on to help, even if it meant taking great risks, even if they did not always succeed. I believe heroes are people who keep on caring for others and helping others, even when they feel hurt, scared, lonely, or so mad they cannot think straight. It takes courage, the courage to do the right thing. And, it takes commitment to become someone a youth can depend on over time.

Practitioners and parents can nurture positive feelings of mastery to overcome the hard times from the past and to honor the successes of family members that all too often were lost in tough times. Life-story work highlights our shared experiences with losses and painful events, and builds on children's and family's successes. Workbooks such as *Real Life Heroes* help foster attachments with caring adults and teach children the value of caring within families and the respect for others that is needed for them to become responsible parents and citizens.

From a larger perspective, troubled and troubling children challenge us all to confront the curse of neglect, the loneliness and alienation of too many children and adults in society. When children are raised with nurture, guidance, and commitment, they learn to value others and contribute. When children are left to grow up with neglect and abuse, they are likely to become neglectful and abusive themselves. Caring adults shape a child's future, and by so doing, they define our neighborhoods, villages, and cities.

Life-story work can be used, not just to tell a child's story, but to rebuild a story of people who cared and will care for a child through his or her lifetime. The heroes in each child's life story are the real people who define what it means for a child to belong to a family and a community.

Appendix A

Important People

Name: ______________________ Date: ______________________

Please think about people in your life and write in their names.

As a Young Child

1. Who helped you at age three or four, when you were sick, if you scraped your knee, or if you were scared at night? ______________________

____

2. Who helped you with homework in elementary school? ______________________

____

3. Who taught you to ride a bike? ______________________

____

4. Who believed in you and thought you could achieve your goals? ______

____

5. Who showed they appreciated your accomplishments, for instance, a good report card, a hit in a baseball game, a great painting in school?

____

____

At Your Current Age

1. If you won $3,000 and a one-week vacation, what would you do? Who would you like to spend your vacation with? ______________________

____

2. Who will really listen to you when you need to talk to someone? ______

____

3. Who could you count to be on your side and to help you in a crisis?

____

____

4. Who believes in you and thinks you can achieve your goals? ________
____
5. Who challenges you to look carefully at your beliefs, your feelings, and what you consider most important?[1] ________
____
6. Who would help you manage to get somewhere or help you with financial support if you needed it?[2] ________
____
7. Who have you helped? ________
____

Five Years from Now

1. Who could you look to for help in a crisis? ________
____
2. Who would still believe in you? ________
____
3. Who could you count on to be on your side? ________
____
4. Who would challenge you to broaden your perspective and keep things in focus? ________
____
5. Who would you like to help? ________
____

Some Final Questions

1. How many people can you think of who cared about you and helped you from the time you were a baby to your present age? Please circle the closest answer:

0 1 2 3 4 5-7 8-10 11-15 16-20 21-30 31+

2. When you think about your life, from the time you were a baby until today, how do you feel? Please circle the number that best shows how you feel:

0	1	2	3	4	5	6	7	8	9	10
(Peaceful)										(Upset)

3. When you think about your life, from the time you were a baby until today, how do you think about yourself? Please circle the number that best shows how you would describe yourself:

0	1	2	3	4	5	6	7	8	9	10
(Good)										(Terrible)

4. At your present age, how many people can you think of who care about you and would help you if you were in serious trouble because, for example, you were so sick you had to go the hospital, or you had to find a new place to live? Please circle the closest answer:

0 1 2 3 4 5-7 8-10 11-15 16-20 21-30 31+

5. What do you think would help make things better? ________________

____

____

____

Thank you for completing this form.

Appendix B

Attachment Ecogram

Family Name: ____
First Names: ________________; ________________; ________________
Dates of Assessment: ____________; ________________; ________________
Dates of Birth: ________________; ________________; ________________
Ages: ______________________; ________________; ________________
Referred by: ____
For Court: Yes/No   Needed by: ________________________

Reasons for Referral

____
____
____
____

Ecogram

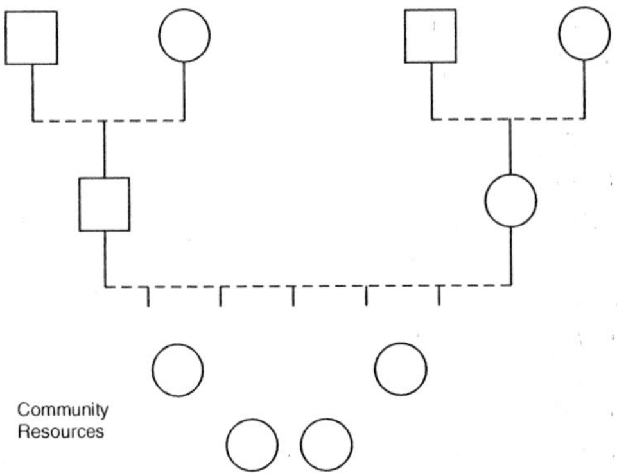

Key: Linkage Symbols

- - - Tentative or partial support, past or present
—— Adult believes, nurtures, and protects child in the present
═══ Adult committed to nurturing and protecting child until maturity

Metaphors (Striking Behaviors, Key Words)

Community Resources

Initial Evaluation

Child	Strengths/Problems

Time Line

Age	Date	Significant Events, Lived with, Services

Assessment

Parents' Goals

Child's Goals

Parent/Family Strengths

Parent/Family Problems

Who could nurture child (primary and backup)?

____
____

Who could protect child (primary and backup)?

____
____
____
____

Who could mentor child?

____
____
____
____

What are the permanency goals and backup plan?

____
____
____
____

Interactional Narrative

____
____
____
____

Essential Services (Denote or Circle)

Building/Rebuilding Attachments

____
____
____
____

Safety Plans (Who, What, When, Where)

____
____
____
____

Alcohol/Substance Abuse Dx and Rx

____

____

____

____

Building Cultural/Religious, Community Connections

____

____

____

____

Trauma Therapy

____

____

____

____

Life-Skills Development

- Self-control (frustration, anger, fear management, impulse control, perseverance, self-soothing): ______________________
  ____
- Parenting (nurture, discipline, developmental expectations, soothing, validation): ______________________
  ____
- Communication (verbal, writing, assertive, understanding others):
  ____
  ____
- Interpersonal relationships (friends, colleagues, partners), conflict management: ______________________
  ____
- Domestic violence prevention (identification, self-protection): ____
  ____
  ____
- Education (memory, attention, concentration, test taking, reading, math): ______________________
  ____
- Employment (vocational/work skills): ______________________
  ____

- Recreation, art, music, dance: ______________________________

  ____

- Helping others, advocacy, leadership: _________________________

  ____

Medical/Health Care/Exercise/Diet

____

____

____

Legal/Court Petitions/Letters to Court/Meetings with Law Guardian/CASA

____

____

____

Life-Story Work

____

____

____

Appendix C

Outline of Assessments and Interventions

I. Engagement
   A. Pass the child's tests
      1. Create safety and basic respect
      2. Talk about what is real without shaming
   B. Recognize child's needs for parents to:
      1. Provide consistency with flexibility
      2. Stand up for child
      3. Implement safety plans
      4. Work with all dimensions of time: past, present, future
      5. Share own life story with child
      6. Help the child understand his or her experiences
      7. React without rage or losing control when frustrated
      8. Tolerate child asserting self
      9. Model problem-solving skills
   C. Recognize parents' needs for:
      1. Support
      2. Time
      3. Safe home
      4. Safe neighborhood
      5. Safe and stimulating schools
      6. Child care
      7. Medical care
      8. Financial resources
      9. Skills and knowledge
      10. Understanding of child's needs
      11. Empathy for child
      12. Child-management skills
      13. Advocacy skills
      14. Self-control: Ability to control regulate own feelings
      15. Sense of humor

II. Assessment
  A. Assess social-emotional development of the child
    1. Consider the child's must successful behavior (e.g., baby-sitting younger children)
      (a) What age is the child's successful behavior typical of?
      (b) What age is the child's problem behavior typical of?
      (c) How old does the child feel?
      (d) When did social and emotional development become stymied?
      (e) What were the key traumas in the child's life at that time?
      (f) What did the child learn from traumas about what can be done, said, seen, and what he or she must do?
  B. Assess attachments
    1. Child's reactions (facial, gestures, actions, affect, concentration, compliance/defiance) before, during, and after visits with parents and significant family members
    2. How child talks about family members (affect, wishes, frequency, desire to see)
    3. How often and for how long child would like to see parents (See Important People survey, Appendix A)
    4. Psychological evaluations including human-figure play, family drawings, Roberts Apperception Test, Projective Storytelling Cards
    5. Interview questions

       If there was a knock at door and it was your ________ (brother, mother, father, grandmother, other significant persons), what would you do?
      (a) Would you let them in?
      (b) What would you say to them?
      (c) What would they say to you?
      (d) What would you do with them?
      (e) When you were sick or hurt, who did you go to?
      (f) Who comforted you?
      (g) Who helped you when you had trouble with schoolwork?
      (h) Who saw the best in you?
      (i) Who believed you could achieve goals, dreams?
      (j) Who gave you hugs when you needed them?
      (k) Who made you feel better if you had a nightmare?
      (l) What were some of the favorite things you did with each person?
      (m) Who did you want to see on holidays celebrated by family?

 (n) If you could not go back home, who would you most want to live with?
 (o) How would parent answer these same questions?
 (p) Where are the child's strongest attachments?
 (q) How much is based on real experiences versus wishes of child?
 (r) Who could parent the child to maturity?
 (s) Who is committed to parenting the child?

C. Trace the roots of a child's struggle
1. Why now? What happened to child leading up to referral or placement?
2. Help the family to share their experience since placement and their hopes (past, present, and future).
3. Learn from the child's behavior and development.
4. At what developmental challenge/age does the child's behavior appear stuck?
5. Does child's struggle trigger dilemmas and impasses for other family members?

D. Map family resources
1. Help each family develop their own map
 (a) What's working?
 (b) Who can help?
2. Draw in lines on Attachment Ecogram (Appendix B) to indicate positive supports for family members
 (a) Who can each family member go to for help in a crisis?
 (b) Who will listen to each family member and validate their experiences?
 (c) What community organizations are involved?
 (d) Who is feeling the pain?
 (e) Who believes child and parents can change?
 (f) Who sees positives in child and parents?
 (g) When have things worked well for child? For parents?
 (h) What was different at that time? Who helped?
 (i) What could help family, extended family, community resources, and practitioners develop safety plans?
 (j) Who is feeling the pain now?
 (k) Who needs to share responsibility?
 (l) Who cares enough to check up on child regularly, signal alarms, bring in help, confront parents if necessary?
 (m) For children in foster placements, are all responsible parties (judges, county attorneys, probation officers, school officials, child protective workers, group-care staff, foster

parents, family therapists) acting in the child's best interests? Is anyone missing?

E. Open up metaphors; the keys to the door
   1. Use our images, feelings, and fantasies.
   2. Where have I felt like this? What does this remind me of?
   3. What are children telling us through their first words, body language, family stories, dreams, and crises?
   4. What is the most prominent behavior? Is it a metaphor for this child's struggle?
   5. What led to first referral, first placement, and current problem?
   6. What grabs you the most?
   7. What in the child's look, actions, words, rules of life, etc. moves you to be concerned?
   8. How would you picture this in a sketch or drawing?
   9. How would you show it in motion?
   10. If time allows sketch how you see the child, using colors, shape, and intensity to show what stands out. Now add yourself to this picture in the same way. Then picture how you would like this to be.
   11. Primary metaphors
      (a) What is our dominant impression of child's behavior as a message?
      (b) How can I frame this as a metaphor that captures family behaviors and offers hope for change?
      (c) How does the child in placement represent his or her family or origin's struggle and experience (basic needs, abandonment messages, traumas, and hopes)?

III. Interventions

A. Develop messages centering on attachment
   1. Identify split messages to the child (or double binds) from the past, which drive dangerous behaviors.
   2. Does the child's behavior reflect unresolved traumas in the family of origin?
   3. Open up lost dimensions of time.
   4. Move beyond "bad" and "good" shame framework.
   5. Frame dual, centering messages that link both sides of a child's response to splitting messages received in previous families.
   6. Tie in loyalty/love and the struggle to end threats of abandonment or violence.
   7. Use metaphors to link messages and the child's struggle.
   8. Make placement, return home, or adoption turning points for family transitions.

(a) Define who will parent a child.
(b) Challenge a child to make choices that earn age-appropriate rights and rewards.
(c) Focus on building enduring attachments based on nurture and guidance.

B. Mobilize a supportive network
1. Start with the child acting out distress
2. Move progressively outward to bring in parents, siblings, extended family, and community resources to encircle child
3. Identify resources (past, present, and future)
4. "Remember" and "encourage" by building support networks and celebrating them at key times
5. Enlist community supports: mentors, sponsors, religious leaders, etc.
6. Overcome myths and fears (e.g., men (brothers) cannot help)
7. Include caring, committed adults to help implement safety plans
8. Add resources by involvement of children and parents as volunteers in community organizations, common interest groups, causes that fight problems afflicting family (NOW, Children's Defense Fund, NAACP, etc.)
9. Connect child: visits, calls, holiday reunions
10. Test who to trust, guarding against impulsive intimacy

C. Empowerment of biological or adoptive families
1. Open up perspectives—beliefs, time frames, generations over time.
2. Take the blame/shame away by understanding impact of child's traumas on family as well as social, historical, and political forces, unspoken privileges, glass ceilings.
3. Enlist resources from family's heritage and ethnic background as links to wisdom and strength.
4. Normalize with activities with other parents (e.g., association-sponsored picnics, trips, ball games, cultural events.
5. Action therapies: project adventure with families, groups, project teams.
6. Family group decisionmaking: empowerment and responsibility for child.
7. Coaching to help families assess strengths and problems, develop goals, avoid shame, access resources, and implement strength-based solutions.

8. Community leadership skill-building, mobilizing parents as advocates.

D. Keep the focus on permanency for every child

1. Set goals with parents as child advocates.
2. Keep goals realistic and focused on what is needed to foster attachments and safe, nurturing homes.
3. Coordinate work with other service providers to focus on attachment, safety plans, and overcoming traumas.
4. Work one step at a time.
5. Help family arrange for school or job training programs that match youth's abilities and needs.
6. Coordinate substance-abuse prevention and treatment tailored to youth: users, abusers, dependency.
7. Predict problems based on past crisis cycles and help parents and caring adults prepare and practice solutions.
8. Double check plans. Who will do what and by when?
9. Develop backup plans for support.

IV. Trauma and Attachment Interventions

A. Develop safety and promote courage

1. What are the child's worst fears?
2. What does the child strive to protect?
3. How can child remain loving and loyal and still feel safe?
4. What messages could parents, relatives, or authorities give to help child feel safe enough to share his or her story of what happened, what he or she saw, heard, and did, and how he or she felt?[1]
5. Develop safety plans to prove to children that they will be kept safe.
6. Who will do what?
7. What will signal that a crisis cycle is starting again?
8. Who can serve as protectors from outside nuclear family to guard against any further abuse or neglect, at home, in the neighborhood, at school?
9. How can they be contacted?
10. Who will check on children as frequently as necessary to maintain safety?
11. Help children learn and practice new skills and test safety plan.
12. Build skills for self-soothing, affect management, safe relationships, parenting, and conflict management.
13. Game therapy for traumatized children to develop skills.

B. Promote bonding between parent and child[2]

1. Parent shows affection to child, even if child becomes tense
2. Physical contact: child on parent's lap
3. Eye contact, touch, movement, smiles, laughter
4. Play to allow child imitates parent (repeated): singing a song, reading a story, nursery rhymes
5. Activities where parent and child work together, putting things away, cleaning, and cooking. Parent can make it fun, even silly, so that when parent laughs, child laughs
6. Opportunities for the child to carry out a task on parent's terms, with reinforcement for success
7. Encourage child to feel, to show feelings, and to explore choices for dealing with feelings. Parent validating child
8. Criticism, scolding limited to less than a minute
9. Unexpected gifts, hugs, kisses, touches
10. Brief praise for affection shown by child
11. Bedtime means a special ritual with parent comforting child (e.g., reading, singing, prayers)
12. Repeating early childhood tasks that the child missed out on in a fun way (e.g., playing baby, rocking, singing, giving child a bottle, nursery rhymes)
13. Help child feel special and part of family during routine and special times with a little special touch, check, nod, and affirmation
    (a) Wake-up time
    (b) Breakfast
    (c) Getting ready for school
    (d) Leaving for school, work
    (e) School time
    (f) After school
    (g) Dinner (preparation, eating time, cleanup)
    (h) Homework
    (i) Fun time with parent
    (j) Bedtime
    (k) Holidays
    (l) Celebrations
    (m) Anniversaries of important events
    (n) Medical appointments
    (o) Weekends
    (p) Vacations

C. Develop meaning and mastery through shared life stories
    1. Develop child's sense of history with songs about his or her life, with life book, photo history books, contact with signifi-

cant others where possible, and time lines[3] of positive and negative events and the people involved.

2. Tell stories of how family members mastered crises and trauma.
3. Build a future by highlighting transitions made by family and child's growth.
4. Celebrate accomplishments and remember important events with rituals and ceremonies, including storytelling.
5. Teach values, heritage, and beliefs with stories.
6. Use metaphor to externalize problem and reduce shame.

D. Use foster care (when needed) as a catalyst for permanency work

1. Begin permanency meetings within first two days of placement.
2. If children are in foster care, make visits with family members the time to work on building or rebuilding attachments, implementing safety plans and proving to the children that things will be different.
3. Show children that staff and foster parents can see and respect their pain and divided loyalty.
4. Coordinate review conferences every four to six weeks to keep time moving within the time limits allowed for permanency work.
5. Work with the messages. Help children face what parents do and do not do.
6. Help children grieve if parents fail.
7. If group care is needed, maximize the best possible relationships a youth can have with extended-family members and provide opportunities to build new attachments.
8. Build long-term connections if a youth cannot live in a family with mentors, relatives, sponsors, foster families.
   (a) Where and with whom will a youth spend holidays?
9. Permanency planning, including:
   (a) Parents' goals
   (b) Child's goals
   (c) Court orders
   (d) Child protective mandates
   (e) Backup plan in place for children in placement or at risk of placement
   (f) Time frame (ASFA, court orders, CPS requirements, managed-care limits)
   (g) Work parents need to do
   (h) Work child needs to do
   (i) Work service providers will do
   (j) Messages to children about all of the previous and how they will be able to see change

10. Review conferences to share progress and revise plans
    (a) Who will do what, by when?
    (b) Services for trauma and attachment therapy
    (c) Day-to-day support services
    (d) Additional work needed

E. Impasse checklist for permanency work
   1. Are any steps missing in previous attachment interventions?
   2. What could help with these steps?
   3. Have you responded to split messages child experienced?[4]
   4. Have you validated dilemmas and strengths shown in metaphor in child's behavior?
   5. Has the child's new family/community network been able to make it safe enough for the child to tell the story and test out safety plans?

F. Self-care for parents and practitioners
   1. Have family members and service providers respected their own needs in this work?
   2. How can I avoid becoming traumatized working with this family?
   3. How can I utilize countertransference as a tool.
   4. Steps caring adults can take
      (a) Take time to care for oneself and keep learning
      (b) Work with a team and supervision
      (c) Recognize stress and secondary PTSD (anger, irritability, feeling overwhelmed, isolating, thinking of children in the middle of the night)
      (d) Recognize and respect limits
      (e) Arrange schedules to carry out responsibilities within time frame
      (f) Prioritize and refer elsewhere when necessary
      (g) Use review conferences to share concerns and work

V. *Post*discharge Services
   A. Respite services with availability of home-based work on a temporary basis
   B. Emergency hotline services with skilled practitioners
   C. Information, referral, and consultation services for families including a directory of skilled practitioners with training in adoption and available to assist adoptive families
   D. Family-centered mental health services including therapeutic interventions for attachment problems, trauma, grief work, and impact on siblings, parents, and family development

E. Case-management services and assistance in accessing specialized services for developmental disabilities, medical problems, and understanding the medical history of children and their biological parents
F. Assistance with adopted children's desire to search and renew (or continue) contact with biological parents
G. Support and advocacy groups for families with similar interests and problems
H. Activities for families such as family trips, days at the ballpark, picnics, or cultural events

Appendix D

Real Life Heroes: A Progressive, Developmental Curriculum

OVERVIEW

Real Life Heroes was designed to help traumatized children build the interpersonal resources needed to reintegrate painful memories without repetition of trauma behaviors. The life story workbook can be used as a phase-oriented protocol to promote a range of creative arts, psychodrama, and other guided interactions that help a child to reexperience the components of early trauma within the embrace of a safe, nurturing relationship with a caring, committed adult.

The workbook provides a structure including time-limited tasks similar to school assignments. This helps normalize the challenge of healing and recovery and also provides clinicians with a framework from which they can add creative and individualized work to desensitize issues for each child. The outline includes key points, strategies, objectives for each phase of the workbook, and suggestions of activities and references to help overcome obstacles to completion. Crises in PTSD are expected, including avoidance. A child's behaviors can be used as a guide to help maintain a balance between resources and painful memories. Clinicians can use the outline to foster development of resources to contain pain and to keep children and caring adults working on rebuilding trust. Completion of tasks in the workbook demonstrates that parents, practitioners, caring adults, and children are committed to overcoming traumas and coping, rather than continuing to hide from the pain or to reenact the past.

Supportive and enduring relationships allow a child to reexperience feelings which go along with memories in a growth-facilitating manner that opens up new possibilities. Each page (and task) is designed to generate affect and communication with significant adults. In use of the life story book, it is important to focus on interactions more than content. Relationships to practitioners and caring adults are critical in this work. With each task, practitioners can help protective adults attune to children and demonstrate their commitment to disempower a child's demons and foster a child's strength and courage within a supportive relationship. Activities provide opportunities for children and parents to relate to one another with nonverbal acceptance and validation. Healing from trauma means reconnecting, right brain to right brain. Facial looks, tone of voice, and touch are critical (Schore, 2003a,b) to demonstrate an adult's attunement and acceptance of a child. Encouraging a caring adult to sit close and gently put his or her arm behind a child is very helpful, as long as this fits the comfort level of the child and his or her developing trust in a caring adult.

Psychological assessment of a child's attachments and social, emotional, and cognitive functioning is critical to guide effective therapeutic interventions. When children have been placed away from their biological parents, or have been threatened with placement, it is important to identify a primary and a back-up caring adult who could serve as the child's primary parent and who would be willing to work with the child on the tasks outlined. The *Real Life Heroes* storybook can be used to help identify a child's hopes for building or rebuilding attachments and thus guide service planning, including visits for children in foster care or in-patient mental health programs and finding caring adults for children.

Before children are reexposed to past traumas, it is important to establish the safety, acceptance, and emotional support needed at the developmental level during which the children were traumatized. A fifteen-year-old who experienced a single trauma and who is able to function socially, cognitively, and emotionally as an adolescent may respond well to work with groups of youths working on skill development with a caring and skillful group leader. In contrast, a youth who has functioned developmentally in the manner of a six-year-old may respond better to the use of games, adventure models, or sports to remaster traumatic incidents and learn new ways of coping (see, for instance, use of game therapies in Chapter 12). A child who was never able to master the basic trust required for a secure attachment as a toddler will usually need to work individually with a therapist and a caring parent figure with interactions which foster reliance and learning to trust a parent or substitute parent. In each case, a therapist can help a child move on from the developmental phase where traumas occurred to develop more age-appropriate skills and perspectives within the new-found safety of therapeutic and family, or substitute family, relationships. Even for older adolescents, it is crucial to connect each youth with persons who will actively and consistently check on him or her, follow up, monitor, exercise authority, and "hassle" the youth enough to show they care.

Each child needs to feel secure enough to reexperience difficult memories and feelings within the safety of a therapeutic relationship. The outline includes safety criteria for work with parents and essential resources to avoid retraumatizing children by exposing them to reminders of the past or current stressful situations for which they are not prepared. It is important to develop safety and basic affect regulation capacity *before* trauma processing (van der Kolk, 2003). Reexposing children to memories of victimization without developing necessary safety and affect management skills can lead to restimulation of overwhelming pain, perceptions of helplessness, and dissociative reactions (Pitman et al., 1991). Too much arousal sensitizes children and associates therapy with pain, confirming the power of the trauma.

Therapy sessions can reinforce confidence through shared activities that emphasize how a child's life is different now and how caring adults will protect a child, even when children reexperience the smells, sounds, images, and feelings associated with past traumas. After sharing memories of difficult situations in Chapter 7, it is helpful to engage caring adults and children in reenactments of these situations to help child and parents reexperience past events in a different way. For instance, a child in therapy can experience the support of a caring parent's arm around his or her back to counter memories of how the smell of a man's cologne and a scowl on a man's face made the child feel vulnerable, alone, and trapped.

In all of this work, it is essential to reinforce the importance of a child's relationships with family members, long-term mentors, and therapists. Techniques and protocols cannot replace the support a child receives from caring adults and skilled practitioners working step by step to help children modulate anxiety, develop skills, and develop solutions to crises that have often left children, their parents, and their grandparents feeling trapped for generations.

INTRODUCTION OF THE REAL LIFE HEROES MODEL

Session(s)

Preparation for conjoint introduction; afterward, therapist works in parallel track with caring committed adults and children; then, if possible, together in conjoint sessions as early as Chapter 3, provided that safety criteria are in place

Key Points and Strategies

1. Use of *Real Life Heroes* as part of comprehensive assessments and interventions with support and supervision for practitioners to adapt this model to meet children's needs

2. Step-by-step approach to avoid overwhelming family members or practitioners
3. Recognition that some children may have never experienced safety or a secure attachment and will by necessity distrust changes and efforts of caring adults
4. Recognition that many families have lived with multigenerational traumas and impairments requiring multifaceted and extended services for children, parents, and grandparents
5. Scheduling of psychological evaluations of attachments, general functioning, and traumas, if not already provided
6. Coordination of skill development with permanency work, trauma and family therapy, and development of family supports
7. Validation of feelings and experiences of family members
8. Commitment of identified adults to care for, guide, and protect child into adulthood
9. Explore child's areas of interests and opportunities to develop creative arts skills (e.g., music, drawing, photography, videography, movement/dance theater arts, clay, etc.) within a strength-based approach that includes instruction, acceptance of youth's creative expression, and, if possible, a long-term mentoring relationship
10. Introduction to impact of trauma and PTSD on children, adults, and families geared to children's age level and understanding
    - How emotional responses protect; subcortical and hormonal responses to ensure survival, how neural pathways become patterns
    - Common responses to life-threatening events: reexperiencing, arousal, avoidance, reenactments; acceptance and value for survival
    - Importance of beliefs for guiding emotional responses
    - Learned skills and resilience
    - Power of connections and attachment; impact of unresolved trauma on trust, belonging, bonding
    - Learning from the past in order to develop skills and heal wounds
    - Power of trauma therapies to rewire neural patterns

Objectives

1. Child agrees to begin *Real Life Heroes* workbook with therapist alone.
2. Caring adults sign commitment/validation page, explicitly giving child permission to share
3. Safety criteria established including the following:
    - Child's disclosures will remain confidential and in accordance with laws requiring reporting of abuse and neglect by practitioners

- Child and parent able to signal when feeling unsafe
- Parents or primary caretakers committed to protecting child
- Child able to manage stress of working in therapy without dangerous behavior

4. Child begins mentoring, skill development program in area of interest

If Experiencing Difficulty

1. Refer children and parents separately to individual therapy to work on safety issues including anger management, domestic violence, substance abuse, PTSD, and mental health impairments
2. Identify supportive and protective adults, advocates, creative arts mentors, etc. who will assure safety for child until parents can be trusted again

CARING ADULT RESOURCE DEVELOPMENT

Sessions

Therapist with caring adult alone; may be combined with psychoeducational groups

Key Points and Strategies

1. Understanding of trauma
2. Split drives between attachment and defense versus abuse/neglect lead to spinning in crisis and dissociation to avoid pain
3. Impact on the child's behaviors
4. Detoxifying trauma for child and adult
5. Taking care of self
6. Developing support for parents with family members, friends, and community groups
7. Self-soothing skills
8. Affect regulation regarding triggers for adult and child
9. Development and practice of self-protection plan to prevent reenactments of traumas
10. Positive beliefs
11. Age-appropriate and experience-based expectations for child
12. Reduce shaming of child and self within context of trauma

13. Parent writes own story using life story book, videotape, photographs, baby books, etc., which addresses all key points in *Real Life Heroes* including the following:
    - Self-description: skills, interests, feelings
    - Heroes/Heroines: models, mentors, how helped others
    - Important people in their lives: who nurtured, guided, protected adults at different ages, people they enjoy being with, people they want to visit
    - Positive memories with significant people
    - Self-soothing images, activities, and experiences
    - Genograms and time lines identifying important events, moves, transitions
    - Lessons learned in overcoming "tough times" ranging from small problems to the hardest times, shared in a way that helps child learn from parent and avoids traumatizing child with parent's experiences
    - Helping others: past, current, and future
    - Making up for mistakes and harm to others
    - Acceptance of own feelings and experiences, lessons learned, and goals for the future for self and family
14. Discussion and practice of how to share parent's life story with child
    - How to keep child safe
    - How to monitor child's reactions
    - How to talk about painful events to child, stressing strengths and resilience
15. Practice how to respond to children in order to rebuild trust
    - Safety messages
    - Affect regulation
    - Supportive tone of voice, facial looks, touch
    - Adding words to feelings

Objectives and Criteria for Involving Caring Adult in Child Sessions

1. Caring adult gives child support and permission to share what he or she experienced
2. Caring adult has validated child's experiences, including traumas involving adults
3. Caring adult committed to protecting child from anyone, even other family members
4. Caring adult identifies how he or she sees child as special and part of his or her life

5. Caring adult can manage own reactions to trauma without re-traumatizing child, able to face traumatic memories and reminders or reenactments. Offer individual trauma therapy for parent, if needed
6. Caring adult demonstrates commitment to protect, provide, and guide
7. Caring adult assures child that both the adult and the child will be safe when the child shares memories
8. Caring adult writes coherent narrative addressing all key points and strategies in *Real Life Heroes* storybook
9. Indication by child in private to therapist that child feels safe to share with caring adult present and wants caring adult in sessions
10. Until accomplished, utilize separate individual sessions, sharing child's work only where safe, with child's consent and with protection established for each disclosure

If Experiencing Difficulty

1. Comprehensive psychological evaluation to identify obstacles and guide services
2. Parent may need intensive individual therapy; often, parents need to show children they are working on overcoming their own traumas in order to help their children. This may involve extended or even lifelong work.

CHAPTER BY CHAPTER, DEVELOPING STRENGTHS

Sessions

Begin Chapters 1-3 with child alone, afterward sharing work with caring adult who has met safety criteria. If appropriate, involve caring adult in sessions to complete Chapter 3 and later chapters, or, if child is more comfortable, continue to work individually with child and share his or her work in separate sessions with parent and child together.

General Guidelines

1. Safety, respect rules established for therapy
2. Contracting with child and guardian
3. Introduce as a special activity that takes courage and makes the hard things easier

4. Utilize *special* markers, colored pencils, etc., reserved for *Real Life Heroes* work
5. Provide comforting, healthy snack of child's choice, e.g., hot chocolate, herbal tea, and chocolate chip cookies
6. Split each session, typically begin with at least one page in workbook followed by other activities
7. Child asked to signal if material becomes too difficult, commitment by practitioners to take a break and respect child
8. Beginning in Chapter 1, utilize a combination of modalities to enhance expression of child's responses for each page, the more the better
    - draw image
    - accentuate facial détails
    - identify tone of voice accompanying image
    - tap out rhythm and intensity to match image (with magic wand or drum stick)
    - identify feelings with words
    - highlight positive beliefs stressing strengths and coping with problems
    - enact with movement, dance, a sports move tied to task (e.g., "happy" dunk shot in basketball, "sad" free throw, "powerful" soccer kick at goal), or with family dolls or homemade puppets representing family figures
9. Monitor feelings state on 1 to 10 scale from calm to worst possible; use of "body scans" to monitor feelings of stress from head to toes
10. Predict and prepare for memories to emerge as a positive sign of child's brain working to heal and become stronger
11. Ask child to write down memories that come up, share them with caring adults, and bring them to next session
12. Utilize Workbook Completion Chart (Appendix E) to chart progress

Objectives and Strategies for Each Chapter

Chapter 1: A Little About Me

Objectives

1. Child can identify feelings in self and others
2. Child can express feelings with words, looks, and gestures

Strategies

1. Therapist identifies messages of support and permission from protective adults to promote safety and comfort for child to express self

2. Child experiments with different modalities to express feelings, wishes, and memories, presented as fun activities
3. Therapist promote ties between kinesthetic, visual, and verbal expression through use of creative arts, physical movement, and nurturing, e.g., rhythm, intonation, physical support, soothing, imagery, etc.
4. Therapist may begin by writing down the child's statements as the child does the "fun" work with drawings, puppet shows, dance moves, etc. This accentuates the therapist's interest and attention to the child as well as their partnership in this important work (Purdy, Personal Communication, 2003).

If Experiencing Difficulty

1. Activities to develop feelings awareness in body and comfort through practice in safe expression of feelings
2. Utilize feelings charts of children with different feelings
3. Exploration of modalities for expression, e.g., music, art, movement, sports, tapping
4. Assess for mandates or messages received by child to block expression
5. Engage permission from significant adults for child to express feelings and beliefs
6. Ensure safety of child to feel and express feelings
7. Work on building self-soothing and calming skills as fun activities

Chapter 2: Heroes

Objectives

1. Child identifies heroes from media, fantasy, books, popular icons
2. Child identifies attributes and actions of people acting as heroes
3. Child identifies real people in his or her life who act as heroes

Strategies

1. Therapist explores characters from books, movies, TV shows, athletes, artists, and other people in the media that child admires
2. Therapist explores child's understanding of heroic individuals associated with child's ethnic group and heritage; child offered selection of storybooks including heroic individuals from own ethnic background
3. Highlight how heroes develop skills over time with practice, including recognition of hero's own fears and weaknesses in every story and how heroes work with allies to overcome obstacles and make up for their own transgressions and problems

4. Utilize stories in the media, autobiographies for children, and interviews with prominent athletes, artists, and representatives of a child's own ethnic group in which these adults share how they overcame adversity, what helped, and what they learned.
5. Therapist invites child to consider people in his or her family and neighborhood who have helped others.
6. Learn from family members and child's heroes how they overcame difficult times, including getting help and working to develop abilities needed
7. Highlight positive beliefs that helped child's heroes persevere and maintain hope

If Experiencing Difficulty

1. Work on finding symbols of hope and mastery by noticing interests, styles, dress, and activities of youth
2. Work with child at developmental where child became stuck, then bring in skills from current age
3. Encourage child to make up a heroes comic book featuring his or her own hero mastering some challenge or, if preferred, develop hero images with puppets, papier mâché, clay, etc.
4. Enact stories or compose hero music, rap songs, drum beats
5. Practice moves of child's heroes from sports, theater, movies, etc. help child see how this feels, then explore through fantasy and enactments how these "powers" could be used to handle different situations
6. Involve youth in activities which offer opportunities to help others, e.g., mentoring programs for younger children, help to senior citizens centers, work in veterinary hospital

Chapter 3: Looking Back

Objectives

1. Child lists factual information about extended family, places lived, and moves between home
2. Child organizes information about life in a meaningful order including good and tough times

Strategies

1. Work with child on factual records to provide safe distance from painful feelings
2. Use of time line and other assignments to highlight positive memories

3. Point out how feeling states change for all of us over time by turning time line horizontally. Highlight upswings in child's life and tie to important people and events.
4. Foster hope for making things better again
5. Use of time line and family tree to trace, foster, and rebuild lost relationships where possible, to grieve lost relationships, and to work on building new relationships
6. Identify missing information, including questions about why a child had to move, but leave sensitive work for later as child develops trust in therapist
7. Tell child that caring adults can help to answer questions as part of work with therapist
8. Engage child to work as a detective with caring adults, extended family, libraries, news media, hospital records, child protective services, and other community resources
9. Arrange telephone calls or, if possible, travel to get "the facts," with safety precautions

If Experiencing Difficulty

1. Utilize safe contacts through letters, e mail, phone calls, or visits
2. If child is not able to deal with why he or she moved, therapists should check with authorities and records on what is known and work to make it safe enough for child to learn what happened
3. Utilize blocks and areas of discomfort shown by child to guide later work, e.g., Chapter 7, once child has developed greater security and trust with practitioner and caring adults. It is often helpful for children to act out with therapists minidramas (after Hughes, 1998b; Becker-Weidman, 2002) in which child asks the therapist, acting as a previous parent figure, the questions he or she has never been able to ask, e.g., why did a previous foster parent send them away?

Chapter 4: People in My Life

Objectives

1. Child recalls people who helped child in the past
2. Child identifies at least three important people and possibilities for reconnecting, including people who cared for child in past and people who child would like to count on now or in the future

Strategies

1. Highlight people who cared for child when he or she was hurt or sick
2. Promote child to imagine visits and fun times child would like to have involving supportive adults

If Experiencing Difficulty

1. Therapist, collaterals, and caring adults work with child on searching for lost extended family, mentors, coaches, teachers, employers, clergy
2. Involvement in outreach centers, religious organizations
3. Promotion of safe, positive connections with mentors, coaches, Big Brothers/Sisters, clergy
4. Promotion of pride in heritage of child's family, including race, ethnicity, and celebrations of culture
5. Provide help to child in grieving losses of adults who are not able or willing to care for child

Chapter 5: Good Times

Objectives

1. Child recovers positive memories lost due to traumas
2. Child shares positive memories with caring adults

Strategies

1. Engage child and share current interests and activities child enjoys doing
2. Engage child to recall and share memories of times when felt good with others
3. Arrange safe interviews with caring adults in extended family and community, recording interviews and developing a visual record of child's past with drawings, photographs, or video

If Experiencing Difficulty

1. Promote fun times with caring adults, trying out new activities children enjoy at the different developmental ages including child's current age and, "just for fun," developmental age where child became stuck
2. Therapist and caring adult videotape or photograph former homes, neighborhoods, and schools, limiting interviews to service providers when no safe family members are available

Chapter 6: Making Things Better

Objectives

1. Child utilizes self-soothing to modulate affective responses to common situations encountered at school, at home, in the neighborhood
2. Child utilizes effective coping skills to manage common situations

Strategies
1. Enhance skills and resources by imagining powers through magic
2. Remembering times when child felt safe and highlighting what helped, who was there, and what child did
3. Highlight what child can do now to help feel better, defining self-soothing skills as similar to sports skills or learning to swim or ride a bike, i.e., difficult at first, but over time with practice they become easy. This can be tied into teaching child about how he or she is training his or her brain, just like an athlete trains his or her body
4. Practice self-soothing skills including body relaxation, focusing attention, imagery, chanting, use of music, use of symbols of caring, and other concrete actions to reduce stress
5. Homework to develop self-soothing skills
6. Consider possibilities to solve problems child brings up and play out with puppets, family dolls, or through role-plays

If Experiencing Difficulty
1. Continue to work on developing affect management skills with activities amenable to child, including breathing exercises with imagery individualized for child; deep muscle relaxation with changes in environment such as lighting, scents, background music; refocusing on comforting stimuli identified in every setting; use of time-out spaces in different situations that child can utilize; developing and practicing "safe place" imagery such as sounds, smells, and scenes; practice songs as meditation; develop sequencing and tonal range with simple musical instruments; try out gestures and develop into movements and simple dances
2. Enroll child in programs that foster self-control and confidence, such as karate, dance, adventure programs, theater arts
3. Refer, if necessary, to anger-management programs
4. Enhance or create comforting objects associated with protective and caring adults, e.g., photos, jewelry, special stones, tiny flashlights, perfume, soft fuzzy stuffed animals, etc.

Criteria for Completion of Life Storybook

To avoid rekindling and strengthening trauma reactions, practitioners, caretakers, and children can work together to build essential skills and resources. These skills and resources provide a foundation for helping children detoxify past traumas and facilitate a child's success in working on Chapters 6 and 7.

Service Providers

1. Recognize and respect family strengths, caring for child, and heritage as well as impact of any abuse, neglect, losses, and traumas
2. Work to demystify and depathologize children's behaviors, including predictable reactions to work on overcoming trauma, the need to grieve losses, pulls and pressure to reenact painful experiences
3. Contract to work with parents, extended family, caretakers, children, and other practitioners to change trauma cycles for the good of all
4. Practice and test viability of safety plans to prevent retraumatization

Parent/Primary Caretakers

1. Modulate own anxiety, anger, and impulses sufficiently to protect child from becoming overwhelmed or needing to "parent" adults
2. Develop and implement safety plans for self and child
3. Validate child's experiences
4. Model and encourage use of words to express feelings and memories

Child

1. Practices and demonstrates affect recognition and safe expression of feelings including calming messages to self, e.g., "this is how *we* keep safe," and self-soothing behaviors
2. Practices and demonstrates positive belief systems promoting support and countering isolation, e.g., "*We* persevere," "*We* help each other," "*We* care," "My family has faced this before and endured," "I am not alone."
3. Understands physiological reactions at appropriate age level
    - Understanding how domestic violence, terrorism, etc., lead to natural human reactions and regeneration of trauma cycles, including hyperarousal, agitation, startle responses, and reexperiencing past sensory experiences (auditory, smell, tactile, visual, motor) in the present as flashbacks
    - How to change cycle from natural fear/flight reactions to energy and recognition of cycles and choices
    - Use of tools and reminders to counter the fear and take charge after "triggers"
4. Demonstrates skills
    - Recognition and expression of feelings with permission and acceptance by significant caretakers
    - Self-awareness of how feeling states change, ability to self-monitor without immediate fear/flight/fight responses
    - Ability to differentiate internal reactions (e.g., hyperarousal) from outside precipitating events

- Ability to associate words with feelings to begin to take control and apply reality-based reasoning
- Ability to manage frustrations and modulate anger sufficiently to avoid harm to self or others
- Ability to manage dangerous impulses
  —Recognition of danger signals, without blocking, avoidance, over- or underreacting, and reenactments of trauma cycles
  —Use of reasoning, planning, checking on own goals, guiding own behavior
- Ability to stop blaming and shaming of self and others
- Ability to focus on one small step at a time
- Ability to reinforce self for small achievements

Chapter 7: Through the Tough Times

Objectives
1. Child utilizes skills and connections (allies) to show steps that could be taken to better manage any repetitions of difficult times in past
2. Child shares some of his or her most difficult memories, based on safety and ability of child to disclose

Strategies
1. Encourage children to see how much they have learned and grown in strength and size since they were little. What things do they now know that can help themselves and help other children?
2. Use of creative storytelling with music, video, movement, pretend radio interviews, puppet or family doll enactments, or psychodrama, emphasizing development of solutions
3. Use of detachment techniques, such as encouraging the child (after Shapiro, 1995) to imagine watching the scene on a movie screen from the back of a large theater or through a thick window, with five inches of bulletproof glass, of a speeding train
4. Use of other distancing techniques from games the child enjoys, e.g., game-card images to help child feel removed from stressful memories and empowered with the help of allies to remain safe. Boundaries around the card can be painted with dark, wide ink. Similarly, the child can be asked to imagine looking at a drawing as if it were a distant screen set up at the far end of a basketball court or football field. At the same time the child can imagine sitting close to friends, strong, protective family members, and other caring adults.

If Experiencing Difficulty

1. Bring in additional supportive individuals child trusts
2. Act out themes from child's memories in different ways, e.g., minidramas
3. Explore how child's heroes would have handled similar situations
4. Play out different endings to child's stories (Gardner, 1975)
5. If child wants to express experiences to an adult but is too frightened to do this directly, invite child to make a phone call to therapist's answering machine or tape recorder in which child is invited to answer questions from therapist about more sensitive issues (Purdy, Personal Communication, 2003). Child can then listen to tape and it can be transcribed and shared with people the child trusts
6. Utilize more intensive trauma therapies, e.g., EMDR adapted for children (Greenwald, 1999; Shapiro, 2001)

Chapter 8: Into the Future

Objectives

1. Child develops positive image and beliefs about self extending into future, including how child can help others
2. Child expresses confidence in attaining goals

Strategies

1. Child draws or enacts future goals for self as shown in significant relationships
2. Child draws and enacts self utilizing desired skills and attributes in the future

If Experiencing Difficulty

1. Practice with art, imagery, body posture exercises
2. Visualize as a book or movie of one's life, highlighting key goals and relationships (see Greenwald, 1999)

COMPLETION OF LIFE STORY WORK

Sessions

Ideally caring adult and child together; child may prefer to work independently with therapist and then share with safe adult.

Key Points and Strategies

1. Children are invited to create their own title page
2. Children are invited to share their storybook with safe, validating adults and children in their families and, as appropriate, with other service providers, mentors, clergy
3. Children are invited to share their stories, or allow portions to be shared anonymously to help younger children going through similar experiences
4. Children are invited to compose a narrative, audiotape, or videotape of their entire life from birth to their current age as a summary and wrap-up to the *Real Life Heroes* workbook highlighting key times in life, what was learned, strengths for overcoming traumas, and goals for the future

Objectives for Completion

1. After completing the life story workbook, children demonstrate ability to
   - Identify people who cared about them in the past and the present
   - Identify people who could help them with problems in the present or the future
   - Share memories and feelings with words, pictures, or action
   - Share stories of how they and significant family members overcame hard times
   - Understand how their behaviors fit into past relationships and experiences and why they did what they did, a "healing story" (Figley, 1989), including a coherent life story tied to feelings and reactions and behaviors
   - Change traumatic experiences from helplessness/failure/shame to acceptance of physical reactions and awareness of how to protect self and loved ones if traumatic situations began again
   - Choose what behaviors to keep and make a list of new skills to learn
   - Share memories of how they helped other people
   - Share goals for how they would like to help other people in the future.
2. By working with children on their life storybook, caring adults demonstrate ability to
   - Identify people who cared for a child in the past
   - Identify people who will validate a child's experiences
   - Identify a child's primary attachments

- Identify important losses for a child and whether the child needs help to grieve
- Identify a child's fears and develop any needed safety plans
- Help a child break down destructive beliefs
- Understand how a child's behaviors fit into past relationships and experiences
- Develop opportunities for children to develop skills in communication, relationships with peers, siblings, parents, and authorities, as well as special talents or areas of interest

Appendix E

Chapter by Chapter, Stronger and Stronger

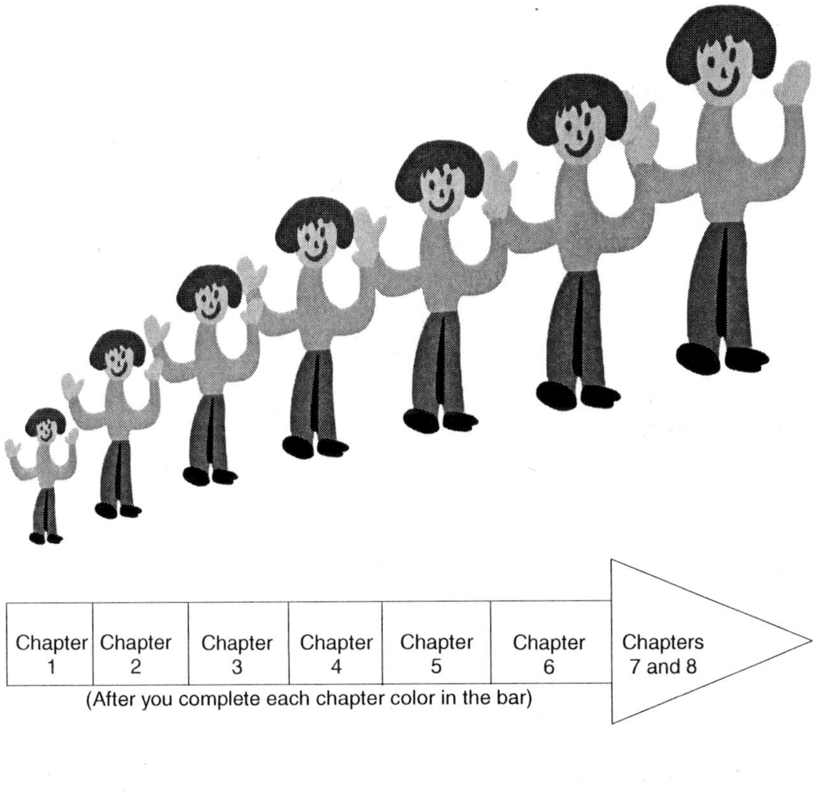

(After you complete each chapter color in the bar)

Appendix F

Utilizing Impasse

In this exercise, two colleagues can help each other learn from a difficult situation. The facilitator uses the following outline to help a colleague expand his or her perspective with images, metaphors, and time to promote possible solutions. Identifying details about clients should be disguised and use of this exercise should be based on the understanding that a practitioner can and will stop at any point necessary for his or her own safety or that of his or her clients (adapted from Kagan, 1996).
Consider an interaction with a child or parent in which you felt some distress.

1. Who was there? ____

   ____

   ____

2. What happened? ____

   ____

   ____

3. Fill in the details of your experience: smells, sounds, gestures, faces, words, intonation . . . ____

   ____

   ____

4. How did you experience messages (verbal and nonverbal) from the child or parent? ____

   ____

   ____

5. Emotional reactions: ____

   ____

   ____

6. Your impulses: ____

   ____

   ____

7. Beliefs about yourself: ____

   ____

Sketch how the child or parent looked, using color, shape, and intensity to show their primary message to you:

1. What metaphors come to mind from this image? ____________________

____

____

Sketch how you looked in this situation, using color, shape, and intensity to show your primary reaction and message to the child or parent (Sometimes it helps to take on the look you felt in front of a mirror, or to ask a colleague to observe you in a role-play):

1. What metaphors come to mind from this image? ____________________

____

____

See if you can condense your experience into an intersection of two or more primary messages, impulses, mandates, or demands

1. ____

____

2. ____

____

Imagine yourself as the child or parent giving the message you received

1. How do you feel in this situation? ______________________________
____
____
2. What are you most afraid of? ______________________________
____
____
3. What is most important to you? ______________________________
____
____
4. How old do you feel? ______________________________
____
____
5. What developmental age would be typical of this behavior? __________
____
____
6. What core developmental stage/conflict does this represent? __________
____
____

Imagine yourself as the child or parent experiencing the messages and impulses you previously listed at this developmental level.

1. How did you learn this was a way of life? ______________________________
____
____
2. Who might have given you these messages? ______________________________
____
____

Try to picture a critical time in the child or parent's life that corresponds to this dilemma. Imagine a dyadic interaction experienced by the child or parent at that age with their own parent(s):

1. Their parents' behavior: ______________________________
____
____
2. Child or parent behavior: ______________________________
____
____

3. Their parents' behavior: ____
____
____

4. Child or parent behavior: ____
____
____

5. What attachment patterns are being demonstrated: anxious/preoccupied, avoidant, ambivalent, chaotic/disorganized? ____________________
____
____

6. What was the primary conflict for you at this developmental age? ______
____
____

7. What would have helped you to develop a more coherent or useful understanding of what happened? ____________________
____
____

8. What would you have wanted to experience to overcome this conflict?
____
____
____

9. Who could have helped you have this experience and understanding?
____
____
____

10. What would have made it believable? ____________________
____
____

Imagine yourself in the role of a person who could have given the child a more positive message at the time of the child or parent's dilemma

1. What messages or actions would have fostered trust and safety? ________
____
____

2. What could have helped the child or parent grieve and overcome any traumas (e.g., messages of apology, a way of understanding what happened, and how the child or parent would be kept safe)? ____________
____
____

3. What may have blocked this from happening? ______________________

4. Return now to the first situation, your dilemma with the child or parent. How did the conflicting messages you received correspond to the traumas and experiences of the child/parent? ______________________

5. How do the conflicting messages and emotional reactions make sense to you? ______________________

6. What would help the child or parent to calm and resolve conflicting messages, conflicts, or traumas? ______________________

7. Who could validate the child or parent's split experience and help contain traumatic messages the child or parent experienced? ______________________

8. What is different now in the child or parent's life that could help him or her overcome the pressures or obstacles that prevented the child or parent from getting a healing message at the developmental age previously identified? ______________________

9. What could make the child or parent feel safe enough in his or her new life to be able to tell his or her story and develop a "healing theory" (Figley, 1989)? ______________________

10. What help from family members would be needed to rebuild attachments and safety from retraumatization? ______________________

11. What supportive services would be needed to make this work? ______________________

12. Who needs to share responsibility? (Who should be helping and is not?) ______________________

13. How can services be integrated? ______________________________

____

____

14. What is needed to maintain safety for everyone involved? __________

____

____

Plan (who will do what by when):

1. ____

____

____

2. ____

____

____

3. ____

____

____

4. ____

____

____

5. ____

____

____

Follow-up review conference schedule:

Appendix G

Game Therapy Illustration

The following outline represents a possible game format that a therapist could consider to develop creative approaches to engage children in work to develop their skills in managing situations without getting into trouble, to help children broaden their perspectives on beliefs and behavioral options, to practice use of different beliefs, to make and own their choices, and to experience different consequences of their choices. This illustration incorporates cognitive behavioral approaches for changing behavior and builds on the creative activities outlined by Cavanagh Johnson (1998) and Eggert (1994) for work with children. The illustration is not intended as a game ready for use, but rather, as an example of how practitioners could work with children to develop their own game.

I. Objectives
   A. Child develops tools to tell trauma story
   B. Child develops power to manage trauma-out-of-control cycle with help from caring adults
   C. Child can verbalize, draw, write, or demonstrate individualized safety plan
   D. Child learns how to succeed without traumatized behavior
II. Key Points
   A. Normalize experiences: everybody faces some forms of trauma, use popular games or activities to engage a fragile child into healing work
   B. Bring in adults who will make it safe to talk about thoughts, feelings, and behavior
   C. Identify triggers to reenactments of trauma
   D. Identify safety plans involving caring adults, with agreed upon signals
   E. Share with parents, protectors, and caring adults
   F. Practice with parents, protectors, and caring adults and encourage adults to validate child and teach positive behavior
   G. Therapist serves as coach
   H. Change game to take power away from negative behavior, to label it, put it aside

- I. Help child look ahead, open up a future, "what happens if the child continues behavior?"
- J. Child makes better choices to win, to change *mis*behavior to winning behavior

III. Instructions

- A. Step one: Make up "Watch Out" cards
    1. Use child's words for names of cards based on child's experiences.
    2. Each card marks a trigger, reminders of past traumas that evoke images, feelings, beliefs, and physiological responses of trauma. For example:
        - (a) People: drawings, photos
        - (b) Places: photos, drawings, locations, rooms
        - (c) Things: objects (e.g., bathtub)
        - (d) Time of day
        - (e) Day of week
        - (f) Months, seasons
        - (g) Holidays
        - (h) Smells: cooking, pets
        - (i) Sounds: voices (male, female, child's, adults', angry, soothing, rhythm, tone, music)
        - (j) Feelings: head, neck, back, stomach, genitals, buttocks, legs, thigh, calves, feet, toes
        - (k) Toxic messages
            - (1) "Don't talk"
            - (2) "You're bad, nasty, no good, evil"
            - (3) "You'll be punished if you tell"
            - (4) "Keep it a secret, just between us"
            - (5) "Look what happened to ______________ when she talked about it"
            - (6) "I never hurt you, I love you"
- B. Step two: Make up "Danger" cards
    1. Use child's words for titles of cards and child's own behaviors that lead to trouble. Sample cards could include:
        - (a) Beliefs
            - (1) "I'm no good"
            - (2) "I'm a loser, and always will be a loser"
            - (3) "I can't win, no sense even trying"
            - (4) "Everybody hates me"
            - (5) "It's everybody else's fault"
        - (b) Actions
            - (1) "Think faster"

(2) "Feel blood rushing, heart pumping, face tighter"
(3) "Thinking of hurting somebody"
(4) "Thinking of hurting self"
(5) "Yelling"
(6) "Cursing"

C. Step three: Make up "Trouble" cards
   1. Can use child's words for what is happening. For example:
      (a) "Cruising for a bruising"
      (b) Threatening
      (c) Running
      (d) Swinging
      (e) Fighting
      (f) Running away
      (g) Stealing
      (h) Taking drugs

D. Step four: Assign power points to each "Watch Out," "Danger," and "Trouble" card
   1. "Watch Out" cards: 1-100
   2. "Danger" cards: 100-200
   3. "Trouble" cards: 200-1,000
      (a) If desired, color or draw pictures on cards to illustrate with symbols

E. Step five: Pick game child likes (illustrated in the following with modifications of Chutes and Ladders® and Life®)
   1. Trace or adapt game board to mark path, starting point, goals, landing spaces for pulling cards
   2. Space out landing spaces for cards to match frequency of child being triggered
   3. Coach: winning strategies behind adapted games
   4. Examples
      a) Chutes Plus Ladders (Ages 4-6)
         (1) Child can make ladders showing safety plans for each chute encountered. Make in advance and use each time you fall down a chute.
         (2) When land on chute, pull Watch Out, Danger, or Trouble card.
         (3) Can match power of cards to size of chute's drop.
         (4) Identify chute as trigger to trauma cycle. After fall, child can pull out ladders with safety plans powerful enough to match power of chute cards (the Watch Out, Danger), or Trouble card drawn for each chute.

(5) Child can use Safety cards to move back up next turn, or wait until find ladder in regular game.

(b) Life in the Real World (Ages 8-12)

(1) Can use red spaces or mark spots. Key to success will be developing powerful safety cards.

F. Step six: Make up Safety cards

1. Can use blank 3" x 5" cards
2. Make a few in advance for every category, then give child choice:
   (a) Can make more in advance or as child goes through game
   (b) Save Safety cards for future games
3. Safety plans need to be as powerful as Watch Out, Danger, and Trouble cards
4. Child can use more than one safety card in a turn to overpower Watch Out, Danger, and Trouble cards
5. Work out details with child, therapist, teachers, relatives and caring adults
6. Child should make up cards using his or her own words. For example:
   (a) Self-talk cards (low power, but can be many of these):
      (1) "Slow down"
      (2) "Stop, think, check my toes, make a plan"
      (3) "I'm okay"
      (4) "Remind self of consequences for trouble" (e.g., detention, lost privileges). These need to be worked out for home, school, and activities.
      (5) "Don't want consequences for trouble"
      (6) "I'm cool"
      (7) "I'm not back in the bad old days anymore"
      (8) "I'm in my new class, new school"
      (9) "I don't have to be perfect"
      (10) "It's okay to feel sad"
      (11) "I will just do my best"
      (12) "I can be good or bad. It's up to me."
      (13) "I can figure this game out!"
      (14) "I know two good things that I am able to do"
   (b) Mantra cards (low to medium power):
      (1) Repeat words from poem or from letter from caring adult
   (c) Attention cards (low to medium power):
      (1) Focus on teacher or friend I like
      (2) Look at picture that makes me feel good

(3) Notice differences from old days when got hurt
(4) Check out my toes, "Do I need to do something else to calm down?"

(d) Action cards (moderate power):
(1) Feel in pocket for symbol from adult who loves me
(2) Practice breathing
(3) Practice muscle relaxation
(4) Practice imagery exercise (e.g., warmth of sun, going to safe place)
(5) Rehearse relaxing song in mind or ask to listen to Walkman ready to play calming music
(6) Play relaxing game
(7) Go to quiet, safe place at home and school

(e) Get Help cards (high power)
(1) Call parent
(2) Raise hand and ask to talk to teacher
(3) Ask to speak to school psychologist or social worker
(4) Sit next to parent
(5) Give nonverbal signal to parent, secret sign (e.g., pull on ear)
(6) Ask for a hug, a wrestling match, a bellybop, and a lift (whatever makes child feel good)
(7) Tell someone you trust something that makes you feel sad; say it softly
(8) Tell someone you trust something that makes you feel scared; say it softly
(9) Tell someone you trust something that makes you feel angry; Say it softly

G. Step six: Play games
1. Children can be challenged to find a way to win the game in no more than ten turns, by incorporating more positive beliefs or helping adult cards. Power points on cards can be adjusted to emphasize strengths and master typical trauma sequences.

H. Step seven: Make your own game
1. Child can develop a second game designing their own game board from start to finish, including pathways and types of power cards.
2. Child can be encouraged to develop a game to help other children, or younger children who experienced the kind of traumas the child lived through
3. Use game to show mastery and establish child as a mentor for others

Safety Steps

Therapeutic games must be adapted to the abilities, needs, interests, and problems of each family and should not be used as isolated interventions. Use of games without addressing the child's family and interpersonal relationships could inadvertently serve to maintain a child (or parents) in dysfunctional roles. Simply repeating a child's traumatic life experiences can serve to perpetuate his or her hopelessness.

A child needs to be able to trust a parent (biological or adoptive) in order to be able to benefit from working conjointly on these games. A conjoint approach should not be used if a parent is unable or unwilling to validate a child's experiences and grant a child permission to honestly express his or her memories and feelings. Validation by a parent is essential for a child to work on rebuilding trust and is a prerequisite for a parent to successfully work on reuniting. When a parent continues to deny abuse and neglect, the child is faced with a conflict between a wish to be close to his or her parent, loyalty to the family, and the reality of his or her own experience. The child may then deny his or her experience; however, the conflict and dishonesty will undermine any work the parent does to rebuild the home. Practitioners need to be well versed in the mandates of the Adoption and Safe Families Act and to be sure that incidents of past abuse and neglect have been addressed by authorities.

Games such as these are also not recommended for psychotic children or children who do not have the capacity to deal with the anxiety created. In these situations, children typically lack a safe relationship with anyone and may be living with injunctions that prohibit any disclosures and leave them living with threats that they or someone they love may be hurt.

For fairly secure and well-balanced youngsters, games may involve very realistic situations. For more anxious or resistant children, it may be necessary to use much more obscure and milder situations and consequences on the playing board, belief cards, and feeling cards. Cards can be carefully selected to utilize less-threatening items or other items may be substituted. However, games should embody the important themes, which affect children and their families.

Therapeutic games work best when used by skilled practitioners working individually with children or youths. Most children will quickly grasp elements of the game that apply to themselves and thus will have an opportunity to deal with personal issues. Individual sessions minimize the contagion effect of children's anxieties on each other.

As with any therapeutic approach, game therapy must be based on a comfortable relationship between practitioner, child, and (if possible) parents. It is important to provide each child with a safe environment where he or she will have opportunities for appropriate ventilation of feelings as well as a great deal of structure and consistent limits. If the child becomes tense or agitated, he or she can be encouraged to express his or her feelings and concerns directly to his or her parents or significant parent figures through letters, tapes, or in conjoint or subsequent sessions. If this is impossible or unsafe, a child needs to be given a sense of hope by authorities that they understand the child's predicament and will not force the child to return to a dangerous home. On-going individual therapy sessions can be arranged to offer the child a special time, place, and relationship within which he or she can safely express intense feelings and learn new behaviors.

Notes

Preface

1. Throughout this book, heroes will be used to refer to both males and females.

Chapter 2

1. Billy and Tommy represent composite descriptions of several real children, their parents, and real incidents. All other individuals described in this book represent individual children and parents I have met; however, details and dialogues have been changed to disguise identities and protect confidentiality.
2. J. F. Masterson, *Psychotherapy of the borderline adult: A developmental approach* (New York: Brunner Mazel, 1976), has written extensively on the formation of split identities and therapeutic approaches for "borderline" personality disorders. Please see R. Kagan, *Turmoil to turning points: Building hope for children in crisis placements* (New York: Norton, 1996, Chapters 4 to 6), for a therapeutic model for helping children in crisis who have experienced such messages.

Chapter 4

1. Please see L. B. Schorr, *Common purpose: Strengthening families and neighborhoods to rebuild America* (New York: Doubleday/Anchor, 1998), for a recent review of a wide-range of effective interventions as well as a discussion of how regulations and funding cutbacks have often limited or destroyed their effectiveness.
2. Please see R. Kagan, *Turmoil to turning points: Building hope for children in crisis placements* (New York: Norton, 1996), and R. Kagan and S. Schlosberg, *Families in perpetual crisis* (New York: W. W. Norton, 1989) for a step-by-step model and framework for permanency-based interventions for traumatized children in child and family services, residential treatment, home-based family preservation programs, foster family care, and psychiatric hospitals.
3. For a discussion of Jewish approaches to atonement, restitution, and punishment, please see L. Kushner, *The river of light* (Woodstock, VT: Jewish Lights Publications, 1990); and L. Kushner, *God was in this place and I did not know* (Woodstock, VT: Jewish Lights Publications, 1994).

Chapter 5

1. Please see R. Kagan, *Turmoil to turning points: Building hope for children in crisis placements* (New York: Norton, 1996), for a detailed outline and case illustrations of permanency work with children in crisis.

2. For further discussion of permanency work, please see R. Kagan and S. Schlosberg, *Families in perpetual crisis* (New York: W.W. Norton, 1989).

3. Please see R. Kagan, *Turmoil to turning points,* Chapter 5, for a detailed illustration of identification splitting messages and a guide to developing dual, centering messages based on a child's need for attachment.

4. Information on the Adoption and Safe Families Act and concurrent planning can be obtained from the National Resource Center for Foster Care and Permanency Planning, Hunter College of Social Work of the City University of New York, 129 East 79th Street, 8th Floor, New York, NY 10021. <www.hunter.cuny.edu/socwork/nrcfcpp>.

5. See R. Kagan, *Turmoil to turning points,* Chapter 4, for a guide to assessing attachments.

Chapter 6

1. As a general resource for adoptive parents, I highly recommend B. A. van Gulden and L. M. Bartels-Rabb, *Real parents, real children: Parenting the adopted child* (New York: Crossroads, 1995).

2. Sue Clary (Personal Communication, 2001), a trainer for adoptive parents at Parsons Child and Family Center, shared this story from her experience raising troubled children in her therapeutic foster home.

3. R. Delaney, *Healing power* (Oklahoma City, OK: Woods 'N' Barnes,1997); R. Delaney, *Fostering changes* (Oklahoma City, OK: Woods 'N' Barnes, 1998); and R. Delaney, *Raising Cain* (Oklahoma City, OK: Woods 'N' Barnes, 1998), provide pragmatic tips from Delaney's clinical experience and successful responses by parents who have adopted children with attachment disorders.

4. Please see D. Hughes, *Building the bonds of attachment: Awakening love in deeply troubled children* (Northvale, NJ: Jason Aronson, 1998), for excellent guidelines for helping foster and adoptive parents manage children with attachment disorders.

5. Please see J. Javorsky, *Alphabet soup: A recipe for understanding and treating attention deficit disorder* (Clarkston, MI: Minerva Press, 1994), for guidelines for communicating effectively with children who show attention-deficit problems.

6. T. Cavanagh Johnson, *Treatment exercises for child abuse victims and children with sexual behavior problems* (South Pasadena, CA: Author, 1998), has developed many excellent activities practitioners and parents can utilize to help traumatized children develop greater impulse control.

7. For a recent review of diagnostic and treatment information on ADHD, please see S. Neuwirth, Attention deficit hyperactivity disorder (U.S. Government Printing Office: National Institute of Health, Publication No. 96-3572, 2001).

8. Many children in foster care have experienced the effects of alcohol, drugs, or severe, life-threatening stress on their mothers while in utero. For an excellent guide to working with fetal alcohol and drug effects, please see Peterson, J., Califano, D., Middleton, S., Vargas-Locato, M., and Marshall, T., *CAN DO!* (Denver, CO: Loving Homes, Inc., 2000).

Chapter 7

1. Please see D. Hughes, *Building the bonds of attachment: Awakening love in deeply troubled children* (Northvale, NJ: Jason Aronson, 1998); T. M. Levy and M. Orlans, Attachment disorder and the adoptive family, in T. Levy (Ed.), *Handbook of attachment interventions* (San Diego, CA: Academic Press, 1998); J. Peterson, *The invisible road: Parental insights to attachment disorder* (Author, 1994); R. Delaney, *Healing power;* and R. Delaney, *Raising Cain* (1998) for detailed guides for building attachments with children with attachment disorders.

2. Please see R. Kagan, *Turmoil to turning points: Building hope for children in crisis placements* (New York: Norton, 1996), Chapter 4, for a guide to assessing a child's attachments and developmental age.

3. Thanks to my father-in-law, Arthur Schwartz, for this game.

Chapter 8

1. Please see "Breaking through the Storm," in R. Kagan, *Turmoil to turning points: Building hope for children in crisis placements* (New York: Norton, 1996), Chapter 11 "Staying alive when the going gets tough," in R. Kagan and S. Schlosberg, *Families in perpetual crisis* (New York: W.W. Norton, 1989), Chapter 11, for guidelines for preventing burn-out and post-traumatic stress with practitioners.

2. Please see R. Kagan, *Turmoil to turning points,* Chapters 4 to 6, for a detailed outline and examples of this approach.

3. Based on messages from Cloe Madanes, Sexual abuse and sex offenders. Workshop presented at Parsons Child and Family Center, Albany, New York, September 28 (1995), and Cloe Madanes, *The violence of men* (San Francisco: Jossey Bass, 1995) for sex-abuse victims. Madanes used the metaphor of breaking a soul apart for religious families and breaking a heart for nonreligious families.

4. See R. Kagan, *Turmoil to turning points,* Chapters 4 to 6, for details.

5. See, for instance, family doll sets of different ethnic groups available from Childswork/Childsplay, Kaplan, and other educational and therapeutic supply companies.

6. For a wonderful melody to accompany this rhyme, see "Autumn to May" in *Peter, Paul, and Mary Songbook* (Miami, FL: Warner Bros. Publications, Inc.).

7. For information, please contact Suzanne d'Aversa, CSW, Coordinator, International Adoption Program, Parsons Child and Family Center, 60 Academy Rd., Albany, NY 12208.

8. For an excellent guide to work with metaphor and ritual, please see G. Combs and J. Freedman, *Symbol, story, and ceremony: Using metaphor in individual and family therapy* (New York: Norton, 1990).

9. These books portray overcoming abusive situations in a frank manner and are not recommended for children who are feeling or acting unsafe. Holes characterizes residential treatment in a negative manner and is not recommended for young children at risk of group-care placement.

10. Please see B. Keefer and J. E. Schooler, *Telling the truth to your adopted or foster child: Making sense of the past* (Westport, CT: Bergan and Garvey, 2000), for a detailed guide to dealing with difficult topics.

Chapter 9

1. Interview on *Meet the Press,* April 23, 2000, CBS News, New York, NY.

2. Please see M. Leichtman, M. Leichtman, C. Barber, and D. Neese, Effectiveness of intensive short-term residential treatment with severely disturbed adolescents. *American Journal of Orthopsychiatry,* 71(2), 227-235 (2001) for an updated model of intensive residential treatment services.

3. The National Court Appointed Special Advocate Association has 900 local community programs in place in the United States (National Court Appointed Special Advocate Association, *Lighting the way: Volunteer child advocates speak out* (Washington, DC: CWLA Press, 2002).

4. The Attachment Ecogram combines genograms and timelines used in family therapy with an ecogram (see A. Hartman, Diagrammatic assessment of family relationships. Social Casework, 59(8), 465-476, 1978).

Chapter 10

1. This is a trick I learned from my father-in-law, Arthur Schwartz.

2. A trick from my uncle-in-law, Jerry Schwartz.

Chapter 11

1. See also B. S. Cain, *Double dip-feelings: Stories to help children understand emotions* (New York: Magination Press, 1990) for children in grades 1 to 5.

2. Please see Rossi, B. *Teacher's Reference Guide: An Introduction to the Teaching Approach Used by YATMA* <rossi@yatma.org> for a model of progressive arts development with children and adolescents that can be offered in conjunction with trauma therapy.

3. This is similar to the cognitive interweave approaches described by F. Shapiro, *Eye movement desensitization and reprocessing,* First and Second editions (New York: Guilford Press, 1995, 2001); and L. Parnell, *EMDR in the treatment of adults abused as children* (New York: W. W. Norton and Co., 1999).

4. Please see F. Shapiro, *Eye movement desensitization and reprocessing* (New York: Guilford Press, 1995, 2001); and R. H. Tinker and S. A. Wilson, *Through the eyes of a child: EMDR with children* (New York: Norton, 1999) for information on use of EMDR.

5. Please see L. L. Lutz, *Concurrent planning: Tool for permanency, survey of selected sites* (National Resource Center for Foster Care and Permanency Planning, Hunter College School of Social Work, New York, April 2000), for an excellent review of concurrent planning and work with ASFA.

Chapter 12

1. Please see M. Straus, *No-talk therapy for children and adolescents* (New York: Norton, 1999), for a wonderful guide and compendium of activities to engage mute, oppositional, rude, and otherwise "resistant" children in psychotherapy.

Chapter 13

1. When therapists have to terminate services, it helps to write children a letter (M. White and D. Epston, *Narrative means to therapeutic ends* (New York: Norton, 1990) sharing both feelings of loss and positive memories recounting how a child and parents overcame challenges. A photograph or memento can also be helpful to symbolize how the therapist saw something special in the child.

2. The meaning of heroes from the ancient Greek. (See C. Vogler, *The writer's journey: Mythic structure for writers* Studio City, CA: Michael Weise Productions, 1998).

Appendix A

1. Adapted from J. M. Richman, L. B. Rosenfeld, and C. J. Hardy (1993). The social support system: A validation study of a clinical measure of the social support press. *Social Work Practice,* 3(3), 288-311.

2. Ibid.

Appendix C

1. See Charles Figley, *Helping traumatized families* (San Francisco: Jossey-Bass, 1989).

2. Adapted from Connell Watkins, The Attachment Center, Evergreen Colorado. See also D. Hughes, *Building the bonds of attachment: Awakening love in deeply troubled children* (Northvale, NJ: Jason Aronson, 1998).

3. See K. Suddaby and J. Landau (1998). Positive and negative timelines: A technique for restorying. *Family Process,* 37(3), 287-297.

4. See Kagan, *From turmoil to turning points: Building hope for children on crisis placements* (New York: Norton, 1996), Chapter 5.

References

Affleck, G. and Tennen, H. (1996). Construing benefits from adversity: Adaptational significance and dispositional underpinnings. *Journal of Personality,* 64(4), 899-922.

Ainsworth, M.D.S., Blehar, M.C., Waters, B., and Wall, S. (1978). *Patterns of attachment: A psychological study of the strange situation.* Hillsdale, NJ: Lawrence Erlbaum.

Amen, D.G. (1998). *Change your brain, change your life.* New York: Three Rivers Press.

American Academy of Pediatrics (1999). Cited by the *Brown University Newsletter* (August), p. 7.

American Psychiatric Association (1994). *Diagnostic and statistical manual of mental disorders,* Fourth edition. Washington, DC: American Psychiatric Association.

Angelou, M. (1969). *I know why the caged bird sings.* New York: Random House.

Athens, L. (1992). *The creation of dangerous violent criminals.* Champaign, IL: University of Illinois Press.

Auerswald, E.H. (1983). The Gouverneur Health Services Program: An experiment in ecosystemic community health care delivery. *Family Systems Medicine,* 1(3), 5-24.

Ausloos, G. (1985). Systemic approach to acting-out youth in and out of placement. Symposium conducted at Parsons Child and Family Center, Albany, NY, April.

Azibo, D. (1989). African-American centered theses on mental health and a nosology of Black/African personality disorders. *Journal of Black Psychology,* 15(2), 173-214.

Bandler, R. and Grinder, J. (1976). *The structure of magic II.* Palo Alto, CA: Science and Behavior.

Barkley, R.A., Edwards, G.H., and Robin, A.L. (1999). *Defiant teens.* New York: Guilford.

Beck, A.T. (1976). *Cognitive therapy and the emotional disorders.* New York: International Universities Press.

Becker-Weidman, A. (2001). Notes on attachment. *Foster families TODAY.* April, pp. 34-36.

Becker-Weidman, A. (2002). Understanding attachment disorder: The broken bond. Workshop presentation, Albany, New York, May 17.

Bensley, L.S., Van Eenwyk, J., Spieker, S.J., and Schoder, J. (1999). Self-reported abuse history and adolescent problem behavior: I. Antisocial and suicidal behaviors. *Journal of Adolescent Health,* 24, 163-172.

Bifulco, A., Brown, G.W., and Harris, I.O. (1994). Childhood experience of care and abuse: A retrospective interview measure. *Journal of Child Psychology and Psychiatry,* 35, 1419-1435.

Blechner, Maris (2002). Talking to children about difficult birth family issues. Presentation for Parsons Adoption Resource Center and the Adoptive Families Coalition, Guilderland, New York, January 8.

Boney-McCoy, S. and Finkelhor, D. (1995). Psychosocial sequela of violent victimization in a national youth sample. *Journal of Consulting and Clinical Psychology,* 63, 726-736.

Boney-McCoy, S. and Finkelhor, D. (1996). Is youth victimization related to trauma symptoms and depression after controlling for prior symptoms and family relationships? A longitudinal, prospective study. *Journal of Consulting and Clinical Psychology,* 64, 1406-1416.

Boszormenyi-Nagy, I. and Spark, G. (1984). *Invisible loyalties.* New York: Brunner/Mazel.

Bowlby, J. (1988). *A secure base: Parent-child attachment and healthy human development.* New York: Basic.

Brazelton, T. (1974). *Touchpoints.* Boulder, CO: Perseus Press.

Brazelton, T. (1997). Introduction. In R. Karr-Morse and M.S. Wiley. *Ghosts from the nursery: Tracing the roots of violence* (p. xiii). New York: Atlantic Monthly Press.

Brewin, J.S., Yule, W., and Williams, R. (1991). Causal attributions and psychiatric symptoms in survivors of the Herald Free Enterprise disaster. *British Journal of Psychiatry,* 159, 542-546.

Brewin, J.S., Yule, W., and Williams, R. (1993) Causal attributions and post-traumatic stress in adolescents. *Journal of Child Psychology and Psychiatry,* 34(2), 247-253.

Briere, J.N. and Runtz, M. (1988). Symptomatology associated with childhood sexual victimization in a non-clinical adult sample. *Child Abuse and Neglect,* 12, 51-59.

Bronfenbrenner, U. (1979). *The ecology of human development.* Cambridge, MA: Harvard University Press.

Brooks, R. (1991). *The self-esteem teacher.* Circle Pines, MN: American Guidance Service.

Brown, M. (1947). *Goodnight moon.* New York: Harper.

Brown, Margaret W. (1991). *The runaway bunny.* New York: HarperCollins Publishers.

Buka, S.L., Stichick, T.L., Birdthistle, I, and Earls, F. J. (2001). Youth exposure to violence: Prevalence, risks, and consequences. *American Journal of Orthopsychiatry,* 71(3), 298-310.

Burton, D., Foy, D., Bwanausi, C., Johnson, J., and Moore, L. (1994). The relationship between traumatic exposure, family dysfunction, and post-traumatic stress symptoms among male juvenile offenders. *Journal of Traumatic Stress, 7,* 83-93.

Calhoun, L., Cann, A., Tedeschi, R., and McMillan, J. (2000). A correlational test of the relationship between posttraumatic growth, religion, and cognitive processing. *Journal of Traumatic Stress,* 13(3), 521-527.

Campbell, J. (1968). *The hero with a thousand faces.* Princeton, NJ: Princeton University Press.

Campbell, J. (1990). Cited by Cousineau, P. (Ed.), *The hero's journey: Joseph Campbell on his life and work.* San Francisco: Harper and Row.

Carlson, V., Cicchetti, D., Barnett, D., and Braunwld, K. (1989). Finding order in disorganization: Lessons from research on maltreated infants' attachments to their caregivers. In D. Cicchetti and V. Carlson (Eds.), *Child maltreatment: Theory and research on the causes and consequences of child abuse and neglect* (pp. 494-528). New York: Cambridge University Press.

Carnegie, D. (1994). *How to win friends and influence people.* New York: Pocket Books.

Carrion, V. and Steiner, H. (2000). Trauma and dissociation in delinquent adolescents. *Journal of American Academy of Child and Adolescent Psychiatry,* 39(3), 353-359.

Carson, M. and Goodfield, R. (1988). The children's garden attachment model. In R.W. Small and F.J. Alwon (Eds.), *Challenging the limits of care.* Needham, MA: Trieschman Center.

Casebeer Art Productions (1989). *Projective storytelling cards.* Reading, CA: Northwest Psychological Publishers.

Casey Family Programs (2001). *It's my life: A framework for youth transitioning from foster care to successful adulthood.* Seattle, WA: Casey Family Programs.

Casey Foundation (2002). *Family to family: Tools for rebuilding foster care; Policies and practices; Shortening children's stays in temporary care, Part one.* Baltimore, MD: The Annie E. Casey Foundation.

Cavanagh Johnson, T. (n.d.). *Helping children with sexual behavior problems—A guidebook for parents.* South Pasadena, CA: Author.

Cavanagh Johnson, T. (1998). *Treatment exercises for child abuse victims and children with sexual behavior problems.* South Pasadena, CA: Author.

Chamberlain, P. (2000). What works in treatment foster care. In M.P. Kluger, G. Alexander, and P.S. Curtis (Eds.), *What works in child welfare.* Washington, DC: CWLA Press.

Charles, K. and Nelson, J. (2000). *Permanency planning: Creating life long connections; What does it mean for adolescents?* Tulsa, OK: National Resource Center for Youth Services, The University of Oklahoma, April.

Cicchetti, D. (1989). How research on child maltreatment has informed the study of child development: Perspectives from developmental psychopathology. In D. Cicchetti and V. Carlson (Eds.), *Child maltreatment* (pp. 377-431). New York: Cambridge University Press.

Cicchetti, D. and Toth, S. (1995). A developmental psychopathology perspective on child abuse and neglect. *Journal of the American Academy of Child and Adolescent Psychiatry,* 34, 541-564.

Clegg, P. and Toll, K. (1996). Videotape and the memory visit: A living lifebook for adopted children. *Child Welfare,* 75(4), 311-319.

Cline, F.W. (1995). *Consciousless acts, societal mayhem.* Golden, CO: Love and Logic Press.

Cohen, J.A., Greenberg, T., Padlo, S., Shipley, C., Mannarino, A.P., Deblinger, E., and Stubenbort, K. (2001). *Cognitive Behavioral Therapy for Traumatic Bereavement in Children: Treatment Manual.* Unpublished manuscript.

Cohen, J., Mannarino, A., Berliner, L., and Deblinger, E. (2000). Trauma-focused cognitive behavioral therapy for children and adolescents: An empirical study. *Journal of Interpersonal Violence,* 15(11), 1202-1223.

Cohen, Y., Spirito, A., Sterling, C., Donaldson, D., Seifer, R., Plummer, B., Avila, R., and Ferrer, K. (1966). Physical and sexual abuse and their relation to psychiatric disorder and suicidal behavior among adolescents who are psychiatrically hospitalized. *Journal of Child Psychology and Psychiatry,* 37, 989-993.

Cousineau, P. (1990) *The hero's journey: Joseph Campbell on his life and work.* San Francisco: Harper and Row

Crittenden, D. and Ainsworth, M.D.S. (1989). Child maltreatment and attachment theory. In D. Cicchetti and V. Carlson (Eds.), *Child maltreatment* (pp. 432-463). New York: Cambridge University Press.

Curry, J.F. (1991) Outcome research on residential treatment: Implications and suggested directions. *American Journal of Orthopsychiatry,* 61(3), 348-357.

Cytryn, L. and McKnew, D.H. (1974) Factors influencing the changing clinical expression of the depressive disorder in childhood. *Journal of the American Academy of Child and Adolescent Psychiatry,* 1, 389-391.

De Bellis, M.D., Baum, A.S., Birmaher, B., Keshavan, M.S., Eccard, C.H., Boring, A. M., Jenkins, F.J., and Ryan, N.D. (1999a). A.E. Bennett Research Award. Developmental Traumatology. Part I: Biological stress systems. *Biological Psychiatry,* 45(10), 1259-1270.

De Bellis, M.D., Keshavan, M.S., Clark, D.B., Casey, B.J., Giedd, J.N., Goring, A.M., Frustaci, K., and Ryan, N.D. (1999b). A.E. Bennett Research Award. Developmental traumatology. Part II: Brain development. *Biological Psychiatry,* 45(10), 1271-1284.

Deblinger, E. and Heflin, A.H. (1996). *Treating sexually abused children and their non-offending parents: A cognitive behavioral approach.* Thousand Oaks, CA: Sage.

Delaney, R. (1997). *Healing power.* Oklahoma City, OK: Woods 'N' Barnes.

Delaney, R. (1998a). *Fostering changes.* Oklahoma City, OK: Woods 'N' Barnes.

Delaney, R. (1998b). *Raising Cain.* Oklahoma City, OK: Woods 'N' Barnes.

Dickens, C. (1980). *A christmas carol.* Mahway, NJ: Watermill Press.

Dickens, C. (1987). *Great expectations.* Oxford: Oxford University Press.

Dolan, Y. (1991). *Resolving sexual abuse.* New York: Norton.

Dreikurs, R. (1964). *Children: The challenge.* New York: Dutton.

Easterbrooks, M.A. (1998). Early foundations of attachment: Opportunities and challenges in infancy and toddlerhood. Conference Presentation, Day Care and Child Development Council of Thompkins County, Inc., Ithaca, New York, November 13.

Eckenrode, J., Powers, J.L., and Garbarino, J. (1997). Youth in trouble are youth typically are youths who have been hurt. In J. Garbarino and J. Eckenrode (Eds.), *Understanding abusive families: An ecological approach to theory and practice* (pp. 166-193). San Francisco: Jossey-Bass.

Eggert, L.L. (1994). *Anger management for youth: Stemming aggression and violence.* Bloomington, IN: National Educational Service.

Elbert, T., Pantev, C., Wienbruch, C., Rockstroh, B., and Taub, E.S. (1995). Increased cortical representation of the fingers of the left hand in string players. *Science,* 270, 305-307.

Erikson, E. (1986). *Childhood and society.* New York: W.W. Norton.

Eriksson, P.S., Perfilieva, E., Bjork-Eriksson, T., Alborn, A.-M., Nordborg, C., Peterson, D.A., and Gage, F.H. (1998). Neurogenesis in the adult human hippocampus. *Nature Medicine,* 4, 1313-1317.

Evans, M.D. (1986). *This is me and my two families.* New York: Magination Press.

Ewing, C. (2001). Keynote address. Parsons Fall Institute, Albany, New York, October 12.

Fahlberg, V. (1979a). *Attachment and separation: Putting the pieces together.* Lansing, MI: Michigan Department of Social Services.

Fahlberg, V. (1979b). *Helping children when they must move.* Evergreen, CO: Michigan Department of Social Services and the National Resource Center for Special Needs Adoptions.

Fahlberg, V. (1991) *A child's journey through placement.* Indianapolis, IN: Perspectives Press.

Fairbairn, W.R.D. (1952). *Psychoanalytic studies of the personality.* London: Routledge and Kegan Paul.

Farber, E. A. and Egeland, B. (1987). Invulnerability among abused and neglected children. In E.J. Anthony and B.J. Choler (Eds.), *The invulnerable child* (pp. 253-288). New York: Guilford Press.

Feshbach, N.D. (1989). The construct of empathy and the phenomenon of physical maltreatment of children. In D. Cishetti and V. Carlsons (Eds.), *Child maltreatment: Theory and research on the causes and consequencxes of child abuse and neglect* (pp. 349-373). New York: Cambridge University Press.

Figley, C. (1989). *Helping traumatized families.* San Francisco: Jossey-Bass.

Finkelhor, D. (1988). The trauma of child sexual abuse: Two models. In G.E. Wyatt and G.J. Powell (Eds.), *Lasting effects of child sexual abuse* (pp. 61-82). Newbury Park, CA: Sage.

Finkelhor D. and Browne, A. (1985). The traumatic impact of child sexual abuse: A conceptualization. *American Journal of Orthopsychiatry,* 55, 530-541.

Finkelstein, N.E. (1991). *Children and youth in limbo: A search for connections.* New York: Praeger.

Finzi, R., Ram, A., Shnit, D., Dov Har-Even, M.A., Tyano, S., and Weizman, A. (2001). Depressive symptoms and suicidality in physically abused children. *American Journal of Orthopsychiatry,* 71(1), 98-107.

Fischer, R.L. (2002). The emerging role of adoption reunion registries: Adoptee and birthparent views. *Child Welfare,* 81(3), 445-470.

Ford, J.D., Mahoney, K., and Russo, E. (2003). Trauma Adaptive Recovery Group Education and Therapy (TARGET-MCS9). Farmington, CT: University of Connecticut Health Center.

Freedman, J. and Combs, G. (1996). *Narrative therapy: The social construction of preferred realities.* New York: Norton.

Freedman, T. (1999). Group says dire poverty on increase. *Times Union,* Albany, New York, December 22, p. F1.

Garbarino, J. (1999). *Lost boys: Why our sons turn violent and how we can save them.* New York: Free Press.

Gardner, R. (1975). *Psychotherapeutic approaches to the resistant child.* New York: Jason Aronson.

Gardner, R. (1986). *Therapeutic communication with children.* Northvale, NJ: Jason Aronson.

Gardner, R. (1993). *Storytelling in psychotherapy with children.* Northvale, NJ: Jason Aronson.

Gelles, R. (1997). *Intimate violence in families,* Third edition. Thousand Oaks, CA: Sage.

Gil, E. (1986). *A book for kids who were abused.* San Francisco: Launch Press.

Gil, E. (1988). *Treatment of adult survivors of childhood abuse.* Walnut Creek, CA: Launch Press.

Gil, E. (1991). *The healing power of play.* New York: Guilford.

Gil, E. (1996). *Treating abused adolescents.* New York: Guilford.

Gold, E.R. (1986). Long-term effects of sexual victimization in childhood: An attributional approach. *Journal of Consulting and Clinical Psychology,* 54, 471-475.

Goldstein, J., Freud, A., and Solnit, A. (1973). *Beyond the best interests of the child.* New York: Free Press.

Gould, E. (1999). Neurogenesis in adulthood: A possible role in learning. *Trends in Cognitive Sciences,* 3, 186-192.

Green, G., Korol, M., Grace, M., Vary, M., Leonard, A., Gleser, G., and Smitson-Cohen, S. (1991). Children and disaster: Age, gender, and parental effects on PTSD symptoms. *Journal of the American Academy of Child and Adolescent Psychiatry,* 30(6), 945-951.

Green, R.L. and Parment, W.L. (1999). *Losing our children: An examination of New York's foster care system.* Albany, NY: New York State Office of Children and Family Services.

Greenberg, M.T., Speltz, M.L., and DeLyen, M. (1993). The role of attachment in the early development of disruptive behavior problems. *Development and Psychopathology,* 5, 191-313.

Greenough, W.T. and Black, J.R. (1992). Induction of brain structure by experience: Substrates for cognitive development. In M.R. Gunnar and C.A. Nelson (Eds.), *Minnesota Symposia on Child Psychology: Vol. 24. Developmental behavioral neuroscience* (pp. 155-200). Hillsdale, NJ: Erlbaum.

Greenspan, S.I. and Lieberman, A.F. (1988). A clinical approach to attachment. In J. Belsky and T. Nezworski (Eds.), *Clinical implications of attachment* (pp. 387-424). Hillsdale, NJ: Lawrence Erlbaum.

Greenwald, R. (1999). *Eye movement desensitization and reprocessing (EMDR) in child and adolescent psychotherapy.* Northvale, NJ: Jason Aronson.

Grinder, J. and Bandler, R. (1976). *The Structure of Magic* II. Palo Alto, CA: Science and Behavior Books.

Gurian, M. (1997). *The wonder of boys.* New York: J.P. Tarcher.

Gurwitch, R.H. and Messenbaugh, M. (Unpublished manuscript). Healing after trauma skills. University of Oklahoma Health Sciences Center, Department of Pediatrics.

Hage, D. (1995). Therapeutic parenting, Part 1. In C.A. McKelvey (Ed.), *Give them roots and let them fly* (pp. 177-214). Evergreen, CO: The Attachment Center at Evergreen.

Hage, D. (2000). Conference Presentation. New York State Citizen's Coalition for Children, Albany, New York, May.

Haight, W.L., Black, J.E. Workman, C.L., and Tata, L. (2001). Parent-child interaction during foster care visits. *Social Work,* 46(4), 325-338.

Handford, M. (1988). *Find Waldo now*. Boston: Little, Brown.

Hanson, R.F., Saunders, B., Kilpatrick, D., Resnick, He., Courch, J.A., and Duncan, R. (2001). Impact of childhood rape and aggravated assault on adult mental health. *American Journal of Orthopsychiatry,* 71(1), 108-119.

Hariri, A.R., Bookheimer, S.Y., and Mazziotta, J.C. (2000). Modulating emotional responses: Effects of a neocortical network on the limbic system. *NeuroReport,* 11, 43-48.

Hartman, A. (1987). Innovations in social work practice. State University of New York at Albany School of Social Work Conference, March.

Hastings, J. and Typpo, M. (1994). *An elephant in the living room.* Northfield, MN: Comp Care.

Hebb, D.O. (1949). *The organization of behavior: A neuropsychological theory.* New York: Wiley.

Heit, S., Graham, Y., and Nemeroff, C.B. (1999). Neurobiological effects of early trauma. *The Harvard Mental Health Letter,* October, 4-6.

Herman, J. (1992). *Trauma and recovery.* New York: Basic Books.

Hesse, E. (1999). The adult attachment interview: Historical and current perspectives. In J. Cassidy and P. Shaver (Eds.), *Handbook of attachment* (pp. 395-433). New York: Guilford Press.

Hesse, E., Main, M., Kelley, Y.A., and Rifkin, A. (2003). Unresolved states regarding loss or abuse can have "second generation" effects: Disorganization, role inversion, and frightening ideation in the offspring of traumatized non-maltreating parents. In Solomon, M.F. and Siegel, D.J. (Eds.) *Healing trauma: Attachment, mind, body, and brain.* New York: Norton.

Hughes, D. (1997). *Facilitating developmental attachment.* Northvale, NJ: Jason Aronson.

Hughes, D. (1998a). *Building the bonds of attachment: Awakening love in deeply troubled children.* Northvale, NJ: Jason Aronson.

Hughes, D. (1998b). Working with attachment disorder: From frustration to hope. Conference presentation, Albany, New York, March 18.

Isabella, R.A. and Belsky, J. (1991). Interactional synchrony and the origins of mother-infant attachment: A replication study. *Child Development,* 62, 373-384.

Jacobsen, T. and Miller, L.J. (1999). Attachment quality in young children of mentally ill mothers: Contribution of maternal caregiving abilities and foster care context. In J. Solomon and C. George (Eds.), *Attachment disorganization* (pp. 347-378). New York: The Guilford Press.

James, B. (1989). *Treating traumatized children.* Lexington, MA: Lexington Books.

Jenson, J.M. and Whitaker, J.K. (1989). Partners in care: Involving parents in children's residential treatment. In R.D. Lyman, S. Prentice-Dun, and S. Gabel (Eds.), *Residential and inpatient treatment of children and adolescent* (pp. 207-227). New York: Plenum Press.

Jewett, C. (1978). *Adopting the older child.* Cambridge, MA: The Harvard Common Press.

Jones, T. and Greenough, W.T. (1996). Ultrastructural evidence for increased contact between astrocytes and synapses in rats reared in a complex environment. *Neurobiology of Learning and Memory,* 65, 45-56.

Kagan, J. (1998). Cited by Efran, J.S., Mitchell, A.G., and Gordon, D.E. Lessons of the New Genetics. *Family Therapy Networker,* (March/April), 27-41.

Kagan, R. (1982). Storytelling and game therapy for children in placement. *Child Care Quarterly,* 11(4), 280-290.

Kagan, R. (1986). Game therapy for children in placement. In C.E. Schaefer and S.E. Reid (Eds.), *Game play: Therapeutic uses of childhood games.* New York: Wiley.

Kagan, R. (1996). *Turmoil to turning points: Building hope for children in crisis placements.* New York: W. W. Norton.

Kagan, R. (1998). *Real life heroes: A life storybook for children.* Author.

Kagan, R. (2000). "My game," rebuilding hope for children in placement. In C.E. Schaefer and S.E. Reid (Eds.), *Game play: Therapeutic uses of childhood games.* New York: Wiley.

Kagan, R. (2003). *Wounded angels: Lessons from children in crisis.* Washington DC: Child & Family Press.

Kagan, R. and Schlosberg, S. (1989). *Families in perpetual crisis.* New York: W. W. Norton.

Kaplan, L. and Girard, J.L. (1994). *Strengthening high-risk families: A handbook for practitioners.* New York: Lexington Books.

Kaplan, S.J., Pelcovitz, D., Salzinger, S., Mandel, F., Weiner, M., and Labruna, V. (1999). Adolescent physical abuse and risk for suicidal behaviors. *Journal of Interpersonal Violence,* 14, 976-988.

Karp, C.L. and Butler, T.L. (1996). *Activity book for treatment strategies for abused children: From victim to survivor.* Thousand Oaks, CA: Sage.

Karr-Morse, R. and Wiley, M.S. (1997). *Ghosts from the nursery: Tracing the roots of violence.* New York: Atlantic Monthly Press.

Katz, L., Spoonemore, N., and Robinson, C. (1994). *Concurrent planning: From permanency planning to permanency action.* Mounlake Terrace, WA: Lutheran Services of Washington and Idaho.

Kaufman, M. (1999). Helping children cope with trauma. *Washington Post,* June 22, pp. 11, 16.

Kazdin, A. (1990). Childhood depression. *Journal of Child Psychology and Psychiatry,* 31, 121-160.

Kliman, G.W. (1996). *The personal life history book method: A manual for preventive psychotherapy with foster children.* San Francisco: The Children's Psychological Trauma Center.

Kliman, G. and Zelman, A. (1996). Use of a personal life history book in the treatment of foster chidren—An attempt to enhance stability of foster care placements. In A. Zelman (Ed.), *Early intervention with high-risk children: Freeing prisoners of circumstance* (pp. 105-124). Northvale, NJ: Jason Aronson.

Kohlberg, L. (1981-1984). *Essays in moral development: Vol. I. The philosophy of moral development. Vol. 2. The psychology of moral development.* New York: Harper and Row.

Kolko, D.J. (1992). Characteristics of child victims of physical violence: Research findings and clinical implications. *Journal of Interpersonal Violence,* 7, 244-276.

Kotulak, R. (1996). *Inside the brain.* Kansas City, MO: Andrews and McMeel.

Kushner, L. (1981). *When bad things happen to good people.* New York: Schocken Books.

Landau, E. (1990). *Teenage violence.* Englewood Cliffs, NJ: Julian Messner.

Lansky, V. (1991). *101 ways to make your child feel special.* Chicago: Contemporary Books.

Lansky, V. (1993). *Games babies play.* Deephaven, MN: The Book Peddlers.

Layne, C.M., Saltzman, W.R., and Pynoos, R.S. (2003). *Trauma/grief-focused group psychotherapy manual for adolescents.* Unpublished treatment manual, University of California, Los Angeles.

Layne, C.M., Wood, J., Saltzman, W.R., and Pynoos, R.S. (1999). *School-based psychosocial program for war-exposed adolescents: Screening and pre-group interview protocol.* Sarajevo, Bosnia, and Hercegovina: UNICEF.

Lazarus, A. (1971). *Behavior therapy and beyond.* New York: McGraw-Hill Book Co.

LeDoux, J. (2002). Synaptic self: *How our brains become who we are.* New York: Penguin.

Lerner, M.D. and Shelton, R.D. (2001a). How can emergency responders help grieving individuals? *Trauma Response.* Commack, NJ: The American Academy of Experts in Traumatic Stress, Inc.

Lerner, M.D. and Shelton, R.D. (2001b). How do people respond during traumatic exposure? *Trauma Response.* Commack, NJ: The American Academy of Experts in Traumatic Stress, Inc.

Levine, M. (1987). *Developmental variations and learning disabilities.* Cambridge, MA: Educators Publishing Service, Inc.

Levy, T. and Orlans, M. (1998). *Attachment, trauma, and healing.* Washington DC: CWLA.

Levy, T.M. and Orlans, M. (2000). Attachment disorder and the adoptive family. In T. Levy (Ed.), *Handbook of attachment interventions.* San Diego, CA: Academic Press.

Lewinsohn, P.M., Clarke, G.N., Seeley, J.R., and Rohde, P. (1994). Major depression in community adolescents: Age at onset, episode duration, and time to recurrence. *Journal of the American Academy of Child and Adolescent Psychiatry,* 33, 809-818.

Linesch, D. (1993). *Art therapy with families in crisis: Overcoming resistance through non-verbal expression.* New York: Brunner/Mazel.

Luthar, S.S., Cicchetti, D., and Becker, B. (2000). The construct of resilience: A critical evaluation and guidelines for future work. *Child Development,* 71, 543-562.

Lutz, L.L. (2000). Concurrent planning: Tool for permanency, survey of selected sites. National Resource Center for Foster Care and Permanency Planning, Hunter College School of Social Work, New York, April.

Lyman, R.D. and Campbell, N.R. (1996). *Treating children and adolescents in residential and inpatient settings.* Thousand Oaks, CA: Sage.

Lyons-Ruth, K., Repacholi, B., McLeod, S., and Silva, E. (1991). Disorganized attachment behavior in infancy: Short-term stability, maternal and infant correlates, and risk-related subtypes. *Development and Psychopathology,* 3, 377-396.

Mackay, H. (2001). Smile: It's free and enriches everyone. *Times Union,* Albany, New York, July 29, p. C-7.

Mahler, M., Pine, F., and Bergman, A. (1975). *The psychological birth of the human infant.* New York: Basic Books.

Main, M. (1991). Metacognitive knowledge, metacognitive monitoring, and singular (coherent) versus multiple (incoherent) models of attachment: Findings and directions for future research. In C.M. Parkes, J. Stevenson-Hinde, and P. Marris (Eds.), *Attachment across the life cycle* (pp. 127-159). London: Routledge.

Main, M. (1996). Introduction to the special section on attachment and psychopathology: 2. Overview of the field of attachment. *Journal of Consulting and Clinical Psychology,* 64, 237-243.

Main, M. and Goldwyn, R. (1998). *Adult attachment scoring and classification systems* (version 6.3). Unpublished manuscript, University of California at Berkeley.

Main, M. and Hess, E. (1990). Parents' unresolved traumatic experiences are related to infant disorganized attachment status: Is frightened and/or frightening parental behavior the linking mechanism? In M.T. Greenberg, D. Cicchetti, and M.E. Cummings (Eds.), *Attachment in the preschool years* (pp. 161-182). Chicago: University of Chicago Press.

Main, M. and Solomon, J. (1986). Discovery of an insecure-disorganized/disoriented attachment pattern: Procedures, findings and implications for the classification of behavior. In T.B. Brazelton and M.W. Yogman (Eds.), *Affective development in infancy* (pp. 95-124). Norwood, NJ: Ablex.

Main, M. and Solomon, J. (1990). Procedures for identifying infants as disorganized/disoriented during the Ainsworth Strange Situation. In M.T. Greenberg, D. Cicchetti, and E.M. Cummings (Eds.), *Attachment in the preschool years* (pp. 121-160). Chicago: University of Chicago Press.

Males, M.A. (1998). Five myths about youth and why adults believe them. *Children's Voice,* (Fall), 27-29.

Malgady, R.G., Rogle, L.H., and Costantino, G. (1990). Hero/heroine modeling for Puerto Rican adolescents: A preventive mental health intervention. *Journal of Consulting and Clinical Psychology,* 58, 469-474.

Malm, K., Bess, R., Leos-Urbel, J., Geen, R., and Markowitz, T. (2001). *Running to keep in place: The continuing evolution of our nations's child welfare system.* Washington, DC: The Urban Institute.

Maluccio, A. and Marlow, W. (1972). Residential treament of emotionally disturbed children: A review of the literature. *Social Service Review,* 46, 230-250.

March, J., Amaya-Jackson, L., Murray, K., and Schulte, A. (1998). Cognitive-behavioral psychotherapy for children and adolescents with posttraumatic stress disorder after a single-incident stressor. *Journal of the American Academy of Child and Adolescent Psychiatry,* 37(6), 585-593.

Masten, A.S. (2001). Ordinary magic: Resilience processes in development. *American Psychologist,* 56(3), 227-238.

Masten, A.S. and Coatsworth, J.D. (1998). The development of competence in favorable and unfavorable environments. *American Psychologist,* 53(92) 205-220.

Masten, A.S. and Curtis, W.J. (2000). Integrating competence and psychopathology: Pathways toward a comprehensive science of adaptation in development. *Development and Psychopathology, 12,* 529-550.

Mayer, M. (1968). *There's a nightmare in my closet.* New York: Dial Press.

McCann, I.L. and Pearlman, L.A. (Eds.) (1990). *Psychological trauma and the adult survivor: Theory, therapy, and transformation.* New York: Brunner/Mazel.

McKinnon, L. (1998). *Trust and betrayal in the treatment of child abuse.* New York: Guilford Press.

Merriam-Webster (2002). *Merriam-Webster's Collegiate Dictionary, Tenth Edition.* Springfield, MA: Merriam-Webster Inc.

Messman, T.L. and Long, P.J. (1996). Child sexual abuse and its relationship to revictimization in adult women: A review. *Clinical Psychology Review,* 16, 397-420.

Miller, A.L., Rathus, J.H., Landsman, M. and Linehan, M.M. (1995). DBT skills training manual for suicidal adolescents. Unpublished manual. Montefiore Medical Center/Albert Einstein College of Medicine, Bronx, NY.

Miller, A.L., Rathus, J.H. and Linehan, M.M. (In press). *Dialectical behavior therapy for suicidal adolescents.* New York: Guilford Press.

Mills, J.C. and Crowley, R.J. (1986). *Therapeutic metaphors for children and the child within.* New York: Brunner/Mazel.

Mitchell, K.T. (2001). Fetal alcohol syndrome and other alcohol related birth defects: Identification and implications. *The NADD Bulletin,* 4(1), 11-14.

Monahon, C. (1993). *Children and trauma: A parent's guide to helping children heal.* New York: Lexington Books.

Moser, A. (1988). *Don't pop your cork on Monday: The children's anti-stress book.* Kansas City, MO: Landmark Editions.

Moss, K. (1997). *Integrating attachment theory into special needs adoption.* Cleveland, OH: Beech Brook.

Munsch, R.N. (1986). *Love you forever.* Scarborough, Ontario: Firefly Books.

Munson, L. and Riskin, K. (1995). *In their own words: A sexual abuse workbook for teenage girls.* Washington, DC: Child Welfare League of America.

Nadeau, K.G. and Dixon, E.B. (1997). *Learning to slow down and pay attention: A book for kids about ADD.* Washington, DC: Magination Press.

National Institute on Alcohol Abuse and Alcoholism (2000). Fetal alcohol exposure and the brain. *Alcohol Alert.* Rockville, MD: U. S. Department of Health and Human Services, No. 50.

Neborsky, R.J. (2003). A clinical model for the comprehensive treatment of trauma using an affect experiencing-attachment theory approach. In M.F.Solomon and D.J. Siegel (Eds.), *Healing trauma: Attachment, mind, body, and brain.* New York: W.W. Norton.

Nichols, M. (1995). *Facing shame so we can find self-respect.* Amherst, NY: Prometheus Books.

Overcash, W., Calhoun, L., Cann, A., and Tedeschi, R. (1966). Coping with crises: An examination of the impact of traumatic events on religious beliefs. *The Journal of Genetic Psychology,* 157(4), 455-464.

Paley, V. (1999). *The kindness of children.* Cambridge, MA: Harvard University Press.

Papolos, D. and Papolos, J. (1999). *The bipolar child: The definitive and reassuring guide to childhood's most misunderstood disorder.* New York: Broadway Books.

Papp, P. (1983). *The process of change.* New York: Guilford.

Pastzor, E.M., Leighton, M., and Blome, W.W. (1993). *Helping children and youths develop positive attachments.* Washington, DC: Child Welfare League of America.

Paulson, G.P. (1987). *Hatchet.* New York: Aladdin Paperbacks.

Pelcovitz , D., Kaplan, S., Goldenberg, B., Mandel, F., Lehane, J., and Guarrera, J. (1994). Post-traumatic stress disorder in physically abused adolescents. *Journal of the American Academy of Child and Adolescent Psychiatry,* 33, 305-312.

Peltzer, D.J. (1995). *A child called it.* Deerfield Beach, FL: Health Communications.

Peltzer, D. (1999). *A Man named dave: a story of triumph and forgiveness.* New York: E.P. Dutton.

Perry, B.D. (2001). The neurodevelopmental impact of violence in childhood. In D. Schetky and E. Benedek (Eds.), *Textbook of child and adolescent forensic psychiatry* (pp. 221-238). Washington, DC: American Psychiatric Press, Inc.

Peterson, J. (1994). *The invisible road: Parental insights to attachment disorder.* Author.

Phillips, Betty W. (1998). Ignore child abuse now, attend to adult social problems later. *Brown University Child and Adolescent Behavior Letter* (August), p 10.

Piper, W. (1961). *The little engine that could.* New York: Platt and Munk.

Pitman, R.K., Altman, B., Greenwald, E., Longpre, R.E., Macklin, M.L., Poire, R.E., and Steketee, G.S. (1991). Psychiatric complications during flooding therapy for posttraumatic stess disorder. *Journal of Clinical Psychiatry,* 52, 17-20.

Pollack, W.S. (1998). *Real boys: Rescuing our sons from the myths of boyhood.* New York: Random House.

Porges, S.W. (1996). Emotion: An evolutionary by-product of the neural regulation of the autonomic nervous system. In C.S. Carter, B. Kirkpatrick, and I.I. Lederhendler (Eds.), *The integrative neurobiology of affiliation.* New York: Annals of the New York Academy of Sciences.

Putnam, F. (2003). Thinking BIG about child trauma: The sciences of prevention and replication. Presentation, Psychological Trauma: Maturational Processes and Therapeutic Interventions, Boston, Massachusetts, May 30.

Quindlen, A. (1991). *Object lessons*. New York: Random House.

Rahano, R. (1998). *Power building strategies for effective treatment to urban families*. Keynote Address, Parsons Fall Institute, Albany, New York, October 10.

Ramachandran,V.S. (1995). Plasticity in the adult human brain: Is there reason for optimism? In B. Julesz and I. Kovacs (Eds.), *Maturational windows and adult cortical plasticity* (pp. 179-197). Reading, MA: Addison-Wesley.

Ramey, C.T. and Ramey, S.L. (1998). Early intervention on early experience. *American Psychologist,* 53, 109-119.

Rattrey, R.S. (1956). *Ashanti laws and constitution.* London: Oxford University Press.

Roberts, G.E. (1986). *Roberts' apperception test for children.* Los Angeles: Western Psychological Services.

Roberts, J. (1994). *Tales and transformations—Stories in families and family therapy.* New York: Norton.

Rojano, R. (1998). Community Family Therapy. Workshop presented at the Sidney Albert Institute Fall Institute, Albany, New York, October 9.

Rosen, I. (1991). Self-esteem as a factor in social and domestic violence. *British Journal of Psychiatry,* 158, 18-23.

Roth, S. and Chasin, R. (1994) Entering one another's worlds of meaning and imagination: Dramatic enactment and narrative couple therapy. In M.F. Hoyt (Ed.), *Constructive therapies*. New York: Guilford.

Rothbaum, B.O. and Foa, E.G. (1996). Cognitive-behavioral therapy for posttraumatic stress disorder. In B.A. van der Kolk, A.C. McFarlane, and L. Weisaeth (Eds.), *Traumatic stress: the effects of overwhelming stress on mind, body, and society* (pp. 491-509). New York: Guilford Press.

Rowling, J.K. (1997). *Harry Potter and the sorcerer's stone*. New York: Scholastic Books.

Sachar, L. (1999). *Holes*. New York: Farrar, Straus, Giroux.

Salloum, A., Avery, L., and McClain, R. (2001). Group psychotherapy for survivors of homicide victims: A pilot study. *American Academy of Child and Adolescent Psychiatry,* 40(11), 1261-1267.

Saltzman, W.R., Layne, C.M., and Pynoos, R.S. (2003). *Trauma/grief-focused group psychotherapy: Supplementary materials*. Unpublished treatment manual, University of California, Los Angeles.

Sanders, C. and Turner, C. (1983). *Coping: A guide to stress management*. Carthage, IL: Good Apple.

Saunders, B.E., Villeponteaux, L.A., Lipovsky, J.A., Kilpatrick, D.G., and Veronen, L.J. (1992). Child sexual assault as a risk factor for mental disorders among women: A community survey. *Journal of Interpersonal Violence,* 7, 189-204.

Schlosberg, S. (1989). When a family experiences placement. In R. Kagan and S. Schlosberg. *Families in perpetual crisis* (pp. 89-105). New York: W.W. Norton.

Schore, A. (1994). *Affect regulation and the origin of the self: The neurobiology of emotional development.* Hillsdale, NJ: Lawrence Erlbaum Associates.

Schore, A.N. (1996). The experience-dependent maturaion of a regulatory system in the orbital prefrotal cortex and the orgin of developmental psychopathology. *Development and Psychopathology,* 8, 59-87.

Schore, A.N. (1997). Early organization of the nonlinear right brain and development of a predisposition to psychiatric disorders. *Development and Psychopathology,* 9, 595-631.

Schore, A.N. (2001). The effects of early relational trauma on right brain development, affect regulation, and infant mental health. *Infant Mental Health Journal,* 22, 201-269.

Schore, A.N. (2003a). Early relational trauma, disorganized attachment, and the development of a predisposition to violence. In M.F. Solomon and D.J. Siegel, (Eds.) *Healing trauma: Attachment, mind, body, and brain.* New York: Norton.

Schore, A.N. (2003b). Regulation of the right brain: A fundamental mechanism of attachment, trauma, dissociation, and psychotherapy. Presentation, Psychological Trauma: Maturational Processes and Therapeutic Interventions, Boston, MA, May 31.

Scott, R.L. and Cordova, J.V. (2002). The influence of adult attachment styles on the association between marital adjustment and depressive symptoms. *Journal of Family Psychology,* 16(2), 199-208.

Seligman, M.E.P. (1973). Fall into helplessness. *Psychology Today,* 7(1), 43-49.

Seligman, M.E.P., Maier, S.F., and Solomon, R.L. (1971). Unpredictable and uncontrollable aversive events. In F.R. Brush (Ed.), *Aversive conditioning and learning* (pp. 347-400). New York: Academic Press.

Sendak, M. (1963). *Where the wild things are.* New York: Harper and Row.

Seuss, Dr. (1940). *Horton hatches the egg.* New York: Random House.

Shapiro, F. (1995). *Eye movement desensitization and reprocessing.* New York: Guilford Press.

Shapiro, F. (2001). *Eye movement desensitization and reprocessing: Basic principles, protocols, and procedures* (Second edition). New York: Guilford Press.

Shore, R. (1997). *Rethinking the brain.* New York: Families and Work Institute.

Siegel, D. (1999). *The developing mind.* New York: Guilford Press.

Siegel, D. (2003). An interpersonal neurobiology of psychotherapy: The developing mind and the resolution of trauma. In M.F. Solomon and D.J. Siegel (Eds.), *Healing trauma: Attachment, mind, body, and brain.* New York: W.W. Norton.

Silverman, M.M. (1989). Children of psychiatrically ill parents: A prevention perspective. *Hospital and Community Psychiatry,* 40, 1257-1264.

Silverstein, O. and Rashbaum, B. (1994). *The courage to raise good men.* New York: Viking Books.

Solomon, J. and George, C. (1996). Defining the caregiving system: Toward a theory of caregiving. *Infant Mental Health Journal,* 17, 183-197.

Solomon, J. and George, C. (1999). The place of disorganization in attachment theory: Linking classic observations with contemporary findings. In J. Solomon and C. George (Eds.), *Attachment disorganization* (pp. 3-25). New York: The Guilford Press.

Somer, E. and Szwarcberg, S. (2001). Variables in delayed disclosure of childhood sexual abuse. *American Journal of Orthopsychiatry,* 71(3), 332-314.

Sorosky, B. and Pannor, R. (1978). *The adoption triangle.* New York: Anchor Press.

Speltz, M.L., DeKlyen, M., Greenberg, M.T., and Gryden, M. (1995). Clinic referral for oppositional defiant disorder: Relative significance of attachment and behavioral variables. *Journal of Abnormal Child Psychology,* 23, 487-507.

Steinhauer, P. (1974). *How to succeed in the business of creating psychopaths without even trying.* Unpublished manuscript. University of Toronto.

Straus, M.A. (1994). *Beating the devil out of them.* New York: Lexington Books.

Straus, M. (1999). *No-talk therapy for children and adolescents.* New York: Norton.

Streissguth, A.P. and O'Malley, K. (2000). Neuropsychiatric implications and long-term consequences of fetal alcohol spectrum disorders. *Seminars in Clinical Neuropsychiatry,* 5(3), 177-190.

Suddaby, K. and Landau, J. (1998). Positive and negative timelines: A technique for restorying. *Family Process,* 37(3), 287-297.

Surrey, J.L. (1991). The "self-in relation": A theory of women's development. In J.V. Jordan, A.G. Kaplan, J.B. Miller, and I. Stiver (Eds.), *Women's growth in connection* (pp. 51-66). New York: Guilford.

Taylor, D. and Alpert, S. (1973). *Continuity and support following residential treatment.* New York: Child Welfare League.

Teicher, M. (2002). Scars that will not heal: The neurobiology of child abuse. *Scientific American,* 286(3), 68-75.

Teicher, M.H., Ito, Y., Glod, C.A., Andersen, S.L., Dumont, N. and Ackerman, E. (1997). Preliminary evidence for abnormal cortical development in physically and sexually abused children using EEG coherence and MRI. *Annals of New York Academy of Sciences,* 821, 160-175.

Terr, L. (1983). Chowchilla revisited. The effects of psychic trauma four years after a school-bus kidnapping. *American Journal of Psychiatry,* 140, 1543-1550.

Terr, L. (1990). *Too scared to cry.* New York: Harper and Row.

Thompson, R.A. and Nelson, C.A. (2001). Developmental science and the media: Early brain development. *American Psychologist,* 56(1), 5-15.

Tinker, R.H. and Wilson, S.A. (1999). *Through the eyes of a child: EMDR with children.* New York: W.W. Norton.

U.S. Department of Health and Human Services, Administration on Children, Youth and Families (2001). *Child Maltreatment 1999.* Washington DC: U.S. Government Printing Office.

van der Kolk, B. (1996). The complexity of adaptation to trauma: Self-regulation, stimulus discrimination, and characterological development. In B. van der Kolk, A. McFarlane and L. Weisaelth (Eds.), *Traumatic stress: The effects of overwhelming experience on mind body, and society* (pp. 182-213). New York: The Guilford Press.

van der Kolk, B. (2003). Posttraumatic stress disorder and the nature of trauma. In M.F. Solomon and D.J. Siegel (Eds.), *Healing trauma: Attachment, mind, body, and brain.* New York: W.W. Norton.

van der Kolk, B. A., McFarlane, A. C., and van der Hart, O. (1996). A general approach to treatment of posttraumatic stress disorder. In B. A. van der kolk, A. C. McFarlane, and L. Weisaeth (Eds.) *Traumatic stress*. New York: Guilford Press.

van der Kolk, B. A., McFarlane, A. C., and Weisaeth, L. (eds.) (1996). *Traumatic stress*. New York: Guilford Press.

van der Kolk, B.A., Perry, J.C., and Herman, J. (1991). Childhood origins of self-destructive behavior. *American Journal of Psychiatry,* 148, 1665-1671.

van Gulden, H. (2001). "Essential skills for working with adoptive families. A post-adoption services conference and training project for human services professionals." Post Adoption Resource Center. Workshop presented for the Parsons Adoption Resource Center, Albany, New York, September 20.

van Gulden, H. and Bartels-Rabb, L.M. (1995). *Real parents, real children: Parenting the adopted child*. New York: Crossroads.

Viorst, J. (1972). *Alexander and the terrrible, horrible, no good, very bad day*. Hartford, CT: Atheneum.

Vogler, C. (1998). *The writer's journey: Mythic structure for writers*. Studio City, CA: Michael Weise Productions.

Waldfogel, J. (2000). Reforming child protective services. *Child Welfare,* 79(1), 47-49.

Waller, M.A. (2001). Resilience in ecosystemic context: Evolution of the concept. *American Journal of Orthopsychiatry,* 71(3), 290-297.

Waters and Deane (1985). Cited by Easterbrooks, M.A. (1998). Early foundations of attachment: Opportunities and challenges in infancy and toddlerhood. Conference Presentation, Day Care and Child Development Council of Tompkins County, Inc., Ithaca, New York, November 13.

Wheeler, C. (1978). *Where am I going? Making a child's life storybook.* Juneau, AL: The Winking Owl Press.

Whitaker, J. and Pecora, P. (1984). A research agenda for residential care. In T. Philpot (Ed.), *Group care practice: The challenge of the next decade* (pp. 71-86). Surrey, England: Business Press International.

White, M. (1989). The externalizing of the problem and the re-authoring of live and relationships. *Dulwich Centere Newsletter,* (Summer), 3-20.

White, M. (1993). Deconstruction and therapy. In S. Gilligan and R. Price (Eds.), *Therapeutic conversations*. New York: W.W. Norton.

White, M. (1995). *Reauthoring lives: Interviews and essays*. Adelaide, S. Australia: Dulwich Centre Publications.

White, M. and Epston, D. (1990). *Narrative means to therapeutic ends*. New York: Norton.

Whitehouse, E. and Pudney, W. (1996*). A volcano in my tummy*. Gabriola Island, BC: New Society Publishers.

Widom, C.S. (1992). *The cycle of violence. Research in Brief.* Washington, DC: U.S. Department of Justice, National Institute of Justice, NCJ 136607.

Widom, C.S. and Morris, S. (1997). Accuracy of adult recollections of childhood victimization: Part 2. Childhod sexual abuse. *Psychological Assessment,* 9, 34-46.

Widom, C.S. and Shepard, R.L. (1996). Accuracy of adult recollections of childhood victimization: Part 1. Childhood physical abuse. *Psychological Assessment,* 8, 412-421.

Wyman, P.A., Sandler, I., Wolchik, S., and Nelson, K. (2000). Resilience as cumulative competence promotion and stress protection: Theory and intervention. In D. Cicchetti, J, Rappaport, I. Sandler, and R.P. Weissberg (Eds.), *The promotion of wellness in children and adolescents* (pp. 133-184). Washington, DC: Child Welfare League of America Press.

Zweibel, A. and Nelson, J. (1999). *The story of us.* CastleRock Entertainment.

Index

THE HAWORTH MALTREATMENT AND TRAUMA PRESS®
Robert A. Geffner, PhD
Senior Editor

REBUILDING ATTACHMENTS WITH TRAUMATIZED CHILDREN: HEALING FROM LOSSES, VIOLENCE, ABUSE, AND NEGLECT. "Dr. Richard Kagan, a recognized expert in working with traumatized children, has written a truly impressive book. Not only does the book contain a wealth of information for understanding the complex issues faced by traumatized youngsters, but it also offers specific interventions that can be used to help these children and their caregivers become more hopeful and resilient. . . . I am certain that this book will be read and reread by professionals engaged in improving the lives of at-risk youth." *Robert Brooks, PhD, Faculty, Harvard Medical School and author of* Raising Resilient Children *and* The Power of Resilience

PSYCHOLOGICAL TRAUMA AND THE DEVELOPING BRAIN: NEUROLOGICALLY BASED INTERVENTIONS FOR TROUBLED CHILDREN by Phyllis T. Stien and Joshua C. Kendall. (2003). "Stien and Kendall provide us with a great service. In this clearly written and important book, they synthesize a wealth of crucial information that links childhood trauma to brain abnormalities and subsequent mental illness. Equally important, they show us how the trauma also affects the child's social and intellectual development. I recommend this book to all clinicians and administrators." *Charles L. Whitfield, MD, Author of* The Truth About Depression *and* The Truth About Mental Illness

CHILD MALTREATMENT RISK ASSESSMENTS: AN EVALUATION GUIDE by Sue Righthand, Bruce Kerr, and Kerry Drach. (2003). "This book is essential reading for clinicians and forensic examiners who see cases involving issues related to child maltreatment. The authors have compiled an impressive critical survey of the relevant research on child maltreatment. Their material is well organized into sections on definitions, impact, risk assessment, and risk management. This book represents a giant step toward promoting evidence-based evaluations, treatment, and testimony." *Diane H. Schetky, MD, Professor of Psychiatry, University of Vermont College of Medicine*

SIMPLE AND COMPLEX POST-TRAUMATIC STRESS DISORDER: STRATEGIES FOR COMPREHENSIVE TREATMENT IN CLINICAL PRACTICE edited by Mary Beth Williams and John F. Sommer Jr. (2002). "A welcome addition to the literature on treating survivors of traumatic events, this volume possesses all the ingredients necessary for even the experienced clinician to master the management of patients with PTSD." *Terence M. Keane, PhD, Chief, Psychology Service, VA Boston Healthcare System; Professor and Vice Chair of Research in Psychiatry, Boston University School of Medicine*

FOR LOVE OF COUNTRY: CONFRONTING RAPE AND SEXUAL HARASSMENT IN THE U.S. MILITARY by T. S. Nelson. (2002). "Nelson brings an important message—that the absence of current media attention doesn't mean the problem has gone away; that only decisive action by military leadership at all levels can break the cycle of repeated traumatization; and that the failure to do so is, as Nelson puts it, a 'power failure'—a refusal to exert positive leadership at all levels to stop violent individuals from using the worst power imaginable." *Chris Lombardi, Correspondent, Women's E-News, New York City*

THE INSIDERS: A MAN'S RECOVERY FROM TRAUMATIC CHILDHOOD ABUSE by Robert Blackburn Knight. (2002). "An important book. . . . Fills a gap in the literature about healing from childhood sexual abuse by allowing us to hear, in undiluted terms, about one man's history and journey of recovery." *Amy Pine, MA, LMFT, psychotherapist and co-founder, Survivors Healing Center, Santa Cruz, California*

WE ARE NOT ALONE: A GUIDEBOOK FOR HELPING PROFESSIONALS AND PARENTS SUPPORTING ADOLESCENT VICTIMS OF SEXUAL ABUSE by Jade Christine Angelica. (2002). "Encourages victims and their families to participate in the system in an effort to heal from their victimization, seek justice, and hold offenders accountable for their crimes. An exceedingly vital training tool." *Janet Fine, MS, Director, Victim Witness Assistance Program and Children's Advocacy Center, Suffolk County District Attorney's Office, Boston*

WE ARE NOT ALONE: A TEENAGE GIRL'S PERSONAL ACCOUNT OF INCEST FROM DISCLOSURE THROUGH PROSECUTION AND TREATMENT by Jade Christine Angelica. (2002). "A valuable resource for teens who have been sexually abused and their parents. With compassion and eloquent prose, Angelica walks people through the criminal justice system—from disclosure to final outcome." *Kathleen Kendall-Tackett, PhD, Research Associate, Family Research Laboratory, University of New Hampshire, Durham*

WE ARE NOT ALONE: A TEENAGE BOY'S PERSONAL ACCOUNT OF CHILD SEXUAL ABUSE FROM DISCLOSURE THROUGH PROSECUTION AND TREATMENT by Jade Christine Angelica. (2002). "Inspires us to work harder to meet kids' needs, answer their questions, calm their fears, and protect them from their abusers and the system, which is often not designed to respond to them in a language they understand." *Kevin L. Ryle, JD, Assistant District Attorney, Middlesex, Massachusetts*

GROWING FREE: A MANUAL FOR SURVIVORS OF DOMESTIC VIOLENCE by Wendy Susan Deaton and Michael Hertica. (2001). "This is a necessary book for anyone who is scared and starting to think about what it would take to 'grow free.' . . . Very helpful for friends and relatives of a person in a domestic violence situation. I recommend it highly." *Colleen Friend, LCSW, Field Work Consultant, UCLA Department of Social Welfare, School of Public Policy & Social Research*

A THERAPIST'S GUIDE TO GROWING FREE: A MANUAL FOR SURVIVORS OF DOMESTIC VIOLENCE by Wendy Susan Deaton and Michael Hertica. (2001). "An excellent synopsis of the theories and research behind the manual." *Beatrice Crofts Yorker, RN, JD, Professor of Nursing, Georgia State University, Decatur*

PATTERNS OF CHILD ABUSE: HOW DYSFUNCTIONAL TRANSACTIONS ARE REPLICATED IN INDIVIDUALS, FAMILIES, AND THE CHILD WELFARE SYSTEM by Michael Karson. (2001). "No one interested in what may well be the major public health epidemic of our time in terms of its long-term consequences for our society can afford to pass up the opportunity to read this enlightening work." *Howard Wolowitz, PhD, Professor Emeritus, Psychology Department, University of Michigan, Ann Arbor*

IDENTIFYING CHILD MOLESTERS: PREVENTING CHILD SEXUAL ABUSE BY RECOGNIZING THE PATTERNS OF THE OFFENDERS by Carla van Dam. (2000). "The definitive work on the subject. . . . Provides parents and others with the tools to recognize when and how to intervene." *Roger W. Wolfe, MA, Co-Director, N. W. Treatment Associates, Seattle, Washington*

POLITICAL VIOLENCE AND THE PALESTINIAN FAMILY: IMPLICATIONS FOR MENTAL HEALTH AND WELL-BEING by Vivian Khamis. (2000). "A valuable book . . . a pioneering work that fills a glaring gap in the study of Palestinian society." *Elia Zureik, Professor of Sociology, Queens University, Kingston, Ontario, Canada*

STOPPING THE VIOLENCE: A GROUP MODEL TO CHANGE MEN'S ABUSIVE ATTITUDES AND BEHAVIORS by David J. Decker. (1999). "A concise and thorough manual to assist clinicians in learning the causes and dynamics of domestic violence." *Joanne Kittel, MSW, LICSW, Yachats, Oregon*

STOPPING THE VIOLENCE: A GROUP MODEL TO CHANGE MEN'S ABUSIVE ATTITUDES AND BEHAVIORS, THE CLIENT WORKBOOK by David J. Decker. (1999).

BREAKING THE SILENCE: GROUP THERAPY FOR CHILDHOOD SEXUAL ABUSE, A PRACTITIONER'S MANUAL by Judith A. Margolin. (1999). "This book is an extremely valuable and well-written resource for all therapists working with adult survivors of child sexual abuse." *Esther Deblinger, PhD, Associate Professor of Clinical Psychiatry, University of Medicine and Dentistry of New Jersey School of Osteopathic Medicine*

"I NEVER TOLD ANYONE THIS BEFORE": MANAGING THE INITIAL DISCLOSURE OF SEXUAL ABUSE RE-COLLECTIONS by Janice A. Gasker. (1999). "Discusses the elements needed to create a safe, therapeutic environment and offers the practitioner a number of useful strategies for responding appropriately to client disclosure." *Roberta G. Sands, PhD, Associate Professor, University of Pennsylvania School of Social Work*

FROM SURVIVING TO THRIVING: A THERAPIST'S GUIDE TO STAGE II RECOVERY FOR SURVIVORS OF CHILDHOOD ABUSE by Mary Bratton. (1999). "A must read for all, including survivors. Bratton takes a lifelong debilitating disorder and unravels its intricacies in concise, succinct, and understandable language." *Phillip A. Whitner, PhD, Sr. Staff Counselor, University Counseling Center, The University of Toledo, Ohio*

SIBLING ABUSE TRAUMA: ASSESSMENT AND INTERVENTION STRATEGIES FOR CHILDREN, FAMILIES, AND ADULTS by John V. Caffaro and Allison Conn-Caffaro. (1998). "One area that has almost consistently been ignored in the research and writing on child maltreatment is the area of sibling abuse. This book is a welcome and required addition to the developing literature on abuse." *Judith L. Alpert, PhD, Professor of Applied Psychology, New York University*

BEARING WITNESS: VIOLENCE AND COLLECTIVE RESPONSIBILITY by Sandra L. Bloom and Michael Reichert. (1998). "A totally convincing argument. . . . Demands careful study by all elected representatives, the clergy, the mental health and medical professions, representatives of the media, and all those unwittingly involved in this repressive perpetuation and catastrophic global problem." *Harold I. Eist, MD, Past President, American Psychiatric Association*

TREATING CHILDREN WITH SEXUALLY ABUSIVE BEHAVIOR PROBLEMS: GUIDELINES FOR CHILD AND PARENT INTERVENTION by Jan Ellen Burton, Lucinda A. Rasmussen, Julie Bradshaw, Barbara J. Christopherson, and Steven C. Huke. (1998). "An extremely readable book that is well-documented and a mine of valuable 'hands on' information. . . . This is a book that all those who work with sexually abusive children or want to work with them must read." *Sharon K. Araji, PhD, Professor of Sociology, University of Alaska, Anchorage*

THE LEARNING ABOUT MYSELF (LAMS) PROGRAM FOR AT-RISK PARENTS: LEARNING FROM THE PAST—CHANGING THE FUTURE by Verna Rickard. (1998). "This program should be a part of the resource materials of every mental health professional trusted with the responsibility of working with 'at-risk' parents." *Terry King, PhD, Clinical Psychologist, Federal Bureau of Prisons, Catlettsburg, Kentucky*

THE LEARNING ABOUT MYSELF (LAMS) PROGRAM FOR AT-RISK PARENTS: HANDBOOK FOR GROUP PARTICIPANTS by Verna Rickard. (1998). "Not only is the LAMS program designed to be educational and build skills for future use, it is also fun!" *Martha Morrison Dore, PhD, Associate Professor of Social Work, Columbia University, New York*

BRIDGING WORLDS: UNDERSTANDING AND FACILITATING ADOLESCENT RECOVERY FROM THE TRAUMA OF ABUSE by Joycee Kennedy and Carol McCarthy. (1998). "An extraordinary survey of the history of child neglect and abuse in America. . . . A wonderful teaching tool at the university level, but should be required reading in high schools as well." *Florabel Kinsler, PhD, BCD, LCSW, Licensed Clinical Social Worker, Los Angeles, California*

CEDAR HOUSE: A MODEL CHILD ABUSE TREATMENT PROGRAM by Bobbi Kendig with Clara Lowry. (1998). "Kendig and Lowry truly . . . realize the saying that we are our brothers' keepers. Their spirit permeates this volume, and that spirit of caring is what always makes the difference for people in painful situations." *Hershel K. Swinger, PhD, Clinical Director, Children's Institute International, Los Angeles, California*

SEXUAL, PHYSICAL, AND EMOTIONAL ABUSE IN OUT-OF-HOME CARE: PREVENTION SKILLS FOR AT-RISK CHILDREN by Toni Cavanagh Johnson and Associates. (1997). "Professionals who make dispositional decisions or who are related to out-of-home care for children could benefit from reading and following the curriculum of this book with children in placements." *Issues in Child Abuse Accusations*